THEORY AND INTERPRETATION OF NARRATIVE SERIES

Narratologies:
New Perspectives
on Narrative Analysis

Edited by

DAVID HERMAN

OHIO STATE UNIVERSITY PRESS

COLUMBUS

Library of Congress Cataloging-in-Publication Data
Narratologies : new perspectives on narrative analysis / edited by David Herman.
p.   cm. — (Theory and interpretation of narrative series)
Includes bibliographical references and index.
ISBN 0-8142-0821-5 (cloth : alk. paper). — ISBN 0-8142-5024-6 (pbk. : alk. paper)
1. Narration (Rhetoric)   I. Herman, David, 1962–   .   II. Series.
PN212.N39   1999
808—dc21   99-19802
                                                                      CIP

Text and jacket design by Paula Newcomb.
Type set in Adobe Minion by Tseng Information Systems, Inc.
Printed by Cushing-Malloy, Inc.

The paper used in this publication meets the minimum require-
ments of the American National Standard for Information Sciences
—Permanence of Paper for Printed Library Materials.
ANSI Z39.48-1992.

9 8 7 6 5 4 3 2 1

Contents

Acknowledgments

More than just a collection of essays, *Narratologies* is its own best argument for the importance of collaborative research on narrative. The task of developing and refining models for narrative analysis is too exacting — and too exciting! — for anyone to try to go it alone. To put the same point another way: as an object of inquiry, narrative is complex enough to accommodate many different perspectives on its structures, uses, and effects. I am therefore grateful to be able to name at least some of the colleagues, friends, and fellow travelers who helped make this volume possible, enriching my own (and I hope the reader's) understanding of stories along the way.

I thank, first, Jim Phelan and Gerald Prince for early consultations that helped give shape to the volume. I also thank Jim Phelan and Peter Rabinowitz for their invaluable advice while I was soliciting, assembling, and editing the essays gathered here. Jim's, Peter's, and Thomas Pavel's careful and extensive reports on a first draft of the volume helped me rethink the Introduction; their reports also enabled contributors to clarify and refine individual essays. To the contributors themselves I offer a blanket statement of gratitude: without their hard work and keen insights, of course, this volume would simply not exist. Further, Emma Kafalenos came up with the wonderful idea of having each contributor provide a brief contextualizing statement that situated his or her argument in the history of narratological research. Marie-Laure Ryan provided useful comments on an earlier draft of the Introduction. Let me mention, too, how great a pleasure it has been to work with Barbara Hanrahan, Director of the Ohio State University Press; with Ruth Melville, the editor who skillfully guided this volume into print; with Jo Ann Kiser, freelance copyeditor for the Press; and with Beth Ina and John Delaine.

More generally, I would like to thank Lubomír Doležel, Emma Kafalenos, Thomas Pavel, Jim Phelan, Gerald Prince, Marie-Laure Ryan, and Walt Wolfram for their collegiality over the past few years. I have not just benefited from their friendship but also taken inspiration from their work. (I am grateful to Gerald Prince more particularly for his suggestions concerning a title for this volume, though I should and do accept full responsibility for any short-comings of the current version.) Thanks are owed as well to the whole linguistics crew at North Carolina State University, including Clare Dannenberg, Elaine Green, Kirk Hazen, Natalie Schilling-Estes, Jason Sellers, Erik Thomas, Tracey Weldon, and Walt Wolfram. Others at North Carolina State and elsewhere, including Amy Coppedge, Linda Holley, Sharon Johnson, Kelly Kincy, Andy Kunka, Jennifer Liethen-Kunka, Veronica Norris, Victor Raskin, and Pam Schubart, also deserve my heartfelt thanks. Further, I thank Walt Wolfram for providing me with access to the computing and photocopying resources of the William C. Friday linguistics lab while I prepared this volume for publication.

Closer to home, I am grateful to Susan Moss for grain-centered meals on Devereux Street and twilights at the Place des Vosges. My thanks as well to Tinker, lover of open windows; Howard and Rebecca Moss, gracious proprietors of the Maison de la Bastide; and Kristin Moss and Bob King, fellow explorers of the River Cèze. Jennifer and Tim Cohen, world-travelers, are much missed, and I am grateful to William Herman for his humor and intelligence. I dedicate my work on this volume to the memory of my mother, Virginia Honor Herman, who told me the first stories.

Introduction: Narratologies
David Herman

1. Two Narratives about Narratology

In 1983, Shlomith Rimmon-Kenan ended her useful (and widely used) guide to narratology and narrative theory, *Narrative Fiction: Contemporary Poetics,* with some remarks on the challenges posed to classical narratology by deconstruction. Rimmon-Kenan expressed hope that deconstruction, at that time a comparatively new development on the theoretical scene, might enrich narrative theory rather than render it obsolete. She thus resisted the idea that her study could be an obituary of the very field it aimed to synopsize and introduce (130). Now, some fifteen years later, Rimmon-Kenan's cautious optimism concerning narratology appears to have been warranted. It seems in short that rumors of the death of narratology have been greatly exaggerated. Recently we have witnessed a small but unmistakable explosion of activity in the field of narrative studies;[1] signs of this minor narratological renaissance include the publication of a spate of articles, special issues, and books that rethink and recontextualize classical models for narratological research; the evident success of the journal *Narrative* (not founded until 1993); and the establishment, in 1994, of the book series to which the present volume belongs. Adapting a host of methodologies and perspectives — feminist, Bakhtinian, deconstructive, reader-response, psychoanalytic, historicist, rhetorical, film-theoretical, computational, discourse-analytic and (psycho)linguistic — narrative theory has undergone not a funeral and burial but rather a sustained, sometimes startling metamorphosis since Rimmon-Kenan published her study.[2] In the intervening years *narratology* has in fact ramified into *narratologies;* structuralist theorizing about stories has evolved into a plurality of models for narrative analysis. These models stand in a more or less critical and reflexive relation to the structuralist tradition, borrowing more or less extensively from the analytic heritage they aim to surpass. It is a major purpose of this volume to trace, in part, the genealogy of current approaches to narrative — to document the extent to which recent work in narrative theory has displaced and transformed the assumptions, methods, and goals of structuralist narratology.

Narratologies thus seeks to complicate two prevalent but competing stories told about the history and evolution of narratology, which originated as an outgrowth of structuralist literary theory in France in the mid to late 1960s. According to the first story, narratology, with its forbidding terminology and mania for taxonomies, stands as a monument to the scientistic aspirations of a high structuralism whose day has long since passed. True, researchers working in the structuralist tradition developed useful schemes for classifying types of narratives; they also introduced a finely grained analytic vocabulary for describing particular effects within a given narrative. Yet as other trends in literary and cultural theory (poststructuralism, feminism, ideological critique) gained prominence, what began as a self-styled science of narrative was, in the space of just a few years, stigmatized as obsolescent. Not everyone, however, thinks that narratology is simply dead. Rather, according to a second, competing narrative, narratology has entered a state of crisis. Recent research has highlighted aspects of narrative discourse that classical narratology either failed or chose not to explore; in consequence, although the structuralist tradition has provided demonstrable gains in the field of narrative analysis (a field still pursued by a significant body of scholars), we must now, according to the story of crisis, recognize the problems of using narratology as a paradigm for further research. Feminist scholars, for example, have suggested that the older narratological categories do not necessarily capture how issues of gender inflect the production and processing of stories. Other researchers have refined our understanding of narratives as complex rhetorical transactions between authors, narrators, and various kinds of audiences. Still other narrative theorists have drawn on fields such as Artificial Intelligence, hypertext, psychoanalysis, film studies, and linguistics (including possible-worlds semantics and discourse analysis) to broaden and diversify our conception of stories and to provide new ways of analyzing their structures and effects.

As these last remarks suggest, the extraordinarily vital and innovative work now being done in narrative studies belies both the story of obsolescence and the story of crisis. Indeed, given the startling transmutation of narrative poetics over the past decade and a half, it may be more germane to speak of a narratological *renaissance* at this juncture. Put otherwise, narratology has moved from its classical, structuralist phase—a Saussurean phase relatively isolated from energizing developments in contemporary literary and language theory—to its postclassical phase. Postclassical narratology (which should not be conflated with poststructuralist theories of narrative) contains classical narratology as one of its "moments" but is marked by a profusion of new methodologies and research hypotheses; the result is a host of new perspectives on the forms and functions of narrative itself. Further, in its postclassical phase, research on narrative does not just expose the limits but also exploits the possibilities of the older, structuralist models. In much the same way, postclassical physics does not simply discard classical, Newtonian models but rather rethinks their conceptual underpinnings and reassesses their scope of applicability.[3]

Collectively, then, the essays assembled in this volume reveal a different way to tell the story about the enterprise of studying stories. Recontextualizing classical narratological models and tools, *Narratologies* suggests that the putative death of (or crisis in) narratology can be better described as a re-emergence—and transformation—of narrative analysis across a wide variety of research domains. As the morphology of the word suggests, a *reemergence* is a secondary origination, in this case a new rethinking of a once-new way of thinking. Postclassical narratology may lack the first flush of heady enthusiasm, the untrammeled excitement of pure discovery, the methodological utopianism of the first great semiological revolution of the 1960s. But it makes up for this with a more sustained reflection on its scope and aims, a fuller awareness of surrounding critico-theoretical developments, a less programmatic and more exploratory posture, a greater willingness to admit that, when it comes to the study of narratives (or anything else!), no one can or should hope to get everything right once and for all. The contributions to *Narratologies* vividly demonstrate, I believe, this ongoing remodulation of narrative analysis. They show that narratology has evolved into a more inclusive and open-ended project that in no way goes back on its original commitment to developing the best possible descriptive and explanatory models. As a whole, therefore, the volume aims to accomplish three overarching goals: (1) to test the possibilities and limits of classical, structuralist narratological models, that is, to assess what sorts of narrative phenomena such models can and cannot illuminate; (2) to enrich, where necessary, the classical models with postclassical models, thereby coming to terms with aspects of narrative discourse that eluded or even undermined previous narratological research; and (3), to achieve goals 1 and 2 through interpretations of particular (literary and other) narratives, thus demonstrating the relevance of postclassical narratology not just for the study of literary and narrative theory but also for critical practice at large. Indeed, it is the collection's dual emphasis on poetics and criticism—its double focus on the systemic features of narrative discourse as well as on features pertaining to individual narratives [4]—that makes *Narratologies* a relevant addition to a series devoted to the theory *and* interpretation of narrative.

The next section illustrates some of the differences between classical and postclassical narratology. I focus on a well-known (indeed, anthologized) instance of narrative analysis based on classical concepts and methods, David Lodge's "Analysis and Interpretation of the Realist Text" (1996[1980]). The provenance of Lodge's essay is important: it was originally a paper presented at "Synopsis 2: Narrative Theory and Poetics of Fiction," an international conference sponsored by the Porter Institute for Poetics and Semiotics at Tel Aviv University in the summer of 1979. As Mieke Bal has described in "The Point of Narratology," the conference was in many ways the high-water mark of classical theorizing about narrative. Centering on Ernest Hemingway's short story "Cat in the Rain," Lodge's essay itself combines theory and interpretation, operationalizing structuralist concepts by making them do interpretive work. It is a skillful and suggestive analysis, one that my own students find useful in their efforts to come to grips both with structuralism and with structuralist narrative theory. But the essay is as interesting for what it does not attempt as it is for what it accomplishes. Taking my cue from the diverse narratologies envisaged by the contributors to this volume, I outline ways in which Lodge's approach can be recontextualized and enriched with ideas developed after the heyday of structuralism. My discussion aims to give readers a sense of narratology as a dynamically evolving field, rather than as a purely taxonomic enterprise that has outlived its at best moderate usefulness.

2. ". . . a richer, more useful, and more complete narratology"[5]

One of the purposes of Lodge's essay is to take stock of models for narrative analysis in the late 1970s; as I discuss in more detail below, Lodge divides these models into three sorts: those developed under the auspices of "narratology and narrative grammar," those associated with the "poetics of fiction," and those used for "rhetorical analysis" of stories. Lodge's essay does more than simply survey the latest theoretical tools then being used by narratologists, however. One of Lodge's own guiding questions is the following: "Is it possible, or useful, to bring the whole battery of modern formalism and structuralism to bear upon a single text, and what is gained by so doing?" (24). Drawing on "Cat in the Rain" as his tutor text, Lodge persuasively argues for the view that it is not just possible but also helpful to synthesize the theory with the interpretation of narrative. He notes the peculiar status of Hemingway's story: on the one hand, "Cat in the Rain" seems to assume a verisimilar relationship between text and reality that "is essentially continuous with that of classic bourgeois realism"; but on the other hand, many readers have found this same narrative "ambiguous, polyvalent and resistant to interpretative closure" (29). The story of an (unnamed) American wife and husband stopping at a hotel in Italy, on the surface "Cat in the Rain" features few reportable actions: as the preoccupied husband reads, the wife ventures out into the rain (unsuccessfully) in search of a cat for which she wishes to provide shelter, and which seems to symbolize in some obscure way everything that the wife yearns for but currently lacks. The story is told by a heterodiegetic narrator, while over the course of the narrative the focalization shifts—crucially, as it turns out— from an external to an internal mode.

Note that in his analysis of Hemingway's story, Lodge makes a compelling case for the usefulness of classical, structuralist theories. For instance, Lodge draws on "the structuralist notion of language as a system of differences and of meaning as the product of structural oppositions" (35) to dispute John V. Hagopian's reading of the man in the rubber cape as a symbol of contraception in the story. Guarding against the rain *can* be an attempt to block the forces of fertility; but Lodge argues that Hemingway is working with a different system of contrasts, one that associates rain not with fertility but with boredom. Further, Lodge makes particularly good use of Genette's idea of frequency, or the relation between the number of times something happens in the story world and the number of times it is recounted in the narrative. He notes that Hemingway's "story tends toward reiteration rather than summary, telling *n* times what happened *n* times or *n* times what happened once rather than telling once what happened *n* times. This is important because it reinforces the definition of the characters according to a very limited repertoire of gestures" (33). Thus the form of the story encodes the repetitiousness, the self-replicating ennui, that is also one of its chief themes. Perhaps the most illuminating section of the essay, though, is Lodge's account of the subtle shifts in focalization that help explain why the ending of "Cat in the Rain" remains ambiguous. Lodge again draws on the work of Genette to distinguish between who speaks (the narrator) and who sees (the place of the focalization). Whereas Hemingway's story is told by a quasi-omniscient heterodiegetic narrator, the tale's focalization is variable, with the perspective shifting from one external to both the husband and wife, to one associated with the wife, to one associated with the husband. Lodge skillfully shows how these shifts in focalization play themselves out in the verbal texture of the story—specifically, through contrasts between definite and indefinite articles. Hence,

> We can now fully understand why the ending of the story is so ambiguous: it is primarily because narration adopts the husband's perspective at this crucial point. Since he did not rise from the bed to look out of the window at the cat sheltering from the rain, he has no way of knowing whether the cat brought by the maid is the same one—hence the noncommittal indefinite article "*a* big

tortoise-shell cat." If however the wife's perspective had been adopted at this point and the text had read . . . "She held a big tortoise-shell cat," then it would be clear that this was not the cat the wife had wanted to bring in from the rain (in which case the definite article would have been used). It is significant that in the title of the story, there is no article before "Cat," thus giving no support to either interpretation of the ending. (34)

Thus Lodge productively implements structuralist theories; his essay demonstrates the interpretive yield of ideas like frequency and focalization, for example.

Tools developed after the heyday of structuralist narratology, however, can help pose questions about Hemingway's story that do not arise in Lodge's discussion. The absence of these questions should not be attributed to an oversight, a mere lack of perspicuity, on Lodge's part. The questions at issue could not be formulated, arguably, from within a classical perspective. We are dealing here with general constraints on research—conditions of possibility for narrative analysis—not with the failings of this or that critic. Thus my aim is to show how postclassical approaches can enrich interpretations of the sort developed by Lodge, not to engage in narratological one-upmanship.

Indeed, Lodge himself makes it clear that narrative theory needs to be situated in a history—a narrative—that traces the evolution of storytelling techniques and of the strategies used to study them. Historically, as Lodge points out, there was a synergistic relationship between the self-conscious experiments of avant-garde novelists, on the one hand, and the developments in linguistics, folklore, and anthropology that led to the development of what I am calling classical models for narrative analysis, on the other hand. The realistic novel typically hid its representational conventions; characteristically, it aimed to create a wholly immersive experience by backgrounding its constructedness and passing itself off as a transparent window on the world. By contrast, experimental fictions foreground their own narrative structures, their status as stories that have been constructed. Such self-conscious fictions thus make palpable the need for tools for narrative analysis. By deautomatizing the experience of stories—by focusing attention on the conventions that cue readers to interpret certain modes of discourse *as* narrative—contemporary writing also prompts the analyst to map narrative structures more explicitly and exhaustively than ever before. Yet, as Lodge notes,

> For a long time these [fictional and theoretical] investigations were pursued on parallel tracks which seldom converged. In the last couple of decades, however, the Anglo-American tradition of formalist criticism, essentially empirical and text-based, theoretically rather underpowered but critically productive,

has encountered the more systematic, abstract, theoretically rigorous and "scientific" tradition of European structuralist criticism. The result has been a minor "knowledge explosion" in the field of narrative theory and poetics of fiction. (24)

Shockwaves from this first narratological knowledge explosion made themselves felt in what Lodge describes as three separate domains of inquiry, each situated at a different level of narrative structure. First, there is narratology and narrative grammar, or the search for narrative *langue* conducted by theorists such as Vladimir Propp, Claude Bremond, Algirdas-Julien Greimas, Claude Lévi-Strauss, Tzvetan Todorov, and Roland Barthes. To invoke terms that Lodge himself does not use at this juncture: this first area of research focuses on the organization of the narrated or the story; that is, the structure of the *fabula* that lends itself to various modes of realization in the *sjuzhet*.[6] Second, there is the poetics of fiction, or "all attempts to describe and classify techniques of fictional representation" (26); for Lodge, the work of both Wayne Booth and Gérard Genette falls under this heading. Such research, studying for example the order in which the events of the story are recounted by the narrator, addresses the relations between the narrated and the narrative, or the story and the discourse, or the fabula and the sjuzhet. Third, there is the rhetorical analysis of fiction, and "[b]y this I mean analyzing the surface structure of narrative texts to show how the linguistic mediation of a story determines its meaning and effect" (27). As defined by Lodge, the rhetorical approach was given impetus by Roman Jakobson's (1971) distinction between metaphor and metonymy (and his association of metonymy with realism), though it also has significant points of contact with Anglo-American New Criticism. This third approach studies discourse-level features of narratives. Note, however, that Lodge's characterization of it does not clearly demarcate rhetorical analysis from the poetics of fiction. Further, as I shall discuss later in this section, and as James Phelan and Mary Patricia Martin's essay in this volume demonstrates, Lodge unduly restricts the scope of rhetorical analysis when he equates it with the study of the tropes or figures of speech used in stories. Rhetorical analysis can be more broadly — and more productively — defined as the study of the forms of narrative vis-à-vis the audiences of narrative.

In fact, the whole landscape of narratological inquiry now displays a different topography than the one Lodge began to map nearly twenty years ago; this is because of the impact of the *second* narratological knowledge explosion currently being propagated across a variety of research domains. The three main investigative tasks identified by Lodge — the formulation of a narrative grammar, the creation of a narrative poetics, and the development of a rhetoric for stories—have evolved, become intertwined, affected surrounding critico-theoretical trends, and in turn been affected by them. There has also been a multiplication of research tasks and of strategies for accomplishing them. Recent developments in fields such as cognitive science, linguistic pragmatics, and discourse analysis, for example, have reinflected the effort to formulate a grammar for stories. In this realm, the guiding questions are perhaps no longer: "Can we construct a formal apparatus capable of generating all and only those discourse units which we call stories? And can we model this apparatus so that it assigns a structural description to the smaller components of such discourse units, accounts for their principles of composition and recursion, and hence yields a formal, rule-based representation of the skills and dispositions bound up with narrative competence?" Such questions have given way to others: "How do formal cues in narratively organized discourse trigger prestored knowledge —for example, knowledge about stereotypical situations and events—in ways that allow people to recognize a story *as* a story in the first place? What formal cues have to be there for this to happen, and why? Do certain kinds of formal cues facilitate narrative comprehension to a greater degree than others? How does narrative competence pertain to the cognitive, verbal, and interactional skills and dispositions bound up with communicative competence generally?"[7] In short, current research indicates that we would do well to ask, not just about story structure as such, but about the patterned, nonrandom ways in which readers and listeners tend to impute narrative structure to certain strings of events presented in discourse. We would also do well to examine ways in which storytellers exploit, for specifically narrative purposes, story recipients' tendency to infer narrative structure from particular kinds of discourse cues.[8]

These brief remarks about the problem of narrative grammar point to a broader reconfiguration of the narratological landscape. The root transformation can be described as a shift from text-centered or formal models to models that are jointly formal and functional—models attentive both to the text and to the context of stories.[9] Increasingly, narrative theorists have focused on the extent to which stories are what they are not because of their form alone, but because of a complex interplay between narrative form and the contexts of narrative interpretation, broadly construed. At stake, then, is an interplay between the way stories are designed and the processing strategies promoted by their design. Depending on the perspective adopted, the nomenclature used, and the level of description chosen, such processing strategies can be characterized in terms of basic hypotheses about causal relations, that is, conclusions about who did what when in a narrative; inferences about a narrator's position relative to the events or about his or her (un)reliability; decisions about which themes in a story take precedence; ways of living out or contesting a more or less implicitly gendered response to certain kinds of narrative structure; modes of resisting or acceding to ideological interpellations encoded in the way a story is recounted; or ethical responses to the values represented, assumed, undercut, ironized, complicated, or reinforced, as the case might be, through various kinds of narrative techniques.

Clearly, the previous list is by no means exhaustive. Nor am I claiming that any one narrative theory (or theorist) can address, all at once, questions about all these facets of narrative interpretation. Rather, I am claiming that questions about all these interpretive strategies fall within the purview of a postclassical narratology, which, as the essays collected here suggest, is now being pursued on many different fronts, in many different styles, and with a wide variety of descriptive and explanatory aims. Thus, what appeared to Lodge to be three discrete projects — *narrative grammar, narrative poetics, narrative rhetoric* — have evolved into interactive dimensions of a single program for narrative analysis. Admittedly, this program is still emergent. But in it, grammar, poetics, and rhetoric can be viewed as only semiautonomous domains; they constitute less a new narratological trivium than a universe of discourse where the foundations and methods of narrative analysis can be rethought. Such rethinking has made it possible to formulate new questions about (the relations between) narrative structure, its verbal, visual or more broadly semiotic realization, and the contexts in which it is produced and interpreted. I have already suggested how cognitive approaches to the problem of narrative grammar indicate the need for integrative, contextually sensitive models: analysis of the structure of stories also requires analysis of discourse-level features and the processing strategies that they trigger. Meanwhile, both rhetorical and feminist approaches to narrative analysis have revealed new ways of linking techniques and contexts. Peter J. Rabinowitz (1977, 1987) has shown how a reader's ability to "get" unreliable narration depends on his or her simultaneous (if somewhat uneasy) participation in two contrasting contexts of reception, the authorial and the narrative audiences. For her part, Susan S. Lanser has argued that Genette's taxonomy of narratorial modes (extradiegetic, homodiegetic, etcetera) needs to be supplemented with a richer description of the contexts of discourse production — for example, an account of whether a given story was designed as public or as private discourse (1991, 620). Such integrative models help explain why narrative poetics and the rhetorical analysis of stories are to some extent conflated in Lodge's essay. It is not that Lodge confused categorically distinct approaches. To the contrary: his tripartite scheme divides up research tasks whose interconnectedness it is easier to see now than when Lodge was writing.

Keeping these general remarks in mind, what do recent developments in narrative studies teach us to ask about Hemingway's story? Or, conversely, what does "Cat in the Rain" suggest about the limitations as well as the possibilities of structuralist models—about their scope of applicability? Given that what Lodge divided up into grammar, poetics, and rhetoric can now be viewed as interrelated profiles of narrative analysis, it is necessary to recontextualize some of Lodge's interpretive strategies; they now open out onto questions to which a more compartmentalized theory of narrative blocked access. For example, at several points in his analysis Lodge draws on the concept of narrative *actant* as it is developed in the work of Greimas in particular. Part of the attempt to formulate a grammar or more precisely a syntax of narrative, actants are names for the basic and general roles (helper, opponent, subject, and so on) that can possibly be assumed by characters in a story.[10] From an integrative perspective, inferences about actants can be grounded in behavioral paradigms that are cognitively based but also always situated in particular sociocultural contexts. Readers or listeners bring these paradigms to stories in their effort to understand them. But narratives relate dialectically to the paradigms: stories are not only susceptible to interpretation via the concept of actants but also, in some cases at least, promote a reconsideration of the concept itself.

Lodge uses Greimas's actantial scheme as a sort of grid for understanding the characters' relationships in the story (30, 31, 32, 37), though he does remark that the ambiguity of the narrative hinders straightforward application of the scheme to the text (30). But it is crucial to note that Hemingway's story orients itself around forces—routine, convention, powerlessness—that impede action, especially on the part of "the wife." It is hard to parse this self-consciously episodic story in terms of classical actantial models; as a narrative that helps readers question the nature and extent of human and especially women's agency, "Cat in the Rain" invites reflection on what it means to help, to oppose, to be a (female) subject. Application of standard behavioral paradigms will be stymied or at least suspended by the highly restricted scope— and the ultimate inconclusiveness—of the wife's effort to rescue the cat. A truly general theory of how stories encode action must allow for such complex modalities of inaction, which themselves constitute ways of acting. By the same token, the theory must account for a narrator's or an author's strategic reduction of human identity to marital roles (the characters are identified only as Americans, never named, and referred to throughout the story as *the husband* and *the wife*). Why does a given narrative foreground a particular type of social role as determinative of—or as a precondition for understanding—the ongoing action? Specifically, why does Hemingway use discourse-level features (in this case, particular sorts of referring expressions) to cue inferences that the wife is who she is, and does what she does, mainly because of her relation to her husband?[11] How does this foregrounding of sociocultural roles bear on classical theories about actants as a route of access to the deep-structural organization of plot? And to what extent does the narrativization of such sociocultural roles also work to naturalize them—to help make them seem built into the *experience* of subjectivity, antagonism, assistance, and conflict, as these things are currently lived by women and men?

Strikingly, then, even as Hemingway foreshortens the complexities of acting out an identity, he develops a kind of anti-plot that prompts readers to rethink what agency is and how actions can or should be recounted. The story's structure may have the effect of gendering certain kinds of (in)action as female versus male; nonetheless, "Cat in the Rain" displays surprising affinities with the women's narratives that, for Lanser, require a rethinking of the basic categories and methods of narrative theory itself. According to Lanser, "The units of anticipation and fulfillment or problem and solution that structure plot according to narrative theorists of plot assume that textual actions are based on the (intentional) deeds of protagonists; they assume a power, a possibility, that may be inconsistent with what women have experienced both historically and textually, and perhaps inconsistent with women's desires" (1991, 623). In other words, Lanser refuses to separate questions about narrative grammar from questions about the contexts in which narratives are designed and interpreted.[12] Her remarks reflect the move toward integration and synthesis that is one of the hallmarks of postclassical narratology; it is this move which allows us to sketch lines of inquiry not pursued in Lodge's account, given its structuralist provenance, its classical orientation.

Similarly, current research on narrative poetics and narrative rhetoric suggests the fruitfulness of thinking about Hemingway's techniques in conjunction with the way they can affect particular kinds of audiences. To put the same point negatively: postclassical narratology highlights the importance of not divorcing the study of Hemingway's narrative strategies ("such matters as tense, person, speech and indirect speech in fictional narrative" [27]) from their contexts of interpretation. Significantly, Lodge does not discuss the role of audience design in storytelling; at stake are ways in which storytellers structure narrative discourse to promote certain kinds of interpretive—cognitive, emotive, evaluative—responses.[13] Thus Lodge cannot formulate a question that has become central to recent work in narrative analysis: how do narrative designs both shape and get shaped by the process of interpretation? In particular, how do Hemingway's techniques acquire meaning from their situatedness in contexts of interpretation? Lodge's analysis teaches us that this situatedness must itself be theorized, on pain of our misdescribing (or perhaps underdescribing) both the narrative techniques and their meaning.

Note that some of Lodge's least persuasive claims about the story occur near the end of his essay, as he comments on Hemingway's ability to achieve "a symbolist resonance [in "Cat in the Rain"] without the use of rhetorical figures and tropes" (35–36). Here Lodge ascribes some quite dubious "connotative meaning[s]" to sentences contained in the opening paragraph of the story. For example, whereas many readers might be inclined to agree that "Americans opposed to other nationalities: index of cultural isolation" is a plausible paraphrase for the sentence *There were only two Americans stopping at the hotel,* there would probably be considerably less consensus about the plausibility of construing *It [the war monument] was made of bronze and glinted in the rain* as follows: "Inert mineral (bronze) opposed to organic vegetable (palm). Rain opposed to good weather. Euphoria recedes" (36). Nor would all readers be likely to agree with Lodge about the significance of the husband's tendency to keep reading while the wife looks out the window at the cat: "The husband is reading, a 'cultural' use of the eyes. The wife is looking, a 'natural' use of the eyes" (36–37). Part of the problem here was identified thirty years ago by William O. Hendricks in his critique of Lévi-Strauss's structuralist analyses of myth and Propp's *Morphology of the Folktale* (1967, 40–51). Specifically, Lodge makes his claims about connotative meanings not on the basis of the story itself, but on the basis of a prior interpretation of what the story, as a whole, means. What is left unspecified is the procedure by which the analyst derives this initial global interpretation from the words on the page. Thus, oppositions and contrasts (for example, nature versus culture, joy versus ennui [36]), supposedly encoded in a story's form, are in actual fact the product of an implicit theory about what the form signifies. In effect, the form is interpreted before it is described—or rather *so that* it can be described. And this at the hands of a structuralist approach that in its early statements purported to yield uniformly reproducible, because wholly explicit, methods of narrative interpretation!

My point is not that Lodge should be blamed for failing to achieve some sort of zero-degree, preinterpretive description of narrative form; my point, rather, is that *no* description is devoid of interpretation, and that insofar as they sometimes suggest otherwise, the structuralist models informing Lodge's account need to be rethought. The search for form and form alone is quixotic at best; at worst it entails a covert projection of time-bound interests, assumptions, and values onto narratives that are then argued to be a *product* of the very interests, assumptions, and values that are being read into them. That said, however, narrative analysts still have the responsibility of working toward the most rigorous formal descriptions possible. It is just that form, now, has to be situated in a constellation of textual and contextual factors in order to be rigorously described. Thus, instead of trying to read off the connotations indexed to a story's form, analysts should study how form is in part the result of contextually situated strategies for reading. These strategies are nonrandomly correlated with textual designs: barring specific textual indications to the contrary, one cannot read a homodiegetic narrative as a story told by a person not involved, in some way, in the events being recounted. Nor does Hemingway's use of past-tense narration permit readers to interpret the actions of his characters as hypothetical forays into a future that the wife and the husband do not yet occupy. But because they are contextualized, the reading strategies in question *are* variable: depending on one's own beliefs and values, one will impute various motives to the wife's concern for the cat, for example.[14] One might also ascribe different kinds and degrees of salience to the narrative techniques used to recount what the wife thinks, says, and does. Why, for instance, does Hemingway employ psychonarration only in connection with the wife? By contrast, why do the husband's thoughts and feelings remain opaque, decipherable only to the extent that they are verbalized in dialogue or realized as physical behavior? Do these differences in narratorial invasiveness, so to speak, derive merely from the story's thematic focus? Or do they suggest something about the system of norms and beliefs associated with the implied author—a system according to which, perhaps, women are the playthings of capricious longings and inarticulable desires, while men think, speak, and act sensibly, though maybe without much sympathy or understanding? If these are in fact the sorts of norms and beliefs undergirding Hemingway's formal designs, what is at stake when a female as opposed to a male reader interprets those techniques, or for that matter a male reader in the late 1990s as opposed to a male reader in the 1920s? Are the techniques "the same thing" in each case? Or does narrative form assume new implications, new meanings, across different contexts, such that form itself must be redescribed (and studied) as form-in-context?

In the foregoing paragraphs, I have raised only a few of the questions about Hemingway's story that can be formulated with the help of a postclassical narratology. Other questions—about the story's underlying structure, its logico-semantic properties, its organization at the level of the discourse, and the way it pertains to the contexts in which it is read—have yet to be asked, let alone resolved. Rather than pursuing my investigation of "Cat in the Rain" further, however, I should now like to widen the scope of the investigation by providing a fuller account of postclassical narratology itself. Specifically, it is time to provide more information about the contents of this volume and about the manner in which it is organized.[15] In the following section, I offer a description of the four main divisions of *Narratologies,* together with a synopsis of all the essays in the volume and an explanation of how each essay relates to the other essays with which it is grouped. My synopses, which are fairly detailed, are designed to indicate how each essay helps rethink classical models and tools; the synopses are also meant to show why *Narratologies* is more than sum of its parts. The volume is, as I see it, less a collection of discrete essays than the collective articulation of a bold new research program for narrative analysis. Postclassical narratology, because it requires pooling the resources of many disciplinary traditions, many kinds of expertise, is something that no single researcher can accomplish, no one perspective define.

3. Directions in Postclassical Narratology

The first part of the collection, "Classical Problems, Postclassical Approaches," focuses on problems and categories that have been foundational to narratological inquiry but that now need to be rethought in more or less radical ways. Such rethinking is an important part of the transformation in narrative theory bound up with the shift from classical to postclassical models. Part I contains an essay by Emma Kafalenos on function analysis, "Not (Yet) Knowing: Epistemological Effects of Deferred and Suppressed Information in Narrative," as well as two co-authored essays: Ruth Ginsburg and Shlomith Rimmon-Kenan's "Is There a Life after Death? Theorizing Authors and Reading *Jazz*," and James Phelan and Mary Patricia Martin's "The Lessons of 'Weymouth': Homodiegesis, Unreliability, Ethics, and *The Remains of the Day*." All three essays indicate how postclassical narratology, by reformulating (ways of asking) basic questions about narrative, reconsiders what stories are and how they can be read, described, analyzed, and, for that matter, *lived*.

Kafalenos's contribution is placed at the beginning of the volume for a reason. The essay discusses concepts—that is, the notions "event" and "sequence"—traditionally used to define what makes a story a story, what distinguishes narrative from other discourse genres, such as arguments, exhortations, and descriptions. The difference between a story and a syllogism is that, whereas arguments unfold as a sequence of propositions, presented linearly according to logico-deductive principles, a narrative is more than just an ordered set of propositions. It is a sequence of propositions used to recount events that themselves occur in a particular temporal sequence. So far, so good. Yet Kafalenos draws attention to a problem that has greatly exercised narratologists ever since Shklovsky distinguished the what (fabula) from the way (sjuzhet) of a story, the matter told from the manner of its telling. Some narratives temporarily defer or permanently suppress information about narrated events, thereby shaping readers' (and analysts') interpretations of the events they purport to represent. Such narratives reveal that events and sequences are reciprocally related, with an event being what it is as a function of the sequence in which it inheres and the sequence taking its identity from the events that constitute it. Kafalenos develops her technique of "function analysis" to give a more precise description of this sort of reciprocity, which had been insufficiently explored by classical narratologists. True, Kafalenos takes her inspiration from the account of narrative functions pioneered in 1928 by Vladimir Propp in *Morphology of the Folktale.* Yet she goes on to synthesize and enrich Propp's ideas with models drawn from Roland Barthes, Tzvetan Todorov, Shlomith Rimmon-Kenan, Meir Sternberg, Menakhem Perry, and Gerald Prince. Reading Balzac's "Sarrasine" and James's *The Turn of the Screw* as case studies, Kafalenos uses function analysis to characterize narrative not merely as a sequence of events but also as a second and parallel sequence of interpretations indexed to—indeed, in some sense constitutive of—the primary event-sequence. Paradigmatically, then, this first essay builds on classical insights but also reflects on their unexploited potentials, as well as their limits of applicability.

Ruth Ginsburg and Shlomith Rimmon-Kenan collaborate on an essay that reconsiders still other concepts that have been central to narrative-theoretical inquiry. At issue, in this case, are the ideas of "narrator" and "author" (including "implied author"). Ginsburg and Rimmon-Kenan begin by noting that classical narratologists bracketed the problem of authorial communication for methodological reasons. Extrapolating from Saussure's synchronic approach to linguistics, structuralist narratologists foregrounded the system of narrative (narrative *langue,* as it were) over individual acts of storytelling produced on the basis of that system (narrative *parole*). Also, by shifting attention away from the referent in favor of the signifier-signified nexus, Saussure set a further precedent for ignoring the biographical author as a factor bearing on the process of narrative communication.

Whereas poststructuralists such as the later Barthes further radicalized these structuralist tendencies, Ginsburg and Rimmon-Kenan draw on the work of Wayne Booth and especially of M. M. Bakhtin to rehabilitate the idea of the author in the form of *author-versions* that are historically and culturally variable. Arguing that the problem of the author is not even thinkable (let alone solvable) in existing narratological frameworks, Ginsburg and Rimmon-Kenan define author-versions in terms of a dynamic complex of relations between authors, texts, and readers. Author-versions are not biographical authors; nor are they co-extensive with narrators, since the narrator "is part of a model designed to account for textual operations" whereas author-versions can be used to get at the production of meaning in stories. Ginsburg and Rimmon-Kenan also discriminate between author-versions and Booth's concept of the implied author, arguing that from a poststructuralist perspective "even the biographical author is 'implied' in the sense of being mediated through texts (notes, diaries, correspondence, interviews, and so forth), and it therefore makes sense to speak of 'author,' *tout court.*" Building on Bakhtin's ideas — in particular, his view of language as a field of dialogic interactions between present intentions, past meanings, and future responses — Ginsburg and Rimmon-Kenan characterize author-versions as subjects-in-process engaging the reader in "a mutuality of subjective consciousnesses." Ginsburg and Rimmon-Kenan then turn to a reading of Toni Morrison's *Jazz* to explore implications of their model, especially its emphasis on author-versions as part of a "subjectivity-forming dynamics." Morrison's polyphonic discourse, its orchestration of multiple narratorial perspectives, reveals the author to be a Janus-like being, conducting the interplay of voices from without yet also emerging from within the fictional world by way of narrative structures and themes.

The other co-authored essay in this section, Phelan and Martin's analysis of the "Weymouth" episode of Kazuo Ishiguro's *The Remains of the Day,* develops the concept of "ethical positioning" to reexamine classical approaches to unreliability in homodiegetic narration. What is more, rather than editing out all traces of their disagreement over the significance of Stevens's reticence toward Mrs. Benn in this episode, Phelan and Martin attach theoretical — and ethical — importance to their own lack of interpretive consensus. As their essay suggests, a hallmark of postclassical narratology is its abiding concern with the process and not merely the product of narratological inquiry; stories are not just preexistent structures, waiting to be found by the disinterested observer; rather, properties of the object being investigated, narrative, are relativized across frameworks of investigation, which must themselves be included in the domain under study. Phelan and Martin's more specific purpose, though, is to articulate a more nuanced model for understanding ways in which narrators (especially first-person narrators) can be unreliable. Their approach combines a rigorous scrutiny of narrative form with an attentiveness to the contexts of narrative reception and, more particularly, the ethics of reading. Phelan and Martin note that Wayne Booth's path-breaking discussion of unreliability in *The Rhetoric of Fiction* has been taken up by so many different critics in so many different ways that the boundaries of the concept are now inconveniently fuzzy. A major problem is that, whereas Booth showed how narrators can be unreliable with respect to facts/events and values, they can also be unreliable with respect to knowledge and perception. In consequence, narrative analysts need an enriched typology that spans unreliable acts of reporting along the axis of facts/events, unreliable acts of evaluating along the axis of ethics/evaluation, and unreliable acts of reading along the axis of perception/understanding. This typology yields six possible kinds of unreliability: misreporting, misreading, misevaluating (= "misregarding"), underreporting, underreading, and underregarding. Revealing Ishiguro's Stevens to be a complexly unreliable narrator, a narrator who is unreliable in different ways at different points during the narration of "Weymouth," Phelan and Martin's discussion also demonstrates how narratives provoke complex, sometimes incommensurable, ethical responses from individual readers. Is Stevens right not to profess what his feelings have been for Mrs. Benn, formerly Miss Kenton? In part because the homodiegetic narration blocks access to "conclusive signals" from Ishiguro, this question cannot be settled once and for all for all readers. Instead, Phelan and Martin use the question to develop a more open-ended model of "ethical positioning." Readers position themselves by bringing their own ethical standards to bear on texts; in the case of unreliable homodiegetic narration like Stevens's, readers' standards help determine which subset of Ishiguro's ethical norms they view as most salient — as most relevant for interpreting the character narrator's behavior and/or words.

The first main division of the book, then, features new approaches to concepts and categories that have been foundational for narratological inquiry. The second section, "New Technologies and Emergent Methodologies," explores whether we need to build new (or at least more expansive) foundations for narratology itself. The three essays included in this section suggest how new technological and theoretical developments have promoted a search for alternative models and metaphors in narrative theory. That search has yielded new strategies for narrative analysis. Marie-Laure Ryan's "Cyberage Narratology: Computers, Metaphor, and Narrative," for example, begins by discussing the specialized vocabulary for which classical narratology has in some quarters become notorious. Even in its classical version, narrative theory borrowed metaphors from fields as diverse as cinema, traditional grammar, transformational grammar, communication theory, geometry, the visual arts, sexuality and psychoanalysis, philosophy, game theory, and feminism. Using a variety of literary narratives to support its claims, Ryan's essay investigates the relevance for narratology of yet another domain of models and metaphors: namely, computer technology and cyberculture. Integrating this metaphorical field into narratology, and drawing on ideas like virtuality, recursion, windows, and morphing, can provide new tools for the study of stories. Thus, as Ryan notes, her primary concern is not to rebuild narratology so that it can handle new genres of electronic writing, such as interactive texts, multimedia stories, and computer games, but to explore what computers can teach us about traditional forms of narrative.

Ryan cites recent discussions of virtual reality and characterizes narrative fiction as "the original VR technology." She also redescribes embedded narratives and departures from the main story line as recursive structures, and then uses the concept of windows (including window structure and window management) to illuminate one of the most neglected aspects of narrative strategy: namely, "how discourse keeps track of concurrent processes, how it unravels the tangled knot of intersecting destinies, how it deals with the spatial mobility of characters, and how it moves back and forth among the various sites where the fate of the story world is being decided." In the final section of her essay, Ryan explores some of the narratological applications of a concept taken from computer graphics; that is, morphing. This is a name for the process by which one image is transformed into another via a number of intermediate frames that gradually remake the source image into the target image. In particular, what classical narratologists called variable focalization and free indirect discourse can be rethought as instances of narratorial morphing. Ryan's postclassical approach proves especially beneficial when it comes to the study of third-person narration. Research in this area has been polarized between mimetic or naturalizing approaches, which regard the third-person narrator as an ontologically complete human being, and the approach associated with the work of Ann Banfield, who argues for the autonomy of fictional narrative vis-à-vis real-world communication. The idea of narratorial morphing points beyond this impasse; it helps reveal that we need not assume, as did some classical narratologists, that a narrator's features are rigidly determined for the entirety of the text. One and the same narrator can morph from a naturalistic personage into a non- or antinaturalistic storytelling strategy, and back again.

The second essay in this section, Uri Margolin's "Of What Is Past, Is Passing, or to Come: Temporality, Aspectuality, Modality, and the Nature of Literary Narrative," focuses in on one of the concepts Ryan associates with cyberage narratology, namely, virtuality. But Margolin concentrates less on the technological source than on the methodological implications of this concept. Specifically, Margolin reconsiders standard models of narrative as a genre thriving on singular past states about whose factivity or certainty readers or listeners can rest assured. Recent developments in both narrative theory and narrative practice have placed such models in question. While narratologists have begun to explore phenomena such as the disnarrated (G. Prince 1988), that is, reports about what did not but might have happened in the story world, we have witnessed a proliferation of avant-garde narratives for which the classical prototype of pastness + factivity + knowledge holds only in part or not at all. These include stories where the traditional retrospective viewpoint of the narrator vis-à-vis the events gives way to a concurrent or a prospective viewpoint, or where the dominant narrative modality shifts from the factive to the hypothetical, optative (may X happen!), or deontic (do X!). Far from being inconsequential oddities, such narratives constitute a modal system that is complementary to the restricted classical model, and they require new tools for their description and analysis.

Margolin finds at least some of these tools in the Tense-Aspect-Modality (or TAM) approach developed in general linguistics. On the basis of this approach, the three crucial dimensions of every reporting act can be defined as "the temporal placement of the event or state relative to the NOW of the viewing act as earlier, contemporary, or later; the event's temporal contour or inner temporal structure: is it seen from the inside or the outside, as a completed unified whole or as being in progress; and the speaker's modal attitude towards his/her claims about it: affirmation and certainty (= knowledge), negation, mere belief (= uncertainty), wish, hope, or command." All narrative propositions can then be viewed as consisting of a nucleus (DO X, HAPPEN Y, BE Z) modified by temporal, aspectual, and modal operators. And the prototypical case of literary narrative, which can be defined in terms of the TAM model as PAST + COMPLETED COURSE OF EVENTS + FACTIVE CLAIM, can be rethought as one possibility within a constellation of other possibilities. This specific type of narrational activity has come to stand metonymically for narrative itself, but it is the task of a postclassical narratology to recontextualize the unmarked case by situating it within a broader system of storytelling strategies. Drawing on narratives as diverse as Henry James's *The Turn of the Screw,* Christine Brooke-Rose's *Amalgamemnon,* E. Y. Meyer's *In Trubschachen,* and Marguerite Duras's *La maladie de la mort,* Margolin reveals the ingenuity with which writers continue to exploit the whole gamut of narrational possibilities. It is time for narratology to "catch up" with the discourse genre it purports to be studying.

Manfred Jahn's " 'Speak, friend, and enter': Garden Paths, Artificial Intelligence, and Cognitive Narratology" continues Margolin's exploration of narratives that resist classical prototypes and so demand new research strategies. The essay shows how so-called "garden path" (GP) narratives can be illuminated through recent developments in linguistic pragmatics, AI, and cognitive science. Again, the impetus for cognitive narratology comes from both narrative theory and narrative practice. On the one hand, quite early on theorists like Meir Sternberg and Menakhem Perry began to supplement classical models with an emphasis on the dynamics of reading. On the other hand, writers as different as James Thurber and Ursula K. Le Guin have created stories that invite strategies for reading which are then revealed to be inadequate or misdirected. Such GP narratives can be viewed as text-sized analogues of GP sentences like *Without her contributions failed to come in,* or *The daughter of Pharaoh's son is the son of Pharaoh's daughter.* Both the sentences and the narratives trap readers or listeners in a misreading that culminates in acutely felt processing failure; an act of reanalysis is needed to recover structure and meaning—to recuperate a structure and a meaning oftentimes at odds with those that *prima facie* seem obvious. Jahn reviews linguistic studies of GP phenomena and examines their function in "simple forms" such as jokes and riddles before moving on to the more complex variants found in narrative. To account for the narrative varieties, Jahn draws on research in AI and cognitive science; relevant ideas include *frames* (ways of characterizing stereotypical knowledge about states and situations), *scripts* (knowledge representations storing stereotypical action sequences), and *preference-rule systems* (models for specific kinds of decision-making processes). As Jahn notes, we strongly prefer to read a text for maximum cognitive payoff. GP narratives, or alternatively, narratives displaying any of a cluster of symptoms associated with garden paths, impede the satisfaction of this preference rule. In consequence, "The garden path is confirmed if the symptom goes away on conscious or unconscious reanalysis, either by switching frames or scripts, or by reshuffling the preference rules." Using Thurber's "The Secret Life of Walter Mitty" and Le Guin's "Mazes" as case studies, Jahn illuminates the cognitive mechanisms underlying the GP effect in narratives; the kinds of narratorial manipulation that trigger and support it; the corrective action needed to recover successful understanding; and the possible cognitive and aesthetic benefits of stories that lead us down these garden paths.

We come to the third main division of the volume, "Beyond Literary Narrative." The primary focus here is not on developing new ways to think about foundational concepts or excavating new conceptual foundations. Rather, the essays in this section show how a postclassical narratology can enrich other fields of study centrally concerned with narrative—all the while being enriched, reciprocally, by those other fields. All three essays thus demonstrate the extent to which postclassical narratology is an inherently interdisciplinary project. For one thing, the concept *narrative* has come to encompass a wide range of semiotic, behavioral, and broadly cultural phenomena; we now speak of narratives of sexuality, for instance, as well as narratives of history, narratives of nationhood, and even, more notoriously, narratives of gravity. But further, historically speaking new developments in narrative analysis often (perhaps usually) occur at the intersection of two or more fields of inquiry—fields only adventitiously divided up into "disciplines" in the first place. Thus Katharine Young explores interconnections between narrative analysis and (the sociology of) medical practice in "Narratives of Indeterminacy: Breaking the Medical Body into Its Discourses; Breaking the Discursive Body out of Postmodernism." My own essay, "Toward a Socionarratology: New Ways of Analyzing Natural-Language Narratives," works toward a *rapprochement* between literary-theoretical and linguistic accounts of narrative. And Lubomír Doležel's "Fictional and Historical Narrative: Meeting the Postmodernist Challenge" draws on the philosophico-logical concept of possible worlds to compare and contrast fictional and historical narratives—to explore just how much fiction-writing and historiography have in common.

Young notes that the narratives told by women undergoing gynecological exams can be better described as "replays" in Erving Goffman's sense. These discourse units are fragmentary, episodic, and open-ended, consisting of clauses that are sequentially but not always consequentially related. A story is begun, only to be abandoned or interrupted. Part of an economy of talk controlled by the physician, women's replays seem to reveal a characteristically postmodern indeterminacy. Yet patient narratives of this sort suggest less a postmodern sensibility of self as fragmentary than a set of strategies used by women to reassemble personal identity outside the constraints of the medical examination. Such "narratives of indeterminacy," in other words, are intendedly incomplete. Not only do they allow the patient to negotiate a verbal exchange in which she has trouble being heard; further, these replays dismantle assumptions about causes and effects, assumptions that would normally be imputed to events in the story world. As the physician touches the patient's body in a more or less invasive fashion, reconstituting that body as an object of medical investigation, the replayed story world thus "provides a spatial anchorage for various narrative presentations, over the course of an occasion or a number of occasions, of a self who is unfolding. The storyteller produces . . . an incomplete, discontinuous, metamorphic, ramifying body, appearing at disjunctive intervals in the same narrative space." In its postclassical setting, then, narrative analysis encompasses the study of how gynecological patients construct the very possibility of a self. Women being examined use stories to negotiate a shifting, often disturbing constellation of visual, tactile, and verbal signals.

Like Young's contribution, my own essay focuses on how storytelling functions as a discourse strategy in particular communicative contexts. My main purpose, though, is to outline a broadly "socionarratological" approach that synthesizes narratology, discourse analysis, interactional sociolinguistics, and cognitive science. Classical narratology was impeded not only by its excessive reliance on Saussurean theories but also by its failure to accommodate developments being advanced by Anglo-American researchers, who from the early 1950s onward turned their attention to units of language beyond the sentence. Traditionally, too, narratologists have devoted most of their attention to literary narratives. By contrast, a postclassical narratology needs to expand its focus to include natural-language data; it also needs to draw on the theoretical (ethnographic, linguistic, cognitive) models used to interpret such data and integrate them with other sociocultural practices. Based on two ghost stories elicited during a sociolinguistic interview with a seventy-seven-year-old female resident of Robeson County, North Carolina, my essay works toward a socio-narratological characterization of stories as speech events both shaped by and shaping communicative practice. Part of my essay uses ideas from cognitive science to rethink classical theories about narrative actants, usually construed as names for the basic and general roles that can be assumed by characters in the unfolding of a story (for example, opponent, helper, sender, or receiver). A narrative, that is, is not just a sequence of events, but a sequence of events performed by (or on) actants whose doings conform to known behavioral paradigms. Cognitive scientists have described how such general paradigms allow processors to make predictions and inferences about emergent experi-ences in terms of experiences already undergone. My analysis suggests that, likewise, storytellers draw on actantial paradigms as a way of promoting infer-ences about who's doing what in the narrated world. Yet this sort of narrative inferencing must be studied not only in terms of formal and cognitive struc-tures, but also as part of a rich, sociocommunicative context in which stories function as modes of interaction.

Lubomír Doležel's study of "Fictional and Historical Narrative" uses re-cent developments in possible-worlds semantics to explain what narratology can gain by opposing the term *discourse* not to *story,* as in structuralist models, but to *possible world.* The point is that the term *possible worlds* designates a more inclusive category than does the term *fictional worlds;* narratives invari-ably evoke worlds, only some of which can be characterized as fictional. This postclassical move puts a check on what Doležel describes as the "narratologi-cal imperialism" of the French structuralists. For Doležel, classical narratolo-gists overextended the scope of the idea of *récit;* by identifying story as what all narratives have in common, the structuralists flattened out differences be-tween text-types and genres, including history, historical fiction, and fiction. Here lie the seeds of a broadly postmodernist theory of history—a theory that conflates historiography and fiction-making.

A crucial turning point was Roland Barthes's 1967 essay "Le discours de l'histoire" ("The Discourse of History"). Eliding the referent and the signi-fied of historical discourse, and arguing that history, like the realistic novel, produces not reality but reality effects, Barthes set the stage for approaches like the one articulated in Hayden White's *Metahistory.* A double equation underwrites such approaches: "plot structuring = literary operation = fiction-making," or, alternatively, "historical narrative = literary narrative = fictional narrative." If they are defined as synonyms of one another, these terms yield a radically constructivist historiography—a historiography that founders, however, on the most traumatic events of the human past, such as the Holocaust. This is where the concept of possible worlds proves useful. As Doležel puts it, "Relocating the problem of fiction and history from the level of discourse to the level of world means asking whether the possible worlds of history and fiction are homomorphous or whether they show some marked macrostructural differences." Doležel catalogues a number of relevant differences; for example, whereas both historical and fictional worlds are necessarily gappy, incomplete, the fiction writer is relatively free to maximize or minimize gaps for stylistic and generic purposes, while the gaps in historical worlds are epistemologically not stylistically constrained. They are determined by the limitations of human knowledge. Only a totalitarian history, as Doležel shows, tries to arrogate the power of *creating* gaps in historical worlds. Doležel also explores what happens when the historical penetrates into fictional worlds and when the fictional intrudes into historical worlds. Such boundary crossings occur in historical fiction, in counterfactual history, and in factual narrative, or the so-called nonfiction novel. In all these settings, narrativization must be distinguished from fictionalization. Enriched by possible-worlds semantics, a postclassical narratology can provide a more precise description of the illocutionary, semantic, and macrostructural indices of fictional discourse; it can also provide a more comprehensive survey and analysis of the features associated with narratives that are not fictions.

The final section of the book, "Narrative Media, Narrative Logics" explores how stories are affected by their modes of transmission, the format in which they are relayed. Two of the essays in this section, Seymour Chatman's "New Directions in Voice-Narrated Cinema" and Robyn Warhol's "Guilty Cravings: What Feminist Narratology Can Do for Cultural Studies," revisit film and television as media for storytelling. As these essays suggest, classical narratology did not exhaustively describe, let alone explain, the narrative logic of what we see (and hear) on both the big and the small screen. A third essay in this section, Gary Saul Morson's "Essential Narrative: Tempics and the Return of Process," radically and provocatively extends the scope of the notion "narrative media" itself; in effect, this essay makes narrative a generalized medium, the medium of media, so to speak.

Morson focuses on an essential though underexplored aspect of narrative, what Bakhtin called its surprisingness or unfinalizability. For Morson, the "eventness" of events, made palpable by stories, is in some sense constitutive of all experience, every possible way of being in the world—however much we might try to repress that fact. Poetics, including classical narrative poetics, is a generic name for the interpretive strategies that have sought to finalize what cannot be finalized; from Aristotle to the present, poetics has tried to reduce dynamic processes to synchronic wholes, to neutralize time itself. Events happen to the characters in narrative, but the reader is invited to view the work as an entirety, spatialized, so that overall patterns are visible. Classical poetics therefore excludes contingency and eventness in principle; and to account for works that call attention to their own eventfulness—works in which contingency is part of the point—Morson develops what he calls "tempics" as an alternative to poetics. Discussing the compositional practices of writers like Fyodor Dostoevsky and Leo Tolstoy, Morson outlines a process-based rather than spatialized model for narrative analysis. Composed serially—in Dostoevsky's case, while confronting debtor's prison and recurrent epileptic seizures—narratives like *The Idiot* and *War and Peace* are steeped in the radical contingency of always only emergent situations. As they wrote, the authors often did not know what would come next. Classical approaches, insofar as they view narratives as structures more or less successfully realized by the storyteller, need to be supplemented with a tempics that studies stories as open-ended, relatively haphazard processes. Morson makes a stronger claim, however. He suggests that, in many research domains, "thinkers . . . have been drawn to [synchronic or structural] models, which, in effect, turn the world into a perfect poem. . . . [T]he chanciness of things, their capacity to develop in unpredictable and messy ways, has been regarded as something to overcome with the right theory." Tempics instead teaches us to view synchrony as a repression of diachrony, system as a way of mastering anxieties about process. From architecture and urban design to the information stored in the genes during the evolution of species: it behooves us to study these things as open-ended processes, stories in the making, and not just as data-sets whose underlying principles of organization must be identified and taxonomized. In this sense, tempics is a way of reading narrative as the medium for knowledge itself, not simply as a discourse genre that can be mediated by various semiotic systems, visual, auditory, or what have you.

Seymour Chatman's essay on "New Directions in Voice-Narrated Cinema" pursues a different strategy for enriching classical accounts of narrative and their media. Studying the role of voice-overs in narrative cinema, Chatman continues and extends in new directions what has become a sustained, extraordinarily fruitful interchange between narrative theory and film studies. Chatman notes that classical narratologists viewed narrative structure as autonomous, independent of any particular medium (words, dance, puppetry, semaphore) in which it might be realized. From a classical perspective, what makes a story a story appears to be determined by what the linguist Louis Hjelmslev called the form of the content plane, not by what he called the form or substance of the expression plane.[16] The key to narrative is the syntax of events, the enchainment, embedding, or alternation of occurrences, not formal or material properties of the semiotic medium in which narrative syntax presents itself. A postclassical narratology, however, is more open to the possibility of "the complicating effect of the medium on the narrative text," as Chatman puts it. Analysts of literary narratives have developed models that, in Rimmon-Kenan's (1989) phrase, neglect the medium; but perhaps because of the technical novelty and formal complexity of cinema itself, film theorists have, all along, more successfully avoided making the same mistake. In narrative cinema, viewer and analyst are faced with two different informational formats, sight and sound, that work concurrently but not always redundantly. Thus the filmic medium, unlike the print medium, is defined by its ability to desynchronize and juxtapose sound and image tracks. *Sound-off* and *sound-over* name two nonsynchronous uses of sound, the first referring to sounds located in the story world but not visible on screen, the second to sounds issuing neither from a visible nor from an off-frame source in the story world. Voices can emanate from a room adjacent to the one currently being filmed; or alternatively, music can cue the audience to make certain inferences about the ongoing action, even when it is impossible to assume that an orchestra inhabits the story world.

Chatman focuses special attention on those sound-overs which are vocal; that is, voice-overs that the audience assumes to belong to a narrator. Such voice-over narration can be used more or less extensively in a film, either as an additional tool exploited by the general cinematic narrator or else as a separate narrational source that takes over the generation of the visual images. Chatman explores innovative, sometimes comic uses of voice-over narration in such recent American films as Terence Malick's *Badlands* and Francis Ford Coppola's *Apocalypse Now.* European and especially French directors, however, have used voice-overs even more ingeniously, exploiting the heterodiegetic voice-over narration rejected by American directors as, presumably, too literary and uncinematic. Discussing such films as Bernard Tavernier's *Un dimanche à la campagne* (*A Sunday in the Country*) and Alain Resnais's *Providence,* Chatman argues that the film medium can facilitate a complex narrative logic, even though few filmmakers have been willing to risk making that logic a prominent part of their films.

The final essay in the volume, Robyn Warhol's "Guilty Cravings: What Feminist Narratology Can Do for Cultural Studies," rethinks both the uses of television soap operas as a medium for storytelling and the logic of narratological inquiry itself. Warhol draws on feminist research that shifts attention from the gender of the author, characters, and narrator to the way stories help structure the gender of their readers and, in the case of soap operas, viewers. Warhol's project requires a reconsideration of the role of close reading in narratology as well as in cultural studies, to which she argues feminist narratology can make a significant contribution. Feminist narratologists have been at the forefront of what Seymour Chatman (1990) calls "contextualist narratology." As Susan Lanser's path-breaking essay "Toward a Feminist Narratology" shows, feminists insist on anchoring stories in particular contexts of production and reception. Whereas the structuralist narratologists sought to describe systems of narrative meaning, not to interpret the meaning of individual narratives, feminist narratologists "borrowed the feminist-epistemological critique of objectivity from the social and natural sciences to object that systems of meaning are never neutral, and that they bear the (gendered) marks of their originators and their receivers." Close reading of individual stories is thus not a return to New Critical (and prestructuralist!) practice, but rather a strategy for ideological demystification. In particular, even though British and American cultural studies have distrusted close reading as a vestige of an apolitical "formalism," feminist narratology's contextualizing approach can reinforce cultural studies' concerns about popular audiences.

Especially important in this respect is the feminist hypothesis that a story not only issues from a gendered source (a woman or a man), but also displays formal elements that work to construct masculinity and femininity in and for its reader. Hence, when Warhol performs a close analysis of one scene from the long-running Proctor and Gamble daytime soap opera *As the World Turns,* she looks not so much for "meaning" (as traditional close reading would do) as for form — specifically for signs of what Warhol thinks of as feminine serial form. As a feminist narratologist, Warhol uses close reading neither to evaluate nor to interpret the text (as old-fashioned formalists would do), but rather to propose a theory of how it works to reproduce gender formally. At issue is the way (scenes from) soap operas function as what Teresa de Lauretis terms a "technology of gender." The sheer popularity and pervasiveness of the television medium make it all the more imperative to study this gender technology; it is an optimal medium for the narrative construction of gender, one of the best brands of "exercise equipment for developing the affective muscles" — "the set of gestures, stances, inflections, postures, and feelings" — "that constitute gender." Warhol's essay thus synthesizes narratology, feminism, cultural studies, and television studies; the result is an enriched model for narrative analysis, as well as suggestive new perspectives on gender and popular culture.

One further feature of *Narratologies* is worth commenting on at the outset. Each contributor has written a brief statement that situates his or her essay in the ongoing evolution of narrative theory. These contextualizing statements are set off in italics and placed at the beginning of each essay; they not only serve as brief "abstracts" of individual articles, but also provide a thumbnail sketch of relevant historical contexts and theoretical background. Read in conjunction with the overview just provided, the italicized statements should help readers span the gap between localized narratological arguments and the larger purpose of the volume: namely, to describe some of the methods and concerns of postclassical narratology, and also to explore how those methods and concerns pertain to what is already a very rich historical and conceptual context. In short, the contributors' statements highlight the dynamic interplay between tradition and innovation that characterizes narrative analysis at the threshold of a new millennium.

Notes

1. Note that I am using the term *narratology* quite broadly, in a way that makes it more or less interchangeable with *narrative studies.* Arguably, this broad usage reflects the evolution of narratology itself—an evolution that the present volume aims to document. No longer designating just a subfield of structuralist literary theory, *narratology* can now be used to refer to any principled approach to the study of narratively organized discourse, literary, historiographical, conversational, filmic, or other.

2. To list just two relevant special issues: in 1990, *Poetics Today* published two issues entitled "Narratology Revisited," edited by Brian McHale and Ruth Ronen; and in 1997 *Modern Fiction Studies* published a special issue on "Technocriticism and Hypernarrative," edited by N. Katherine Hayles. (For complete bibliographic information about works cited in abbreviated form here and in the contributors' essays, please consult the master bibliography included at the end of this volume.) Among the many recent articles and books that have promoted a rethinking of classical narratological models are those written from a feminist perspective (Susan S. Lanser's *Fictions of Authority,* Kathy Mezei's *Ambiguous Discourse,* and Robyn R. Warhol's *Gendered Interventions*); those written from linguistic, sociolinguistic and psycholinguistic perspectives (Peter Dixon and Marisa Bortolussi's "Prolegomena for a Science of Psychonarratology," Monika Fludernik's "Narratology in Context" and *The Fictions of Language and the Languages of Fiction,* David Herman's "Textual *You* as Double Deixis in Edna O'Brien's *A Pagan Place*" and "Towards a Formal Description of Narrative Metalepsis," Uri Margolin's "Narrative 'You' Revisited," Gerald Prince's *Narrative as Theme,* and Shlomith Rimmon-Kenan's "How the Model Neglects the Medium"); those written from a cognitive perspective (Manfred Jahn's "Frames, Preferences, and the Reading of Third-Person Narratives," Fludernik's *Towards a "Natural" Narratology,* Herman's "Scripts, Sequences, and Stories" and "Pragmatic Constraints," and Marie-Laure Ryan's *Possible Worlds, Artificial Intelligence, and Narrative Theory*); those written from a logico-philosophical perspective based on the concept of possible worlds (Lubomír Doležel's *Heterocosmica,* Herman's "Hypothetical Focalization," Ryan's *Possible Worlds, Artificial Intelligence, and Narrative Theory,* and Ruth Ronen's *Possible Worlds in Literary Theory*);

those written from a rhetorical perspective (Adam Zachary Newton's *Narrative Ethics,* James Phelan's *Narrative as Rhetoric,* and Peter J. Rabinowitz's *Before Reading*); and those written from a postmodernist perspective that stresses the ludic, nonformalizable, and anti-totalizing forces and effects of narrative (Andrew Gibson's *Towards a Postmodern Theory of Narrative,* Patrick O'Neill's *Fictions of Discourse,* and, somewhat more tangentially, Jean-François Lyotard's *The Postmodern Condition*).

This list does not purport to be exhaustive; it does not include all the ways in which classical narratology has begun to be rethought or, for that matter, all the titles that could be grouped under the modes of rethinking that I did mention. (For additional approaches to the rethinking of narratology and narrative theory, see the diverse essays collected in such recent edited volumes as Ann Fehn, Ingeborg Hoesterey, and Maria Tatar's *Neverending Stories,* James Phelan's *Reading Narrative,* and James Phelan and Peter J. Rabinowitz's *Understanding Narrative.*) Nonetheless, taken together with the essays assembled in this volume, my list of titles does suggest something of the richness and variety of the work now being done in the field of narrative studies. The term *postclassical narratology* designates this growing body of research, which has revitalized and transformed structuralist narratology in ways that the present volume tries to assess. See the next note for more on the contrast between classical and postclassical models for narrative analysis.

3. The idea of postclassical theory and its relation to classical theories were major themes at a colloquium on "Mathematics and Postclassical Theory" sponsored in the fall of 1993 by Duke University's Center for Interdisciplinary Studies in Science and Cultural Theory. For my understanding of the relation between classical and postclassical models, I am particularly indebted to Arkady Plotnitsky's remarks on that occasion. In their introduction to the special issue of the *South Atlantic Quarterly* based on the colloquium, Barbara Herrnstein Smith and Plotnitsky offer the following general characterization:

> While the term "postclassical theory" can be given a range of meanings in relation to more or less radical developments in [mathematics and science as well as contemporary cultural and literary theory], [e.g., developments] such as experimental and theoretical discoveries in quantum physics or significantly revisionary accounts of evolutionary dynamics in contemporary theoretical biology, its use here is intended primarily to evoke the various critical analyses and efforts at reconceptualization (again, more or less radical) that have emerged in the humanities and the social sciences around a cluster of quite general but problematic concepts, notably, *knowledge, language, objectivity, truth, proof, reality,* and *representation,* and around such related issues as the dynamics of intellectual history, the project of foundationalist epistemology, and the distinctive (if they are distinctive) operations of mathematics and science. (371–72; see also Plotnitsky, "Complementarity")

Plotnitsky and Herrnstein Smith go on to point out, moreover, that "the postclassical logic of undecidability may be applied to the very opposition between classical and postclassical. For this opposition, too, cannot be established once and for all, either theoretically or historically; nor can any hierarchy be established unconditionally between its constituents. Across the spectrum of the history or, speaking more postclassically, *histories* of modern mathematics, science, and theory . . . there is an immensely complex and sometimes undecidable interplay between that which is classical and that which is postclassical" (386–87). Although they are grounded in the specialized domain of narrative theory, the essays in *Narratologies* engage in this same broad project of (postclassical) reconceptualization. For one thing, the contributors focus on a cluster of concepts— *narrative, narrator, (implied) author, unreliability, event, sequence, temporality, actant, fiction, history, process, form, medium*— that are both historically and conceptually systematic with the "quite general but problematic" ideas identified by Herrnstein Smith and Plotnitsky. For another, the reader will discover throughout the volume a complex interplay between classical, structuralist accounts of narrative and the models and vocabularies that have evolved as strategies for rethinking the structuralist accounts.

4. It should be pointed out, however, that this (classical) distinction between narrative and narrative*s* is based on methodological assumptions reconsidered by several of the essays in the collection, including Ruth Ginsburg and Shlomith Rimmon-Kenan's, Robyn Warhol's, and my own.

5. This is a phrase taken from Susan S. Lanser's "Towards a Feminist Narratology" (1991, 614).

6. Lodge does discuss the distinction between fabula and sjuzhet but associates it exclusively with the second avenue of narratological inquiry, the poetics of fiction. Historically, however, theorists working on narrative grammars have made the same distinction. They have concerned themselves mainly with story structure, which Greimas, for example, construed as "a limited number of principles of structural organization of narrative units, complete with rules for the combination and functioning of those units, leading to the production of narrative objects" (1971, 794; compare Rimmon-Kenan 1983, 6–28).

7. It may be helpful to identify some of the representatives of these two contrasting approaches to the problem of narrative grammar, though of course I have sketched the contrast in very broad terms and it does not hold up at all points; that is, the two approaches are not always and everywhere antithetical. Research conducted under the auspices of the first approach includes Thomas Pavel's *La syntaxe narrative des tragédies de Corneille* and *The Poetics of Plot;* and Gerald Prince's *A Grammar of Stories,* "Aspects of a Grammar of Narrative," and (in part) *Narratology.* The second approach is represented by research such as Monika Fludernik's *Towards a "Natural" Narratology,* Herman's "Scripts, Sequences, and Stories" and "Toward a Socionarratology" (in this volume), Jahn's "Frames, Preferences, and the Reading of Third-Person Narratives," and Ryan's *Possible Worlds, Artificial Intelligence, and Narrative Theory.*

8. See, for example, Jahn's " 'Speak, friend, and enter' " (in this volume) and Herman's "Limits of Order."

9. Similar characterizations of this shift toward contextualism in narratology can be found in Chatman's *Coming to Terms,* Lanser's "Toward a Feminist Narratology," and Warhol's "Guilty Cravings" (in this volume).

10. For more on the syntactic or quasi-syntactic orientation of structuralist research on actants, see Herman's "Existentialist Roots" and "Pragmatic Constraints" and Pavel's "Literary Narratives."

11. In this connection, note that Lodge does not comment on the sexism evident in much of Carlos Baker's paraphrase of "Cat in the Rain": " 'From the window of a hotel room where her husband is reading and she is fidgeting, a young wife sees a cat outside in the rain. When she goes to get it, the animal (which somehow stands in her mind for comfortable bourgeois domesticity) has disappeared. This fact is very close to tragic because of the cat's association in her mind with many other things she longs for: long hair she can do in a knot at the back of her neck; a candle-lighted dining table where her own silver gleams; the season of spring and nice weather; and of course, some new clothes' " (29).

12. To put this same point another way, in an integrative approach models for narrative grammar will encompass both a narrative syntax and a narrative pragmatics, both a theory of narrative structure and a theory of narrative processing.

13. In talking about "audience design," I draw on the work of the sociolinguist Allan Bell, who describes style-shifting in discourse (e.g., switching stylistic registers from the formal to the informal or vice versa) as a strategy for accommodating diverse audiences. The audiences in question can be spatio-temporally proximate or distant, present or absent, interlocutors or merely those listening on. See the excellent discussion in Walt Wolfram's and Natalie Schilling-Estes's *American English: Dialects and Variation*, chap. 8.

14. In this connection, note how Carlos Baker's implicit allegiance with "the young husband" shapes his interpretation of the whole story. Specifically, Baker does not foreground the possibility that the wife seeks out the cat *mainly* because her husband has failed to provide her with emotional support and genuine companionship. For Baker, the husband comes across as merely "preoccupied," while the wife's yearnings are "irrational" (Lodge, 29).

15. With the exception of Katharine Young's "Narratives of Indeterminacy," which is an expanded and modified version of a chapter from her book *Presence in the Flesh*, all the essays collected here are new, written specifically for this volume and in support of its attempt to rethink classical models for narratological research.

16. This position is articulated by Gerald Prince in "Aspects of a Grammar of Narrative" (50–51). For a different perspective, see Herman, "Scripts, Sequences, and Stories" (1052–53).

PART ONE

Classical Problems, Postclassical Approaches

1 | Not (Yet) Knowing: Epistemological Effects of Deferred and Suppressed Information in Narrative

Emma Kafalenos

A function, according to Vladimir Propp, is "an act of a character, defined from the point of view of its significance for the course of the action" (1968, 21). Propp's recognition in 1928 of a disjuncture between an event and its function, as Lubomír Doležel discerns, marks a crucial moment in the development of a poetics of narrative. Doležel introduces the terms "functional equivalence" and "functional polyvalence" (1990, 144) to describe the possible relations between events and functions: One function can be expressed by different events (functional equivalence); one event can represent different functions (functional polyvalence).

Functional polyvalence is the underlying principle of function analysis, *a procedure I have developed. When Propp says that a function is an act defined according to its significance for the course of the action, he does not specify who determines the significance of the act. I heighten the instability inherent in functional polyvalence by assigning the interpretation of significance to the perceiver: a reader or someone listening to a story, a character watching events unroll, an individual contemplating events in our world.*

In the present essay I use function analysis to develop a theory that is both specific to narrative and in accord with the manner of reading that Roland Barthes uses connotation and starring to accomplish in S/Z — the study in which he crosses the boundary from a structuralist to a poststructuralist approach. My purpose, like Barthes's, is to remain attentive to the plural as a means to subvert univocal readings. But where Barthes more generally refers to the "moderately plural" or the "readerly" (1974, 6, 4), my concern is the finite nature of narrative and the effect on meaning of narrative representations that begin and end. I postulate contradictory interpretive procedures — resulting in sequences of events and sequences of interpretations that often do not correspond—as a means to elude epistemological closure even in nar-ratives that conclude.

In experiments beginning at Black Mountain College in 1949 and continuing during the 1950s at Yale, the artist Josef Albers demonstrated that a given piece of colored paper will be seen sometimes as one color and sometimes as a sur-prisingly different color. Interpretations of pigment as color, Albers showed, depend on the context in which the pigment is perceived: the color or colors next to which a given color is placed when viewed.[1] Similarly, interpretations of a given event depend on the context in which the event is perceived: the events that precede and follow it in the sequential set of events in which it is encountered.

When the set of events one knows about is incomplete, whether the miss-ing information is temporarily deferred or permanently suppressed, one's in-terpretation of a known event may differ from what it would be if deferred or suppressed information were available. Analyzing the epistemological effects of temporarily or permanently missing information in narrative—i.e., any representation of sequential events—helps us to understand how we process information about sequential events in the world as well as in novels, plays, biographies, ballets, and films. Moreover, when information is deferred or sup-pressed, the resultant gaps provide windows through which to observe how narratives—whether fictional or not[2]—shape interpretations of the events they represent.

The set of events one knows about at a given moment depends in large part on a perceiver's spatio-temporal position. One learns about events either through observing them, which requires one's presence at the time and place where they occur, or through channels of communication that are open at the time and place where one is.

Channels of communication are diverse: conversations, e-mail, a sixteenth-century manuscript written by a Bolognese nun, a recently published book on the history of Hong Kong. Which channels are open for a given individual de-pends in part on who the individual is—her interests, her visual acuity, what languages she speaks, how tired she is at the end of a particular day. But as important as these and other aspects of individuality are, none overcomes the exigencies of time and place. One can read a centuries-old document, for ex-ample, only if the original or a copy of it survives into one's own time, and is placed within reading distance of one's eyes. To watch a broadcast of the day's network news requires being near a television set at the time of the broadcast. This necessary correlation between the spatio-temporal position of a perceiver and the set of events that the perceiver can know about generally obtains, readers assume, not only for people in the world but also for characters in narratives, and for character narrators — narrators who present themselves as inhabitants of the world they describe.

Because our spatio-temporal position determines to such a degree which events we have information about at a given moment, it is not at all uncommon that the sequence in which we learn about events is different from the chronological sequence in which the events occur. Sometimes information about a given event is deferred; we learn that an event has occurred only after we already know about events that happened at a later time. Sometimes information about an event is suppressed; we never find out what happened. Because the effects of a perceiver's spatio-temporal position on the information that is received apply to characters in narratives and to character narrators, as well as to people in our world, characters and character narrators are also subject to instances in which information about events is temporarily or permanently missing.

For readers, the set of events that one knows about at a given moment in the process of reading depends not only on how much a narrator knows, but also on how much a narrator tells. Character narrators, whose information is restricted to what characters in their spatio-temporal position can know, and unrestricted narrators both have the power to withhold information that they possess. In Meir Sternberg's terms (1978, 260ff.), narrators may be *omnicommunicative* or *suppressive*.[3] Thus for readers, information may be deferred or suppressed in situations in which an unrestricted narrator or a character narrator chooses not to reveal information, as well as in situations in which a character narrator does not (yet) have the information and for that reason cannot reveal it.

Missing information matters because we interpret and reinterpret events, from moment to moment, on the basis of the information that is available to us at that moment. We understand events, I shall argue, by viewing them as elements in chronological and causal chains of events. First we organize the events we know about in a chronological sequence, and then we look for possible causal relations among the chronologically ordered events. We consider whether there is an event or events in the sequence we have constructed that could have caused subsequent events, or been caused by prior events. When information that an event has occurred is deferred or suppressed, the event is missing from the chronological sequence that perceivers construct. If the missing event is crucial, the causal relations that seem to obtain among the known events are different from the causal relations one would be able to perceive if information about the missing event were available.

Narrative theory provides tools that help to explain this process of perceiving and interpreting events. A narrative is a representation of sequential events. The representation is a process in which events are revealed successively, one after another. Readers who perceive the represented events conceive a parallel sequence in which the identical events occur in chronological order. The Russian Formalists named the two sequences *sjuzhet* (the representation) and *fabula* (the chronological sequence abstracted from the representation). As I use the terms, a fabula is made by readers from information found in a sjuzhet.[4]

Positing sjuzhet and fabula as parallel sequences permits conceiving instances of deferred or suppressed information as gaps in one or both sequences. Sjuzhet/fabula relations illuminate gaps. Gaps provide windows through which the separate identities of a sjuzhet and its fabula are often easier to perceive than in other circumstances. In this essay I analyze the effects of gaps in sjuzhets to explore how we process information about sequential events.

My ideas about the effects of deferred and suppressed information have developed under the influence of two important books on gaps in narratives: Shlomith Rimmon-Kenan's *The Concept of Ambiguity—The Example of James* (1977) and Meir Sternberg's *Expositional Modes and Temporal Ordering in Fiction* (1978). Although the two theorists accomplish different purposes— Rimmon-Kenan defines a specific form of structural ambiguity available to narrative, which she locates in certain late works by Henry James, and Sternberg explores the artistic effects of the placement of expositional material in a sjuzhet—both theorists analyze relations between sjuzhets and fabulas to explain the effects of specific narrative texts, and both illuminate relations between sjuzhets and fabulas by investigating gaps.

As part of their analysis of the relations among elements of narrative, both theorists distinguish between temporary and permanent gaps in information, and differentiate between the two types according to whether the gaps are located solely in sjuzhets or also occur in fabulas (Rimmon-Kenan 1977, 48; Sternberg 1978, 51). Since a chronological fabula (according to the definition I am using) is made by readers from information obtained by reading a sjuzhet, a fabula can contain only those events that a sjuzhet either explicitly states as having occurred, or provides information to permit a given reader at a given reading to deduce as having occurred.

In instances in which an event is suppressed (permanently missing) in a sjuzhet, there is a gap in the sjuzhet where the information might have been included, and a corresponding gap in the fabula at the location in the chronological sequence where the event would have occurred. A gap in fabula occurs whenever an event is permanently suppressed in a sjuzhet; if a sjuzhet gives no indication that an event has taken place, a reader will not include the event in the fabula she makes. In instances in which an event is deferred (temporarily missing), there are two gaps in the sjuzhet: one where the information would have been revealed if it were not deferred, and *another* where the information is later revealed ("a double chronological displacement—both when opened and filled in"; Sternberg, 241). But there is no gap in the fabula, because, finally, when the reader reaches the conclusion of the sjuzhet and places the last events revealed into the chronological fabula she is assembling, the previously missing piece is available to be included.

The idea that one can distinguish between temporary and permanent gaps through the presence or absence of a gap in fabula is grounded in the Formalist/early structuralist view of fabula as a material: a set of events from which a sjuzhet is made. Because a fabula (in this view) is conceived as finite (a finite set of events), it can be assumed to be available as a totality for analysis. Both Sternberg and Rimmon-Kenan move beyond this position. In Rimmon-Kenan's analysis of James, which we will consider later in greater detail, she addresses the question of how a sjuzhet reveals a fabula—and in the instances she studies more than one fabula—thereby reversing the perspective from the Formalist view of fabula as a material to be shaped into a sjuzhet, to a view of sjuzhet as revealing its fabula(s). Sternberg considers the effects for readers of the placement in sjuzhets of (temporarily withheld) expositional material, thereby addressing the relations between sjuzhet and fabula from the perspective of the reader and also considering the effects of temporary gaps on the process of reading, as the set of events revealed to the reader gradually expands.

When I define fabula as a construct that readers make from a sjuzhet, I do so as a theoretical move designed to shift emphasis from the Formalists' issues, where further analysis has largely been blocked by later theorists' problematizing of concepts including the "intent" and the "identity" of the "author," to epistemological issues that can fruitfully be pursued. My goal in the present essay is to lay the groundwork for a theoretical perspective that preserves for narrative much of the open-ended play of signification characteristic of life. By assigning the constructing of fabula to perceivers (including readers), I open the possibility not only of comparing individual perceivers' fabulas but of directly addressing the instability of a fabula as it grows and changes during individual perceivers' process of perception. Further, I provide a vocabulary that permits detailed analysis of individuals' shifting interpretations of events perceived in successive unstable fabulas. I also complicate the issue of gaps, in two ways.

Both Sternberg and Rimmon-Kenan analyze gaps (1) that readers are aware are gaps, (2) in literary narratives. Because my topic in this essay is the epistemological effect of gaps, I will analyze interpretations of known events, and compare interpretations of one set of known events to another slightly different set of known events, without much regard for whether a given perceiver is aware of the gaps in her vision. My interest in the epistemological effect of gaps also extends beyond literary narratives to any representation of sequential events, and even to individual experiencing of the world, which I think we conceive as a sjuzhet or sjuzhets, and interpret by creating fabulas, which continue to grow and which we reinterpret, perhaps throughout the duration of consciousness.

To consider the effects of deferred and suppressed information on interpretations of known events, I take as examples two literary narratives, and hope to demonstrate an interpretive process that will be recognized as familiar, as a way of "reading" events in one's world as well as in narratives. The two narratives are *Sarrasine* (1830) by Honoré de Balzac and *The Turn of the Screw* (1898) by Henry James. I have chosen them in part because both have been discussed so often that many people in addition to specialists in the nineteenth-century art story have read them. I do not propose to offer yet another reading of the two works; instead I draw from them examples of interpretations of sequentially perceived events.

Both works present a narrative world in which the story of another narrative world is told. This structure offers an embedded set of events (the events of the contained story), which is perceived from three locations: by characters in the contained story, by characters in the containing story, and by readers. Perceivers at the three locations are looking at the same events. Not every event, however, can be perceived from every location, nor are events revealed in the same sequence to perceivers at each location. Thus we can test the effects of suppressed and deferred information by comparing interpretations by perceivers at different locations.

1.

Before turning to the two texts, however, I need to define the terms *interpretation* and *interpreted events* as I am using them, and to do so I draw upon Louis O. Mink's work on modes of comprehension in history and fiction. Mink defines *comprehension* as "an individual act of seeing-things-together" (1970, 553), or, more precisely, as a grasping "in a single act, or in a cumulative series of acts, the complicated relationships of parts which can be experienced only *seriatim*" (548). Mink proposes that there are perhaps no more than three fundamental modes of comprehension. The one that concerns us here is the *configurational mode* in which "a number of things may be comprehended . . .

as elements in a single and concrete complex of relationships," for example, as "a particular configuration of events" (551).[5]

According to Mink, then, to comprehend events as a configuration is to grasp a number of events as a single complex of relationships. Mink sees this grasping as "a single act, or . . . a cumulative series of acts" (548). I agree, but the act can be analyzed from two complementary perspectives: as a grasping both that and how events in a configuration are related.

Understanding that events are related requires at least some understanding about how they are related. For one to be able to grasp a number of events as a configuration entails being able to grasp individual relationships between event and event, and between event and configuration. These individual relationships, when combined, form the network of relationships that seeing-events-together implies. The two perspectives I distinguish are two aspects of the same act, but the distinction is important in defining the act. I use the term *interpretation* to denote the act of seeing a given event in relation to the configuration of events in which one comprehends it. By defining interpretation with reference to a configuration of events, I am indicating that I assume that interpretations of events are contextual and depend on the other events in the configuration in which a given event is perceived. I assume that an interpretation of an event may change whenever the configuration in which it is perceived expands (or decreases) in response to new information.

Moreover, I assume that we interpret an event as if both the event and the configuration in which we perceive it were completed actions. I turn again to Mink, who analyzes cognition in terms of the temporal position of the perceiver in relation to the perceived event(s). While we are reading a story or watching "a game in progress, such as a cricket match," he discerns, we can "follow understandingly what we could not predict or infer" (545). Distinguishing between anticipation and retrospection, Mink argues, correctly I think, that "an historical narrative does not demonstrate the necessity of events but makes them intelligible by unfolding the story which connects their significance" (545). He summarizes: "It is not following but *having followed* which carries the force of understanding" (545 note 9; his emphasis).[6]

Like Mink, I see interpretation as a form of comprehending events that have occurred; we interpret events after the fact in a given configuration. But since my interest is not restricted to accounts of historical events in our world, but includes events in fictional worlds, and anticipated events in our world, I diverge from Mink's position in one respect. I argue that we interpret events retrospectively, as if they had occurred, whether or not they have occurred in one or another world, because we interpret events in the same manner — *as if* retrospectively, in relation to the configuration in which we perceive them—whether they take place in our world, in a narrative world, or in our imaginings as something that might or might not take place.

In previous work I have introduced what I call *function analysis,* adopting the term *function* from Vladimir Propp. A function, in Propp's words, is "an act of a character, defined from the point of view of its significance for the course of the action" (1968, 21), or defined "according to its consequences" (67). To define an event according to its consequences is to interpret it retrospectively, and in relation to other events in a configuration. Shifting Propp's emphasis to reflect my own concerns, I define a function as an interpreted event: an event that is retrospectively interpreted in relation to the events in the configuration in which it is viewed. I assign the act of interpretation to the reader in the first article I wrote on the topic (1997), and then in a later article I include, in addition to readers, the characters through whose perceptions readers view the narrative world (1995). In the present essay I broaden the field again to include, among those who interpret events as functions, readers who interpret events in a narrative world, characters who interpret events in their own or another narrative world, and people who interpret events in our world—where often we are left to determine which events to comprehend as a configuration without the guidance of novelist, playwright, or historian.

From Hayden White's work I develop an image of events in our world as a piece of cloth, or a ribbon, from which the historian cuts a segment. The placement of the cut guides interpretations. According to White: "The same event can serve as a different kind of element of many different historical stories. . . . The death of the king may be a beginning, an ending, or simply a transitional event in three different stories" (1973, 7). In my terms, the placement of the cut shapes interpretations by determining which events will be included in the configuration in relation to which the death of the king is interpreted.[7]

From Tzvetan Todorov I adopt the concept that the large-scale pattern of narrative is a movement from an equilibrium, through a period of imbalance, to an equilibrium that is similar but never identical to the first (1968, 96). Like Todorov, I see this cyclical pattern not as a rule to govern the shape of a story but as an abstraction—like a kilometer or a mile—that permits measuring the difference between for example, a novel that traces two complete cycles (equilibrium-imbalance-equilibrium-imbalance-equilibrium) and another novel that traces only a segment of the cycle, say from imbalance to equilibrium.

From the thirty-one functions that Vladimir Propp discerned in the Russian fairy tales he analyzed, I select eleven functions that recur in narratives of various periods and genres.[8] These eleven functions name stages in the segment of the cycle that extends from imbalance to equilibrium. I retain Propp's names for the eleven functions in my model,[9] and provide definitions that are developed from his but more abstract, and designed to reveal the general situations underlying the specific conditions of the stories he studied:

> Initial equilibrium [not a function]
> A (*or* a)   disruptive event (*or* reevaluation of a situation)
>> B request that someone alleviate A (*or* a)
> C   decision by C-actant[10] to attempt to alleviate A (*or* a)
> C′   C-actant's initial act to alleviate A (*or* a)
>> D   C-actant is tested
>> E   C-actant responds to test
>> F   C-actant acquires empowerment
>> G   C-actant arrives at the place, or time, for H
> H   C-actant's primary action to alleviate A (*or* a)
> I (*or* I$_{neg}$) success (*or* failure) of H
> K equilibrium

The six functions in the left margin delineate stages in one complete cycle: the move from an initial equilibrium to a motivating disruption (A or a), and then, through the four primary functions of the C-actant (C, C′, H, I), to a new equilibrium (function K). The functions that are indented are included in some narratives but not in others. They can be omitted without fragmenting the cycle.

An ordered set of functions is a semiotic system of interdependent concepts and terms, a set of words to talk about interpretations of events in relation to the configurations in which they are perceived. I propose the eleven functions listed above as a vocabulary. I recognize that there is many a nuance in interpretation that this set of signifiers does not permit naming. Even more problematically, signifiers, once available, can shape not only expression but thought. Nonetheless I offer this vocabulary as a means to sketch, if yet in rough outline at least in greater detail than previous approaches have permitted, the epistemological effects of deferred and suppressed information on interpretations of events, for characters in narratives, for people in the world, and for readers of narratives.

2.

The opening section in *The Turn of the Screw* provides an introductory frame that remains unclosed; there is no parallel scene at the end of the novella. But the section gives information, to James's readers as well as to Douglas's listeners, that the governess's account of events at Bly does not contain, including information that the governess does not know at the time of the events that she describes. The framing scene offers its information through the double lens of two men whose interaction with each other indicates a mutual respect that reinforces, for readers, the authority of both as sources of trustworthy information. Specifically, a first-person narrator quotes and summarizes—and offers as factual data—prefatory remarks that his friend Douglas makes to the people to whom Douglas reads the manuscript that the governess entrusted to him decades previously, before she died.

The two men convince us, I think, at least as we begin to read, that they know how less sophisticated people, like the governess, think. She is twenty, the youngest daughter of a poor country parson, taking service for the first time. Her prospective employer, they tell us, "struck her, inevitably, as gallant and splendid, but what took her most of all and gave her the courage she afterward showed was that he put the whole thing to her as a favour, an obligation he should gratefully incur" (James 1995, 25). The favor he asks is that she take complete charge of his deceased brother's orphaned children, and under no circumstances consult him.

Given this information, most readers probably interpret the governess's otherwise cryptic statement at the beginning of her manuscript about having "ris[en], in town, to meet his appeal" (28) initially in this way:

A   the children are a heavy burden to employer
B   employer asks governess to relieve this burden
C   governess decides "to meet his appeal"
C' governess sets out for Bly
G   governess arrives at Bly
H   governess takes charge of the children

According to this interpretation the governess is the C-actant who decides (function C) and then begins to act (function C') to alleviate her employer's function-A problem, which she is aware of because he asks her (function B) to relieve his burden.

Because Douglas has told his auditors, and thus readers know, that the governess will not see her employer again after she accepts the position, we may find somewhat pathetic her willingness to assist her employer in his desire so completely to shirk his responsibilities, particularly when she admits that she often thinks how charming it would be if he were to appear "at the turn of a path . . . and smile and approve. I didn't ask more than that—I only asked that he should *know* (37; James's emphasis). The governess cannot know that he will never appear;[11] it is the possibility that he may that sustains her infatuation.

The governess's infatuation is the first premise of Edmund Wilson's influential early study of the novella. Perceptively noting that the scene in which the governess wishes that her employer might appear immediately precedes the scene in which she first sees a ghost, Wilson proposes a causal relation between the two scenes. If the governess is sexually repressed, Wilson suggests (after reminding us that she is the daughter of a country parson), then her infatuation may have led her to have "conjured up an image who wears the master's clothes but who (the Freudian 'censor' intervening) looks debased, 'like an actor,' she says" (1948, 91). Peter Quint, in this view, is the governess's employer, in neurotic disguise. The governess's situation, as Wilson describes it, can be represented by these functions:

A   father's occupation ensures daughter's sexual repression
a   governess is infatuated with employer (lower-case a, indicating internal disruptive event)
A   governess sees visions
B_{neg} governess is isolated at Bly, with neither white knights nor psychoanalysts nearby whom she can ask for help

Wilson's world view is not unlike that of the two men in the introductory framing scene. Although from ontologically disparate worlds, all three are sophisticated, perceptive, experienced men of the world in the worlds they inhabit. The governess's view of her situation is very different from Wilson's, and the difference is in this instance not the result of a specific piece of information that one has and the other does not, but in the governess's very lack of experience. If she is sexually repressed she is too naive to know it. If she needs an analyst she is aware only that other people need her. According to her interpretation, immediately after the second time she sees Peter Quint, the children are in danger and she is their best available protector. The words she chooses indicate that interpretation: Peter Quint has come, she says, "not for me [but] for someone else" (James 1995, 43); she tells Mrs. Grose she will not leave the children to go to church because she is "afraid [for them] of *him*" (45; James's emphasis). These functions represent her interpretation:

A   Peter Quint has come for one or both children
C   governess will try to protect the children
C′   governess stays with the children instead of going to church

In the same scene, moreover, the governess establishes with Mrs. Grose the relationship that from the governess's perspective seems to continue throughout the rest of the narrative. Just after she tells Mrs. Grose that she is afraid "of *him*," she "made out in [Mrs. Grose's face] the delayed dawn of an idea I myself had not given her. . . . I thought instantly of this as something I could get from her" (45). Mrs. Grose begins to ask questions (function D), to which the governess responds (function E). By the end of the scene Mrs. Grose has identified the apparition as Peter Quint, and informed the governess that Peter Quint is dead (function F). Function F represents the acquisition by a C-actant of something—some object or information—that will be of assistance in alleviating a motivating function-A disruption. In this instance Mrs. Grose provides new information that the governess does not have. In ensuing conversations Mrs. Grose sometimes offers nothing more specific than an opportunity for discussion, which permits the governess to say aloud what she has been thinking—but this too the governess seems to perceive as a form of assistance (function F) from Mrs. Grose.

To the governess at the time that the events are occurring at Bly, it seems to me, Mrs. Grose seems as trustworthy as Douglas seems to readers during a first reading. Both Mrs. Grose and Douglas seem credible for the same reason: just as Douglas knew the governess while she was alive, Mrs. Grose knew Peter Quint and Miss Jessel. Many readers, I think, will see the following sequence of functions as a representation of the governess's interpretation of the events at Bly at the time they occur, perhaps even until the final scene:

A   ghosts threaten the children
C   governess decides to protect the children
C′   governess stays with the children instead of going to church
D   Mrs. Grose asks questions
E   governess answers Mrs. Grose's questions
F   Mrs. Grose provides information and discussion that help the governess
H   governess acts repeatedly to protect children

Rimmon-Kenan defines structural ambiguity, in her brilliant analysis of ambiguity in James, as "the coexistence of mutually exclusive *fabulas* in one *sjužet*" (1977, 41). Specifically in *The Turn of the Screw* she discerns: "Take the governess as a reliable interpreter of events, and you have one story. Take her as an unreliable neurotic fabricator of non-existent 'ghosts of the mind' and you are reading a diametrically opposed narrative" (119).

For readers to be able to construct two fabulas from one sjuzhet, some of the scenes the sjuzhet offers will need to be open to being read as one event in one fabula and another event in the other fabula (the governess sees real ghosts; she fabricates "ghosts of the mind"), but other events will occur in both fabulas. At least some of the events that are common to both fabulas will be interpreted in one way in one fabula and another way in the other fabula. Functions are interpretations of events. Where structural ambiguity exists, I propose, one or more events must fill one function in one fabula and a differ-ent function in the other fabula. Structural ambiguity offers a radical—perhaps even a limit-case—situation in which an event is interpreted differently in one, than in another, configuration.

The scene near the end of *The Turn of the Screw* where the governess and Mrs. Grose find Flora near the lake, and then the governess sees Miss Jessel on the opposite bank, offers an example. The governess says to Flora, "She's there, you little unhappy thing . . . and you see her as well as you see me!" (James 1995, 70), to which Flora responds by denying that she sees anybody or anything. Ad-dressing the governess, Flora continues, "I think you're cruel. I don't like you" (71), and then asks Mrs. Grose to take her away from the governess. Finally the governess says to Flora, "I've done my best, but I've lost you. Goodbye." (72).

Both the governess's and Flora's interpretations of what is occurring are revealed. As we have previously understood, the governess sees herself as a C-actant who is trying to protect the children from the ghosts she thinks have invaded their lives. The governess interprets her behavior in this scene as her major effort to vanquish Miss Jessel (function H), which fails (function I_{neg}). Flora, on the other hand, interprets the governess's behavior in this scene as cruel (function A), and asks (function B) Mrs. Grose to protect her from the governess.

For readers, if we have decided that the governess sees ghosts that are there, then we interpret this scene as she does: as a function H that concludes in an unsuccessful I_{neg}. If we have decided that there are no ghosts, we can inter-pret this scene as Flora does: the governess's ill-founded behavior has created a function-A situation for Flora, who asks Mrs. Grose to assume the C-actant role. The very same behavior can be read as a function H moving to an unsuc-cessful I_{neg}, or as a function A moving to a function B. These are very different interpretations of the function of the governess's behavior in this scene.

As Rimmon-Kenan perceives, ambiguity in *The Turn of the Screw* is in part an effect of the first-person narration; without independent confirmation the reliability of a character narrator's perceptions and conceptions cannot be con-firmed (1977, 119). Second, in this novella as in the other narratives by James in which Rimmon-Kenan locates structural ambiguity, ambiguity arises, as she skillfully demonstrates, as the effect of an "equilibrium of singly directed clues [which support one hypothesis—e.g., there are ghosts, and contradict the alternative] and the presence of doubly directed clues [which simultaneously support both alternatives—e.g., the governess's behavior in the scene at the lake]" (101). In addition, the ambiguity of *The Turn of the Screw* can be seen, by readers and Douglas's listeners, as the result of permanently suppressed pieces of information that the introductory framing section has given us reason to assume will be revealed. The account the governess writes covers the period from her arrival at Bly to the death of Miles. The chronological fabula that readers construct, from information in the introductory section and in her account, extends from at least a couple of years before her arrival at Bly to many years thereafter. The framing section draws attention to the gaps in information in the periods both before and after the governess's stay at Bly.

The gap that follows the governess's account stretches from the moment when, in her words, Miles's "little heart, dispossessed, had stopped" (James 1995, 116), to approximately a decade later when Douglas, who is ten years younger than the governess (she is twenty when she goes to Bly), finds her at home when he "com[es] down the second summer" (23) from Trinity. In terms of scenic treatment, which we know mattered to James, the gap extends from a scene in which the governess is holding a probably dead boy, to a scene in which she is entrusted with the care of a living girl, Douglas's younger sister. In terms of interpreting the final scene of the manuscript, James's entire suppression of the events of the decade in question effectively presents readers with an uninterpreted event. An uninterpreted event is an event to which no function has been assigned.[12]

We do not know what Miles dies of, and the diagnosis is important because the manner of death might indicate cause. Nor do we know the effects, if there are any, of his death; the configuration of events in which to interpret this event is incomplete. Moreover, interpretations of the event by characters in the narrative world are withheld. The governess's manuscript stops without indication of how she interprets the final scene and her role in it. Nor are we given at that time or later any knowledgeable, authoritative view. We do not even know whether the person who entrusts Douglas's sister to the governess is cognizant of the events of ten years before. Perhaps no one other than Douglas, who is very young when he meets the governess and finds her "most charming" (23), is in possession even of her version of the events at Bly. Retrospectively, we probably trust him (and the frame narrator who quotes him) less than we did on first reading, because of his failure to address the question that his listeners must surely have asked: please explain what happens to Miles.

Because the event comes to us uninterpreted it encourages interpretations. Peter G. Beidler, who summarizes the critical history of the narrative, cites more than a score (1995, 141–44), including these four recurring possibilities: (1) Miles is not dead; or (2) Miles is not dead, and ten years later is called Douglas (our minds have a tendency, I suggest, to perceive uninterpreted events as if they have not occurred); (3) the governess succeeds in getting Miles to confess (if we interpret the governess as the C-actant we see this as function I, a successful concluding event) and thus Miles dies free from Peter Quint's control (function K); (4) the governess suffocates Miles, or frightens him to death (if we interpret the governess as the C-actant we see this as I_{neg}, an unsuccessful concluding event—the governess does not achieve her goal, and will have no further opportunities to try).[13]

However one chooses to interpret this event, a knowledge of it instigates retrospective reinterpretations of previous events, probably including events at Bly that preceded the governess's arrival. During our reading of the governess's manuscript we see the events she sees from her spatio-temporal position. When we attempt to construct a chronological account of the events that occurred prior to her arrival, we become aware of how much information we do not have. We may also begin to think about how the events at Bly might appear to the children, from their spatio-temporal position. The children were sent to Bly, we remember, two years before the governess, and immediately following the untimely death of their parents in India. The children would view their lives, I suggest, as one disruptive event following another:[14]

A	loss of both parents
A	sent to a new place (Bly)
A	either (1) the disappearance and death of Miss Jessel and Peter Quint, if the two have had a supportive relationship with the children, or (2) being controlled and then haunted by Miss Jessel and Peter Quint
A	uncle has no patience for children; he disappears
A	new governess arrives; they are now in the care of an inexperienced twenty-year-old and the illiterate Mrs. Grose
A	Miles sent down from school (and no other arrangements for schooling are considered)
A	the new governess sees ghosts—that is, either (1) the children are possessed and the governess cannot save them, or (2) the governess's mental disturbance leads her to see evil in her charges
B_{neg}	there is no one the children can ask for help
C, C′	the children court the governess's good will by their incredibly beautiful behavior
$I_{neg} = A$	as beautifully behaved as the children are, the governess continues to think they are possessed
A	little Miles dies or is murdered
A	little Flora is hysterical

A? C'?   Mrs. Grose carries off Flora—that is, either (1) the final disruptive
event (A), or (2) a last hope for Flora's survival (Mrs. Grose as C-
actant, trying to save Flora)

Although the events that the children see and that the governess sees include many of the same events, the configuration of events in relation to which
they interpret specific events is not the same, in part because the children's
spatio-temporal position leads them to interpret the events at Bly from the
time they arrived, and with reference to their memories of why they were sent
there. The governess on the other hand considers (and writes about) the events
at Bly from the time she arrived, and with reference to her memories of why she
accepted her position there. The two interpretations are obviously very different, and thereby illustrate the possibility that a given event can be interpreted
as one function in one configuration and as a different function in another
configuration. When the configuration changes, interpretations shift.

3.

Narratives guide readers to discern a particular configuration in relation to
which to interpret given events. Readers are led to include in a configuration
certain revealed events and not others, primarily by the relation between a
sjuzhet and its fabula—a relation that is illuminated by gaps. The gaps with
which we have been concerned in *The Turn of the Screw* are for the most part
permanent (suppressed)—gaps in fabula. There are so many gaps in the fabula
because the sjuzhet reveals only a few events that precede or follow the governess's summer at Bly, and those few events are spread over a long period of time.
The fabula extends for decades. This particular fabula can nonetheless be conceived as one single line. We can see this fabula as a single linearity because we
are given enough information that we can arrange in chronological sequence,
reasonably accurately, every event we learn about—from the arrival of the children at Bly to the frame narrator's transcribing the governess's manuscript.

Within this linear fabula, the governess's manuscript traces only a short
segment, no more than a few months. This compression of duration in the governess's text guides readers to assemble as a configuration the events that are
available to the governess to assemble as a configuration; thus the governess
and readers (at least on first reading) tend to interpret events in relation to the
same configuration.

In *Sarrasine,* on the other hand, the gaps with which we will primarily
be concerned, both in the framing narrative and the contained narrative, are
temporary. The contained narrative, to which we will return, illustrates a gap-
producing pattern of sjuzhet-fabula relations that we did not see in *The Turn*

of the Screw. The framing narrative, however, creates a temporary gap in much the same way that James's novella creates a permanent gap, through a sjuzhet that traces only a segment of a single linear fabula.

As Roland Barthes has discerned, the framing narrative of *Sarrasine* exemplifies the narrative contract. The bargain in this instance is between the narrator (of both the framing narrative and the contained narrative)[15] and his companion, Mme de Rochefide. The narrator will tell a story (the contained narrative, about Sarrasine and la Zambinella), and in return, his companion indicates, she will permit him a night of love.[16] In Barthes's words: "Here, the [contained] narrative is exchanged for a body (a contract of prostitution); elsewhere it can purchase life itself (in *The Thousand and One Nights,* one story of Scheherazade equals one day of continued life); . . . in these exemplary fictions . . . one narrates in order to obtain by exchanging" (1974, 89).

A contract indicates that both parties to a transaction want to exchange something for something; both parties are motivated by a desire (function a) to possess something. But a contract can be reached only when the two parties want different things—each wants something that the other happens to possess. For both parties the motivation is a function of desire, but the object that is desired by each party is necessarily different. In *Sarrasine,* readers are ultimately given enough information to be able to recognize both characters' motivating desires. But although Mme de Rochefide's desire is chronologically subsequent to the narrator's desire, we learn about her desire first, because of the sequence in which the sjuzhet reveals information.

As we begin to read the narrative, on a first reading, we discover initially Mme de Rochefide's motivation. The narrator's companion is fascinated by the painting she sees at the party to which the narrator has taken her: an Adonis, who she says is "too beautiful for a man" (Balzac 1974, 232; *114).[17] When the narrator tells her that the portrait "was copied from the statue of a woman" (232; *117), she asks whom it depicts, adding impetuously "I want to know" (232; *119). He responds: "I believe [*je crois*] that this Adonis is a . . . a relative of Mme de Lanty" (232; *120). Readers interpret these statements, I suggest, according to the following functions:

a   companion wants to know the identity of the model for the Adonis
B   companion asks narrator who the model is
C   narrator decides to tell her
C' narrator begins to reveal information[18]

These functions that I think represent readers' initial interpretations probably also represent the narrator's companion's interpretation. Her interpretation of the further events that conclude the framing narrative is probably as follows:

G   narrator arrives the next evening and is shown to the "small, elegant
      salon" (234; *148) where she receives him
H   narrator tells story
I_neg companion finds story unsatisfactory, tells narrator to leave

Readers, however, if they continue to think about the fabula of the framing
narrative, may remember that the party takes place in a house that is familiar to
the narrator but that his companion is visiting for the first time, and, if so, they
may then consider that although the sjuzhet begins at the party, the fabula must
contain an earlier event, in which the narrator invites the woman he brings: a
woman he describes when he first mentions her in the story as "one of the most
ravishing women in Paris" (228; *59). I suggest that the following functions
represent the interpretation of the other party to the bargain, the narrator:

a   narrator's desire for Mme de Rochefide
C   narrator decides to try to win Mme de Rochefide
C′   narrator invites Mme de Rochefide to party
D   his companion is fascinated by the Adonis
E   narrator tells her the portrait was copied from the statue of a woman
F   his companion's interest empowers the narrator to trade the story she
      wants for a night with her
G   narrator goes to the small salon where she receives him
H   narrator tells story
I_neg narrator's story does not please; she tells him to leave

If we compare the interpretations I ascribe to the two characters, we see that
the functions assigned to events are in some cases different. For example, Mme
de Rochefide's request for information about the identity of the model for the
Adonis is a function B in her interpretation and a function F in the narrator's
interpretation.

The differences in the two characters' interpretations are the result of differences in the configuration in relation to which each is interpreting perceived
events. For readers, the companion's interpretation is the one we are apt to
perceive first, because the sjuzhet introduces us initially to her configuration.
Although the narrator's desire (for Mme de Rochefide) chronologically precedes Mme de Rochefide's desire (for a story), we are slower to recognize the
narrator's motivation, for several reasons.

First, the information that the narrator considers Mme de Rochefide "ravishing" and that it is he who has brought her to the ball is deferred in the
sjuzhet until well after the reader's curiosity about the de Lanty household is
firmly aroused. Second, the two pieces of information about Mme de Roche-

fide are revealed (and she herself first appears) at the same point in the sjuzhet that the ancient, decrepit figure whom the narrator's story claims is la Zambinella is first seen. In fact, the first sign of Mme de Rochefide in the sjuzhet is her "stifled laugh" (227; *54) in response to the ancient figure—in comparison to whom we are thereby guided to see her initially as a subordinate character, as primarily a lens through which to show readers just how horrifying the old creature looks to her unaccustomed, young eyes.[19] Third, the narrator's desire for Mme de Rochefide (his function-a motivation, as I interpret it) is never explicitly stated in the sjuzhet, although the reader can deduce as a probability that if he finds her "ravishing" and has invited her to the ball, he has invited her *because* he finds her ravishing.

Nonetheless, like the events in *The Turn of the Screw*, the events of the framing narrative of *Sarrasine* can be conceived as a single linear fabula. Although we can interpret the events according to two motivated sequences, Mme de Rochefide's and the narrator's, we can nonetheless arrange all the events we learn about in the framing narrative reasonably accurately in chronological sequence. In *Sarrasine*, in the framing narrative, the sjuzhet guides readers to interpret the situation initially as the companion does, by revealing the events of her configuration first. Readers are slower to understand the narrator's interpretation because information about the events that the narrator probably interprets as his motivating function a, his C-actant's decision, and his initial C′ action is in part deferred in the sjuzhet and in part left for readers to deduce and never explicitly stated. As a result, I suggest, at least on first reading, we listen to the story he tells (the contained narrative) and consider its effect with our attention more directly focused on Mme de Rochefide's desire than on the narrator's.

In the contained narrative, the information that is deferred—that la Zambinella is not a woman but a castrato—is so central that the temporary withholding of the information motivates the primary action as well as interpretations by readers and the narrator's companion. The young French sculptor Sarrasine, sent to Rome to study, naively enters an opera house in the Papal States, where he perceives in the prima donna an ideal beauty; she seems "more than a woman, this was a masterpiece" (238; *227). Naivete, I suggest, is one type of restricted configuration. Sarrasine does not know that la Zambinella is a castrato, nor that in the Papal States no women are permitted on the stage. Thus he interprets her as the woman to whom he will devote his life:

a   Sarrasine falls in love with la Zambinella
C   Sarrasine decides to win her love ("To be loved by her, or die" [238; *240])

C'   Sarrasine accepts an invitation to meet her ("I'll be there" [241; *289])

G   Sarrasine arrives at the mansion where the performers are assembled

H   Sarrasine tries to win her love

I_{neg} = A   he cannot succeed: she is a castrato; this knowledge motivates a new sequence

C, C', H   Sarrasine tries to destroy the statue for which she was the model and to kill la Zambinella

I_{neg} Sarrasine is killed by la Zambinella's protector's henchmen

Only near the end of the narrator's story, when Sarrasine finally learns that the woman he loves is a castrato, is la Zambinella's condition—and her interpretation of her existence—simultaneously revealed to Sarrasine, readers, and the narrator's companion. Prince Chigi tells Sarrasine: "I am the one, monsieur, who gave Zambinella his voice. I paid for everything that scamp ever had, even his singing teacher. Well, he has so little gratitude for the service I rendered him that he has never consented to set foot in my house" (250; *470). In what Barthes calls this "whole little anterior novel" (1974, 186), we see revealed a set of prior events and are permitted to glimpse la Zambinella's interpretation of the life-altering event of his childhood:

A   Prince Chigi's "gift" of la Zambinella's voice—i.e., the prince pays for surgery to castrate a boy soprano; the boy (la Zambinella) is far from grateful

B_{neg} the surgery cannot be reversed; there is nothing for which to ask; there can be no resolution

From the perspective of la Zambinella, all later events are interpreted in relation to a configuration that includes his castration. The configuration in relation to which Sarrasine interprets events does not include information about la Zambinella's castration until just before the end of the story and a few hours before Sarrasine's death. The difference in the information each has available explains their different interpretations of ongoing events; their different interpretations motivate their actions, with grave results.

The information about la Zambinella's castration can be kept for so long from Sarrasine because of his naïvete. The information is kept from readers (and from the narrator's companion) by the perspective—the spatio-temporal position—that the narrator adopts to tell his story. The narrator tells the story through Sarrasine's focalization; Sarrasine's perceptions and conceptions are reported in the narrator's words.[20]

The temporary withholding of information from the reader and the narrator's companion is the effect in this instance of a relation between sjuzhet and fabula for which we have not previously in this essay seen an example. In the contained narrative of *Sarrasine,* the events that are revealed cannot be conceived as a single linear fabula. We cannot arrange all the events we learn about in an accurate chronological sequence. For the years in which Sarrasine is growing up in France and la Zambinella is growing up in Italy, we have some information about specific events in both characters' lives, but no information about the temporal correlations between the events of one life and those of the other life. We do not know, for example, whether la Zambinella was castrated before or after the Good Friday when Sarrasine carved an impious Christ; we cannot determine where to intercalate the events of one character's life into the chronological sequence of the other character's life.

In situations such as this, I suggest, we conceive two linearities: two young people in two different places undergo parallel apprenticeships that lead to mastery in their different art forms. I see these as separate linearities, which come together and can be thought of as one line only after the two characters meet, during the period when they interact. When the information a sjuzhet reveals leads readers to construct a fabula that includes more than one linearity, an entire linearity can be temporarily deferred, even without anyone's suspecting at the time that information is being withheld.[21]

4.

We have now seen the two available patterns in which gaps in fabulas can occur, whether the missing elements are temporary (in fabulas constructed during reading, with gaps that will later be filled in) or permanent (the gaps are never filled in). A fabula that contains gaps is either a single linearity with missing segments (for example, *The Turn of the Screw,* the framing narrative of *Sarrasine*), or two or more parallel linearities, with at least one entire linearity missing (for example, the contained narrative in *Sarrasine*). Either pattern reveals certain events and withholds others, and thereby guides narrators' audiences, including readers, to include certain events and omit others in the configuration they are assembling.

Readers construct fabulas as they read. Each version of fabula that readers construct during the process of reading is a configuration. Readers interpret events as they are revealed in relation to the configuration they have assembled at that stage in their reading. As the fabula one creates grows and extends, the configuration in relation to which one interprets events expands. Interpretations shift as one reads *because* the configuration changes.

To summarize: Narrative is a representation of sequential events. Representations of sequential events are incremental, in most cases successive, and necessarily perceived successively.[22] The sequence in which events are revealed in a representation guides the contents of the configuration that perceivers establish. The power of the configuration to govern interpretation, which I have used function analysis to demonstrate, can be immense. Because of the effects of sequential perception on the configuration one establishes, and of the configuration on interpretation, any sequentially perceived representation of sequential events — *any narrative* — (necessarily, unavoidably) shapes interpretations of the events it represents.

Sternberg proposes that in literary narratives both the suppression of information and its subsequent disclosure "have to be quasi-mimetically accounted for, so as to avoid the reader's indignation at being 'cheated' (this motivation of the temporal ordering usually taking the form of shifts in point of view, notably shifts from indirect or external to direct or internal presentation" (1976, 308).[23] Similarly, Menakhem Perry perceives that "examples of 'distorting the order of the *fabula*' . . . are usually cases where the text does conform to a 'natural'-chronological sequence [such as] the 'natural' sequence of an 'external' occurrence; the 'natural' sequence of a character's consciousness; the sequence within a block of information transmitted from one character to another, etc." (1979, 39–40).

In both theorists' examples, I suggest, anachronies[24] are motivated by focalization — the writer's selection of whose perceptions and conceptions readers will be permitted to know. In *The Turn of the Screw*, as we have seen, gaps are the effect of the interplay between two focalizations: the governess's detailed account of a few months' events and the frame narrator's much more general grasp of a few temporal signposts spread over a period of decades. In *Sarrasine*, the narrator's focalization at the time the events are occurring (in the framing narrative) and the restriction to Sarrasine's focalization (in the contained narrative) similarly explain gaps. Focalizers' perceptions are limited by their spatio-temporal position in the narrative world, and by personal characteristics that guide them to attend more closely to some events than to others.

Whether focalization is restricted to one or another character, or a narrator occasionally reveals one or another character's perceptions and conceptions, or a narrator's own perceptions and conceptions are the only ones revealed, the information that is available to a reader as she progresses through a narrative text depends on whose perceptions and conceptions are revealed from moment to moment as the text unrolls. What I am proposing in this essay is that in narratives manifest as text, whether fictional or not, representation shapes interpretation according to this causally linked sequence: (1) focalization controls which events are revealed and in what sequence in the representation;

(2) the sequence in which the representation reveals events guides the formation of a configuration; (3) the configuration shapes interpretation.

5.

At the beginning of this essay I discussed the effect of the spatio-temporal position of an individual in our world on the information available to that individual. Whether we think of a narrative in which the focalization is restricted to
a single character whose perceptions and conceptions are revealed, or we think
instead of a narrative in which a narrator presents a finite number of events
from an external perspective, with or without commentary, the quasi-mimetic
nature of the sources of information in narrative (I borrow Sternberg's term
and concept [1976, 308]) ensures that a reader's sources of information about
events in a narrative world and an individual's sources of information about
events in our world are not dissimilar. Readers of narratives, characters in narratives, and individuals in the world establish configurations from available
information and interpret the function of events in relation to those configurations. Gaps matter because deferred or suppressed information is not available
to be included in a configuration, and the absence of the information in the
configuration may affect interpretations of known events.

For characters in narrative worlds and individuals in our world—but less
often for readers, particularly readers of fictional narratives—interpretations
motivate actions, and actions change the configurations in relation to which
further interpretations will be made. As a result, the distinction between deferred and suppressed information is often less important for individuals and
characters than for readers. For the character Sarrasine, for example, the distinction is almost irrelevant. The gap in Sarrasine's information about castrati
is temporary. But because he has this gap in his configuration when he meets
la Zambinella, he falls in love with the semblance of a woman and adopts as
his aesthetic touchstone for female beauty a being who is not female. The subsequent disclosure of the previously deferred information does not and cannot
rectify the situation that Sarrasine's previous ignorance has brought about. In
our world as well as in characters' worlds, temporary gaps have effects that are
easily seen.

Suppressed information can be differentiated from deferred information
only with reference to a point beyond which no further information can become available. Representations of sequential events—narratives—come to an
end and stop. Hayden White writes about the problem "of 'concluding' an
account of *real* events; for we cannot say, surely, that any sequence of real
events actually comes to an end, that reality itself disappears, that events *of*

the order of the real have ceased to happen" (1980, 26; his emphasis). The case that White makes—that the historian's selection of a segment of the historical record for representation unavoidably shapes readers' attitudes toward represented events—is supported by my concept of the configuration and its effect. An account (any account) represents some events and not others, and thereby guides the configuration that readers establish and in relation to which they interpret the function of the represented events. In a finite account, fictional or not, suppressed events leave permanent gaps in the configurations that readers establish and in relation to which they interpret revealed events. Like the effects in our world and in characters' worlds of both temporary and permanent gaps, the effects of permanent gaps in finite narratives are also easily seen.

The effects of temporary gaps in finite narratives are not as easily perceived. Certainly, as we have seen, a fabula grows moment by moment as one reads, and the sequence in which events are revealed affects readers' experience during the process of moving through a text. Temporary gaps color the experience of reading. Suspense, for instance, is the result of temporary gaps that arouse desire and withhold satisfaction during the process of reading. A more difficult question is whether, and how, temporary gaps shape readers' interpretations in ways that endure beyond the final pages of the text. I shall argue that they do: that narratives shape interpretations of events through the selection of events to be represented, as White perceives, and also through the sequence in which those events are revealed.

Previous studies that suggest that temporary gaps in finite narratives have a permanent effect approach the topic from several perspectives. Menakhem Perry traces an effect of the opening pages on readers' decisions about how to read the rest of the text: "The first stage of the text-continuum . . . creates a perceptual set—the reader is predisposed to perceive certain elements and it induces a disposition to continue making connections similar to the ones he has made at the beginning of the text. What was constructed from the text as the reading began affects the kind of attention paid to subsequent items and the weight attached to them" (1979, 50). As I read this passage, Perry is describing a process in which one of the ways that readers respond to the first pages of a narrative they are beginning to read is by adopting a set of principles by which to determine what kinds of information, and how much information, to include in the configurations they are starting to establish. I think that the principle of selection that Perry discerns is important to explaining how readers establish configurations. We have seen the significance of configurations in guiding interpretations of events.[25]

Both Perry (53ff.) and Sternberg (1978, 93ff.) have summarized and analyzed studies reported by psychologists who designed experiments to determine the effect on interpretation of the sequence in which information is perceived. These studies document the *primacy effect:* our tendency to accept as valid the information we are initially given, even when that information is contradicted later in the same message. When we read a narrative, we interpret events (in my terminology) as functions. If the primacy effect obtains for readers of narratives, and I concur with Sternberg and Perry that it often does, then our initial interpretation of the function of an event may endure even after we have been given information that contradicts it. In the terms I am using in this essay: a function is an interpretation of an event in relation to the configuration in which it is perceived. The primacy effect suggests that the interpretation may endure after the configuration in relation to which the interpretation was made has changed.

During the process of reading a narrative, I propose, we interpret events according to two simultaneous procedures. One procedure is the one I have been discussing throughout this essay: we interpret events as functions in relation to the configurations we have established at the moment that the event is revealed to us. The other procedure is the thought process that traditional narratology has taught us to perceive: we construct a fabula by arranging in chronological sequence all the events that the text we are reading reveals.

Temporary gaps in narratives can draw attention to and elucidate situations in which the two interpretive procedures produce contradictory readings. When we construct a fabula, we include information that is deferred but later revealed; temporary gaps have no effect on the final fabula that readers construct after they finish reading a text. Temporary gaps do, as we have seen, affect the configurations that readers establish as they read, and thereby readers' initial interpretations of events as functions. These first interpretations may endure because of the primacy effect.

The result is that events sometimes simultaneously carry two or more, often conflicting, interpretations as functions: the function we initially assign in relation to an incomplete configuration, and the function that the position in a completed fabula implies. Sometimes, even, we interpret an event according to the function that seems appropriate in an incomplete configuration, and then retain that function as our interpretation after we become fully cognizant of a larger configuration, where we would immediately interpret the event as a different function if only we recognized the need to reinterpret. In effect, we accurately perceive a completed fabula, but continue to interpret the function of an event in relation to an earlier incomplete configuration. Contradictions like these can occur, I suggest, often without our being aware of them, in our conceptualized version of a narrative we have finished reading.

I am proposing that an individual reader sometimes simultaneously holds contradictory interpretations of the function of an event, without necessarily recognizing the contradictions. One way to explore possible contradictions is to consider the sequence in which we forget what we have read. I suggest that readers of this essay join me in thinking about a narrative read several months or years ago, so that we can compare our present conception of it with our conception of it during the first days after reading it. Our grasp of fabula is most thorough and detailed during the period just after one finishes reading, and the influence of the completed fabula on readers' interpretations of events as functions is thus at its strongest at that time.

The character Pierre Menard, in Jorge Luis Borges's story that bears his name, proposes that a reader's recollection of a book read long ago, which through the passage of time is "simplified by forgetfulness and indifference, can well equal the imprecise and prior image of a book not yet written" (1964, 41). The "imprecise . . . image" that readers are eventually left with is often, I suggest, a function: an interpretation of a few (perhaps only vaguely remembered) events, often attached to a character as an interpretation — perhaps expressed in the form of a judgment — of that character's actions.

In instances in which a reader interprets an event in the completed fabula as a different function than she interpreted it in a previously revealed, incomplete configuration, it can be interesting to consider which interpretation endures after the passage of time. If the function that endures is the function that interprets the event in the completed fabula, then we can assume that the primacy effect fades and is replaced by later, more complete information. But if the function that endures is the function that interpreted the event in an incomplete configuration revealed early in the sjuzhet, then that finding corroborates the primacy effect and lends support to my theory that readers can simultaneously hold contradictory interpretations of the function of a given event. We need to allow for variation of course, from one narrative to another, from reader to reader, even from one reading to another reading by a given reader, in how disjunct a given reading can be.

But in my own experience, whenever I think of *The Turn of the Screw* (and if some months have passed since I last read it), I immediately envision the governess as innocent and vulnerable, and as valiantly devoting her youthful energies to C-actant activity that addresses existing problems. the children's uncle's "burden," the children's needs. This view of the governess, which is always the first thing about the novella that I remember, is in stark contrast to my considered opinion, if I am pressed to decide, which is that the governess's behavior causes a dangerous function-A disturbance: she seriously damages one child and is responsible for the death of the other. I would not permit this governess to care for a young person for whom I was responsible. Now my view of the governess as ardently devoted to saving her charges is in accord with my initial interpretation of the function of her behavior and is thus reinforced by the primacy effect, whereas my negative judgment of the effects of her actions is supported—to the degree that any judgment of a narrative characterized by structural ambiguity can be supported—by the fabula(s) I have constructed when I reach the end of the text.

Similarly, when I find in an article on *Sarrasine* the question of why the narrator would go home and write up this particular adventure,[26] I realize that this excellent question is not one that I have ever thought to ask. Again, I suggest, the primacy effect is at work. As we have seen in the section earlier in this essay on *Sarrasine,* the object of Mme de Rochefide's function-a desire (for information about the painting) is clearly stated in the sjuzhet well before readers are given sufficient information to deduce the narrator's function-a desire (for Mme de Rochefide). Thus the sjuzhet guides readers to be more aware of and more interested in the fulfillment of her desire than his. For this reason, I suggest, I read the narrator's story of Sarrasine as a function-H fulfillment of *her* desire (in addition to reading it as a wonderfully told story). Then, when I read the concluding pages, my attention is taken by Mme de Rochefide's very ungracious response to the narrator's attempt to please her: her self-pity, her too slight tolerance for intellectual discomfort, her abrupt dismissal of the narrator.

But I had not thought about why the narrator would choose to tell a story in which he fails to win the woman he desires, and fails moreover because the story he tells her does not please her. This gap in my thinking occurs even though I have constructed a fabula according to which the narrator tells Mme de Rochefide a story as *his* function-H attempt to win her. But although I have conceived and can describe two fabulas (one motivated by her desire, the other by his), the primacy effect, apparently, without my having been aware of it, has led me to respond to the narrator's story according to the interpretation I initially gave it: as a function-H effort to satisfy Mme de Rochefide's desire. Since my attention is caught up by her response to the story, I fail to consider how the narrator feels in response to his I_{neg} failure to please her.

Situations in which a first interpretation of an event as a function is in contradiction to the function of an event in a completed fabula are by no means limited to narratives in which the sequence of the representation diverges from the chronological sequence of fabula. Any sequential representation reveals information piece by piece. Interpretations are made in relation to available information, and the information available to readers during the process of reading is necessarily less than the information they will have acquired after they read on.

Life, moreover, in contrast to narrative, offers endless versions of fabulas that serve as configurations in relation to which we interpret, reinterpret, or—in response to the primacy effect—fail to reinterpret given events. Prejudice, for instance, can be analyzed in relation to the primacy effect: as a clinging to initial interpretations of the function of events in one or another of our inherited stereotyping "master-narratives"[27]—a prior interpretation that seems to block our ability to interpret real actions we have the opportunity to see played out by people whose race, gender, sexual preference, or religion is other than our own. What psychoanalysis hopes to accomplish, I suggest, can be seen as an effort to overcome the primacy effect: to change the function of a previously interpreted event by encouraging a reinterpretation in relation to the expanded configuration available to an adult patient and analyst. In contrast to life, finite narratives offer only a limited plural, as Roland Barthes tells us in S/Z, and many finite narratives offer a far more limited plural than the two from which I have drawn examples in the present essay. In Barthes's view, nonetheless, to which I subscribe, the goal of "interpret[ing] a text is not to give it a (more or less justified, more or less free) meaning, but on the contrary to appreciate what *plural* constitutes it" (1974, 5; his emphasis).

The explanation of readers' interpretive procedures that I am proposing is in accord with the goal Barthes describes. While I accept that a narrative that concludes may finally reveal a stable fabula, I argue that interpretations of the function of given events are as dependent on context as interpretations of the color of given pigments in Josef Albers's experiments. I emphasize the instability of a fabula as it grows and expands during the process of reading, and I propose that contradictions—between the functions readers assign to events as they read, and the functions that the position of the event in a completed fabula indicates—permit readers of narratives to participate in an endless play of signification.

Such a view of narrative supports a theoretical position that narrative is not a univocal mode of communication. It explains readers' intuitive experience that their interpretations change long after they have read the final pages of a narrative. And it preserves for narrative some of the instability—the condition of being subject to change—that characterizes and enriches interpretations of events in our world.

Notes

I would like to thank David Herman, William Bruce Johnson, Roland Jordan, James Phelan, and the two anonymous readers for the Ohio State University Press for their helpful comments on earlier versions of this essay.

1. Albers published his findings in *Interaction of Color* in 1963. The original edition is in the form of a box containing some 150 color illustrations in several dozen folders, and an eighty-page book. Later editions include reproductions of only a few of the illustrations.

2. Although I argue in this essay that all narratives shape interpretations of the events they represent, I do not intend to imply that in other respects I make no distinction between fiction and nonfiction. Marie-Laure Ryan salvages the distinction, I think, by brilliantly extending her earlier work on possible worlds to locate the source of evaluation firmly outside the individual text: "The reader evaluates the truth value of the text by comparing its assertions to another source of knowledge relating to the same reference world. This source of knowledge can range from sensory experience to information provided by other texts." Her argument is that "whether accurate or inaccurate, texts of nonfiction stand in a competitive relation with other texts and other representations because to the reader they offer versions of the same reality [whereas] fictional texts do not share their reference world with other texts" (1997, 166–67).

3. Gérard Genette, who notes approvingly that Sternberg uses these two terms to distinguish between types of omniscient narrators, adds that the terms are equally applicable to "focalized narratives" (1988, 78, note 8), which of course they are.

4. More specifically, I conceive a sjuzhet as a manifestation of sequential events in any medium and as incorporating, in addition to the components of the medium itself, the temporal factors of sequence and duration and frequency in the form in which they are manifested, all aspects of character beyond agency, and focalization. Following the distinction initially introduced by Genette (1980, primarily chap. 4 and chap. 5) between the narrative *voice* that speaks and the *focalization* that perceives and conceives, I include focalization as a component of sjuzhets manifest in any medium, and voice as a component of sjuzhets manifest in a medium that incorporates language. I conceive fabula as unexpressed in any medium: a chronologically ordered abstraction of the events and agencies a sjuzhet reveals to a perceiver.

Although I use the Russian terms to avoid the shifting signifieds of *récit* (often translated as *plot*)—a term that when paired with *discours* (discourse) is comparable to fabula and when paired with *histoire* (story) is comparable to sjuzhet—my definitions incorporate refinements introduced by post-Formalist theorists and are influenced by Shlomith Rimmon-Kenan's analyses [esp. 1976, 35–36 and 36 note 2] of the increasingly explicit definitions of French narratologists, including Claude Bremond's recognition [1964, 4] that what I term fabula is medium-free.

5. The other two modes that Mink proposes are the *theoretical* (in which a number of objects are comprehended "as instances of the same generalization") and the *categoreal* (in which a number of objects are comprehended "as examples of the same category") (1970, 550). Mink's early and very interesting essay on the relations between history and fiction comes to my attention through a reference by Abiola Irele, who defines narrative as "a mode of meditation . . . on immediate experience" (1993, 168), which is a definition with which I would not disagree.

6. Mink argues that the distinction between anticipation and retrospection may be more than a mere difference in temporal perspective: "We know that the difference between past and future is crucial in the case of moral and affective attitudes; we do not fear something that is over and done with, nor feel regret for something not yet undertaken. My thesis is that the difference is crucial as well for cognition: at least in the case of human actions and changes, to know an event by retrospection is categorically . . . different from knowing it by prediction or anticipation. It cannot even, in any strict sense, be called the 'same' event, for in the former case the descriptions under which it is known are governed by a story to which it belongs, and there is no story of the future" (1970, 546).

7. The historian Peter Burke perceives that "[a] narrative history of the First World War, for example, will give one impression if the story ends at Versailles in 1919, another if the narrative is extended to 1933 or 1939," and suggests that it "might be worth following the example of certain novelists, such as John Fowles, and providing alternative endings" (1992, 240).

8. Although I have derived my eleven-function model by considering which of Propp's thirty-one functions interpret events in the narratives from various periods that I read and teach, I draw attention to similarities between the set of functions in my model and those in two of the three five-function logically ordered sequences A.-J. Greimas uncovered in his analysis of Propp's morphology (Greimas 1983, 228), as well as those in the three core sequences in Paul Larivaille's extension of Greimas's model (Larivaille 1974, 376, 383); but I also note that my model is closer in spirit to the concise five-category plot-grammar devised by Thomas Pavel (1985b) to depict, in convincing representations of the causality of fabula, causally related sequences as interconnected trees. I choose a sequential model in order to trace the diachronic nature of readers' experience.

9. With one exception. I substitute C′ (C prime) for Propp's arrow signifying departure, to avoid a recurring symbol to which no ASCII code is assigned and to reinforce the connection between a decision to act (function C) and the act that reveals it (function C′).

10. By definition, function C is the act of the C-actant: the actant who decides to ameliorate A (or a). For the duration of any one sequence, the role of the C-actant is played by a single character (or a single group of characters acting together). In narratives containing more than one sequence, the role of the C-actant in one sequence may be played by a different character from the one playing the C-actant role in a second sequence.

11. Although the governess writes her account after the fact, in a past tense, the focalization is hers at the time that the events are occurring.

12. An uninterpreted event stands in contrast to an empty function. Empty functions represent events in the narrative world that are suppressed in the representation except for their consequences—e.g., *they lived happily ever after* (Kafalenos 1995, 133). My concept of empty functions and uninterpreted events has its origins in Gerald Prince's fascinating analysis of types of negation in narrative in "The Disnarrated" (1992, 28–38).

13. Success (or the lack of it), in function analysis, indicates only that a C-actant's intentional acts alleviate (or fail to alleviate) the motivating function-A situation; no moral judgment is intended.

14. Expressed in one formulation or another (e.g., *I had a salmon day today; whatever I tried to do I felt as if I were swimming upstream*), the sensation is familiar to everyone: that for a given period of time, the onset of which is often marked by a specific event (ever since the children's parents died . . .), everything has gone wrong. In function analysis, this interpretation of the way one's own or someone else's life has been going is represented by successive function-A events.

15. Genette comments that "to [his] knowledge . . . the situation of a *double narrator* occurs only . . . in *Sarrasine*." In his terminology, "the extradiegetic narrator [of the framing narrative] himself becomes intradiegetic narrator [of the contained narrative] when he tells his companion the story of Zambinella" (1980, 229 note 42).

16. The contract, as Ross Chambers perceives, "is as close to being explicit as decorum allows: in accepting the very intimate circumstances of the rendezvous in which the narrator reveals the secret she wishes to learn . . . Mme de Rochefide accepts her part of the bargain" (1980, 218). Mme de Rochefide even arranges the setting: a small salon in her home, softly lit and with a fire in the fireplace; she is seated on a sofa, the narrator on cushions at her feet.

17. I cite passages from *Sarrasine* in English translation only, and give page numbers that refer to the fine translation by Richard Miller that is part of his translation of Roland Barthes's *S/Z*. But to facilitate locating citations in French, I also include the lexia numbers (preceded by a star) that Barthes assigns to the fragments I cite.

18. Whether the information that the narrator reveals is indeed about events he knows to have occurred, or whether he begins at this moment to invent a story to tell his companion, to earn her gratitude, is another question. Readers of Balzac's story who have seen the film *L'année dernière à Marienbad* (*Last Year at Marienbad*), with screenplay and dialogue by Alain Robbe-Grillet, may find suspicious the narrator's hesitation and pause before he provides even the most general information.

Henrik Ibsen's *The Master Builder* raises similar suspicions in the scene near the end of Act I when Solness finally acquiesces to Hilda's claim that he kissed her ten years before, then asks what happened next. In all three works a character attempts a seduction by telling a story about previous events that may or may not have occurred in the potential seducer's world.

19. Although my emphasis here is on the ways in which this passage defers readers' understanding of the narrator's desire for Mme de Rochefide, her primary role in this extremely beautifully constructed story *is* to serve as a lens through which to show how horrifying the events of the narrator's story appear to a first-time listener.

20. The distinction between voice (who speaks) and focalization (who perceives and conceives), which was introduced by Genette (1980, esp. chaps. 4 and 5), seems most useful in two situations that *Sarrasine* illustrates: where one character's conceptions and perceptions are revealed in someone else's words (e.g., in *Sarrasine* in the con-

tained narrative), and where a character's perceptions and conceptions at the time of an ongoing set of events are revealed in that character's words *at a later time* (e.g., in *Sarrasine* in the framing narrative, in which the narrator maintains suspense by revealing no more than he knew at the time of the events he describes).

21. As Chambers discerns, the narration is not fully restricted to Sarrasine's focalization all the way to the end of the telling. Chambers locates the change as beginning after the narrator's companion's second interruption, after which she and readers are "free[d] . . . from absolute subjugation to Sarrasine's point of view" (1980, 228). His example, two paragraphs later in Balzac's text, is the response to Vitagliani's telling Sarrasine, "Go ahead; you need fear no rivals here" (Balzac 1974, 243; *331). Chambers perceives, and draws attention to "the shift in narrative point of view which is now able to notice (although Sarrasine does not) the malicious smiles which accompany Vitagliani's equivocal remark" (1980, 229).

22. Even in instances in which two or more events are represented simultaneously in a visual medium, we view the events successively if, and as long as, we conceive specific increments as separate events. As soon as we move to a broader perspective—e.g., we stand back to view the overriding shape of the mountain in the background—we are no longer perceiving separate events, although we may do so again thereafter. Often the painter (or choreographer, or cinematographer) uses one or another technique of the medium to guide the sequence of perception. In certain Postmodern works the sequence of perception—and thus the "work" one perceives and one's interpretation of it—shifts from viewing to viewing. On the power of a fixed visual image to represent a narrative, see my "Implications of Narrative in Painting and Photography" (1996).

23. I cite the early version of this essay because in the revised version (in *Expositional Modes and Temporal Ordering in Fiction* [1978, 218]) Sternberg leaves out the phrase in which he suggests that a quasi-mimetic explanation for gaps may be motivated by a desire to keep readers satisfied, which is an important idea in the argument I am developing.

24. I use the word as Genette does (1980, 40), to indicate situations in which the sequence of the representation diverges from the chronological sequence of fabula.

25. Perry continues: "It is not only the relative weight of items in the following stages which is affected. . . . The details of the sequel are assimilated as best they can into a prepared framework where they undergo an assimilative change of meaning: had this material *stood on its own* it would have had other implications than those now activated" (1979, 50; his emphasis). An "assimilative change of meaning," I suggest, is a way of describing the effect of a configuration on interpretations of events that are perceived in relation to it, which we have been discussing throughout this essay.

26. Per Nykrog asks in addition two related questions: for whom the narrator writes, and why the narrator gives Mme de Rochefide the last word (1992, 439). Of course Nykrog recognizes (as do I) that the story we read was written not by the narrator but by Balzac, which in no way lessens the interesting speculation his questions raise about the character narrator's motivation.

27. In *The Postmodern Condition,* Jean-François Lyotard posits and analyzes "grand" narratives of legitimation. My ideas about how master-narratives (abstract but pervasive sets of judgments or world views) can influence readers' interpretations of written narratives, as well as individuals' interpretations of events perceived in the world, have developed in conversations with Teresa Carson, who is writing a dissertation on a related topic, and whom I thank.

Is There a Life after Death?
Theorizing Authors and Reading *Jazz*
Ruth Ginsburg and Shlomith Rimmon-Kenan

This essay is an attempt to rethink the problem of authors and author-ship against narratological and poststructuralist accounts. Based on Saussurean linguistics and the structuralist enterprise, classical narra-tology bracketed authors for methodological reasons. Reacting to those approaches as well as to phenomenological models of the cogito, *post-structuralists like Barthes and Foucault radicalized the notions of sign and subject, launching an attack on the author. They set out to destroy the concept of a single origin and owner of the text, of an authority that controls and limits its meaning. Ousting the tyrant they glorified the liberated reader of the orphaned text.*

A re-reading of classical narratology with Wayne Booth and espe-cially M. M. Bakhtin in mind opens up a different perspective on authors. Historicizing and contextualizing such notions as author, im-plied author, and narrator, we argue for the advantages of the idea of "author-versions," defined in terms of a dynamic complex of re-lations between authors, texts, and readers. Against the backdrop of ideological-political changes that reaffirm the agency and responsibility of subjects, we explore how author-versions can help rethink classical narratological approaches to authors, narrators, readers, and the re-lationships between them. Specifically, we sketch a narrational process in which authors producing fictional worlds create themselves as open subjects. This process entails a probing of authority, responsibility, and freedom.

Toni Morrison's Jazz *illuminates the same process in an especially compelling way. In the novel, author, narrators, characters, and readers alike undergo a gradual change involving the renunciation of authority and knowledge. Opening up to surprising facets of the other, partici-pants in the narrational process create hitherto unforeseen possibilities in the represented world. Both the relaxation of authoritative control and the freedom-granting recognition of others bring home the need for a new, contextually oriented conception of authors as Janus-like—as doubly directed beings defying borders (for example, the border between the textual and the extratextual) and challenging comfortable distinctions (for example, narrator versus author). As* Jazz *suggests, author-versions orchestrate the process of narration from the outside yet simultaneously emerge from within the fictional world by way of both thematic and structural designs.*

Why Author?

In 1968, the Author was publicly put to death. In his funeral oration, Barthes eloquently portrayed the deceased. This memorable portrait of an authoritarian tyrant, exercising arbitrary control over subjects and texts, has become a classic of contemporary thought. In a struggle for freedom, this oration was taken to be the weapon dealing the deathblow to what in retrospect can be seen as only one version of author. In this essay, we attempt to explore and theorize the problematics surrounding the concept of author and to outline one particular version, not necessarily entailing murder. We shall then read Toni Morrison's *Jazz* in dialogue with this version, in which the hero-author[1] develops a more benign relation to subjects and texts—one of relaxing authority and encouraging their freedom.

1.

To present the alternative we are concerned with, as well as for our own contribution to that alternative, we need to historicize and contextualize the debate in which we wish to intervene. The immediate historical context concerns structuralism (with its narratological offshoot) and poststructuralism, two partly overlapping intellectual movements of the sixties and seventies. Of the varied facets of this complex context we shall foreground those which bear directly on problems of authority, control, and freedom, restricting our exploration to literary texts.

True, authority, control, and freedom are notions that did not feature as such in classical narratology. From this point of view, the latter could perhaps have remained external to our account. Nevertheless, classical narratology is highly relevant, since it anticipated later attacks on the Author. More importantly, the above notions can be seen, retrospectively, as implicit in it. These implications can best be extrapolated from the insights of structural linguistics on which narratology founded its own models.

As is well known, Saussure based his structural linguistics on the central concepts of system, structure, and sign. These are manifested in distinctions that invite the methodological bracketing of authors, namely, *langue* versus *parole,* synchronic versus diachronic, signifier versus signified, sign versus referent. Just as linguistics advocated the study of *langue* — the general system of language (with its surface and deep structure) — so narratology insisted on the study of the general laws taken to govern all narratives. No individual can be taken to create, author, or even enunciate *langue,* as distinct from *parole.* Further, the correlate synchronic bias in linguistics has led narratologists to a universalistic conception of the excluded Author, blinding them to diachronic changes which may give rise to different versions of authors. The contours of linguistics (and therefore of narratology) were also limited in a way that left referents out, the biographical author being one such referent.

These linguistic-narratological concepts not only severed traditional ties with authors but also involved a subordination of subjects in general to systems. Being "spoken" by language rather than speaking or owning it, the speaking subject was subjected to the laws and constraints of the language s/he did not author. These positions were also implicit in the Saussurean notion of the sign where the relation between signifier and signified, as well as that between sign and referent, was defined as arbitrary; that is, convention-bound. Obviously, convention imposes a limitation of freedom for the speaking subject. Later adaptations and modifications further radicalized the dual nature of "sign," relating the problem of meaning to that of subjects, thus triggering an escalation from methodological to ideological attacks on the author.

Once the concept of the sign was taken up by other disciplines, primarily anthropology and psychoanalysis, Saussure's cohesive duality became a split in both sign and subject. The split, now exposing a signifier and a signified precariously yoked together, destabilized faith in the reliability of the sign as an indicator of binding meaning. Moreover, when "I" (or "author," for that matter) is no longer securely tied to a concept of subjectivity, it is not only emptied of all subjective meaning-possibility, but becomes a mere grapho-vocal gesture. One cannot say "I" without risking the slippage of the "self" formerly signified by it. Such a view completely undermines the ideas of self-expression and intention, two traditional attributes of authors. With "I" forever lost to oneself, no user of language could lay claim to ownership of language and control of meaning. No longer a move directed to distance an author-other outside, the conflict was now raging in language itself, splitting the subject-sign to confront the subject-other inside.

Since this radicalization logically leads to the impossibility of authors as originators of binding meaning, how can one explain the emotionally charged tone of Barthes and his followers? Logic would lead to the "death" of the author in any case. The vehemence of the attack was determined not only by the far-reaching implications of structuralism but also by the philosophical background of those leading the struggle. As Sean Burke has so convincingly shown, it was

[T]he intersection between phenomenology and structuralism, however, [that] produced an iconoclastic and far-ranging form of antisubjectivism. Having been schooled in phenomenological method, and having seen two of the great sciences of the human subject—anthropology and psychoanalysis—dispense with the subject under a structuralist sign, Barthes, Foucault, and Derrida were not content with simply sidelining the authorial subject as in earlier formalisms. A phenomenological training had taught them that the subject was too powerful, too sophisticated a concept to be simply bracketed; rather subjectivity was something to be annihilated. Nor either could they be content to see the death of the subject as something applying merely to the area of literary studies. The death of the author must connect with a general death of man. At the limit, therefore, between phenomenology and structuralism the discourse of the death of the author as we know it comes into its being. An era of theory is under way in which language is "the destroyer of all subject"—the author of literary studies, the transcendental subject of philosophies of consciousness, the subject of political theory, psychoanalysis, anthropology. (1992, 14)

The Author this discourse set out to destroy had to be experienced as a threat to justify this kind of attack. A portrait of the Author's threatening figure can be extracted mainly from Barthes's "The Death of the Author" (1977a[1968]) but also from one strand in Foucault's "What Is an Author?" (1984[1969]). In both, the authorial subject becomes perforce a menace to the freedom of meaning. At once human ("the human person," Barthes 1977a, 143) and divine ("the Author-God," 146), this subject is single ("a single person," 143), and endowed with interiority (144; Foucault 1984, 102). Temporally anteceding the text, he is its origin, privileged owner and authority, controlling and limiting its meanings. In Foucault's words, "[T]he author is . . . the ideological figure by which one marks the manner in which we fear the proliferation of meaning" (119). In other words, the construction of meanings in the process of reading is, *a priori,* restricted by him. Reacting against this control, it is partly in the name of readers that Barthes needs to kill the author: "The birth of the reader must be at the cost of the death of the author" (1977a, 148). And partly in the name of the shared notion of text and writing (*écriture*). In this view, "text" cannot be thought of as a finite, closed object; it is a process of production, an "anonymous," "*stereographic plurality*" of the signifiers that weave it" (Barthes 1979, 76–77). "Text" therefore, entails "the effacement of the writing subject's individual characteristics." The author "must assume the role of the dead man in the game of writing" (Foucault 1984, 102, 103), must become the absence that enables it.

The murderous language directed at the author—explicitly by Barthes, implicitly by Foucault—arouses associations of other struggles, psychological and political. It sometimes reads like a chapter from *Totem and Taboo* and a political class manifesto alike. The "off with his head" outcry is aimed at the author-king-father-bourgeois so that the reader-subject-son-revolutionary will share and enjoy hitherto forbidden spoils (meanings, mothers, and economic resources). The terminology informing the *oedipolitical* struggle over the body of the text as a source of endless *jouissance* is as heavily gendered as it is saturated by deadly fear. The coupling-copulation of reader and text can produce a proliferation of meanings only if the author's prohibition is transgressed.

History has shown—not least through such Authors as Barthes, Foucault, Derrida—that authors are immune to all kinds of attack, no matter how violent or by whom. Indeed, the logic of discourse against authors (Derrida would say, any discourse) seems to be of the type that inadvertently invites the return of the excluded into its own domain. There is, for instance, an inconsistency in Barthes concerning the very notion of subject and an asymmetry between the characteristics attributed to the deposed author and those granted to the enthroned reader. Is the newly born reader a subject? If so, what is the justification for excluding the author *qua* subject and replacing him by another subject? And if the reader is claimed to be a different kind of subject, why can't the author also be conceived of differently? Why does he have to remain single, unified, authoritarian? And why can't the proliferation of meaning be attributed to him as well?[2] While Barthes's polemical manifesto invites subversive questions not asked in it, Foucault's declaredly historical approach leaves the door wide open for authors. This aspect of his essay, which is discussed in greater detail below, relativizes the notion of author; or more precisely, what Foucault calls the author-function, which is "characteristic of the mode of existence, circulation, and functioning of *certain* discourses within a society" (1984, 108; our emphasis). It is his historical considerations that lead him to the conclusion, or hope, that in the modern period a kind of writing has instituted itself where "the work, . . . possesses the right to kill, to be its author's murderer, as in the cases of Flaubert, Proust, and Kafka" (102). In his view, the modern text has preceded the modern critic, who, Foucault hopes, will eventually join it in "a form of culture in which fiction would not be limited by the figure of the author" and "the author function will disappear" (119). In contrast to this vision of an authorless future, thirty years after Foucault we witness, within contemporary literature, a whole gamut of texts which renounce "the right to kill." On the contrary, they militantly foreground the agency and responsibility of the author, without the seeming correlative of authority and suffocating control. These texts are a product of an ideological-political climate which exerts pressure to affirm the subjectivity of those who have been deprived of it for too long. Before allowing theory to declare its disappearance, a subject has to *be*.

2.

The foregoing historical sketch can now be considered an indirect answer to the initial question "Why author?" What motivates the need to revive a concept that seemed methodologically a superfluity to some, ideologically an anathema to others? The motivation is both historical-political and theoretical. Attacks on the concept of author as well as attempts to readmit it into theory concern the production of meaning, an issue evaded by classical narratology. A shift from a description of textual operations to a discussion of the concept of author in relation to meaning entails for us a parallel shift in our theoretical agenda. The desire to contemplate ways of understanding problematizes the very notion of the literary text as an unmediated, stable object, and with it the pseudoscientific aspirations of literary theory. Therefore, we do not aim to find a place for "author" within classical narratological models, nor to devise a new model which will integrate the frequently used narratological *instances* in a new way. Rather than constructing a model which aspires to the status of an objective, reliable, and unambiguous description of states of affairs, we have conceived our project as a testing out of a cluster of problems surrounding the concept of author. Eschewing finalizing formulations, we foreground the process leading from question to question. We believe that the process itself is a mode of theorizing in the course of which both the researching subject(s) and the object of study undergo continuous transformation. Theory thus becomes a junction between a subject-in-process[3] and an object-in-process, in short, what Bakhtin might call a dialogue.

In line with this general view, we propose to displace the question "What Is an Author?"—raised and subverted by Foucault's essay—grappling instead with three possible queries. Each addresses the complex of author-meaning on a different level and from a different angle:

1. Is there a capital-"A" author?
2. What does "author" signify?
3. In what sense can "author" be conceptualized as subject-in-process?

In response to the first question we wish to dispel the impression potentially created by the capital "A" of one universal concept of author. We argue,
instead, for versions of authors (lower case, plural), convention-bound and
subject to change. Different (literary) texts, different generic formulations,
under different historical conditions, have been created-produced-written and
received-consumed-read with different versions of authors in mind. Such versions range from a posited sole source of meaning, an originator of truth, to an
anonymous, effaced transmitter of tradition, from the objective reporter to the
political *engagé*. From this perspective, the convicted Author is but one such
version. Indeed, this insight can be detected in Barthes and Foucault, even
though they often—Barthes more so than Foucault—tend to identify this version with author in general.

Our insistence on author-versions calls for further inquiry, leading on to
the second question: What does the signifier "author" signify? Since there is a
marked tendency, in the current political climate, to revive the importance of
the biographical author, we feel the need to stress that for us the signified of
"author" is a concept, though not a narratological one. Unlike classical narratological concepts, operating within clearly demarcated borders, it is precisely
the transgression of "inside"/"outside" borders that characterizes "author."
Thus, "author" is both an agent responsible for the text and a position within
it. From the traditional perspective of hierarchy, the status of "author" is an
oxymoron. Foucault hints at the problematic nature of the concept when describing what he is dealing with as "the manner in which the text points to
this 'figure' that, at least in appearance, is outside it and antecedes it" (1984,
101). What for Foucault is relegated to the status of an "appearance" seems
to us a characteristic of the concept. "Author" is a heterogeneous "threshold-
concept," pointing inside and out, before and after simultaneously. "Our theories," Gary Saul Morson states, "have no way of describing this phenomenon,
which therefore seems paradoxical or impossible" (1994, 95). This reinforces
our search for a mode of theorizing, commensurate with the unsettling phenomena it explores and the concepts it employs.[4]

The closest we can come to a description of the Janus-like concept of author
is by talking about it in terms of relations. Obviously, "author" is a relation
to a specific text which it creates and is created by. Similarly, it is a relation
to "reader," an indispensable reading partner, a set of implied reading instructions, constructing the reader and constructed by it.[5] The result is a triadic relation, distinct from the dyadic transaction between reader and text proposed
by reader-response theories. Hence, the relation is one of a triple mutual transformation. Mutual transformation also characterizes the relation between the
outside facing "author" and the outside facing "reader." "Reader" approaches

text with anterior expectations as to its author, based on generic conventions, ideological climate, and the like. In the course of the "reader"'s interaction with the unfolding text, these expectations may undergo modifications, intensifying the reciprocal dynamics of the relationship.

It is the differences in the nature of the relationship that constitute different author-versions. What relationships characterize the specific version described in our third query as "subject-in-process"? "Author" as subject-in-process seems to arise in relation to the growing number of texts in which the rights of subjects of all kinds is a central issue. Although the subjectivity of the author can be gleaned from other versions as well, and "process" certainly underlies the notion of relations, this version foregrounds both — subjects and processes. Moreover, in this version the author-subject is not conceived of as an *a priori* given entering a process or as a finished product issuing from it. On the contrary, it is almost co-extensive with the process itself. It is therefore characterized by an increased dynamism and openness. The Janus-like nature of this subject's "face" is also extremely conspicuous: on the one hand, facing the fictional world, and on the other, turning out toward author and community. Indeed, it is this latter aspect that most acutely arouses the readers' anterior expectations. In accordance with these, readers regard the authors of such texts as politically committed, giving voice to a community, thereby intervening in reality. Without relinquishing their early expectations, readers continuously develop, nuance, and modify them. In this particular version, the modifications tend to concern the ongoing probing of relative freedom, authority, responsibility, and control. It does so by questioning the role of knowledge and the right to define others and speak for them. In contradistinction to the father figure against which Barthes, Foucault, and others rebelled, this "subject-in-process" evokes maternal associations of responsible, nonpossessive, caring love.

3.

Our responses to the queries raised above are informed by Bakhtin, first and foremost. However, before expounding on our debt to him, we would like to engage in a dialogue with one strand in Foucault's "What Is an Author?" and the relevant terminological apparatus in narratology and in the rhetorical narrative theory represented by Wayne Booth. Foucault deals with the difficulties surrounding "author" by characterizing it as "a certain functional principle" operative in our culture (1984, 119). The historical-contextual thrust of this move is close in spirit to ours, and we might have been tempted to use the term "author-function" rather than "author-version," all the more so since Foucault avoids a capital-A author. However, several reasons led us to hesitate. First, Foucault's project is, of course, much broader than ours. He aims at rewriting history as the history of discourse, using the author-function as a touchstone for a typology of discourses, their status and mode of existence. In spite of our historical perspective, we do not presume to write an overall history; all we attempt to do is intervene in the debate surrounding the concept of author in literary studies. Second, Foucault regards this function as operative in literary contexts only since the seventeenth century. In his view, "[T]here was a time when the texts we today call "literary" . . . were accepted . . . without any question about the identity of their author" whereas "a reversal occurred in the seventeenth or eighteenth century" and "literary discourse came to be accepted only when endowed with author function" (109). Although it is thus a historically contingent recent phenomenon, it nevertheless gained control in our culture, according to Foucault. Author-versions, conceived as indispensable to the process of production and reception of meaning, are necessarily operative in all periods, in all texts — even anonymous ones.[6]

Our discussion of author-versions in terms of changes in relations is also akin to one aspect of Foucault's author-function. However, while the relation we emphasize is between "author," text, and "reader," Foucault — in accordance with his general project — claims that the "relationship (or nonrelationship) with an author, and the different forms this relationship takes, constitute . . . one of [a set of] discursive properties" (117). Interestingly, the beginning of his essay declaredly sets out to study "the relationship between text and author" in a context dangerously evoking the biographical writer. This may be why he hastens to delimit "this 'figure' that, at least in appearance, is outside [the text] and antecedes it" (101). Like many treatments of "author," Foucault's work encounters its double-facedness, pointing inside and outside simultaneously in a way we try to do justice to via a "threshold-concept." What plays the connecting role between inside and outside for him is the "author's name." It is neither the author's person, nor even his "figure," that functions in relation to a text and endows it with the "author-function"; it is rather "the author's name," an element of discourse, that "manifests the appearance of a certain discursive set and indicates the status of this discourse within a society and culture" (107). The inherent difficulty of finding a suitable concept to handle the inside/ outside quality of the phenomenon of "author" is apparent in Foucault's essay in the proliferation of terms he uses. "Author," "author's persona," "figure of author," "writing subject," "narrator," "name of the author," even "alter ego" and "self," all are used in turn. The attempt to trace borders between these cognates and the relations they conjure leads to a clear-cut separation, a scission in which Foucault situates the author-function: "It would be just as wrong," he states, "to equate the author with the real writer as to equate him with the fictitious speaker; the author function is carried out and operates in the scission itself, in this division and distance" (112). Eager to avoid any psychological or anthropomorphic associations, he posits a separating gap, creating a function of author securely bound to the order of discourse.

"Author-versions" allows us, on the other hand, to be less wary of the two-sided "author." As we have already pointed out, this does not lead us to a confusion of "author" with the biographical writer, nor, as we hope to establish, to a collapse of "author" with narrators. Although in reintroducing authors through their versions we deliberately transgress the borders of the text, we wish to make clear that this move in no way intends to dismiss "narrator," a notion which has proved a very fine descriptive tool. It is therefore important to distinguish between the classical narratological notion of "narrator" and our "author." "Narrator," we remember, is part of a model designed to account for textual operations, whereas "author," in our sense, concerns the production of meaning. Consequently, whereas the "narrator" is an *instance* inside the text, the "author" looks both ways, inside and outside. Such transgression of borders could not be tolerated by narratologists, nor could they risk a scission on the brink of the text. They had to fill in the gap with a series of agencies, devised to account for the utterance and its composition, without transgressing the borders of the text (for example, Brooke-Rose's "Narrator's-meta-text" and "author's-meta-text," 1981). It may be worth noting that even in classical narratology the neatness of the category of "narrator" is sometimes disturbed. While personified character-narrators could be clearly distinguished from authors, nonpersonified, third-person ones potentially put the distinction in doubt. First-person narrators are equally problematic, most strongly in autobiographical fiction, the shifter "I" seeming to invite the identification with the real author. Such disturbances may be taken as yet another argument against the bracketing of authors in narratology, and hence as further motivation for our project.[7]

"Narrator" is not the only category we wish to distinguish clearly from our "author"; the "implied author," both as employed by narratologists and by Booth, is another such concept. Chatman distinguishes between narrator and implied author thus: "Unlike the narrator the implied author can *tell* us nothing. He, or better, *it* has no voice, no direct means of communicating. It instructs us silently, through the design of the whole, with all the voices, by all the means it has chosen to let us learn" (1978, 148). Chatman's implied author, then, though a silent instructor, is neither a speaker nor a subject. Later narratologists, carrying the argument to its logical extreme, insisted on the "implied author" being a construct "inferred and assembled by the reader from all the components of the text" (Rimmon-Kenan 1983, 87). This static construct differs from our "author," a participant in a dynamic process.[8] Moreover, whereas the above construct is explicitly nonanthropomorphic, our concept leaves room for the human-like as one aspect of "author."[9]

In this framework, it is interesting and refreshing to rediscover Booth, who originally coined the term "implied author" (1983[1961]). We realize, in retrospect, how much closer in spirit both his concept and his deliberations are to ours than the orthodox narratological formulations. This surprising affinity between our postnarratological exploration and Booth's prenarratological one may perhaps suggest something about the spiral evolution of intellectual climate: it is precisely to those features of Booth's theory that provoked narratological criticism that we now return in our reconsideration of narratology. A prominent feature in Booth's work is his search for a concept that will "satisfy" by being "as broad as the work itself but still capable of calling attention to that work as a product . . . rather than a self-existing thing" (1961, 74). In a similar vein, we search for a concept that will "satisfy" by its comprehensiveness, bridging levels rather than delimiting them. The need to encompass and bridge leads Booth to emphasize dynamic relations, the particular relation between reader and author being central to his understanding of the rhetoric of fiction. In addition, Booth's "implied author" is clearly anthropomorphic: it is a "he" who creates, chooses, and evaluates all that there is in the work. Although — as we show below — our grounds for "humanizing" the "author" differ from those of Booth, our "author" too has anthropomorphic attributes.

If with the hindsight of history our "author" emerges — almost against our expectations — as akin to Booth's "implied author," why don't we adopt his term? Our first reason hinges, precisely, on the changes which made the "implied author" into a construct — changes from which we beg to differ. Second, from a certain poststructuralist perspective, even the biographical author is "implied" in the sense of being mediated through texts (notes, diaries, correspondence, interviews, etc.), and it therefore makes sense to speak of "author," *tout court.*[10] In fact, Barthes's comment in regard to the novelist's signature might lead to a similar conclusion. The author "becomes a 'paper author'" he says. "[H]is life is no longer the origin of his fables, but a fable that runs concurrently with his work. There is a reversal . . . the work of Proust and Genet allows us to read their lives as a text" (1979, 78–79). Third, our reluctance to adopt Booth's term also stems from pronounced differences, in spite of the similarities, between his view and ours. Although the concept of "implied author" was at least partly designed as a distinction from the biographical writer, the real individual, Booth's definition retains an indissoluble bond between the two (1961, 70–71). Indeed, he sees the former as so many "official versions" of the latter (71).[11] This strong link with the "individual" underlies the anthropomorphic impulse in Booth. Moreover, the "individual" for him is a "self"—the "author's second self" (71), implying constancy, unity, coherence, continuity. Accordingly, this "second self" can be discussed in terms of "character" (215), a better, "ideal," trustworthy version of "the real man" (75). By contrast, despite our vocabulary, our notion of "author" is not necessarily linked to any biographical individual. Not a "character," and certainly not "ideal," no moral value or norm is attached to this "author." Nor do we conceive of it in terms of a constant self. It is rather thought of in terms of a continuously changing subjectivity, an aspect of particular importance to us with regard to the version analyzed through *Jazz*.

Continuous changes are another way of talking about the dynamism constitutive of our concept of "author." Booth also emphasizes dynamism, though of a different kind. The dynamism in Booth pertains to the relationship between the implied author, the real author, and the real reader (71). In our theorizing, dynamism envelops the entire network of reciprocal relations in which the whole and each participant is potentially in constant change. This potentiality of change signals another difference, not only in the scope but also in the kind of dynamism. According to us, "author"—in particular as "subject-in-process"—is not a constant but a becoming, in and by the interaction with the other participants. Booth, on the other hand, describes a process of discovery, where both the author and the reader gradually find out about the given particular implied author. The "implied author" is finally the means by which the author's rhetoric is implemented and revealed.

4.

Our own emphasis on processes and becoming is mainly influenced by Bakhtin (1905–75). Bakhtin is crucially important to the development of our thinking not in the particularities of his theories—he strongly objected to "theoretisms"—or in his terminology. It is rather his world view, perhaps even general philosophy, that helped us shape some of our ideas. Therefore our dialogue with him, unlike our preceding "dialogues," does not take the form of an examination of similarities and differences. It is an exposition of his outlook as an acknowledgment of his overall influence. A full introduction of his thought, as it developed over the span of fifty years, is far beyond the scope of this paper. We shall have to limit ourselves to pointing out the elements to which we are most indebted, especially those of direct relevance to the problem of the author.[12] The focus of Bakhtin's study was concrete processes rather than abstract models. In a polemic against Saussure (in particular, from the thirties onward), he explores language in its concrete sociohistorical manifestation. By concrete manifestation he refers to both people and the world they live in. Seen from the perspective of the human, the social and the historical at once, concrete language is conceived of as a dynamic, heterogeneous, diverse phenomenon. It is never considered in the isolation of a single sentence or the structure underlying it, but always as part of a discursive social context. As such, Bakhtin claims, it is never neutral and never orphaned. Further, he came to believe that although humans are born into a linguistic environment that precedes them, they are answerable for the way they process language as part of their inner speech and use it in dialogue. They have relative freedom and full responsibility for their speech. Meaning in language is always contextually dependent, produced in the complexity of a dialogic interaction of present intentions with both past meanings and expected future responses. Human self-conscious subjectivity evolves in a double process of assimilation of preexistent language(s) and dialogic negotiation of meanings with other subjects.

This brief, necessarily slanted presentation of Bakhtin's view of language — based primarily on *Discourse in the Novel* (1981b[1936]), of his so-called middle period — is intended to highlight the notions of heterogeneity, interaction, dialogue, freedom, and responsibility which inform it. Such an attitude to language also allows a new approach to the problem of ownership, so relevant to the question of the author. Above all, although assigning to language as great an importance as Foucault does, Bakhtin would hardly share the latter's indifference to Beckett's question: " 'What does it matter who is speaking,' someone said, 'what does it matter who is speaking' " (in Foucault 1984, 101). For Bakhtin it matters indeed, as it clearly does for many authors active today.

The problem of authoring occupied Bakhtin from the very beginning. And, as Morson has put it, he "used the *relation* of the hero of a work to its author as a figure for the *relation* of a person to the world" (1994, 88; our emphasis), the concrete social, historical world. Narrative literature, the novel in particular, is a laboratory where these relations could be examined. With time, the "world" he thought of was more and more the linguistic environment, "linguistic" always retaining its concrete character of spoken heteroglossia and never turning into an abstract structure. As questions of freedom and responsibility in dialogic human relations came to predominate in his writing, Bakhtin had to modify the models he devised for the description of such relations. But throughout, the idea of the author as a subjective consciousness in a process of creating an other consciousness and relating to it remained central.

In Bakhtin's early deliberations, in "Author and Hero in Aesthetic Activity" (1990[1920–23]), the author, as creator of the artistic whole and its governing consciousness, was conceived of as having complete control. This was a result of the author's essential excess knowledge and outside position, a necessary condition for the aesthetic creation of a hero. The author, in this model, possesses complete preknowledge of an utterly preconceived hero, who can become a hero of aesthetic value only under this condition. Nevertheless, even when the defined hero is denied freedom of choice, the author is not perceived in authoritarian terms. On the contrary, his "divine" aspect is that of a Christian, grace-bestowing, merciful, loving, motherly god rather than a tyrannical one. And his "human" attitude to the hero is examined in terms of a basic reciprocity of I-other, I-thou. An outside, loving, vision of the hero is not only an aesthetic necessity, it is that which endows a person with validity and value. "I myself cannot be the author of my own value," Bakhtin famously claims, "just as I cannot lift myself by my own hair. The biological life of an organism becomes a value only in *another's* sympathy and compassion with that life (motherhood)" (1990, 55; our emphasis. See also, in particular, 50–51).

As is well known, dialogism as the *sine qua non* of human conscious subjectivity and life dominated Bakhtin's thought from the thirties on. The notion of human life and language as inherently dialogic enabled him to think of authoring in a way that could cope more successfully with the problem of human freedom and mutual responsibility. He offered his clearest formulations of his idea in the revised version of *Problems of Dostoevsky's Poetics* (1984[1963]). In initiating the polyphonic novel, Dostoevsky-as-creating-author became the model of a radically new, egalitarian, relation of author to the world of created heroes:

> Thus the new artistic position of the author with regard to the hero . . . is a *fully realized and thoroughly consistent dialogic position,* one that affirms the independence, internal freedom, unfinalizability, and indeterminacy of the hero. For the author the hero is not "he" and not "I" but a fully valid "thou," that is, another and other autonomous "I" ("thou art"). (Bakhtin 1984, 63; his emphasis)

No longer a reified, finite object, the hero is designed—and, for Bakhtin, there is always an author's artistic design—as human discourse that must be given full freedom to reveal itself, to mean. The author's discourse must, therefore, orient itself dialogically to the hero's discourse, be "in intimate contact" with it, "and yet at the same time not fuse with it, not swallow it up, not dissolve in itself the other's power to mean" (64). The hero is approached as a living consciousness, actually present, capable of choice and surprise. The paradox of freedom, as artistic design, is the gist of the polyphonic novel. A never-ending process of intersubjective relation, of a mutuality of subjective consciousnesses, is its expression.

Throughout these stages of development, Bakhtin clearly distinguishes the author with which he is concerned from the biographical writer, on the one hand, and the fictional speaking agents, on the other. The latter are for him but one manifestation of the author's overall position regarding the created, fictional world. It goes without saying that Bakhtin's "author" reveals himself, first and foremost, through the discourse in the novel. From a Bakhtinian perspective, discourse always expresses a world view and is always directed toward a discourse of an other. World view and direction are inscribed in stylistic attitudes like *skaz,* parody, stylization, irony, as well as in the manners in which speech is relegated to other agents. Additionally, since the author— even in the polyphonic novel—also retains the outside position that underlies his capacity to design, the principles informing this design clearly manifest him. These principles concern, above all, the axiological categories of time and space, dominating, in his view, the organization of the fictional world and the characters within it. Time, for Bakhtin, subsuming space in the novel, structures the "meaning that shapes narrative" (1981a, 250).[13]

It may be illuminating to recall briefly how narratology handled potentially similar features. The quotation of speech was discussed, in narratology, under the heading of "narrators," and severed from problems of world view. Style was completely sidelined. Characters were related neither to world view nor to time-space but—labeled "functions"—were subordinated to the succession of events. Time was not discussed in relation to value but as a technique organizing text-time versus story-time. The axiological dimension was assigned to the implied author and often studied as the "norms of the text," rather than as the values of the represented world and the subjects inhabiting it. Bakhtin, for whom literature was always the concrete, experimental field of philosophy, was above all concerned with values, relating the work as a whole to a complex world view, or ideology.

5.

Having suggested that different author-versions are an effect of changing relations between authors, texts, and readers, it is no wonder that we have been tempted to read a contemporary novel, Toni Morrison's *Jazz,* in this light. What relations then characterize this specific version, allowing a subject in process to emerge? Here, the "author"'s attitude towards the fictional world seems to be at the opposite pole from the one Barthes attacked. Far from being the tyrant he portrayed, Morrison's author is neither single, nor unified or homogeneous. "It" is tolerant, plural, heterogeneous. Moreover, this "author," dispersed into many voices, is positioned on the threshold. On the one hand, the orchestration of the great number of narrators, identifiable or unidentifiable, in juxtapositional analogies is an aspect of design; that is, of an outside view of a whole. On the other hand, although narrators are obviously within the fictional world, in this text they also pull outward, in two complementary ways. Thematically, all the narrators are engaged with problems of authoring. Structurally, at times an unidentified voice becomes audible, not only explicitly dealing with problems of authoring and writing but openly imitating the voice of the outside, "real" authoress. Short of naming itself "Toni Morrison," it does everything to create that illusion. Being thus both inside and outside, this impossible, Janus-like author defies borders and challenges comfortable distinctions. Because this aspect is so conspicuous in *Jazz,* we focus on it, at the expense of other manifestations of the author. To emphasize the subjectivity-forming dynamics we shall single out a freedom-granting process undergone by author, narrators, characters, and readers alike: a gradual renunciation of authority and knowledge, combined with an opening up to surprising facets of the other.

At the center of *Jazz* is a case of murder in which middle-aged Joe Trace shoots his young lover, Dorcas, in a fit of jealousy. Adding insult to injury, the outraged (and perhaps demented) betrayed wife, Violet, slashes the dead girl's face during the funeral ceremony. Felice, Dorcas's friend, causes them to reevaluate and accept their life together. This all too common criminal event, presented in the opening lines of the text as an open and shut case, carries with it anterior expectations pertaining to authors in genres of detective and pulp fiction, converging on the problem of knowledge. These preliminary expectations undergo modifications which put in doubt the value of the very search for this type of knowledge. With the pivotal enigmas of who-done-it-and-why seemingly solved, the initial presentation becomes subject to improvisations. It is told and retold as different versions of a story of loss, quest for recognition, and reconciliation. These are attempts at a better understanding rather than "knowledge" of self and intersubjective relations. The versions are improvised by a gossipy neighbor, an external narrator, character narrators (Violet, Joe, Dorcas, Felice), a Morrison-like voice, and more. This very proliferation of narrating agents provokes—and thwarts—a narratological desire to attribute each textual segment to an origin or owner (see Mbalia 1993, 623–46, for such an attempt).

The novel begins with a first-person neighbor-narrator who "knows" the characters: "Sth, I know that woman. She used to live with a flock of birds on Lennox Avenue. Know her husband too" (3).[14] "Knowing" in the sense of "being acquainted with" soon becomes an uncanny omniscience concerning past, present, and future, external behavior as well as inner thoughts. For example, when Felice enters Violet's house, looking almost exactly like Dorcas, the narrator tentatively authors a future story as a repetition of a triangular relationship, another "scandalizing threesome" (6). The narrator's obsession with knowledge about others also screens an anxiety about self-exposure: "But I do know how to take precaution. Mostly it's making sure no one knows all there is to know about me. Second, I watch everything and everyone and try to figure out their plans, their reasonings, long before they do" (8).

Opposed to the narrator's declared knowledge in the opening is Violet's reported ignorance concerning Dorcas: "Violet didn't know anything about the girl at first" (5). Out of ignorance, she embarks on a quest for knowledge: "So she decided to love — well, find out about — the eighteen-year-old" (5). She questions everybody, talks to teachers who knew Dorcas, pesters the girl's aunt. She even tries to *be* the girl by imitating her dance steps. Finally, she acquires a framed photograph of Dorcas and puts it on the mantelpiece as an object of adoration for her and her husband. This is what Violet's knowledge and love are like: they close off, frame and fix the other always in the same posture, in short — repeating an act of murder.

And this is what authoritative knowledge of the other could have become in the novel as a whole. However, things do not turn out this way. Toward the end, Felice's entry into Joe's and Violet's life almost verbatim repeats the anticipation of the opening (197–98). Yet, instead of becoming a "scandalizing threesome," the second triangle is redemptive. Seeing this, the (same?) narrator expresses surprise at the unpredictability of the characters and criticizes the arrogance involved in her initial presumption of knowledge:

> So I missed it altogether. I was sure one would kill the other. I waited for it so I could describe it. I was so sure it would happen. . . . I was so sure, and they danced and walked all over me. Busy, they were, busy being original, complicated, changeable — human, I guess you'd say, while I was the predictable one, confused in my solitude into arrogance, thinking my space, my view was the only one that was or that mattered. (221)

The "others" are busy "being human," and being human means being original, changeable and surprising — a challenge to the haughtiness of being "so sure." A/the narrator now openly declares the limitations of her knowledge, imagination, and arrogant solitude, seeing herself as inferior to the characters in these respects. She, who tried to know without being known, now realizes that she is the predictable one, while the others are changeable, hence unknown. Together with this lesson in humility, she also gains an insight into the nature of love:

> I saw the three of them, Felice, Joe, and Violet and they looked to me like a mirror image of Dorcas, Joe, and Violet. I believed I saw everything important

they did, and based on what I saw I could imagine what I didn't: how exotic
they were, how driven. Like dangerous children. That's what I wanted to believe. It never occurred to me that they were thinking other thoughts, feeling
other feelings, putting their lives together in ways I never dreamed of. (221)

In the opening pages of the novel, Violet's desire to love and master through
knowledge was derided, precisely by a narrator who proclaimed her own
knowledge of Violet: "Maybe she thought she could solve the mystery of love
that way. Good luck and let me know" (5). At the end, the narrator does learn
the mystery of love from Violet. This is partly because Violet gave up the framing, finalizing attitude toward the other, gave back Dorcas's framed picture to
her aunt, stopped seeing Felice as a mere repetition of Dorcas, and even admitted, "I'm fifty and I don't know nothing" (110). But it is also because the
speaking subject has come to realize the impossibility of imagining what she
didn't see on the basis of what she did. She becomes aware of the problematic
nature of the narrative plot-conventions underlying any prediction. Such real-
izations enable her to intuit the releasing power of a love that lets things be
"another way" (219). From an initial relation between a narrator who "knows"
and an ignorant Violet who tries to know and foreclose, the novel has evolved
to a narrating position which renounces knowledge, authority, and foreclosure
and to a Violet capable of teaching "the mystery of love."

A similar renunciation of knowing authority for the sake of the freedom of
the other occurs in the two versions of the Golden Gray story.[15] This time, however, the anterior expectations are clearly connected with racial stereotypes,
and their modification involves a liberation of the individual from the label of
the group. The white-looking Golden Gray, a mulatto of an earlier generation,
is on a quest for his black father's recognition. On his ride, he collides with the
bleeding, pregnant Wild (Joe's mother, it later transpires) and reluctantly lifts
her onto his horse. The narrator comments: "That is what makes me worry
about him. How he thinks first of his clothes, and not the woman. How he
checks the fastenings, not her breath" (151). At the back of the narrator's mind,
it seems, is a stereotypic image of squeamish whites, and she goes on recounting the very different—courageous and honorable—story she believes Golden
Gray to be rehearsing for his father. Her narration is strewn with expressions
like: "He is avoiding her, I know" (152), "I know he is a hypocrite" (154), "But
I know better" (154).

This version of the story soon crumbles, and the narrator faces the limitations of her knowledge and imagination:

What was I thinking of? How could I have imagined him so poorly? Not
noticed the hurt that was not linked to the color of his skin, or the blood that

beat beneath it. But to some other thing that longed for authenticity. . . . I have been careless and stupid and it infuriates me to discover (again) how unreliable I am. (160)

The juxtaposition of the two versions dramatizes a dilemma of authoring: how can one speak for a community without labeling it and stereotyping the individuals who belong to it? The challenge is to represent a group while respecting the freedom and diversity of its members. It is for this purpose that any version must be seen as open and provisional: "I may be doomed to another misunderstanding" (161), the narrator reflects on the revised version. For the same reason, narrators must renounce authority, speak not about a character, but with him:[16] "Lie down next to him, a wrinkle in the sheet and contemplate his pain and by doing so ease it, diminish it" (161). She wants "to be the language that wishes him well" (161), freeing him to be himself and hoping he will succeed. Not an authoritative and possessive motherly passion which, we know from *Beloved,* is "a killer," but a caring and releasing maternal love. Language here creates a subject-to-subject "wishing well" relationship between itself, those who speak it, and those who are spoken by it.

It seems, then, that narrating, often a means by which a subject creates him/herself, here engages the problem of authoring, creating the other, and with it the self. A growing consciousness of the intrinsic connectedness of narration, subjects, and freedom develops as *Jazz* unfolds and multiplies narrators. Yet, this process is manifest not only where human agents are concerned; the novel has another heroine—the City, Harlem of the nineteen twenties.[17] Although some of the discourse about the City is identical in style with that of the various first-person narrators, it is often infiltrated by a totally different, elevated, poetic erotic voice. The song of the City personifies it as a seductress, hospitable to the millions who "entering the lip of the City" were "dancing" all the way to her. Celebrated, the temptress "was speaking to them" while she "danced with them, proving already how much [she] loved them," and "they could hardly wait . . . to love it back" (32).

No longer a conventional literary background, the City becomes a subject, a partner in a love relationship. This sense of mutual love promotes in the characters a feeling of empowerment, of freedom—even encouragement—to be "their stronger, riskier selves" (32). At the same time, another voice intimates, from above, the illusory nature of the experience: "I like the way the City makes people think they can do what they want and get away with it" (8). The illusion to which they surrender themselves completely—"a fascination, permanent and out of control"—entices them into feeling "more like themselves, more like the people they always believed they were" (35). And the dream is not only of self-realization but also of self-sufficiency, the latter entailing a ne-glect of other: "[T]hey love that part of themselves so much they forget what loving other people was like" (33).

Exposing the hypnotic influence of the lover-City, who deluding, lets "you think you're free" (120), the narrator condescendingly claims to know better. Even though she screens herself behind the City as an active agent, the voice of authority is unmistakable through the framing generalizations: "That's the way the City spins you. Makes you do what it wants, go where the laidout roads say to. . . . You can't get off the track a City lays for you . . . you always end up back where you started" (120).

At the end, the voice becomes suggestively identifiable with that of Morri-son outside. After unmasking illusion, from above, she now realizes her own entrapment in self-deception. Rather than seeing through the characters' fas-cination, she too, "crazy about the City" (7), succumbed to its charms. The double-edged passion lured her into the belief that she "was taking precaution" to be herself and control her life; what she lost in the process was a recognition of others, and thus herself:

> I ought to get out of this place. Avoid the window; leave the hole I cut through the door to get in lives instead of having one of my own. It was loving the City that distracted me and gave me ideas. Made me think I could speak its loud voice and make that sound sound human. I missed the people altogether. (220)

In addition to the human failure, missing the people also implies an inca-pacity to create characters in transformation. For the Morrison-like voice, the failure to make the City and the people authentic is a collapse of initial ambi-tions. A similar transformation of expectations occurs in the reading process. Readers come to this text with a preconception of an engaged, militant woman-author, whose writing is part of a political struggle intended to give voice to a particular group of people. Giving voice is understood as a weapon in the fight for freedom. The modifications this author-version undergoes spring from an apprehension of the role of the other: one can truly speak for others only when freeing them to speak for themselves.

The author of *Jazz* emerges as neither an *a priori* given nor a finished prod-uct; it evolves as an open subject-in-process, free and freeing. But freedom, too, is revealed in the novel, as much more complex than our preconceptions would allow. We approach such a novel with an expectation to witness libera-tion unequivocally celebrated. However, we gradually come to see freedom's darker side, abandonment. Abandonment, painfully experienced by characters and narrators alike, signals the dangers of unrestrained liberty. Autonomy, as it emerges at the end, is a complex combination of freedom and constraint-as-security, of being "wide open" and yet "snug" (221).

The ambivalent concept of liberation thus plays a problematizing role in the represented world. Beyond this role, it significantly enriches the political "message" which readers might have expected. To be sure, there is in *Jazz* a manifesto-level, calling for black liberation and equality. However, the awareness of the other side of freedom renders even this political desire more complex, counteracting abandonment through a restraint constitutive of both self and community. What is more, Morrison also practices what she preaches. An interplay between freedom and constraint does not only emerge from the thematics of this novel; it is also its compositional principle. The principle, of course, is borrowed from jazz music, which is based precisely on free improvisations on a given theme.[18] The novel is structured as a session in which different voices improvise on a theme common to all. Morrison as author becomes indeed a composer of jazz, and *Jazz*.

Notes

1. To solve the intricate problem of gender for a discussion of authors and narrators we have decided to use the masculine in the first parts of the essay, because this is the practice in the theories we deal with. We switch to the feminine in the analysis of *Jazz*, since both the text and our context-sensitive theorizing promote this hypothesis.

2. Burke's project is to demonstrate how the author reenters the discourses that excluded him. Stronger, he shows how the author has never really been dead.

3. The term "subject-in-process" was coined by Julia Kristeva, though our use is different from hers.

4. Barthes, writing in a different context, is nevertheless close in spirit to our deliberations here, when he expresses the necessity to find "a new language" for "the new object"—the *Text*. He says this: "These propositions [regarding the *Text*] are to be understood as enunciations rather than arguments, as mere indications, as it were, approaches that 'agree' to remain metaphoric" (1979, 74).

5. Clearly, "reader" is a concept of the same order as "author." Since this essay centers on "author," we cannot follow the analogous implications for "reader."

6. We are aware of the possibility that, from Foucault's perspective, our position may itself be an effect of the modern era, which does not tolerate literary anonymity (Foucault 1984, 109).

7. Since talking about the author is not yet fully accepted, and talking about narrators often involves the disturbances mentioned above, the term "narrative-voice" has gained currency these days (see, for instance, Norton 1993, who, it seems, uses the term to bridge between the biographical author and narrators).

8. There are, of course, later theorists (e.g., Brooks 1984, Morson 1994, Phelan 1989)

who try to account for various aspects of narrative progression. However, they are not— strictly speaking—narratologists, nor is their analysis primarily focused on the author.

9. Paradoxically, the same narratology that so forcefully excluded human agents has personified texts, attributing to them human characteristics.

10. This statement is inspired by a much more complex argument put forward by Moshe Ron during personal communications with us.

11. Clearly, what Booth means by "version" is limited to the implied-author/real-author relationship, whereas our author-version describes the whole complex.

12. For attempts at full presentations of the Bakhtinian corpus the reader is referred to Clark and Holquist 1984, Holquist 1990, Morson and Emerson 1990, and Gardiner 1992. We are fully aware of the hazard involved in trying to extricate from Bakhtin only those notions that have to do with language and literature, insofar as they touch on the question of author. Although simplistic, such a move is, unfortunately, necessary.

13. Bakhtin's discussion of time is, of course, part of his concept of chronotope.

14. All references are to the Plume edition of 1993.

15. Mbalia (1993, 640–41) and Bower (1992, 13) also discuss the narration of the Golden Gray episode. Mbalia addresses the alternative versions of the episode but not in terms of anterior expectations concerning racial groups and individuals. Bower dismisses the whole episode as irrelevant to the novel, a point which our analysis shows we cannot accept.

16. This is the position Bakhtin attributes to Dostoevsky as polyphonic author (1984, 63).

17. Chadwick-Joshua (1995, 168–80) has also discussed the role of the city in *Jazz,* though from a different perspective.

18. We were often tempted, throughout this essay, to discuss the function of music, so important and so beautifully handled, in this novel. Of particular relevance to our discussion would be the tracing of the analogy between the City and its music. This, as well as many other musical aspects, is unfortunately beyond the scope of this essay. Mbalia (1993, 624, 639–41) and Rodrigues (1993, 733–54) have discussed the functioning of music in this novel, though not in relation to the City.

3 | # The Lessons of "Weymouth": Homodiegesis, Unreliability, Ethics, and *The Remains of the Day*
James Phelan and Mary Patricia Martin

This essay proposes to revise one concept of classical narratology, unreliable homodiegetic narration, and to use that revision as part of its exploration of an issue that has recently become prominent in narrative studies, the ethics of reading. The essay's method is to establish a recursive relationship between its theoretical investigations and Kazuo Ishiguro's The Remains of the Day, *approaching the narrative through the lenses provided by theory but remaining open to ways in which the narrative requires revisions of the theory that may in turn provide further illumination of the narrative.*

With the first issue, unreliable homodiegetic narration, we suggest that Ishiguro's narrative leads us to three important revisions of the classical approach: (1) With any character narrator, the relation between the character functions and the narrator functions may not always be seamless, and thus, we cannot always infer a narrator's reliability or unreliability on the basis of what we learn about his or her character. (2) Unreliability occurs not just along the axes of facts/ events and values/judgments but also along the axis of knowledge/ perception. (3) By attending to unreliability along these three axes and to the kind of readerly activity unreliability evokes, we distinguish six different types. Our taxonomy is intended to be heuristic, a way of refining our perceptions of a very complex phenomenon rather than a way of making narrative conform to a predetermined grid of theoretical possibilities.

With the second issue, the ethics of reading, we develop and illustrate an approach to what we call "ethical positioning," a term that refers both to the ways in which narrative technique and structure position hypothetical audiences in relation to the narrative and to the ways in which individual readers inevitably read from particular positions. This approach leads us to argue that while a text invites particular

*ethical responses through the signals it sends to its authorial audience,
our individual ethical responses will depend on the interaction of those
invitations with our own particular values and beliefs. We illustrate
this point through the analysis of our own disagreement about the appropriate ethical response to Ishiguro's Stevens at the very climax of his
narrative.*

1. "Weymouth": Claims and Contexts

In "Weymouth," the final installment of Kazuo Ishiguro's *The Remains of the
Day,* an elderly butler named Stevens recounts the climactic moments of his
life, a narrative situation in which the familiar distinction between experiencing-I and narrating-I is especially relevant. As experiencing-I, Stevens is so
overcome by commingled feelings of love and loss, recognition and regret that
his heart breaks. As narrating-I, Stevens is so complexly reliable and unreliable that Ishiguro places the authorial audience[1] in a very challenging ethical
position. Furthermore, Stevens's narration is so richly layered that classical
narratology's account of unreliability cannot do either him or Ishiguro justice.
Indeed, during "Weymouth," Ishiguro deftly and unobtrusively offers a lesson
in sophisticated homodiegesis and its relation to the ethics of reading, a lesson
that his audience needs at some level to register in order to feel the depth and
power of Stevens's experience. In this essay, we shall seek to unpack the details
of that lesson, paying close attention to how Ishiguro's technique guides our
inferencing, where it leaves us to our own devices, and how both the guidance
and the freedom affect our ethical engagement with Stevens. Ishiguro's lesson
will lead us to consider two new theoretical models: (1) a comprehensive, rhetorically based account of unreliability; and (2) a rhetorical approach to ethical
criticism that links matters of form and technique to the responses not just of
the authorial audience but also to flesh-and-blood readers.[2]

2. Reliably Reading the Unreliable Stevens

Almost four decades ago, in his 1961 study *The Rhetoric of Fiction,* Wayne C.
Booth gave a name to the narrator whose word cannot be taken straight, when
he introduced what has come to be one of the most widely invoked distinctions
of classical narratology: a narrator is *"reliable,"* Booth writes, "when he speaks
for or acts in accord with the norms of the work (which is to say the implied
author's norms), *unreliable* when he does not" (1983, 158–59). Booth goes on to
explain that a narrator may be unreliable about either facts (the axis of events)
or values (the axis of ethics) and to describe the special communication — the

"communion and even . . . deep collusion" (307) — between implied author and audience that goes on behind an unreliable narrator's back. Since 1961, narrative theorists have engaged in some debate about the meaning and usefulness of the term "implied author" as part and parcel of elaborations and refinements of Booth's work, and critics have conducted extensive debates about the reliability of individual narrators such as Nelly Dean, Nick Carraway, Marlow, and the governess in *The Turn of the Screw*. Strikingly, however, there has been virtually no debate about the efficacy of the reliable/unreliable distinction itself and no comprehensive account of the varieties of unreliability.[3] Learning the lessons of Weymouth will involve reexamining both the distinction and the nature of unreliability, but first we should locate the final installment of Stevens's narration within the overall shape and direction of *The Remains of the Day*.

Stevens tells the story of his trip in the summer of 1956 from Darlington Hall in eastern England to the West Country, where he meets with his former co-worker, Miss Kenton, who has recently written to him in some distress about her marriage. Stevens has been having some problems with his new staff plan for Darlington Hall, and he reads in Miss Kenton's letter a desire to return to her old post and, thus, a solution to his staffing problems. Ishiguro arranges Stevens's narration into eight distinct installments that recount the successive events of his trip; each act of narration, except "The Prologue" and "Weymouth," also leads Stevens into memories of his more distant past. This arrangement means that Stevens narrates each installment from a different place, both literally and emotionally, because in those memories Stevens almost unwittingly conducts an examination of his life. More specifically, the act of narrating leads Stevens to reflect on key moments in his life, on his three significant relationships with others — his father, Lord Darlington, and Miss Kenton — and on the two main ideals that have consistently guided his behavior: (1) a great butler always acts with dignity; and (2) a butler's greatness depends on his loyal service to a distinguished household. Acting with dignity means always remaining in control of a situation and one's emotions, never giving way to sorrow, love, sympathy, never literally or metaphorically "removing one's clothing in public" (1990, 210). Loyal service to a distinguished household means striving to be part of the great affairs of the world through service to one's distinguished employer. As Stevens moves, mile by mile, day by day, and narrative installment by narrative installment toward his meeting with Miss Kenton, he shows intermittent signs of recognizing the deficiencies of his ideals.

It is the meeting itself that leads him simultaneously to recognize and to regret just how seriously mistaken his ideals have been and how much he has foolishly sacrificed for them. Ishiguro's difficult task is to communicate the psychological complexity, emotional richness, and ethical difficulty of Stevens's climactic realization by means of Stevens's generally reticent and often unreliable narration. Part of our purpose is to show how well he succeeds.[4]

Early in Stevens's meeting with Miss Kenton (now Mrs. Benn), he learns not only that she does not want to return to Darlington Hall but also that she had recently "returned home and [that] Mr Benn had been very pleased to have her back" (233). Stevens comments:

> I am aware, of course, that such matters were hardly any of my business, and I should make clear I would not have dreamt of prying into these areas were it not that I did have, as you might recall, important professional reasons for doing so; that is to say, in respect to the present staffing problems at Darlington Hall. In any case, Miss Kenton did not seem to mind at all confiding in me over these matters and I took this as a pleasing testimony to the strength of the close working relationship we once had. (233–34)

This passage is a case of unreliable narration: as we shall see, Ishiguro's audience infers a great deal more from Stevens's narration than the butler is aware that he is communicating. But adopting the approach of classical narratology toward that unreliability will not adequately explain our inferencing. That approach would have us take four steps: (1) determine through evidence either in the passage or in the larger context of the narrative that unreliability exists; (2) specify the kind of unreliability it is—about facts, values, or both; (3) link the unreliability to inferences about the narrator as character; (4) reflect on the kind of communion established among implied author, narrator, and authorial audience. The main problems arise in steps 2 and 3.

The seven previous installments of Stevens's narration have cumulatively indicated that although he does have legitimate professional reasons for inquiring about the state of Miss Kenton's marriage, he has even more pressing personal ones. Indeed, the authorial audience recognizes that Stevens's professional purpose is actually a pretext for his personal interest in finding out how Miss Kenton now feels about him. For similar reasons, we can also infer that Stevens's pleasure in Miss Kenton's "confiding in [him] over these matters" is a reminder not just of their former close professional relationship but also of the intimacy that they once shared and that he has been hoping, without ever quite admitting it to himself, they could share again. Yet, Stevens's narration here is an accurate and honest report of his motives *as he understands them.* Or to put the point another way, the passage is reliable *as far as it goes;* the problem is that it doesn't go far enough. Recognizing that Stevens here is both reliable and unreliable in this way also means recognizing that trying to locate the unreliability only on the axis of facts or that of values may be inadequate to the complexity of the passage.

Given what we know about Stevens and what he tells us, we can infer that he is seriously either underreporting or underreading his motives here. By "underreporting," we mean that Stevens does not admit to his narratee what both he and the authorial audience know about his personal interest. If he is underreporting, the unreliability does exist along the axis of ethics: Stevens is being intentionally deceptive. By "underreading," we mean that he does not consciously know—or at least is not able to admit to himself—what we infer about his personal interest. If he is underreading, then the unreliability exists along neither the axis of ethics nor the axis of events but along a different axis, one that previous work on unreliability has not sufficiently noticed: the axis of knowledge and perception.[5]

One way to determine whether Stevens is underreading or underreporting is to follow step 3 of the standard approach and examine the link between narrator and character. This method initially produces a clear result: Stevens is underreading. His strict adherence to a code of dignity, which for him has meant denying his feelings, has prevented him from obtaining conscious awareness of those feelings. Thus, it is very much in character for him to locate the motive for his questions to Miss Kenton in professional rather than personal reasons. But if we continue to examine the relation between the roles of narrator and character, the situation becomes less clear. Shortly after this passage, Stevens admits that Miss Kenton's report of being content with her life breaks his heart. We will have much more to say about this moment, but for now we just want to note how it complicates the authorial audience's decisions about Stevens's unreliability. Because Stevens the narrating-I speaks in the present tense—that is, at the time of the narration, after the anagnorisis of Stevens the experiencing-I—the standard approach would now lead us to conclude that he is not underreading but underreporting. Although he says, "I am aware," he clearly leaves out much that has entered his awareness by the time of the narration.[6]

Faced with these conflicting conclusions, our analysis may go in one of several directions. If we choose to follow the standard approach, we have two choices: either (1) account for the conflict as a positive contribution to Ishiguro's narrative project, a step that would require explaining how the project benefits from our reading the passage as both underreading and underreporting. Or (2) conclude that Ishiguro has mismanaged the narration here, at best producing an incoherent view of Stevens and at worst cheating by making Stevens appear to be underreading when in fact he is underreporting. Alternatively, we could bracket the standard assumption and seek to explain—even perhaps resolve—the conflict by turning back to the detailed workings of Ishiguro's technique. If we arrive at a satisfactory account, then we will also have to conclude that there is a significant limitation in the standard approach, a limitation connected with its failure to realize an important point about homodiegesis: homodiegetic narration, even in the realistic mode, does not require—indeed, we would go so far as to say cannot require—full coherence between the character-narrator's dual roles.

Let us consider the choices Ishiguro faces in his handling of Stevens's narration in "Weymouth" as he builds to the climactic moment. As with all the other installments, Stevens narrates the events of his meeting with Miss Kenton shortly after they occur; in this case, he is narrating "two days since my meeting with Miss Kenton" (231). Thus, Ishiguro either can have Stevens's narration be informed on every page by the awareness Stevens achieves as character late in the scene or he can have Stevens the narrator retain his general lack of awareness until Stevens the character experiences his painful éclaircissement. The choice, in a sense, is whether to destroy the climax by following the dictum that says there should be full coherence between the roles of narrator and character or to abandon the idea of full coherence and build to the climax. Understood this way, the choice is an easy one.

But why shouldn't the choice be seen as cheating once the hypothesis about underreporting becomes available? Because the hypothesis that Stevens is underreading not only makes the narrative better—it fits with what Ishiguro needs—but it also conforms to our experience of the narrative progression. As we read the passage, we do not know that Stevens will achieve his breakthrough; consequently, we assume that Stevens the narrator, like Stevens the character, is operating with the level of knowledge he has achieved by the end of the previous installment. That assumption renders the passage perfectly intelligible while also making it even more powerful: the reminder of Stevens the character's inability to articulate fully his motives underlines the magnitude of his later self-recognition. And because we experience his narration as underreading before we can entertain the hypothesis that it is underreporting, the departure is rhetorically effective. The more general conclusion, then, is that homodiegesis allows the lack of full coherence between the roles of character and of narrator when that lack both serves the larger purposes of the narrative and when it is registered only after the incoherence operates.

3. Six Types of Unreliability

We would like to expand on these two lessons about unreliability in "Weymouth," especially the lesson about the axes of unreliability, and derive some more general conclusions about the variety of ways in which homodiegetic narrators can be unreliable. Over time Booth's term has become so generally

accepted that critics now use it without citing its source; while this development is a sign of the influence of Booth's discussion, it also has led to greater
imprecision. Some critics restrict their use of "unreliable" only to narrators
who are untrustworthy reporters of events, while others use it to mean unreliable in any way. And other terms such as "imperceptive," "naive," and "de-
ceitful" have been introduced.[7] Like Booth's, our taxonomy is a rhetorical one,
focused on the relations among implied author, narrator, and authorial audience — and on the activities of the narrator as teller and those of the authorial
audience as re-interpreter of what is told. Given these emphases, we propose to
broaden Booth's original definition beyond just the axes of events and of values:
a homodiegetic narrator is "unreliable" when he or she offers an account of
some event, person, thought, thing, or other object in the narrative world that
deviates from the account the implied author would offer. (To be more rigorous, though, alas, more convoluted, we could say "deviates from the account
the authorial audience infers the implied author would offer, excepting the
point that the implied author knows that the narrator is a fictional construct.")
We want to broaden the definition for two reasons: (1) regardless of the axis all
deviations require the authorial audience to infer an understanding of the narration different from that offered by the narrator; (2) as we shall argue, there
is a strong family resemblance among deviations, and, indeed, one kind of de-
viation will often be accompanied by its kin. Consequently, we prefer to label
all deviations with the single term "unreliable" and then differentiate among
kinds of unreliability rather than multiplying terms for kinds of narrators.

As Booth's initial account and our analysis of the passage from "Weymouth" indicate, narrators may deviate from the implied author's views in their
roles as *reporters,* as *evaluators,* and as *readers* or *interpreters.* And as we have
seen, the metaphor of axes of unreliability helps to differentiate among these
kinds: unreliable reporting occurs along the axis of facts/events; unreliable
evaluating occurs along the axis of ethics/evaluation; and unreliable reading
occurs along the axis of knowledge/perception. The activity of the authorial
audience allows us further to distinguish kinds of unreliability. Audiences perform two qualitatively different actions once they determine that a narrator's
words can't be taken at face value: (1) they reject those words and, if possible,
reconstruct a more satisfactory account; or (2) they do what we have done
with the passage from "Weymouth" — accept what the narrator says but then
supplement the account. (Although it is possible to distinguish a third option
here, namely "subtracting from" the narrator's account, as, for example, when
we have a narrator given to overstatement, we find "subtraction" or "discount-
ing" similar enough to "rejecting and reconstructing" that we do not create a
separate category of unreliability to describe it. When we add to a narrator's

account, we have a stable base on which to do the addition; when we subtract, we don't have the same stability. In trimming the narrator's inflated account, we have to decide what should go and what should remain.)

Combining the activities of narrators and audiences, then, we identify six kinds of unreliability: misreporting, misreading, misevaluating — or what we will call misregarding — underreporting, underreading, and underregarding. Misreporting involves unreliability at least on the axis of facts/events. We say "at least" here because misreporting is typically a consequence of the narrator's lack of knowledge or mistaken values; it almost always occurs with misreading or misevaluating. When Stevens says that he stood outside Miss Kenton's door and heard her crying after she learned of her aunt's death, he is misreporting. When he later corrects the report to say that he was in that position on the night she became engaged, we understand that his misreporting was a consequence of his mistaken value system, which denies the importance of his own emotions and so initially leads to a memory which locates all the dolorous emotions of the scene in Miss Kenton. Misreading and misregarding may occur either by themselves or in combination with other kinds of unreliability. Misreading involves unreliability at least on the axis of knowledge/perception. When Stevens says that "any objective observer" will find the English landscape "the most deeply satisfying in the world" (28), he demonstrates a misperception analogous to his saying that "any objective observer" would find English cuisine the most satisfying in the world. Since his descriptions of the landscapes, however, are both accurate and sincere, one might argue either that the misreading exists by itself or, as we would, that the misreading is also sign of a mistaken value system that finds "unobtrusiveness" to be one of the greatest virtues. Misregarding involves unreliability at least on the axis of ethics/evaluation. When Stevens rationalizes his lying about having worked for Lord Darlington, he is misregarding: his claim that "Lord Darlington was a gentleman of great moral stature" is not only untrue but his denials suggest that at some level of consciousness he knows it is untrue.

Similarly, underreporting, underreading, and underregarding occur at least on the axes of event/fact, understanding/perception, and ethics/evaluation respectively. Underreporting, which Genette calls paralipsis, occurs when the narrator tells us less than s/he knows. When Stevens reports that he has denied working for Lord Darlington but defers telling us about Lord Darlington's disgrace, he is underreporting. Not all underreporting, however, constitutes unreliability. At several places in the narrative, including later in "Weymouth," we learn from the dialogue of other characters but never from Stevens's direct report that he is crying in public. On those occasions, Stevens is underreporting his emotions, and this underreporting is a telling sign of the reticence of his character but it may or may not be an instance of unreliability—depending on whether we decide that he expects his narratee to infer from the scene that he has been crying.[8] As we have seen in the passage from "Weymouth," underreading occurs when the narrator's lack of knowledge, perceptiveness, or sophistication yields an insufficient interpretation of an event, character, or situation. Underregarding occurs when a narrator's ethical judgment is moving along the right track but simply does not go far enough. A possible instance of underregarding, one that we shall return to, occurs when Stevens entertains the idea, at the very end of "Weymouth," that "in bantering lies the key to human warmth" (245).

Having sketched this taxonomy, we want to emphasize some important points about its possible uses and abuses. As our illustrations from *The Remains of the Day* indicate, a given narrator can be unreliable in different ways at different points in his or her narration. As we have also seen, a narrator can also be unreliable in more than one way at any one point in his narration, and indeed misreporting will almost always be accompanied by another kind of unreliability. Furthermore, even where the unreliability initially seems to be of one kind (located along only one axis), once the authorial audience makes inferences about the relation between the narrator's unreliability and his or her character, the unreliability is likely to reveal itself as multifaceted. Finally, in many cases the border between types, especially that between two types identified by the same root (for example, misreporting and underreporting) will be soft and blurry rather than hard and firm. For these reasons, this taxonomy should not be regarded as a new set of tools for an aging Procrustes but rather as a heuristic device designed to sharpen our perceptions of individual acts of unreliable narration. At the same time, recognizing these different kinds of unreliability allows us to move away from the common assumption that reliability and unreliability are a binary pair, that once any unreliability is detected all the narration is suspect, and, instead, to recognize that narrators exist along a wide spectrum from reliability to unreliability with some totally reliable on all axes, some totally unreliable on all, and some reliable on one or two axes and not on others.

4. Telling, Acting, and the Ethics of Reading

As Ishiguro builds to Stevens's climactic realization in "Weymouth," the inferences he asks his audience to make become more complicated and the lessons of the narrative expand to the domain of ethics. Ishiguro guides our inferences not only through Stevens's underreporting but also through the extensive dialogue. Because the inferencing is so complex, we will review the major steps leading to Stevens's moment of recognition. As they wait for the bus that will take Miss Kenton back to her husband, Stevens explicitly requests her permission to ask "something of a rather personal order" (237), namely, whether she is "ill-treated in any way" (238). Stevens begs her forgiveness for asking but says it is something he's been concerned about for a long time and that he "would feel foolish if [he] had come all this way and seen you and not at least asked you" (238). After Miss Kenton assures him that "[m]y husband does not mistreat me at all in any way," Stevens remarks that, then, "one is rather mystified as to the cause of your unhappiness" (238). Miss Kenton revises his question, saying that she understands him to be asking something of an even more personal order, "whether or not I love my husband." She explains that, although she initially got married only to conduct "another ruse . . . to annoy you," she has grown to love her husband. However, she adds this reflection:

> "But that doesn't mean to say, of course, there aren't occasions now and then — extremely desolate occasions — when you think to yourself: 'What a terrible mistake I've made with my life.' And you get to thinking about a different life, a *better* life you might have had. For instance, I get to thinking about a life I may have had with you, Mr Stevens. And I suppose that's when I get angry over some trivial little thing and leave. But each time I do so, I realize before long — my rightful place is with my husband. After all, there's no turning back the clock now. One can't be forever dwelling on what may have been. One should realize one has as good as most, perhaps better, and be grateful." (239)

Stevens's response contains the climax:

> I do not think I responded immediately, for it took me a moment or two to fully digest these words of Miss Kenton. Moreover, as you might appreciate, their implications were such as to provoke a certain degree of sorrow within me. Indeed — why should I not admit it? — at that moment, my heart was breaking. Before long, however, I turned to her and said with a smile:
> "You're very correct, Mrs Benn. As you say, it is too late to turn back the clock. Indeed, I should not be able to rest if I thought such ideas were the cause of unhappiness for you and your husband. We must each of us, as you point out, be grateful for what we *do* have." (239)

Moments later, Stevens and Miss Kenton part, and as she goes, Stevens notes that "her eyes had filled with tears" (240).

Drawing on our previous inferences about both Stevens and Miss Kenton, we can recognize that much is going on beneath the surface of the scene. Miss Kenton's move to speak more directly and frankly only reveals the thinnest layer of the deep subtexts operating here. Just as Stevens's narration is marked by underreporting and underreading, his dialogue and Miss Kenton's are marked by some combination of what we might call underdisclosing (the character-to-character equivalent of underreporting—they say less than they mean and so convey less to each other) and indirection (they say less than they mean but convey their meaning anyway). Reading the dialogue requires the same kind of inferential activity that reading Stevens's narration does.

Ishiguro wants us to recognize that Stevens's question to Miss Kenton about being ill-treated is the first personal question he has ever asked her. But we also infer that it is a pale reflection of the question that he really wants to ask, though he himself does not yet fully realize what that question is. Miss Kenton's revision of his question shows that she recognizes both of these facts, even as that revision, despite its move toward greater disclosure, also stops short of the real question. Miss Kenton's additional remarks about the life she might have had with Stevens then constitute her answer. That question, of course, is "Do you still love me?" and Miss Kenton's answer is "I used to love you, and, indeed, I loved you more than I love my husband now, but my feelings have altered and it's now too late for us to think about a future together." Stevens's heart breaks precisely because, in the "moment or two [it took] to fully digest these words of Miss Kenton," he is registering their subtext. He not only still loves Miss Kenton but his trip and his reminiscences have made his feelings more acute even as they've led him to value those feelings more. Reading the scene, we feel our hearts about to break in sympathy.

Part of the power of the scene derives from how Ishiguro orchestrates the movement of Stevens's narration from underreporting back to reliable reporting. Ishiguro uses the extreme formality and self-distancing rhetoric of the statement, the "implications [of Miss Kenton's words] were such as to provoke a certain degree of sorrow in me," to mark it as underreporting. Consequently, Stevens's shift to the frank, plain-spoken acknowledgment, "Indeed—why should I not admit it?—at that moment, my heart was breaking," stands out as his most directly honest statement in the narrative. Yet even here Ishiguro requires us to infer a lot beyond what the statement directly asserts: Stevens's admission is simultaneously (1) a realization that he loves Miss Kenton—and, indeed, has loved her for years; (2) an acknowledgment that she has told him what he had hoped was true and what he had undertaken the journey to find out, namely, that she too had loved him; and (3) an expression of his belief that he has lost his chance to have her return that love. Thus, the moment when he fully acknowledges to himself that he loves her is also the moment that he realizes he is too late. In the authorial audience, our knowledge of Stevens's character and situation has been greater than his own throughout the whole course of the narrative. As the trip has progressed, however, Stevens has gradually, albeit inconsistently, moved toward what we know. In this sentence, Ishiguro not only shows that Stevens now knows his heart as well as we do but also that Stevens comprehends more about his situation than we are likely to do in the "moment or two" he takes "to fully digest" Miss Kenton's speech.

In his speech to Miss Kenton, however, Stevens does not disclose any of what he comprehends but rather replies in a kind, if conventional, turn toward closing off the topic: "You are very correct . . . , it's too late to turn back the clock. . . . You mustn't let any more foolish ideas come between yourself and the happiness you deserve." This discrepancy between Stevens's narration and his speech (his telling as narrator and his acting as character) deepens the emotional poignancy of the scene: his heart breaks but he doesn't let her know. At the same time, the discrepancy increases the complexity of the ethical demands the scene places upon its readers. Before taking up those demands in detail, we would like to sketch and situate our way of discussing the ethics of reading.

Our approach has most in common with the work of Wayne C. Booth and of Adam Zachary Newton.[9] Each of them, like us, wants to root ethics in narrative itself. Indeed, Booth emphasizes the pervasiveness of ethics in critical responses to literature, and Newton says that he wants to conceive of "narrative *as* ethics." Each of them moves, in his own way, from narrative to theoretical treatments of narrative and then back to narrative. In Booth's case, those theoretical treatments can be found in his own earlier work on the rhetoric of literature. His title *The Company We Keep* (1988) and his main metaphor in that book, books as friends, grow out of his earlier exploration of the way that writing and reading make possible a meeting of minds between author and reader. *The Company We Keep* moves beyond Booth's earlier major emphases on the cognitive, the aesthetic, and the emotive aspects of that meeting to the contemplation of how our values are engaged as we read, especially the ethical dimension of desiring as the text invites us to desire, and what the ethical consequences of those engagements are likely to be. *The Company We Keep* also gives greater emphasis to the communal nature of ethical response, suggesting that the activity of discussing the ethics of texts, what Booth calls co-ducing, is more important (ethically) than getting the text "right."

Newton investigates the "ethical consequences of narrating story and fictionalizing person, and the reciprocal claims binding teller, listener, witness, and reader in that process" (1995, 11), an investigation that leads him to describe three kinds of ethical structure in narrative: the narrational, the representational, and the hermeneutic. Narrational ethics are those associated with the telling; they occur along the line of narrative transmission from author to narrator to narratee to reader. Representational ethics are those associated with "fictionalizing person" or creating character. Hermeneutic ethics are those associated with reading and interpreting, the obligations readers and critics have to the text. Newton synthesizes work of Mikhail Bakhtin, Stanley Cavell, and Emmanuel Levinas as he does his analyses, borrowing especially Bakhtin's concept of *vhzivanie* or live-entering (empathy with the Other without loss of self), Cavell's concept of acknowledging (being in a position of having to respond), and Levinas's of Saying (performing a telling) and Facing (looking at or looking away).

While we share much with Booth and with Newton, we do not want to adopt Booth's overarching metaphor of books as friends, because it seems too limiting, or Newton's idea that narrative is equivalent to ethics because that seems not to recognize all the other things narrative is as well. Like Booth and Newton, our focus is on the ethics of reading, on how the very act of reading entails ethical engagement and response, but we focus more than either of them do on the links among technique (the signals offered by the text) and the reader's cognitive understanding, emotional response, and ethical positioning.[10] Indeed, the central construct in our approach to the ethics of reading is *position*, a concept that combines *acting from* and *being placed in* an ethical location. Our ethical position at any point in a narrative results from the dynamic interaction of four ethical situations: (1) that of the characters within the story world; (2) that of the narrator in relation to the telling: the different kinds of unreliability, for example, represent different kinds of ethical positions; (3) that of the implied author in relation to the authorial audience; and (4) that of the flesh-and-blood reader in relation to the set of values, beliefs, and locations that the narrative invites one to occupy. While the ethical dimension of reading engages our values and judgments, it is deeply intertwined with cognition, emotion, and desire: our understanding influences our sense of which values the text is calling forth, the activation of those values influences our judgments, our judgments influence our feelings, and our feelings our desires. And the other way around.

Thus, from our perspective, coming to terms with the ethical dimensions of the discrepancy between Stevens's telling and his acting in response to Miss Kenton involves addressing the following interrelated questions: Should Stevens have spoken differently to Miss Kenton, should he have told her that his heart has broken as she spoke? How does Ishiguro guide us to answer that question, both through signals in the scene and through the patterns of ethical reasoning he has previously established in the narrative? What are the consequences of our once again being in the position of knowing more about the characters and their situations than they do about themselves? How is this positionality related to our emotions about and desires for Stevens? The first three questions show how deeply intertwined the ethical positions of character, narrator, and implied author are: answering one implies an answer to the others. But none of the questions has a clear answer. On the one hand, Stevens's speech to Miss Kenton appears to be one more failure, one more instinctive choice for dignity over honest emotion. Earlier in the narrative, Ishiguro has shown Miss Kenton asking Stevens with both exasperation and justice, "Why, Mr Stevens, why, why, why do you always have to *pretend?*" (154; emphasis hers). Consequently, his pretending yet once more, on this occasion when his feelings are so strong and when he seems to have recognized something of the cost of his habitual pretending, seems to be a clear signal from Ishiguro that Stevens's self-understanding is still limited.

On the other hand, given the specific nature of Miss Kenton's revelation — "I loved you once but I now am content with my husband" — Stevens's decision not to speak about his own feelings can be understood as an act of unselfishness. This position becomes clearer if we imagine the likely consequences of his telling Miss Kenton how he feels. To say to her that his heart is breaking is not just to tell her that he loves her but also implicitly to appeal for help. And that appeal for help would, in effect, be an abuse of his new self-knowledge, an act in which he took his new awareness of the consequences of his own failures and used it to ask for relief from the very person those failures have most hurt in the past. The lesson of "Weymouth" for him is that he has lost any right to make such an appeal. Both Miss Kenton and Stevens are right: it is too late to turn back the clock.

Perhaps we can resolve the conflict between these views of Stevens's action and Ishiguro's signals about it by expanding our view of the scene to include Miss Kenton and the motives of her speech. Again we need to pay attention to the way the speech involves both disclosure and indirection. If, as we have argued, she is aware that her speech is indirectly answering Stevens's question about whether she still loves him, then she may be using the speech to appeal to him indirectly as well: "I'm willing openly to acknowledge that I did love you and still think about what-might-have-been; are you willing to reciprocate and, for once, talk about your feelings — not because I want to leave my husband but because I want to hear you talk about the past?" This view of Miss Kenton, then, would support the reading that the discrepancy between Stevens's telling and his acting is another wrong choice for dignity over honest expression of feeling.

But other elements of the scene point to another reading of the speech. Ishiguro sends us many signals that Miss Kenton takes control of their meeting: she comes to find Stevens at his hotel, rather than waiting, as they had planned, for him to come to her house; she asks most of the questions during their meeting and otherwise does more to direct the flow of their conversation; as we have seen, she takes the step of translating Stevens's question about being mistreated to one about whether she loves her husband, and she answers firmly and clearly that she does. The speech about what-might-have-been, then, is not an indirect appeal for an acknowledgment of Stevens's feelings but a further step in Miss Kenton's taking control. Its message is "let me be perfectly clear about the difference between the past and the present: I did love you, as even you must have figured out; further, as you may have seen in my letters over the years, I've occasionally wished we'd had a life together; but don't get any wrong ideas; I'm past all that and want to go on with the life I have." On this account, the last thing Miss Kenton wants to hear from Stevens is that his heart is breaking.

In short, we find that we cannot resolve the ambiguity of Stevens's ethical position at this point in the narrative because we cannot clearly determine Ishiguro's relation to Stevens. And our inability to make that determination is a direct consequence of the homodiegesis. While Ishiguro's rendering of Stevens's character and his narration has guided us to the complicated series of layered inferences that we have traced here, that rendering simultaneously prevents us from reading through the drama of the scene and its narration to Ishiguro's own position on the discrepancy between Stevens's acting and his telling. The most logical way for Ishiguro to resolve the ambiguity of the scene—to have Stevens disclose his motives for his response to Miss Kenton—is not really an option. First, it's not plausible that Stevens, given the way Ishiguro has characterized him, would disclose those motives, even if he knew them. Second, such a disclosure, even an unreliable one, would undesirably reduce the emotional intensity of the scene, which depends so much on what is not said.

To find such ambiguity in homodiegetic narrative is of course not a surprising phenomenon; even finding it at the climax of a narrative is not unheard of. (Can you say *The Turn of the Screw?*) Finding it, however, in the climax of an artfully constructed narrative that has depended on the reader's inferring clear, albeit complex, conclusions about the character narrator is a rare occurrence, certainly one that deserves further comment. Precisely because the narrative has, for most of its trajectory, rewarded rather than blocked our efforts to discern Ishiguro's positions behind Stevens's narration, this ambiguity has further consequences for our interpretive efforts: it transfers the responsibility for disambiguating the scene, and especially for coming to terms with the ethics of Stevens's action, from Ishiguro and the signals in the narrative to the flesh-and-blood reader.

In other words, to say that the authorial audience cannot disambiguate the scene is not to say that flesh-and-blood readers won't feel compelled to resolve the ambiguity, and it is also not to say that they will have difficulty finding one account more persuasive than the other. On the contrary, the pressure of the prior experience with the narrative is more likely to make it difficult for the flesh-and-blood reader who resolves the ambiguity one way to see the force of the argument for resolving it the other. Our own experience follows this pattern: Mary Pat is convinced that the right thing for Stevens to do is to let Miss Kenton see what he is feeling, while Jim remains persuaded that, in keeping silent, Stevens has done the right thing. Our extended conversations about the book and the scene, what Booth would call our coductions, have led us to recognize the persuasiveness of each other's case, but each of us in our heart of hearts believes that he or she has the better reading. In fact, we each initially saw our own readings as self-evident and were surprised to discover that what was so self-evident was not shared.

It is possible of course that the most compelling explanation of this phenomenon is that each of us has a wide, stubborn streak, but we would like to propose an alternative account, one that would apply not just to us in this reading situation but also to other readers in other situations. Our account emphasizes not only the links among homodiegesis, the cognitive, the emotive, and the ethical but also those between the patterns of the narrative and the flesh-and-blood reader's agency. Because the homodiegesis blocks our access to conclusive signals from Ishiguro and so transfers the responsibility for disambiguating the scene to the flesh-and-blood reader, the deciding factor in how we each carry out that responsibility is *our individual ethical beliefs as they interact with our understanding of Stevens as a particular character in a particular situation.* In other words, our own ethics play a crucial role in shaping our response to the scene, but those ethics do not supply abstract rules of behavior for us to slap on Stevens and his situation. Instead, our own individual ethical standards influence our view of which subset of Ishiguro's ethical norms is most relevant to this scene. In a sense, we each ask "What does Ishiguro think is the right thing for Stevens to do here?" and we find persuasive answers in a particular subset of the norms he has previously established. That the answers and the norms underlying them are different indicates the influence of our different ethical beliefs—or at least of our different hierarchy of such beliefs. For Mary Pat, Ishiguro's emphasis on the costs to both Stevens and Miss Kenton of Stevens's pretending is what is most salient. For Jim, Ishiguro's emphasis on Stevens's past selfishness is what matters most. While we might each think that we are getting out of ourselves and entering into Stevens's situation, we nevertheless continue, as our differences show, to carry our own ethical standards with us.

We are aware that our particular difference fits what some might predict on the basis of gender: of course the woman wants Stevens to express his feelings, and of course the man wants him to keep those feelings to himself. While we would not want to deny that gender has some effect on our beliefs, we would resist any single-cause explanation of our difference, since our ethical beliefs, like those of most people, have developed from a multitude of sources and causes, including experience, religious training, education — and reading narrative. We make this point not to move this essay toward autobiography but rather to underline the multifarious relations among the narrative texts and our responses to them.

5. Knowledge, Desire, and the Narratee

Regardless of how we individually resolve the ambiguity of the climax, there is another dimension of our ethical positioning that deserves attention. In this scene, as in the one depicting the events on the night Miss Kenton gets engaged, Ishiguro gives us knowledge about Stevens that Miss Kenton does not have. In that earlier scene, Stevens remembers that he stood outside her room, convinced that she is inside crying:

> As I recall, there was no evidence to account for this conviction — I certainly had not heard sounds of crying — and yet I remember being quite certain that were I to knock and enter, I would discover her in tears. I cannot remember how long I stayed standing there; at the time, it seemed a significant period, but in reality, I suspect, it was only a matter of a few seconds. For, of course, I was required to hurry upstairs and serve some of the most distinguished gentlemen of the land. (226–27)

Stevens here corrects his earlier report that he stood outside Miss Kenton's room convinced she was crying after she had learned about her aunt's death. The psychological dynamics of Stevens's memory are telling: Stevens's misremembering is another sign of his repression of feeling. Where the earlier report locates Miss Kenton's sorrow in something external to Stevens, this scene locates it in Stevens himself: he is both its cause and its secret sharer. Indeed, he may even be projecting his tears onto Miss Kenton; shortly after he has been standing outside her room, we learn through the dialogue with young Mr. Cardinal that Stevens is himself crying. (Strikingly, however, while Stevens may be misreporting the facts about Miss Kenton here, we can be confident that she has not really wanted to leave Darlington Hall and marry Mr. Benn: earlier that evening, she indirectly appealed to Stevens to tell her that she should not go out.) That Stevens is able to recall this scene now is a sign of how his journey — both geographically across England toward Miss Kenton and temporally across decades of memory — is leading him to admit where he went wrong. Now that he reports the more accurate memory, we make new inferences about a future they once might have had together: if Stevens were to knock and enter or if

Miss Kenton had opened her door and found him standing outside it, the entire course of their lives would have been changed. The scene is excruciating to read because their "whole dreams" hang by a thread and Miss Kenton is not even aware of that fact. What, then, about our ethical position as readers who know what Miss Kenton does not?

Our knowledge has two main effects, one connected with ethical responsibility, the other with desire. With the privilege of this knowledge comes a certain temptation and a certain responsibility. The temptation is to feel omniscient, or at least so superior that we begin to look down at both Stevens and Miss Kenton, these foolish Brits who simply can't talk directly to each other; or we may decide that if they can't see the value of the relationship they treat so cavalierly, they don't deserve to be together. But these temptations are balanced against the demands our superior knowledge places on our sense of justice. In Stevens's case, justice means recognizing his desire to knock as well as his fear of the consequences of knocking. Indeed, recognizing his near breakthrough at this moment also means recognizing how close he came to having a very different life, a recognition that leads to empathy rather than superiority. In Miss Kenton's case, justice means recognizing how conflicted she must have felt: in love with Stevens but despairing of ever having him acknowledge his own feelings or even the possibility that anything matters to him beyond his service to Lord Darlington. She loves but knows that her beloved is someone whose emotions, while deep, are only expressed through indirection. The effect of exercising this responsibility is to deepen our sympathy for each of the characters and to intensify our desire for Stevens to act. But this desire itself exists alongside the knowledge, implicit in the retrospective nature of the narration, that Stevens does not knock. So even as our desire is activated, we know it cannot be fulfilled.

Nevertheless, this understanding of the scene allows us to regard the final meeting in "Weymouth" as Stevens's finally deciding to knock on Miss Kenton's door, a recognition that in turn increases our desire for them to make a satisfactory emotional connection (though, given our own awareness of the passage of time, not necessarily an acknowledgment of their mutual love). In Mary Pat's reading, Stevens's failure to share his feelings, after traveling so far to knock and after having Miss Kenton open the door in her speech, again frustrates our desire. Miss Kenton has again opened herself to Stevens, and he ought to reply in kind; his feelings would not be a burden for her; she would welcome—and he owes her—the acknowledgment of their mutual regret for the life they now realize might have been. Consequently, the pain of Stevens's broken heart is doubled. And Miss Kenton's tears as she boards her bus are the objective correlative of the reader's unfulfilled desire. In Jim's reading, Stevens's knocking and Miss Kenton's answer give a twist to the reader's desire: although the emotional connection is not complete, something new has happened between them. Although Miss Kenton does not know all that Stevens is feeling, she does understand what it means for him to knock, however tentatively, and she can feel the tenderness with which he treats her throughout the scene. Her tears, then, signify her own recognition that if he'd acted this way twenty years before, her life would be different. In that important respect, her knowledge catches up with ours.

Despite their differences, both readings agree that our desire for Stevens remains unfulfilled, at least to some extent, and both lead to the conclusion that Stevens's anagnorisis leaves him with little to build on: he is brokenhearted about Miss Kenton and ashamed of his association with Lord Darlington. The final segment of the narrative, however, offers some consolation both to Stevens and to us. Again it will be helpful to recall the details of the scene.

Narrating the event right after its occurrence, Stevens tells of meeting an elderly gentleman on the pier at Weymouth who turns out to be a retired butler. Significantly, in light of his earlier denials to others, Stevens tells this butler that he worked for Lord Darlington and then suddenly breaks into tears and confesses his feelings of professional failure: comparing himself to Lord Darlington, Stevens says, "I can't even say that I made my own mistakes. Really—one has to ask oneself—what dignity is there in that?" (243). Stevens's companion, without being asked, advises Stevens that he needs to stop looking back and start looking ahead because "the evening's the best part of the day" (244). Stevens takes this advice to heart, and, inspired by the happy laughter of the crowd enjoying the evening on the pier at Weymouth, decides that he shall take up the art of bantering because it just may be "that in bantering lies the key to human warmth" (245).

If Ishiguro was not cheating in his handling of Stevens's narration leading up to the climax, surely he is cheating here. By what rule of literary probability can Ishiguro justify having Stevens meet a retired butler who just turns out to give him wise and consoling advice? We think that Ishiguro uses this last segment, including the seeming contrivance of Stevens's meeting with his "curious companion" to call attention to our experience as readers of this narrative and to readerly desires that have not yet been fulfilled.

In a number of ways, this section is set apart from the others in the novel. It is told in the present tense. Stevens's conversation with his new acquaintance is curiously intimate, its tone more like that of Stevens's narration than any other dialogue. As the two butlers share a cheerful conspiracy of "secrets" and "know-how," we are reminded of the professional camaraderie Stevens has consistently assumed with the narratee, as this reflection reveals: "The hard reality is, surely, that *for the likes of you and I,* there is little choice other than to leave our fate, ultimately, in the hands of those great gentlemen at the hub of this world who employ our services" (244; our emphasis). The retired butler, in other words, is a figure of the narratee — and he speaks as if he knows Stevens's whole story. Indeed, the conversation he has with Stevens roughly reiterates the trajectory of Stevens's prior narrative. Stevens's early reflections on the nature of greatness in a butler are recalled in the memories they share of professional life, and his gradual reexamination of his dedication to Lord Darlington results in the disillusionment he openly confesses to the sympathetic stranger. The greatest cost of Stevens's dedication is, of course, the life that he has missed with Miss Kenton, and we hear echoes of their final parting in the advice from Stevens's companion: "Don't keep looking back . . . make the best of what remains" (243–44).

In providing this figure of the narratee and this rough recapitulation of Stevens's story, Ishiguro also provides us some consolation after the deeply painful experience of the climactic scene. Since the narratee is only minimally characterized, he functions as a stand-in, first, for the authorial audience, and, second, for flesh-and-blood readers. Thus, the butler is ultimately a stand-in for us. When Stevens not only listens to but heeds the advice we would like to give him, some of our desire is finally satisfied. The emotional satisfaction of having Stevens's reality partially conform to our desire and the ethical satisfaction of seeing Stevens resolve to make something of the remains of his days combine to relieve the bleakness of his final situation. His anagnorisis has led not just to his pain but also to a new direction even at this late period in his life.

In other ways, however, Ishiguro keeps the final scene within the boundaries of realism he has observed in the rest of the narrative. Stevens's remark that "in bantering lies the key to human warmth" is an example of underregarding, a sign that he still has much to learn about the sharing of human emotion. Bantering can convey warmth but it does not equal the warmth generated by the intimate and frank disclosure of thoughts and feelings among people who trust each other. (If bantering were *the key* to human warmth, then male locker rooms would be the warmest places in the world.) Nevertheless, it is progress for Stevens to be underregarding rather than misregarding or misreading, and his resolution to seek greater human warmth in his life is more significant than his overestimation of bantering. In the final move of the narrative, then, Ishiguro shows Stevens trying to build on his new self-knowledge without showing him as an unrealistically transformed character. We can have some hope for the remains of his day, even as we ought not have any illusions about how much he has lost.

Ishiguro's communications to us, by contrast with Stevens's, are themselves a generous offer to share human warmth. Although the veil of fiction and the filter of Stevens mean that he is not engaging in direct disclosure about himself, he is, nevertheless, sharing his concerns about lives not lived, sacrifices made for the wrong reasons, whole dreams irredeemably lost. And that sharing is one that implies a deep trust in our ability to read the disclosures behind his many strategies of indirection — and, in the key moment of the narrative, to fend for ourselves. *The Remains of the Day,* in that respect, is itself an ethical act of the highest order.

Notes

1. The term was coined by Peter J. Rabinowitz to refer to the author's ideal audience. In this essay, the first-person-plural pronoun will often be used to describe the responses of the authorial audience. This audience is synonymous with "implied reader" but distinct from both the narratee (the audience addressed by the narrator) and the "narrative audience," the observer position that flesh-and-blood readers occupy within the world of the fiction. For further discussion, see Rabinowitz 1977 and 1987, Phelan 1996.

2. In a very fine essay on Ishiguro's technique, Kathleen Wall also recognizes that Stevens's narration provides challenges to existing theories of unreliable narration, but our rhetorical model places greater emphasis on the reader's activity than does her more strictly formal model. Consequently, our discussion moves toward the ethics of reading, while hers moves toward the relation between contemporary ideas of subjectivity and unreliability. While we find much to admire in her essay, we also disagree, for reasons that will become evident, with some of her general conclusions, particularly the points that the novel "deconstructs the notion of truth" (1994, 23) and that at the end of this century authors are more likely than those at its beginning to be "concerned with the causes and consequences of split subjectivity than with values" (38).

3. For examples of the different attitudes toward the category of "the implied author," see Seymour Chatman 1990, which includes a chapter "In Defense of the Implied Author," and another on "The Implied Author at Work," and Gérard Genette 1988, which contends that the category is unnecessary. Shlomith Rimmon-Kenan's (1983) discussion of reliability and unreliability is a good illustration of the widespread acceptance of Booth's distinction: a reliable narrator, she writes, is one who offers "an authoritative account of the fictional truth," while an unreliable narrator is one whose account "the reader has reasons to suspect" (100).

4. Terrence Rafferty's review of the novel in *The New Yorker* provides an instructive contrast to our analysis. For Rafferty, Stevens and his unreliability are too easily seen through, rendering the novel too neat and bloodless. We want to argue that Rafferty's view derives from underreading not just the subtlety of the technique but the depth of psychological insight and emotional sensitivity it contains.

5. For an important exception, see Riggan 1981. Naive narration such as we find in *Adventures of Huckleberry Finn* is typically unreliable along this axis. For a discussion

of Twain's novel that calls attention to the unreliability resulting from Huck's lack of "cultural literacy," see Elizabeth Preston (1997).

6. This information, regardless of how we decide the question of unreliability, establishes the passage as an instance of what Genette calls paralipsis: the narrator not telling as much as he or she knows. Our question is about how to read the paralipsis, what kind of effect it has on our understanding of the narrative. For related discussions of paralipsis and its effects, see Phelan's (1996) discussions of Hemingway's "My Old Man" and *A Farewell to Arms*. For more on these passages in Ishiguro's novel, see Wall.

7. Commenting on Stevens, Daniel Schwarz, for example, writes, "Stevens is more an imperceptive than unreliable narrator; he is historically deaf to his implications rather than untruthful" (1997, 197).

8. It is also arguable that all narrators report less than they know, since narration necessarily involves selecting from among the welter of events, thoughts, feelings, and experiences that make up the raw material of "what happened" those that are most salient for the narrator's account. But we distinguish this general condition of narrative from the underreporting of what is clearly salient.

9. Booth and Newton are themselves part of a broader ethical turn in literary studies over the past decade, a phenomenon that should be seen in relation to other, larger developments in the institution. The ethical turn is part of the general reaction against the formalism of Yale-school deconstruction in the wake of the revelations of Paul de Man's wartime writings; it is also compatible with, though distinguishable from, the continuing power of feminist criticism and theory and the rising influence of African American, multicultural, and queer criticism and theory, all of which ground themselves in sets of ethico-political commitments. The ethical turn in narrative studies is also part of a growing attention to the uses of narrative across the disciplines and in "everyday life."

From this perspective, we can see J. Hillis Miller's work on ethics as an effort to address the connection between the formal concerns of Yale deconstruction and the turn toward ethics. That ethics becomes, for Miller, another way of doing deconstruction is testimony to both the power and limits of deconstruction's conception of language as undecidable. We can also see Martha Nussbaum's philosophical investigation into narrative's capacity to offer thick descriptions of moral problems and moral reasoning as a rich instance of interdisciplinary interest in narrative. For other important work, see Geoffrey Harpham and the recent issue of *PMLA* devoted to ethical criticism.

10. In this connection, the difference between this essay and Newton's analysis of *The Remains of the Day* is instructive. He focuses on a number of ethical issues either enacted in the narration or dramatized in the action — "looking away," "leaving home," "throwing voice," and others — but his analysis is very much text-centered rather than reader-centered. Booth's attention to the way in which narratives ask readers to follow a pattern of desires is more in line with what we do here, but again we offer more systematic attention to the reader's ethical positioning by the text and by his or her own values.

PART TWO

New Technologies and Emergent Methodologies

4 | Cyberage Narratology: Computers, Metaphor, and Narrative
Marie-Laure Ryan

What is the role of metaphor in narratology? Does its use condemn the discipline to be a virtuoso solo performance in textual interpretation, or is it compatible with the ambition of narratology to build a sharable basis for a systematic, objective study of narrative that relates to the texts of its corpus much in the same way that linguistics relates to language? This essay tries to debunk two myths: one that claims that metaphor is incompatible with a scientific approach, and another that denies distinctions between metaphorical and literal language.

Since the early sixties, narratology has steadily widened its scope by borrowing concepts from a variety of fields: traditional grammar, transformational grammar, optics, the cinema, psychoanalysis, formal semantics, game theory, social theory, and feminism. Here I propose to expand the metaphorical repertory of narratology to a domain that owes much of its vitality and ability to market its ideas to its own skillful use of metaphor: cyberculture and computer technology. Through the development of four concepts inspired by computer programming— virtuality, recursion, windows, and morphing—I hope to substantiate the claim that in narratology, as in other disciplines of the physical and social sciences, analogical thinking is the force that reveals new perspectives and moves knowledge forward. But if metaphor blazes trails into unknown areas, it takes the literal designation of technical vocabulary—such as Genette's terminology—to divide, explore, map, and administrate the conquered territories.

From its very beginning, narratology has been affected by a case of split personality: is it art or science, literary criticism or discourse analysis, interpretation or description? One of the issues that divide the two conceptions of the discipline is the appropriateness of metaphor. An offshoot of structuralism, narratology was originally driven by the ambition to raise literary studies to the degree of scientific rigor and technical precision that structuralist linguistics was supposed to have achieved. (Remember Levi-Strauss's claim that linguistics should be regarded as a "pilot-discipline" in the social sciences.) Since scientific precision begins with adequate tools, the first task of the emergent discipline was to develop a technical jargon custom-made for the investigation of narrative phenomena. The terminology introduced by Genette (*homodiegetic, heterodiegetic, analepsis, prolepsis*) is as close to literal expression as language will ever get: it would be necessary to unearth long-forgotten Greek etymologies to find any metaphorical resonance. But the vocabulary of narratology was quickly invaded and enlivened by borrowings from other fields: traditional grammar[1] (Todorov's assimilation of characters, properties, and events to nouns, adjectives, and verbs), transformational grammar (deep structure, surface structure, transformations), geometry (figures, semiotic squares, triangles, and wheels), optics (point of view, focalization), the cinema (camera-eye narrative, panning, zooming in and out), the visual arts (framing), topography (story space and discourse space, domains, boundaries), sexuality and psychoanalysis (narrative desire, seduction, climax), mathematics (chaotic systems), philosophy of language and formal semantics (possible worlds), game theory (moves), postmodern social theory (Foucault's Panopticon), and feminism (distinguishing typically male and female narrative structures; gendering the narrator).

The question of the legitimacy of metaphor has created a split between a formal descriptive narratology inspired by discourse analysis and cognitive science and a speculative discourse about narrative conceived by its practitioners as a virtuoso performance in postmodern theory. The detractors of metaphor argue that borrowings from other fields involve an inevitable distortion of the original concept, since not all of their features can be transferred to the new field. Figural language is just a "way of speaking" that covers up the lack of a proper, unambiguous designation. Partisans of figural language, especially those of a deconstructionist persuasion, retort that there cannot be proper designations, because meaning arises through semantic displacements, and language is "always already" metaphorical. In this vein, Harry Shaw has argued that most narratological concepts conceal metaphors, including that of narrator (1995, 98).[2]

Linguistics and philosophy of language, though by no means unanimous on the topic, offer more nuanced accounts of the role of metaphor in language than does deconstruction. The position I personally endorse states that if language expands through figural displacements, it does so from a core vocabulary of etymologically nonanalyzable terms (kinship words, basic commodities, numericals, directional and temporal terms). Moreover, once a metaphor passes into common language, it becomes for the speakers a literal designation, out of which other metaphors may be developed. As Richard Rorty observes: "Old metaphors are constantly dying off into literalness, and then serving as a platform and foil for new metaphors" (1989, 16). This process of regeneration encapsulates the truly creative moment in the use of language. Thinking is analogical as much as it is logical, and it is by recycling words and extending their scope that language and thought can map new territory.

In the present essay, I hope to substantiate this claim by expanding the metaphorical repertory of narratology to yet another domain: cyberculture and computer technology. My primary concern is not to initiate the broadening of the scope of narratology that will be required to deal with the new genres of electronic writing, such as interactive texts, multimedia stories, computer games and text-based virtual reality (MOOs and MUDs), but to survey what computers can teach us about traditional forms of narrative. By selecting computer science as source of analogies, I am not only focusing on a technology which will have a great impact on how we read, what we read, and whether or not we read — all questions of crucial importance to the survival and development of literary narrative — I am also drawing inspiration from a field whose ability to market its ideas and imprint itself on the popular imagination is strongly indebted to its own skillful use of metaphor. Ever since a malicious insect found its way into one of those giant metal boxes that housed the computers of the early forties and wreaked havoc in its logical circuits, the field of computer science has demonstrated its vitality through an unparalleled metaphorical creativity: bugs, viruses, and snails (as in mail); garbage, trash compaction, wastebaskets, and recycle bins; surfing and navigating the Net; lurking on a user-interest list or starting a flame war — the list could go on and on. These terms have now become part of a fashionable jargon that brands its users as aspiring members of the elite fraternity of digital cognoscenti, but one should not underestimate the heuristic value of metaphor: it is the ability of computer science to absorb and adapt concepts from everyday life that has enabled it to transform the computer from an intimidating number-crunching device into a user-friendly, multipurpose machine. The lesson of this growth and self-renewal through metaphorical creativity should not be lost on narratology.

The four items to be discussed in this essay — virtuality, recursion, windows, and morphing — are therefore not obscure technical terms crafted for narrow purposes, but concepts and images themselves borrowed by computer science from other areas, and awaiting new life in a third incarnation as narratological tools. In the first three of these entries I revisit topics whose exploration I have initiated elsewhere (1987, 1991) while in the fourth I venture into what is for me a new territory.

1. Virtuality

By introducing the concept of virtuality into the study of narrative, we are not so much *borrowing* an idea from the computer field as activating a way of thinking that has energized many domains of contemporary culture. Virtuality is very much a *topos* of the current *Zeitgeist,* what Brian McHale would call a dominant. The idea of virtual reality (VR) has had such an impact on the popular imagination that the term virtual has become a trademark of cyberculture, almost a synonym of electronic: "virtual technologies" is broadly used to designate all applications of computer technology, from the Internet to goggle-and-glove VR. But before it turned into a buzz word applicable to virtually (!) everything, and therefore to nothing, virtual had a precise technical meaning in computer science. The user who programs a computer in a higher-level language, such as C or LISP, is said to communicate with a virtual machine because the physical machine can only understand instructions coded in binary form. The program must therefore be translated into machine language before it can be executed. But from the point of view of the user, the virtual machine is "as good as" the actual machine. This concept of virtuality—which has many more applications in computer architecture—connotes the ideas of "as if," of "passing as," of lacking authenticity. It embodies the fascination of postmodern culture for the fake, for copies that kill the desire for the original. A computer program that lets the user compose images of bouquets and send them through e-mail to a loved one is tellingly called "Virtual Flowers." But there is more to virtual than an opposition to "the real thing." Etymologically, virtual derives from *virtus,* Latin for strength, manliness, and virtue. In scholastic Latin, *virtualis* designates the potential, what is in the power (*virtus*) of the force. In this philosophical sense, the virtual is not that which is deprived of reality, but that which possesses the potential, or force of developing into actual existence. The classical example of the virtual as potentiality is the mode of existence of the oak in the acorn. Just as an acorn can develop into many different oaks, depending on environmental factors, a virtual object can be actualized in many different ways. Computers are virtual machines in this sense of "many in one," because the same hardware can support a variety of software programs which fulfil many different functions. Insofar as VR projects are interactive simulative systems, the virtual as potential is no less important to VR technology than the idea of fake. A simulation is not a static representation of a specific state of affairs, but a "garden of forking paths" (to paraphrase the title of a short story by Borges), containing *in potentia* many different narrative lines threading together many states of affairs. Through the choices of the user, every session in the simulative system will send the history of the virtual world on a different trajectory. Moreover, when the function of the VR system is to teach the user how to manage real-world problems (for instance, flying an airplane), the exploration of the potential inherent to *this* world becomes the *raison d'être* of the the simulation's fakery. To paraphrase Aristotle's definition of the purpose of the literary work of art: "It is not [the VR system's] business to tell what happened, but the kinds of things that would happen—what is possible according to possibility and necessity."[3]

Both aspects of the virtual play a role in narrative theory. Through its power to conjure an imaginary world to the imagination and to create an emotional involvement in the fate of nonexisting characters, narrative fiction may be the original VR technology. Theorists describe the reader's experience of the fictional text in many pertinent terms—suspension of disbelief (Coleridge); being lost in a story (Nell 1988); transportation into another world (Gerrig 1993); engaging in a game of make-believe (Walton 1990); and mental simulation of the represented events (Walton 1997)—all images linking the text to a fake reality. But the narrative text (not just the text of narrative fiction) also puts into play the virtual as reservoir of potentialities. From the point of view of the reader, a narrative is like a musical score waiting to be performed. For the sake of convenience critics talk about *the* textual world, but insofar as this world is produced by the reader's act of imagination, the text contains *in potentia* as many worlds as there are different ways to flesh out the given information into a vivid mental representation.

The virtual as potential can also be used to describe the mode of existence of narrative itself. Some scholars regard narrativity as inseparable from the concept of a narrator engaged in an act of storytelling. This definition excludes nonverbal forms of narrative, unless one postulates the rather *ad hoc* concept of a metaphorical narrator for such genres as drama, movies, and the visual arts. (The case of voice-over narration shows that there *can* be a narrator in film, but the above definition makes a narratorial presence necessary.) Another approach, better suited to deal with various media, consists of viewing narrativity as a cognitive frame into which readers process texts, authors shape materials, and the human mind categorizes experiential data. Whereas the first approach regards verbal realization as a necessary condition of narrativity (it denies the existence of "untold stories"), this view accepts various degrees of actualization, from the purely virtual narrativity of a life situation all the way to a hypothetical full realization of the narrative frame in a discourse that makes completely explicit its configuration and leaves the reader no other alternative than a *specific* narrative construction (a likely disaster from an artistic standpoint!).[4] Whether the frame is traditionally conceived in terms of plot, or, as Monika Fludernik has recently suggested (1996b), in terms of human experience this view legitimates the attempt to seek underlying narrative patterns in texts that do not present themselves as a narrative act and do not exhibit the surface features of narration, such as lyric poetry or certain forms of postmodern fiction.

The concept of virtuality also finds application in the analysis of individual narratives, especially on the level of story.[5] In the late sixties and early seventies, Todorov and Bremond pointed out that events that do not happen are as important to the understanding of narrative as events reported in the factual mode. Any "narrative grammar" (or semiotic system designed for the description of plots) should therefore contain operators specifying the mode of existence of the states and events that determine the development of the story. Under modality Todorov had in mind such categories as *optative* (wishes), *obligatory* (duties and commitments), *conditional* (promises and threats), and *predictive* (anticipated events). Narratologists working in the framework of possible-world theory (Eco, Pavel, Doležel, and myself) extended this repertory by breaking apart the semantic universe of narrative into a realm of facts (what I call the textual actual world), and one of possible worlds created by the mental activity of characters: the potentially actualizable worlds of knowledge, desire, obligations, anticipation, goals and plans, as well as the alternative worlds of pretense, dreams, hallucinations, and embedded fictions. A story's intrinsic tellability—the quality that makes certain plots produce ever new versions—is to a large extent a function of its ability to deploy a rich field of virtualities. Even though the realistic narrative can actualize only one itinerary on the "garden of forking paths" of the virtual, it takes an appreciation of the paths not taken and of those that are still open for the reader to be caught in narrative suspense. As I have suggested elsewhere (1991), the themes of error, deceit, failure, broken promises, violated interdictions, and goals achieved in unexpected ways are intrinsically more productive than their opposites because they trace at least two paths on the narrative map. It is not without reason that outlining divergent possibilities is one of the most common advertising strategies on the blurbs that adorn the cover of paperback novels: "A case that started small is exploding into a thunderous multi-million dollar war of nerves, skill, and outright violence—a fight that could cost one young lawyer his life, or turn him into the biggest rainmaker in the land" (blurb for John Grisham's *The Rainmaker*). While there is no doubt as to which possibility will be realized (the one that fulfils the reader's desire for vicarious success), it is the risk inherent to the other branch that keeps the reader spellbound.

Nothing could be less suspenseful than a one-path narrative, in which a character forms a goal, constructs a plan to achieve it, and executes this plan according to all expectations, except perhaps a narrative that offers no glimpse whatsoever into the characters' motivations. As philosophers have argued (von Wright 1967), human action only becomes intelligible when the actuality of the physical gesture is interpreted against the virtual background of goals, projections, fears, and rejected lines of actions. A narrative that remains entirely focused on the actual/observable (like the camera-eye narratives of modern literature) allows neither anticipation of what is to come, nor, in extreme cases, interpretation of the gestures as action. In Flann O'Brien's *At Swim-Two-Birds*, or in certain monologues by Beckett (*The Unnameable*), characters perform gestures and talk, but there is no apparent purpose to their speech and behavior. In these works, the reader does not ask "What is he going to do next?" but "What is he going to say next?"[6] In the true spirit of postmodernism, language is all that remains to the show. It is well known that postmodern narrative challenges the idea of an intelligible reality by letting the virtual proliferate out of control and engulf the factual, but in these two examples a sense of absurdity and disorientation is reached in the opposite way, by isolating the factual from the virtual horizon that normally gives it significance. In both cases the text disrupts the classical ontology of a universe grounded in the neat opposition of one actual to many possible worlds.

Traditional narrative lives not only from the contrast between the actual and the virtual but also from the interplay of the two forms of virtuality: the potential, which can be actualized in the same world, and the counterfactual, or fake, which can only be enacted in an alternative reality. This subject is too vast to be adequately treated here, but let me present it through a few examples. In *Don Quixote*, the reader is warned from the very beginning that the hero's obsession with chivalric romances is the escape of a sick mind into a fake reality, but the plot itself lives from the Don's stubborn belief that these novels describe a potential that can be achieved in the world of everyday life. In *Waiting for Godot*, the reader or spectator gradually comes to the conclusion that Godot exists only in the mind of the characters, but Vladimir and Estragon remain faithful to an interpretation that places his arrival in the domain of the virtual-as-field-of-possibilities. When it is treated in a realistic, rather than an allegorical manner, the interplay between the two forms of virtuality accounts for some of the most poignant situations of narrative fiction. In James Joyce's "Eveline," the heroine conceives the plan of escaping her condition of enslavement to an abusive father by eloping with a sailor to the New World. The opportunity seems too good to be true, and some readers may wonder whether the lover and his offer are not the construct of a desperate mind. (Eveline's mother died in a condition of insanity, and the technique of internal focalization casts a doubt on the reliability of the heroine's mental representations.) It is only in the last episode, when Frank, the lover, physically appears on the narrative scene, that "the reader" (as represented by my own experience) becomes convinced that Eveline's plan to elope has a foundation in the textual actual world. But it is also in this last scene that the virtual-as-potential disintegrates into a virtual-as-counterfactual: rather than boarding the ship with the man who loves her, Eveline remains tied to the shore by a paralyzing fear. In this dramatic scene, the loss of opportunity is punctuated by the slow ticking of the narrative clock. Every passing second intensifies the reader's desire to see Eveline escape her condition, but also frustrates this desire, as it brings the "could be" closer to the "could have been."[7]

2. Recursivity, Stacks, Pushing, and Popping

In the jargon of computer programming, the term of recursion describes the mode of operation of algorithms that activate a copy of themselves in order to accomplish a task. The activated copy is "pushed" on top of a "stack" of waiting programs and interrupts the execution of the "calling program" (as I call the version that does the activation). When the copy produces a result, it is "popped" from the stack, its output is fed back into the calling module (now occupying the top of the stack), and the program continues its run using this data as input. Since the copy may in turn activate a copy of itself, the process can be repeated any number of times, and the stack can grow to any height (limited only by the configuration of the system).[8] To avoid infinite recursion, and produce concrete results, it is therefore necessary to define a halting condition. Some mathematical definitions of functions are inherently recursive; for instance, in the famous series known as Fibonacci's numbers, the value n of the series is the sum of the values of the function for $n - 1$ and $n - 2$. The recursion is halted by attributing a fixed value to the first two terms of the series: when $n = 1$ and $n = 2$, the value of Fibonacci (n) is 1. To compute Fibonacci (3) we must first compute Fibonacci (2) and Fibonacci (1), each of which returns the value 1. Adding these two values, Fibonacci (3) produces 2 as output. (I leave it to the reader to continue the series; the solution appears in this endnote.[9]) Recursive functions are responsible for the beautifully complex images that have been made familiar by fractal geometry. In these images, every detail is a reflection (a *mise-en-abyme*, to use narratological terminology) of the entire picture. The virtually infinite complexity of the texture of clouds and rocks, of the branching system of a tree, or of the asperities of a coastline can all be generated through a mathematically simple recursive process that draws tiny clouds, rocks, trees and coastlines inside the larger picture. While recursive functions have been known for a long time, it took the speed of computers to calculate and plot them to a sufficient degree of recursion to reveal their intricate beauty.

The phenomenon of recursivity is well known to narratologists in at least one of its forms: the framing, or embedding, of stories within the story. The phenomenon of embedding could also be described through the computer-inspired metaphor of stacking and the accompanying operations of pushing and popping: every time the text enters a new level, it "pushes" a story on a stack of narratives awaiting completion; every time a story is completed, it is "popped," and attention returns to the previous level.[10] All the levels of the stack must be cognitively accessible to the reader—otherwise she could not form a global representation of the narrative or adequately assess the function of the current level—but only the top level is narratively active, in the sense that it must be brought to a satisfactory closure before discourse can return to the representation of the preceding level. (It would be ungrammatical to resume narration on a level other than the top one.) The metaphor of recursion is thus used in this essay to describe the same phenomenon as embedding, but it does so from a dynamic perspective. As a spatial metaphor, embedding presents narrative as a picture that can be instantly grasped as a whole, and it tells nothing about the temporal succession of elements. The analogy with the computer concept of recursivity, which implies the metaphor of objects being pushed on and popped from a stack, introduces a temporal dimension that makes it possible to describe the structure of expectations created by the process of self-replication. The notion of "current level" of the stack shows where the reader is "now" at any given moment of the narration, and where she expects to be when the unit of this level is completed.

As I have suggested elsewhere (1991), the boundaries that delimit recursively embedded narratives from their calling environment can be of two types: the crossing of illocutionary boundaries involves a change of narrator, and marks a new speech act; while the crossing of ontological boundaries involves a transportation to a different reality, such as the worlds of dreams, illusions, fantasies, or fiction. A "story within the story" thus involves one type of boundary when it concerns the same world as the discourse of the preceding stack level (example: a character telling about his past), and two types of boundaries when it transports the reader into a new fictional world (the stories told by Scheherazade in the *Arabian Nights*).

But narrative recursivity is a wider phenomenon than overt framing. As Gerald Prince has observed, "Any narrative is made up of little narratives" (1992, 22).[11] This idea is allegorized and dramatized in a recent science fiction novel by Neil Stephenson, *The Diamond Age, or, A Young Lady's Illustrated*

Primer, through a technique analogous to the procedure by which the users of the computer program *Chaos* explore the fractal images generated by Mandelbrot or Julia functions: the user blows up a detail of the screen, and discovers the same pattern on a smaller scale. In the novel, a "street urchin" named Nell fortuitously comes into possession of the most technologically advanced artifact yet invented: an interactive book that projects the reader into the story world and produces a didactive narrative that transposes her real-life situation into fictional (in this case, fairy-tale) action. When Nell first opens the book, it reads to her a dry summary of the whole story. With each successive session, however, an element of the outline is blown up into full narrative life: "She found herself reading the same story, except that it was longer and more involved, and it kept backtracking and focusing in on tiny bits of itself, which then expanded into stories in their own right" (1996, 135).[12] This recursive expansion is not only described but also implemented through the novel's top-down (from whole to parts), and therefore not strictly chronological, presentation of Nell's fictional adventures.

In its most basic form, narrative recursion involves neither illocutionary nor ontological boundary crossings: the little stories that make up the stuff of narrative are reported by the same narrator, and they concern the same world. In a complex narrative, the relation of constituents may follow two syntactic patterns: an iterative one, comparable to paratax in the sentence, and a more properly recursive one, similar to hypotax. In iterative structures, little stories succeed each other on the same narrative level, and each of them must terminate before the next one begins. The iterative structure is illustrated by episodic narratives, such as the *Bildungsroman,* or in more recent literature, by the proliferating narratives of Gabriel Gárcia Márquez and of much of third-world, postcolonial literature. In the recursive pattern—which occasionally combines with iteration—little stories are a structural component of a larger constituent, to which they contribute input. The trademark of this pattern is a sense of interruption: each new story is pushed on a stack of unfinished stories, and upon completion, returns information necessary to the continuation of the lower level. (Here "level" corresponds to a cognitive focus, to the aspect of the story world currently being offered to the reader's attention, rather than to a discrete ontological domain, reference field, or narratorial speech act.) While iterative structures respect the forward movement of time, recursive embedding typically sets the narrative clock back to some point in the prehistory of the current situation. The prototypical example of recursive narration is the performance of those verbose conversational storytellers who, under the pretext of narrating the embarrassing thing that happened to Susan at her cousin's wedding, regress to Susan's problems with her boss, how the boss met his wife, why his wife does not get along with her mother-in-law, and so on, until the whole town becomes part of the story. It usually takes a formulaistic expression to halt the recursion and steer the narrative back to the announced topic: "but where was I?," "anyway," or the delightfully self-contradictory "to make a long story short."

In its minimal form, recursive narration is a summary of the past life of a character. Here is an example from Isak Dinesen's tale "The Supper at Elsinore": "Old madame Baek, *who had herself been married for a short time to a sailor, and had, when he had drowned, reëntered the service of the De Coninck family as a widow*, thought it a great pity that neither of the lovely sisters had married" (1972, 218; my italics). The private tragedy of Mme Baek could have been a story in its own right, but the text only mentions it to explain how Mme Baek came to be the caretaker of a house abandoned by the De Coninck family. In a standard case such as this one, the content of the recursively embedded story is treated as mere background information. In another example from the same text, the narrator is almost apologetic about the interruption inherent to the technique, and promises a quick return to the main narrative line: "But there was another girl of Elsinore whose story may rightly be told, very briefly, in this place" (231). (The story itself takes twenty-five lines.) The narrative function of this embedded story is to illustrate the attitude of the de Coninck sisters toward the lovers of their brother. In the hands of a writer as keenly aware of narrative teleology as Isak Dinesen, narrative recursion is mostly a means to consolidate the logical and psychological motivation of the main narrative line. In yet another case, however, the connection of the embedded story to the main plot line becomes problematic. When the text regresses to the youth of Mme Baek and narrates her relation to the great poet Ewald (234ff.), the purpose of recursive narration is not to shed light on the current events, but to sharpen the portrayal of the housekeeper, as well as to enliven the evocation of the historical setting. Through this episode, a secondary character is momentarily brought into the spotlight, and acquires a human density that is normally reserved for the main protagonists.

In its fullest realization, the emancipation of embedded stories from the main narrative line leads to a subversion of the distinction between story and discourse. In *Tristram Shandy*, recursive narration turns into lengthy digressions, and the lengthy digressions, far from supporting a plot, use the plot as life support, as verbal performance becomes the point of the novel. In the utilitarian, background-sketching uses of the device, the recursively embedded story mentions events without conveying a sense of a "narrative now": the reader expects the interrupting narrative to be popped from the stack for the narration to return to the plot line that forms the real focus of the text. When recursion becomes emancipated, however, the content of the stacked-up story is brought to life in an imaginary present, and the reader loses sight of the foreground/background distinction.

It is through the application of the recursive principle that narrative resolves the conflict between the necessary closure of its form and the openness of its subject matter: life, experience, and history. Every narrative cuts a stretch of finite length from the infinite fabric of time and plays it back for the reader. Whether the main narrative tense is the present or the past, the reader lives this narrated time as a moving present and becomes in imagination a witness of the events. The limits imposed by narrative on the time continuum are both necessary and arbitrary: necessary from a pragmatic and artistic point of view, since telling cannot go on forever, and since a well-formed story must have, according to Aristotle, a beginning, a middle, and an end; but also arbitrary, if one remembers that every initial state has a prehistory, every conclusion has an implicit sequel, and every event in the middle has ramifications that fall outside the narrative window. By stretching representation beyond the main story line, beyond the events selected for reenactment in the narrative present, recursive narration helps narrators cope with the sense of proliferating stories that Italo Calvino so eloquently captures in *If on a winter's night a traveler:*

> I am producing too many stories at once because what I want is for you to feel, around the story, a saturation of other stories that I could tell and maybe will tell or who knows may already have told on some other occasion, a space full of stories that is simply my lifetime, where you can move in all directions, as in space, always finding stories that cannot be told until other stories are told first, and so, setting out from any moment or place, you encounter always the same density of material to be told. (1981, 109)

As I hope to have shown through this brief discussion, the concept of recursivity and the accompanying notions of push and pop on a stack of waiting narratives touch upon many important narratological problems and open many areas of investigations: the characterization of different narrative styles, from the flat narration of a chronicle to the deeply recursive approach of the baroque *roman à tiroirs;* the reader's sense of the narrative now and the correlated distinction between foregrounded and backgrounded events; the cognitive processing of narrative (how many levels of stacked-up stories can human memory handle); the storyteller's strategies for alleviating or increasing the sense of interruption created by recursion; the question of narrative teleology (when does recursive narration fulfil an explanatory role, and when, having grown beyond this function, does it move into the foreground?); and the relevance of the notion of scale to describe the nature of the reader's involvement:

Is interest mainly focused on the grand narrative of the macrolevel, or is the text being read for the sake of the little stories?

3. Windows

In the computer field, the metaphor of window is associated with an operating system that allows the user to run many programs simultaneously, to determine which one(s) will be shown on the screen, and to specify the size of the visual frame in which they appear. As I read my e-mail, for instance, my word-processor is running in the background (together, of course, with "Windows," the operating system). If I want to answer one of the letters, I close the window of the e-mail program, open a window on the word-processor, type my answer, copy it into a buffer accessible to all programs, close the word-processor window (without terminating the program), reopen the e-mail window, and paste in the answer. (This rather complicated procedure allows me to circumvent the fact that my rather antiquated e-mail connection does not let the user correct typos.) The basic idea behind the computer use of the window metaphor is that, at any given time, there is more going on than what can be shown on the screen. The user can only engage actively with one process at a time, and view perhaps one or two more, but it is the concurrent operation of a number of different processes, both seen and unseen, that determines the global state of the system and keeps the computer operating.

Narrative theory did not need inspiration from Bill Gates's software products to find applications for the concept of window. In the preface to *The Portrait of a Lady,* Henry James writes:

> The house of fiction has in short not one window, but a million—a number of possible windows to be reckoned; every one of which has been pierced, or is still pierceable, in its vast front, by the need of the individual vision and by the pressure of the individual will. . . . These apertures . . . have this mark of their own that at each of them stands a figure with a pair of eyes, or at least with a field-glass, which forms, again and again, for observation, a unique instrument, insuring to the person making use of it an impression distinct from any other. (1970, ix; quoted from Jahn 1996, 251)

Developing this passage into a theory of focalization, Manfred Jahn suggests that "the 'watchers' standing at the windows of the 'house of fiction' are narrators. Their primary activity, apart from the piercing of walls, is the contemplation of . . . the storyworld" (1996, 251). Since the openings in the wall of the house of fiction are observing minds, the various windows can represent character consciousness as well as narratorial perception. The omniscient narrator can thus choose between two modes of observation: he can pierce his own window into the wall, or he can take advantage of an existing window and represent the story world from the angle of the character associated with this particular position. This character becomes, in standard narratological terminology, the focalizer or reflector, and his consciousness functions as "a screen, an intermediate window opening onto the narrative world" (252). This narratological use of the concept of window owes nothing to computers and operating systems. But the analogy can be tightened if we consider that life, the subject matter of narrative, is a massively parallel machine. The Borgesian image of the "garden of forking paths" describes not only the relation of the actual to the virtual within the conceptual domain relevant to the understanding of narrative, but also the pattern of individual life histories within the domain of the actual. Just as a computer may run several programs concurrently, a narrative may develop several plot lines; and just as a program may receive input from another program, the outcome of a line of actions may be affected by another sequence of events taking place at the same time but in another location. If we map a reasonably well-developed and complex narrative, the resulting graph will be a tapestry of converging and diverging, splitting and merging strands. But if life is parallel, its narration is sequential. The concept of window can help us describe one of the most neglected aspects of narrative strategy: how discourse keeps track of concurrent processes, how it unravels the tangled knot of intersecting destinies, how it deals with the spatial mobility of characters, and how it moves back and forth among the various sites where the fate of the story world is being decided.

In order to define what I have called a story-line window (1987)—to keep the concept distinct from the above-mentioned windows of focalization—let me return to the metaphor of the house of fiction. I visualize the narrator as sitting inside the house and looking through the windows toward the story world. Every window thus frames a different segment of space. Let us imagine, furthermore, that the house can rotate like one of those revolving restaurants on top of a needle-shaped tower, so that the observer can follow the movements of a character through story space without shifting position. At some point, however, the observer will be forced to move to a different window in order to record a scene. Imagine that the moving window followed Emma Bovary from her life with Charles in Yonville to her escape with Léon to Rouen. The narrative presents Emma's actions through a continuous report (we never lose sight of her), but as the scene shifts from Yonville to Rouen, Charles moves away from the window, and Léon moves into its frame from the outside. For the narrative to return to what Charles is doing in Yonville during Emma's sojourn in

Rouen, it would be necessary for the observer to move to a different window, one that remains focused on Yonville. The window shift is made necessary by the parallelism of the life histories of Emma and Charles.

This interpretation of the window metaphor opens two complementary areas of investigation:

1. *Window structure.* Given a specific plot, mapped as a temporally ordered sequence of states mediated by events, the window structure determines how many different frames are necessary to present the story. A narrative necessitates as many windows as there are distinct branches in the plot; a branch, in turn, consists of a sequence of events that can be recorded in one narrative "take" (to explain the computer-inspired metaphor through a more familiar one borrowed from the cinema). Consider for instance the plot of the well-known fable "The Fox and the Crow." Since the entire story can be told without losing sight of the fox, the window structure necessitated by the plot comprises only one frame. Now contrast this case with the famous story by O. Henry, "The Gift of the Magi." Here the telling of the story requires at least two windows, since the paths of the two protagonists first run together, then split and merge again. A window shift will be necessary to move from Jim selling his watch to buy an ornament for Della's hair to Della selling her hair to buy a chain for Jim's watch. The number of windows in the basic structure increases proportionally to the number of main characters and the breadth of the slice of life captured by the narrative.

To count the number of windows in these two examples I have appealed to the reader's intuitive grasp of what constitutes a loss of continuity in the narration, but this intuition can be supported by a more rigorous definition. A window shift occurs in two situations. In the first case, a narrative state results from the merging of two distinct plot lines; if the narrative has followed one line up to this point, it must backtrack to the other line. The typical example of this case is when a new character with a narratively significant past enters the stage, forcing the narrative to set the clock backward in order to represent this past.[13] The other case of window shift is when the narrative jumps to a parallel plot line, causing all the discourse referents to be changed at the same time. The classical example of this case is a transition from a scene showing x and y at a to a scene showing w and z at b. If the narration moves from showing x at a (Della selling her hair in town) to x and y at b (Della and Jim offering each other presents at their house), some continuity is maintained through the referent x. We can imagine that the observer remained at the same window, but fell asleep for a moment, so that Della's return to her house was not recorded. Another way to maintain some type of referential continuity is through the location: a narrative can shift from x and y at a to z and w at a. These two possibilities distinguish two types of windows. The first, *moving windows,* focuses on characters and follows them through space and time. The unity of these windows does not require a constant referent. A window following x can end up following y and losing sight of x if at a certain point in the narrative x and y are both framed by the window. The second type, *static windows,* frames a specific site and records the coming and going of characters within constant spatial limits. Static windows are typical of the theater, especially if the play observes the classical rule of the unity of location, but they are also represented in those verbal narratives that tell the story of a place through an extended period of time, such as Ivo Andríc's *The Bridge on the Drina.*

2. *Window management.* While window structure determines the number of windows needed, given what events have to be told, window management describes how narrative discourse handles the succession of frames and marks the transitions. Window management is thus to window structure what discourse is to story: a given window structure can be managed in several different ways.

The study of management begins with a repertory of the stylistic devices that mark the boundaries between windows. These devices include space-shifting expressions such as "Meanwhile," "Not far away from the castle, in a humble cottage," "At about the same time, on another planet"; time-shifting ones, such as "Many years earlier, at the turn of the century, the de C. had been a powerful family," "Let me tell you what strange twist of fate had brought this beggar to the scene"; illocutionary transitions marking embedded narratives: "They all listened intently as the sailor began his story: 'I was born, etc'"; typographical signals (chapter breaks, paragraph breaks); and changes of stage setting in the theater. In (post)modern literature, window shifts can even be left totally unmarked: in *Le sursis* by Sartre, for instance, the narrative switches every few sentences, and without paragraph breaks, to what different characters are simultaneously doing in various locations.

As these examples of transitions demonstrate, window shifts can create spatial or temporal discontinuities (or both). These discontinuities can be handled in two ways: by lateral or by embedded windows. A lateral window moves to a different braid in the plot (with possible moving back in time) without creating a stack structure; when the window closes, or when its representation is suspended in mid-action, the narrative can turn to any other braid in the plot, and there is no way to predict what the next window will show.[14] In a computer-programming language, a shift to a lateral window would be effected by a simple GOTO statement. With embedded windows, on the other hand, the new window is pushed on top of a narrative stack, and the reader knows exactly to which scene and to which time the narrative will return, once the current window is closed. The analogous programming language command is the procedure call, which combines a GOTO with a return address. The category includes not only the clearly framed stories through which characters tell about their past, but also the cases of recursive embedding discussed in the previous section.

In its minimal form, an embedded window is a retrospective summary of the past of a character, such as the evocation of Mme. Baek's marriage and widowhood quoted in the previous section. In such a case, the narrative conveys information relative to a side branch in the plot — what led Mme. Baek to become available as caretaker — but it does so in the pluperfect tense, without resetting the clock. This suggests two modalities in the presentation of narrative windows: the actual mode, which transports the reader to a new *here* and/ or *now;* and the virtual mode, which minimizes the evocation of the second story line, and remains anchored in the same spatio-temporal point of reference (that is, deictic center) as the surrounding narration.

With these definitions in place, we can distinguish several types of window management:

— *One-window narratives, with occasional embedded windows.* These narratives follow the life of one central character, and avoid discontinuities by virtualizing the windows relating to the lives of other characters. Most first-person narration falls into this category, since to maintain credibility, the narrator must either be on the scene, or summarize in virtual windows what is a matter of general knowledge.

— *Many-windows narratives that minimize the number of shifts.* These narratives follow a complex system of interwoven destiny lines, but they maintain a sense of continuity by staying with one line until it merges with another. Many of the great panoramic novels of the nineteenth century — those of Tolstoy, Dostoevsky, Balzac, Stendhal — adopt this economy.

— *Narratives with a limited number of separate windows but frequent window shifts.* In this case the narrative moves back and forth between two or more story lines, presenting them in many installments. This structure is exemplified by Isabel Allende's *Eva Luna.* Alternating chapters are devoted to the life of Eva Luna in South America and of Rolf Carlé in Europe, until their paths run together, and one window absorbs the other. An extreme case of this category is the above-mentioned novel by Sartre.

— *Narratives with many small windows.* While the preceding type segments the presentation of its windows, this type cuts up the lives of characters into many discontinuous but self-enclosed sketches focused on different times and places. Practitioners of this technique, which has been compared to cinemato-graphic montage, include André Malraux (*La condition humaine*) and Toni Morrison (*Beloved*).

—*Narratives that systematically present parallel plot lines as embedded narratives.* The life story of a newly encountered character could be told in a narratorial voice, by resetting the narrative clock backward, but in works such as *The Arabian Nights* or Jan Potocki's *Manuscript trouvé à Saragosse,* the past of the major characters who walk onto the stage is almost always presented through a first-person narration.

—*Narratives with simultaneous visual windows.* In an attempt to overcome the sequentiality of language, some avant-garde narratives (for instance Arno Schmidt's *Evening Edged in Gold*) opt for a newspaper-style layout, in which parallel strands in the plot are captured in separate boxes or columns. Each area of the page is devoted to events taking place in a certain location, and the page as a whole becomes a map of the story world.

—*Narratives with configurable visual windows.* Electronic texts go one step further in the spatialization of language by letting the user define the number and size of the windows that appear on the screen. Commonly found in word-processing programs, this feature is also exploited in hypertext fiction. In Michael Joyce's *Afternoon,* the text can be broken up into any number of windows, and the exploration of the forking paths that make up the hypertextual network can be pursued as simultaneously as reading will allow. (No spatial presentation can however overcome the temporality of the reading process.)

Since my use of the metaphors of window, embedding, and recursivity in the preceding discussion may have blurred the distinction between these concepts, let me conclude this section with a recapitulation which I hope will lead to a clarification of their entangled relations.

A *window* is a narrative unit delimited by what can be shown of a textual world in one "take," as the narrative recording device follows certain objects or focuses on a location for a specific time span. The evolution of the contents of the window must follow the directionality of time. Window shifts are the processes by which narrative moves from one strand in the plot to another. They are formally marked by a jump to another time and place, or by a setting backward of the narrative clock.

The concept of *recursion* and the accompanying metaphor of the *stack* are used in this essay to describe the dynamics of embedding. All instances of embedding represent a window shift, since they involve either referential discontinuity or the exploration of the prehistory of the current situation, but the case of narratives that work alternately on several parallel strands demonstrates that not all window shifts involve embedded elements.

Framing finally is a type of recursive embedding in which the replicated unit is clearly separated from its context through illocutionary or ontological boundaries: a different speech act, or a recentering into a different world. As Isak Dinesen's stories suggest, not all cases of narrative recursion involve framing.

4. Morphing

In contemporary culture, transformation is everywhere: in TV advertisements, in special-effects movies, in toys (transformers), in holographic pictures, in body politics (sex-change operations, cosmetic surgery), in the location of political boundaries, in religious discourse, in New Age philosophy and advertising rhetoric. We are constantly urged to be born again; to open ourselves to spiritual growth, to welcome life-changing experiences, to "take three simple steps to a slimmer new you." This fascination for metamorphosis, for an ontological system composed of more fluid categories, is reinforced by the postmodern doctrine of the subject: we are told that identity is no longer to be found in a stable foundation located in the depth of interiority, but in the embracing of a multiple, "decentered" self constantly recreating itself through the performance of many roles.

One of the phenomena that best capture the spirit of the time is the visual effect known as morphing. This term of computer graphics refers to the technique of turning an image into another through a number of intermediary frames that gradually alter the features of the starting image into those of the target. Visual media are so influential on the culture of this late century, and morphing lends itself so well to magical realism, one of the dominant imaginative paradigms of contemporary fiction, that one should expect many attempts to emulate the effect in recent and future narratives. The theme of transformation is admittedly as old as myth, perhaps as narrative itself, but in order to qualify as morphing, transformation must be so progressive that the reader or spectator realizes only retrospectively that one form has been replaced by another. This excludes instantaneous changes, such as Gregor Samsa's awakening as a giant vermin in Kafka's *Metamorphosis,* the successive reincarnations of the narrator of Günter Grass's *The Turbot* into many historical characters, or the quintessential fairy tale prince being turned into a frog.

To speak of narrative morphing inevitably involves a certain degree of metaphorical displacement, since the special effect must be transposed from the visual to the verbal domain. On a scale of decreasing literalness, we can distinguish the following types:

1. Gradual transformation of objects involving their visible shape.
2. Gradual transformation involving mental, ontological, or taxonomic features (what "kind of individual" the affected character is).
3. Symbolic transformation of individuals.
4. Transformations of a purely technical nature, affecting the mode of narration and the identity of the narrator.

The focus of my discussion will be the morphing of this fourth type, but to situate the problem, let me briefly illustrate the three other types. It is not easy to find examples of the first category because reading a description of how one shape is slowly turned into another is much less appealing than watching the process on a screen. Uri Margolin has found a rare example of this most literal type of narrative morphing in Ovid's *Metamorphoses:*

> When Ovid portrays arborification (human beings turning into trees) . . . he always has the process start from the ground up, so that the [character] can still speak and think for a while and be aware of what is befalling him/her. In the story of Myrrhea, the incestuous mother of Adonis [book 10 of *Metamorphoses*], he goes one step further. Myrrhea is transformed into a tree while she is pregnant, but she still retains a distended womb; she undergoes labor, and she/the tree is moist with falling tears. (1995, 11)

In the second category, morphing affects being rather than appearance. In Kafka's short story "Report for an Academy," an ape retraces the stages of his becoming human, though he retains the body of an ape. In Donald Antrim's recent novel *One Hundred Brothers,* the narrator, one of a hundred brothers meeting for an annual family reunion, is transsubstantiated into a "Corn God" and plays the sacrificial role in a ceremony of death and rebirth that rejuvenates the group for another year. According to the logic of ritual thinking, the transformation must be real, not just symbolic, for the ceremony to exercise control over vital energies.

In the third type of morphing, characters progressively become "like something else," though they do not undergo transformation in any literal sense. An example is Richard Powers's *Galatea 2.2.* In the novel, a Turing test is organized between a computer that has been taught by the narrator to think like a human and a young female student who has rejected the narrator's love. Each of them produces an essay on Shakespeare's *The Tempest,* and a judge must decide which one is the computer and which one is human. While the student produces a brilliant New Historicist reading of *The Tempest* "as a take on colonial wars, constructed Otherness, [and] the violent reduction society works on itself" (1995, 326) — all suspiciously fashionable positions in today's academic circles—the machine can only whisper her love for the narrator and die. The machine has morphed into an unpredictable human overcome by emotion and the woman has become a programmable machine incapable of love, the feeling traditionally viewed as the trademark of humanity.[15]

In all these examples, morphing is both a theme and a technique of presentation associated with it: transformation is enacted without being explicitly mentioned, and no sharp boundaries are drawn between the former and the latter state. In my last category, narratorial morphing, the technique emancipates itself from the theme of physical or mental transformation. Morphing does not affect a character or an object within the world of the narrated, but the virtual individual presupposed by the act of narration. To introduce the topic, however, let me present an example that hovers on the borderline between the thematic and the technical.

In Bharati Mukherjee's novel *The Holder of the World,* a contemporary American woman—the wife of an Indian computer scientist engaged in a VR project—undertakes to reconstruct the life story of Hannah Fitch, a seventeenth-century Puritan woman who emigrates from the New World to England and from England to India, where she becomes the mistress of a Hindu prince. The story is mostly told in the hypothetical, third-person mode appropriate to historical biography. But toward the end of the novel, the narrator enters a VR system which transports her onto the scene of the events she is trying to re-create. At first, the pronoun *I* still refers to the narrator—or to her VR counterpart—since she describes Hannah as being seen for the first time: "She is a beautiful woman, more Pre-Raphaelite than I had imagined, with crinkly golden hair" (1993, 281). But when Hannah addresses the referent of this I, she uses the Christian name of her own Indian servant, Hester, who shortly thereafter is wounded on a battlefield. From this moment on, the narratorial center of consciousness merges with Hester's. The scene of the servant's death is told from a first-person perspective which lends greater vividness and immersive power to the narration. The whole episode is a first-person equivalent of the strategy through which third-person narrators slip into the consciousness of characters in free indirect discourse (I use this term for both represented speech and thought). The passage can therefore be read as an allegory of the morphing process that underlies third-person narration with variable focalization. The artificiality of the VR system underscores the conventional character of a narrative technique whose felicity conditions cannot be met in the real world.

My suggestion to regard variable focalization and the use of free indirect discourse as an instance of narratorial morphing may seem far-fetched, but a number of intermediary examples fill the territory between the literal transportation of Mukherjee's narrator into a foreign consciousness and the metaphorical transformation of third-person narrators into the characters whose perspective they represent:

1. *Morphing of the narratee.* In Italo Calvino's *If on a winter's night a traveler,* the narrative YOU appears in the first sentence to refer to the actual reader: "You are about to read Italo Calvino's new novel, *If on a winter's night a traveler*" (3). As the narrative develops, however, this YOU is drawn into the fictional world and gradually acquires distinctive features that differentiate him from the real-world reader. In the last sentence, his gender emerges as male: "You stop for a moment to reflect on these words. Then, in a flash, you decide you want to marry Ludmilla" (259). From my personal point of view as a female reader, the referent of the narrative YOU has morphed during the course of the novel from woman to man, and from real-world individual to fictional character.

2. *Morphing of the narrator into author (and back).* This process is typical of the postmodern metafictional novel. The narrator of John Fowles's *The French Lieutenant's Woman* appears successively, and without apparent breach of continuity, in the reference of the pronoun *I* (liberally used throughout the text), as an observer located on the scene of the narrated events, as a twentieth-century social historian who chronicles the past as true fact, and as a modern-day writer who confesses having invented all of the characters.

3. *Morphing of the narrator from character to nonindividuated third-person narrator.* Gustave Flaubert's *Madame Bovary* begins as a classical first-person narration told from the point of view of an observer character: "We were at prep, when the Head came in, followed by a new boy not in uniform and a school-servant carrying a big desk" (1992, 1). After this brief appearance, however, the narrator vanishes, and the rest of the story is presented in a third-person narration alternating between narratorial point of view and character focalization (predominantly Emma's). The first-person beginning blends so smoothly into the third-person narration that most readers simply forget about the ephemeral and weakly profiled narratorial figure.[16]

In all these examples, narratorial morphing involves some kind of transgression: of natural laws (Mukherjee's time travel), of logic ("I" becoming another person), of taxonomy (Calvino's transgendering), of ontological boundaries (reader becoming character; narrator becoming author), and of pragmatic constraints: first-person and third-person narration are different language games, creating different sets of expectations, and the morphing of the narrator from one type to another opens up an entirely new field of possibilities. It is, for instance, only after the disappearance of Flaubert's narratorial figure that the novel resorts to character focalization and psychonarration, two devices normally associated with a nonindividuated narrative voice.

Migrating into the center of consciousness of other characters and occupying their spatio-temporal coordinates in the fictional world is semantically much less consequential for impersonal third-person narrators who are by definition deprived of physical attributes than it is for individuated first-person narrators. Because the third-person narrator is a fundamentally amorphous, bodiless entity, "he"[17] can borrow any body, rent any consciousness and speak through any foreign voice without breaking any rules, for there are no rules specifying what ontologically incomplete entities can say. In this passage of *Madame Bovary,* for instance, the third-person narrator looks at the mind of a character from his own omniscient point of view; the telltale sign is that he knows what the character ignores: "Léon never knew, as he forlornly left the house, that she had just stood up to gaze after him through the window" (86). A few lines later, the narrator evaluates past events through the mind of Emma: "She fancied that she had pushed him too far away, that the moment was gone, that all was lost" (86). The novel also includes sarcastic statements presupposing an opinion that can only be attributed to a narratorial or authorial subjectivity: "[Monsieur Homais] is doing infernally well; the authorities handle him carefully and public opinion is on his side. He has just received the Legion of Honour" (286); objective reports stating what is a matter of general knowledge rather than recreating perception (the last sentence of the previous quote, taken factually); and passages focalized by an anonymous collective observer located on the scene: "Then was seen stepping on to the platform a little old woman, moving timidly, and apparently cringing deep into her shabby clothes" (120). In other third-person narratives (for example, Gogol's *The Overcoat*), observations presupposing omniscience co-exist with declarations of ignorance. One of the remarkable features of third-person narration with variable focalization is how impossible it is from a pragmatic point of view, and yet how easily it is accepted by the reader. Within the confines of third-person narration, morphing is processed as a normal aspect of the narrative mode, and the migration of the narrator into many selves has no impact on the reader's assessment of the distance between the real and the fictional world. Variable focalization and free indirect discourse are indeed the technical trademarks of the realistic novel.

The use of the concept of morphing to describe the finely grained and infinitely varied modulations of the third-person narrative voice introduces an element of flexibility into a domain whose theorization has split narratology between two doctrinaire and bitterly opposed factions: those who regard the third-person narrator as an ontologically complete human being and those who want to do away with the concept; those, in other words, who want to naturalize fictional language by forcing it into the parameters of a real-world speech act, against those who want to affirm the autonomy of literature with respect to real-world communication.

The first of these two schools literalizes the metaphor of narrator by attributing to third-person narrators all the properties of an embodied individual. Susan Lanser insists for instance that gender is a fundamental feature of all types of narrator, even when the text does not specify any such property. The gender of the impersonal third-person narrator usually ends up being inferred from the gender of the author: some critics refer to the narrator of *Pride and Prejudice* as "she," and so would they, presumably, with the narrators of George Sand and George Eliot. It is of course impossible to tell whether or not the narratologists who advocate a necessary gendering of the narrator for ideological reasons actually engage in an act of imagination appropriate to their theoretical position. Do they mentally picture the narrator of *Pride and Prejudice* as an embodied female observer, hiding behind the curtains of drawing rooms or invisibly following the heroines on their walks through the English countryside? It is not my intent here to prevent readers from fleshing out their mental representations of third-person narrators, if this act of imagination helps them get immersed in the fictional world (though I don't see how these readers would reconcile human embodiment with superhuman omniscience). But I object to any theoretical attempt to legislate over my own act of imagination by imposing on me what I regard as a needlessly specific representation. I am certainly not misreading Jane Austen if I do not picture the narrator of *Pride and Prejudice* as a woman, though I would indeed be missing a necessary semantic feature of the text if I failed to gender Roquentin, the first-person narrator of *La nausée*.

The other school of thought, represented by Ann Banfield's "non-narrator" theory of narration, adheres to an extreme literalism. If there is nobody telling the story, because the narrator has no name and no physical properties, why postulate a narrator at all? For Banfield, a text must have one illocutionary source (1 TEXT/1 SPEAKER principle), and an expression must represent one center of consciousness (1 E/1 SELF). Since the sentences of free indirect report of speech and thought represent the self of a character, they cannot at the same time express a narratorial subjectivity. These sentences are therefore instance of "pure," objective narration, and they do not participate in a communicative transaction between a speaker and a hearer. In this pure narration, the text does not pass as the representation of a narratorial cognitive act, but as the unmediated unfolding of events in the reader's field of perception. Insofar as the formula 1 TEXT/1 SPEAKER prescribes that the entire text must be ascribed to the same source, the presence of a single sentence of free indirect discourse throws the entire narration into the non-narrator category. As Monika Fludernik has observed, however (1993, 381), it is not uncommon for narratives to contain both character focalization and narratorial statements of a highly subjective nature. Omniscient third-person narrators can say "I," dialogue with the reader, ironize, moralize and pontificate (Tolstoy's "All happy families") — in short, express their subjectivity without acquiring the ontological status of the first-person narrator. In contrast to Banfield's model, a morphing theory allows the narrator to enter foreign minds without depriving him of a mind of his own.

While the naturalizing approach denies any difference between first- and third-person narration, Banfield's model denies any resemblance. Both treatments suffer from the same shortcoming: they presuppose that the features of the narrator must be rigidly determined for the entire text. In one case he has none, in the other he has all the features of a regular human being. In a morphing theory, by contrast, the third-person narrator is basically nonindividuated and nonembodied, but "he" can acquire any conceivable temporary features. This approach cannot be contradicted by the data, because it guarantees absolute freedom of expression. While Banfield's model precludes any expression of narratorial subjectivity in the third-person mode, the concept of morphing can fully accommodate the case she wants to account for: the occasional emptying of the center of consciousness and the effacement of the narrator behind the narrated events.

More importantly, perhaps, the dynamism inherent to the idea of a morphing narrator provides a response to an objection recently raised against classical narratology in the name of postmodern ideology. In *Towards a Postmodern Theory of Narrative,* Andrew Gibson accuses narratology of being obsessed with form, of viewing everything in terms of spatial models, of reducing all phenomena to static geometrical schemata (1996, 5); of being blind to the forces, or textual energies, that continually create new forms out of old ones — briefly, of being incapable to deal with the temporality of form, a phenomenon more concisely described as trans-formation. "To think of narrative and its movement in terms of force . . . is to conceive of it as a constant folding into and unfolding out of form" (66). The narratological treatment of voice in particular is criticized for the assumption that "a narrator is a character present in a mystifying singleness throughout her or his discourse" (164). In his rejection of narratological taxonomies and schemata, however, Gibson seems to forget that force can only be apprehended in its interaction with form: we don't see the wind itself, we only see its effect on objects. (I wonder what would be the general shape of a theory of narrative force uncontaminated by formalism: verbal description, cinematic representation, computer simulation, or musical transposition?) Narrative energy has to work on something, and it takes a good dose of theoretical prejudice to exclude a priori from this something the formal categories so thoroughly worked out by narratology. All it takes to reconcile formalism with energetics is to recognize that formal categories need not frame the entire text and reduce it to uniformity. Just because some narratologists have attempted to define modes of narration and types of narrators on the global level does not mean that the categories thus obtained cannot apply to the local level, evolve throughout the text, and combine with other forms into complex structures. By modulating narrative voice and allowing narrative modes to blend into each other, the concept of morphing not only frees the text from the "mystifying singleness" of the narrator, it also gives dynamism to form, and visibility to force.

If narrative is force and form, so is narratology. I propose to regard the complementarity of these two notions as a model of what could be the relations of metaphor to technical terminology in both narrative theory and the social and physical sciences. Metaphor is the force that conquers new territories, reveals new perspectives, and moves a discipline forward. Many of the scientific revolutions that impose new paradigms originate in a global metaphor that radically reconfigures the domain under investigation. In the linguistic field, for instance, the Saussurean model rests on the metaphor of language as a self-enclosed system of solidary elements (if one disappears, all of its substance will go to its neighbors), while the Chomskyan model develops the metaphorical opposition of depth versus surface. More modestly, metaphors can provide new viewpoints on some local problems and redescribe some of the data without revolutionizing the entire field. But insofar as a new metaphor creates a new perspective, it does not work in harmony with other metaphors. What happened for instance to the idea of system of signs in transformational grammar? Some metaphors come in pairs, and neatly divide the phenomena to be described among themselves (for example, the Apollonian and the Dionysian), but in most cases, their relation is one of competition. A case in point is what has come to be known as complementarity in theoretical physics. As Niels Bohr has shown, light can be described as either a wave function or as material particles, and each approach offers insights that would be unreachable from the other, but objectively speaking, light cannot be at the same time a wave and a set of particles. The results obtained by adopting each of the two conceptualizations may be complementary, but the conceptualizations themselves are mutually exclusive.[18] The four metaphors discussed in the present essay are not as blatantly incompatible, because each of them maps only part of the territory of narratology. But within the whole field, they do not interlock neatly like the pieces of a jigsaw puzzle. Their respective areas overlap in some cases (windows and recursion), or they constitute self-enclosed domains to which the other metaphors have little to contribute (virtuality and morphing). My use of metaphors from the computer field is more what Claude Levi-Strauss would call a *bricolage* than an attempt to draw a global analogy between narrative structures and computer architecture. Important computer concepts such as hardware and software, RAM and ROM, bits and bytes, direct and indirect addressing, arrays and linked lists were simply left out of my discussion because I could not find useful analogies with narrative phenomena. But if the choice of metaphors is the result of *bricolage,* this does not preclude a systematic mapping of their territory. The observations allowed by a certain metaphor are relative, since metaphor is a perspective, and a given phenomenon can be described from an infinite number of different angles, but two observers sharing the same spatial coordinates should contemplate the same panorama, and within this panorama, distinguish the same shapes. It is the role of narratological formalism to describe the phenomena that can be objectively observed under a particular metaphorical perspective. If metaphor blazes trails into new areas of investigation, it takes the literal designations of technical vocabulary to divide, explore, map, and administrate the conquered territories.

Notes

1. I wish here to draw a distinction between metaphorical and literal uses of linguistic terminology in narrative theory. The former rest on the assumption that narrative is structured like a language, while the latter find their justification in the fact that language is the medium of narrative. The literal category includes notions such as reference, speech acts, tense, and deixis.

2. I personally do not see why the first-person narrator should be considered a metaphor, but I find this approach justifiable in the case of impersonal, third-person narration, because this mode does not involve the visible presence of an embodied and individuated speaker/writer figure.

3. *Poetics* IX.1; quoted from Pavel (1986, 46).

4. I conceive this fully actualized narrativity as something like the plot outlines produced by computers: "One day, a lady of the court named Andrea wanted to have some berries. Andrea wanted to be near the woods. Andrea moved to the woods. Andrea was at the woods. Andrea had some berries because Andrea picked some berries. At the same time, Lancelot's horse moved Lancelot to the woods. This unexpectedly caused him to be near Andrea. Because Lancelot was near Andrea, Lancelot loved Andrea. Because Lancelot loved Andrea, Lancelot wanted to be the love of Andrea" (S. Turner 1994, 199). (Note however that even this outline is not fully explicit, since it does not state that Andrea wants to be near the woods because berries are found in woods.)

5. For lack of space, I will not discuss two interpretations of virtuality that relate to

the level of discourse. One is treated in Uri Margolin's contribution to the present volume: narratives presented in the conditional mode. The other (discussed in Ryan 1995) consists of telling a story in a specular mode: rather than stating directly that events happened, the text describes their representation, or mirror image, as captured by a reflective device contained in the textual world, such as a painting, photograph, novel, movie or TV show. This interpretation of virtuality activates the optical sense of the term.

6. I am here quoting from memory a critic whose name I do not remember.

7. I am of course aware of the relativity of my reading. In a survey of the reactions of a group of undergraduate students to the story, I was surprised to find out that quite a few—mostly female honor students—regarded Eveline's decision as the best choice for her future, and downplayed the drama of the last scene. This divergence of interpretations brings further evidence of the inherent virtuality of the literary text.

8. "Stack overflow" is the standard error message when the system crashes, whatever the reason.

9. The series goes 1, 1, 2, 3, 5, 8, 13, 21, 34, etc.

10. Another narratologist who resorts to the concepts of pushing and popping is Mary Galbraith. In discourse analysis and computational linguistics, their use was pioneered by Rachel Reichman.

11. Generative models of narrative such as Prince's or Pavel's account for this phenomenon through the occurrence of the same symbol (Episode, Move, or simply Story) on the left-hand and right-hand side of rewrite rules. This means that a component of an Episode, Move, or Story can be filled with one of these categories, either directly or indirectly, after other rules have applied. Similarly, in Chomsky's generative grammar, components of a sentence (S) can be rewritten as S:

$$S \rightarrow NP + VP$$
$$NP \rightarrow S$$

This property of recursivity is what enables grammars to generate sentences or narratives of infinite complexity.

12. "She," in this passage, does not refer to Nell but to an actress who interacts with her by reading on a screen the script generated by the book, and whose voice is relayed to Nell through a computer network. But Nell undergoes the same experience as the performer as far as the temporal unfolding of the story is concerned.

13. One may wonder why I count moving back in time (analepsis) and not moving forward (prolepsis) as window shift. The reason is that for a scene to be perceived as prolepsis it must be followed by an analepsis; otherwise, it would be a simple "fast forwarding" of the narrative tape. It is therefore the analepsis that creates the prolepsis.

14. Or if there is a stack, it consists of only two levels: the top is occupied by the currently opened window, and the bottom includes all the previously shown windows. Popping of the top level can return to any of these windows.

15. In an ironic twist, however, the judges are quick to recognize the student's essay as the product of a human mind.

16. As Genette has pointed out, far more dramatic, but equally smooth, alternations

between first- and third-person narration are found in Proust's *A la recherche du temps perdu.* In Flaubert the first-person narrator is easily forgotten because he only appears as a nondifferentiated member of a group (the schoolmates of Charles Bovary), but in Proust he is the focus of the novel.

17. My use of the pronoun "he" carries no gender implications. I could not use he/she, because this presupposes gendering, and "it" is incompatible with consciousness and linguistic ability.

18. The terms of "wave" and "particle" can be regarded as metaphors, though many scientists view them as literal technical designations, because they function as the natural language translations of mathematical formulas. As Fritjof Capra has argued in *The Tao of Physics,* mathematics is the literal language of science, and all verbal formulations are transpositions meant to facilitate communication, both with the general public and within the scientific community.

5 | Of What Is Past, Is Passing, or to Come: Temporality, Aspectuality, Modality, and the Nature of Literary Narrative

Uri Margolin

The paradigm case of narrative, as described in classical narratology, consists of the PAST + FACTIVE + COMPLETIVE triplet. In other words, the states, actions, and events portrayed are supposed to be past as regards the temporal position of the global narrating voice or consciousness, and hence recounted in retrospect. Their status is that of known, established facts. Finally, sequences of actions are supposed to have run their full course, allowing their patterning as meaningful wholes. This model, however, is far from universal in its applicability to literary practice. Even retrospective narration portrays states and events with nonfactual status: negative facts (what did not happen), counterfactuals, possibilities not realized, unresolved indeterminacies as to whether certain events took place, and unconfirmed hypotheses or conditionals. Even more importantly, we are witnessing the contemporary rise of narratives where the traditional retrospective viewing position of the narrator vis-à-vis the events is replaced by the concurrent (with uncompleted sequences of events) or the prospective one, and where the governing modality often shifts to the hypothetical, the optative (may X happen!), or the deontic (do X!). These newer varieties cannot be dismissed as nonstandard oddities or deviations—first, because they too, like standard narratives, portray dynamic situations, and, secondly, because they are too numerous.

There is consequently a need for a much broader, integrated model of narrative where the standard classical case will form just one variety among many, and not necessarily the basic or privileged one. Such a revised unified model will require an anchoring in a broader or more fundamental framework for its defining parameters, and may lead to a revised or even new view on the very nature of narrative as a semiotic product. In what follows, I sketch out tentatively a revised model, based on the Tense-Aspect-Modality approach in general linguistics.

One central claim of my model is that the canonic form of any narrative proposition consists of a nucleus (= the event or state being described) and three operators, which define the temporal position of the nucleus, its inner temporal contour (completed or in progress), and its reality status (actual, nonactual, hypothetical, indeterminate, counterfactual, wished for, ordered into being), with all three operators being specified relative to the temporal perspective and mental attitude of an overall narrator or focalizer.

If this model is accepted, narrative itself needs to be redefined. It is now seen to portray not dynamic situations per se, but rather the key factors and operations involved in the mental representation (= cognitive mapping) of dynamic situations, and the different possible configurations these factors can assume. On the metatheoretical level, such a view constitutes a shift from the structuralist to the cognitive paradigm, where the results of structuralist narratology are reinterpreted and inscribed into a more comprehensive vision, that of the "age of cognitive science" (Mark Turner's term).

There is one way for an event to be actual, and numerous ways for it to be less than that. (Chung and Timberlake 1985, 241)

Each deep narrative structure [can] be actualised according to a number of different modes, of which the indicative, governing conventional narrative realism, is only the most familiar. Yet other possible narrative modalisations: [the conditional], subjunctive, optative, imperative and the like, suggest a heterogeneous play of narrative registers. (Jameson 1981, 165)

1.

1.0 The standard, canonical, or prototypical narrative, as defined in classical theories of narrative, is one which revolves around that which has already occurred and been completed in the story world, in other words, around states, actions and events that are past from the viewpoint of the global narrating position. This kind of narrative is told by the textual voice or personalized narrator as a known fact within the story world, and thrives on certainty or factivity. One succinct formulation of this view is provided by the philosopher David K. Lewis: "In the world of the story, the act of story telling is truth-telling about matters whereof the teller has knowledge" and further: "[Within this world] the story is told as known fact" (Lewis 1978, 40). But how canonical is this form really? Serious doubts or challenges seem to issue from both current literary practice and current theory. Recent developments in narratology have clearly shown that even in standard retrospective narration there are zones of the dis-narrated, that is, sets of claims as to what has not happened (G. Prince 1988); mention of possibilities that existed at a given point but were not actualised in the subsequent course of events (Beaugrande 1981; Ryan 1986); unresolved in-determinacies as to whether or not certain events took place at all, and, even if they did, what their precise nature was; and past acts of focalization by narrative agents that are presented as merely hypothetical, conditional, "iffy" (Herman 1994a). While these findings necessitate a modification *cum* expansion of the classical model, its general validity has been put into much more radical ques-tion by the contemporary rise of narratives, from short stories to novels, whose overall governing mode of viewing is either concurrent with the events being narrated ("present tense narrative"), prospective ("future tense narrative"), conditional, optative, or deontic. (For concrete examples, see section 4.)

1.1 Several crucial questions immediately arise: (1) First and foremost, can one construct an alternative model of narrative that, while necessarily more complex than the classical one, will be able to provide a comprehensive, inte-grated, and unified map of narrational varieties, both traditional and contem-porary? To be theoretically sound, such a model will have to treat the numerous aspects and forms that fall outside the classical model not as oddities, devia-tions, or leftover phenomena, but as options and possibilities built into this very model, and on equal footing with the classical forms. Moreover: the dif-ferent varieties will have to be described or defined by means of a uniform set of theoretical concepts, parameters, or categories, and will have to be related to one another in terms of a coherent system. If this requirement can be satisfied, one would have, as an added bonus, the possibility of describing in a cogent and explicit fashion the modifications or transformations involved in moving from one narrational variety to another.

(2) Assuming such a unified model can be constructed, what wider or more fundamental currently available theoretical framework (cognitive, linguistic, philosophical) can be adduced as its conceptual foundation or underpinning, and where should one look for it?

(3) What contextual motivation(s), cognitive or aesthetic, can one provide for the enormous preponderance within literature of the past + fact + knowl-edge prototype, as well as for the current rise of alternative paradigms of nar-ration? This question is not as trivial as it may sound, given the widespread use in nonliterary contexts of concurrent or "live" reporting, of future and condi-tional discourses (social, political, and economic scenarios and forecasts), and

of manuals of instructions of all sorts ("If you want to be financially independent at 55, do X and Y").

(4) Finally, what wider implications could such a model have for our understanding of the very nature of narrative as a semiotic product?

In the present article, I shall try to sketch out some initial tentative answers to these four questions. These answers should be treated as suggestions or proposals for further elaboration, and not as an attempt at "narrative encirclement." A second, closely related goal, would be to provide a systematic characterization of concurrent, prospective and conditional narratives in terms of the general model adopted.

1.2 As we all know, contexts of discovery and of justification are radically different in their internal structure. My own quest for answers to the preceding four questions has proceeded from 1 to 3 to 4, and only then did I expand into 2. But the presentation of my tentative answers will be much more perspicuous and effective if one begins with 2. This would be in line with the currently held view that the study of literary narrative is ultimately a subdomain of the study of narrative discourse in general, be it everyday oral, journalistic, historiographic, or fictional. One would want to identify an underlying framework that takes into account in equal measure the basic philosophical and semantic issue at hand, namely, our experience of things in time, and its discursive or linguistic manifestations. I believe such a framework is provided by the Tense-Aspect-Modality (TAM) approach that has risen to prominence within general linguistics in the last two decades (a few examples out of many are Bybee et al. 1994, Bybee and Fleischman 1995, Dahl 1985, Frawley 1992, Givón 1984, Hopper 1982, Shopen 1985, Tedeschi and Zaenen 1981). The basic tenets of this approach are as follows: (1) A narrative can be viewed initially as containing a report about actions, events, and states of affairs in some domain or universe of discourse. (2) All reporting is undertaken from a specific viewing position, narrative perspective, subjectivity or experiencing mind. (3) The three basic dimensions of every reporting act are the temporal placement of the event or state relative to the NOW of the viewing act as earlier, contemporary, or later; the event's temporal contour or inner temporal structure: is it seen from the inside or the outside, as a completed unified whole or as being in progress; and the speaker's modal attitude toward his/her claims about it: affirmation and certainty (= knowledge), negation, mere belief (= uncertainty), wish, hope, or command (see Slobin and Aksu 1982, 186). If we pursue this line of reasoning one step further, we could accordingly envision every narrative proposition as consisting of a nucleus (DO X, HAPPEN Y, BE Z), to which several operators are attached, concerned with its viewer-relative temporal, aspectual, and modal features. The specific profile of a narrative proposition, as well as its full information content, can be described only if all four factors (nucleus and three operators) are taken into account. And the same applies to the characterization of a connected narrative discourse as a whole. The foregoing cognitive or epistemic dimensions are encoded in natural languages in terms of tense distinctions, aspectual ones (perfective/imperfective, completive/incompletive, simple/progressive) and modal forms, particles, and expressions. There is of course no 1–1 mapping between surface grammatical features and the underlying semantic, cognitive, or pragmatic factors. The (cor)relation between tense and time for example has been the subject of ongoing debates in linguistics, and it is widely recognized that tense, especially in extended discourse, is multifunctional. To mention just one well-known fact: the "historical present," which equates viewing time and event time, is employed for the description of events that are past as regards speech time, and of which certain knowlege can be possessed. Nevertheless, such verbal features are indispensable clues for our construction of the three dimensions, and are practically the only means of access to these dimensions in a narrative that creates rather than reflects both its viewing situation and its topic entities (story world).

If we accept this model, we immediately realize that the standard or prototypical literary narrative, defined as past + completed course of events + factive claim, constitutes one particular constellation of the three basic dimensions, one extreme of a whole range of possibilities, and does not possess any theoretical primacy, even though historically it can be viewed as the unmarked case of narration. As a matter of fact, many options are available in the system, all equally falling under the umbrella term of narrative or narrational activity. In principle, the three dimensions are independent variables. All the same, common sense tells us that a speaker's epistemic stance toward a reported event, say one of certainty or mere belief, is often intimately linked with its temporal status with respect to the speaker's temporal position (past versus non-past). Similarly, the representation of an activity as completed or incomplete will often depend on whether or not it is concurrent with speech time (present versus not-present). In what follows, I will therefore take the temporal placement of the event or action relative to the narrative speech act as the basic dimension and as point of departure for the ensuing discussion.

2.

2.1 *Retrospective narration.* When a narrated course of events is textually presented as anterior, as having been completed prior to the moment of viewing, we are obviously dealing with narrative retrospection, with a reconstruction of what has gone on earlier, with a configuring of earlier states and events into a totality with global coherence and significance. All relevant facts are already there, so to speak, and so are their interrelations. The time line of the actions is bounded as regards both initial and terminal phases, and certain and complete knowledge about them can be available to the narrator. Notice that the availability of such knowledge to the narrating instance is itself only an option, and literary retrospective narratives do exist where the narrator dwells instead on his or her lack of knowledge, his or her uncertainty as regards the very occurrence or nature of some crucial past events. On the other hand, retrospective narration is the only form of narration where unqualified factive claims can dominate and unequivocally define the story world. This is actually one of, if not *the* one specific defining features of retronarration, so it is only natural that most authors employing this temporal stance would also employ this mode. But even here positive claims, though dominant, are not all that matters.

2.2 Oftentimes, that which did not occur, happen, or exist, when viewed against a background of textually defined probabilities and expectations, or against the inscribed norms and regularities of the story world, is as significant. Such negative facts (= it was not the case that P), when explicitly referred to by the narrator in a mode of certainty (the so-called *modus realis*), define the sphere of the disnarrated (G. Prince 1988). The disnarrated may include not only external states and actions, but internal ones as well, relating to the sphere of knowledge and belief (that which was not known to or believed by one or more narrative agents), to the sphere of obligations (failure to do what should have been done), and to that of wishes (failure to wish that which could or should have been wished for).

2.3 Another way in which negative facts can be expressed in the context of retronarration is by means of counterfactuals or contrary-to-fact conditionals. A simple example is: "If she had been quicker in expressing her love for him, then he would have stayed with her." In ordinary language, unlike formal logic, an "if . . . then" conditional structure implies that whenever a speaker is ready to accept the antecedent as a true part of a story, s/he would also recommend to include the contents of the consequent as part of the same story. In contrary-to-fact conditionals, the falsity of the antecedent, indicated by grammatical means, yields the first negative fact. Because of the usual association between the "if" and "then" clauses, a strong suggestion is further made— although this does not follow logically—that the contents of the "then" clause are also false in the story world. Although counterfactuals, strictly speaking, are only about what was not the case, they often encourage us to think that

what did not happen was still possible at some point, and could have been part
of the reality of the story world, had things gone otherwise. In other words,
they lead us to the realm of possibilities within the story world.

2.4 Retrospective narratives often make claims about possibilities that
positively existed at a given point in the action sequence, but that were not
actualized. To be narratively significant, such possibilities are often presented
not in isolation, but as true alternatives to that which did happen or take place,
in other words, as roads open but not taken. A prototypical formulation would
be a concessive clause: "Although she could marry a rich man, she decided to
marry her hometown sweetheart instead." Such roads not taken define a set
of alternative courses of events or virtual scenarios with respect to the story
world, a zone of possibilities not actualized, things that could have existed but
did not and so on. This zone is circumscribed and demarcated relative to a
framework of positive facts, that is, possibilities that were realized (Ryan 1986).
Note that claims about situations that could occur but did not can be as factive and certain in this context as claims about what did and did not happen.
In other words, it is an objective fact of the narrated domain (not a mere conjecture), known to the narrating voice with absolute certainty, that a particular
possibility actually existed at a specific stage of the events. Such epistemic certainty about both possibility and its nonrealization is a function of the narrator's later temporal position, which enables him or her to survey the situation
in a comprehensive manner and define the total sphere of action in the light
of later developments and final outcomes. Logically speaking, the subsequent
realization or nonrealization of possibilities that exist at a particular story state
could remain unknown, and their very existence itself may also be presented
in a merely hypothetical rather than asserting manner such as "She may have
had a chance to marry a rich man."

Positive and negative facts, counterfactuals and possibilities not actualized
jointly define what was the case in the reference world according to the narrator. The propositions that express these states of affairs are precisely those to
whose truth the narrator is strongly committed, and which s/he asserts in an
unqualified manner, the so-called *realis* mode, as certain knowledge.

2.5 Some existents, properties, and relations, actions, and events in the
narrated domain may be referred to by the narrating voice in the *irrealis* mode,
that is, a mode of epistemic doubt and uncertainty: X may or may not have
happened, existed, or been thus and so; a narrative agent may or may not have
known certain things; the course of events was precipitated by A, B, or C, but
it is not clear which of them it actually was; some say that P was the case, others
claim it was Q, but it is impossible to decide between these incompatible claims.
In all such cases we are dealing with narrative propositions qualified or modal-

ized by the narrator as "Possibly thus and so." Our last example, for instance, would read "possibly P (hence possibly not-P) or possibly Q (hence possibly not-Q)." Once a claim is qualified as "possibly," "probably," "allegedly," or the like, it immediately turns from a factive claim into a mere belief, hypothesis, conjecture, or unconfirmed assumption about some aspect of the story world. In other words, the narrating voice is not ready or able to commit him- or herself to the truth of the proposition under the scope of the modal operator. While the nature and extent of the hypothetical-conjectural, of what is merely possibly the case, varies in different retrospective narratives, we are all familiar with a whole genre, that of *conte fantastique,* defined by the built-in unresolved hesitation between positing a natural agency, often psychological, and a supernatural one as the motivating force behind some central events (for a classical study see Todorov 1970). But once again, retronarratives exist where the zone of indeterminacy is reduced to zero, so that all explicit narratorial claims are fully factive in nature. Furthermore, the lack of certainty, hence the indecision, as to whether something happened, was of a certain nature, and so on, is presented in retronarration as strictly epistemic, not ontological. Narrator and reader may be unable to resolve certain doubts because of the narrator's incomplete information state, not because the narrated domain is inherently indeterminate. It is precisely the temporal closure of the narrated domain, coupled with the assumption about the purely epistemological nature of any indeterminacy in it, which has led naive, and sometimes not so naive, readers to insist that unequivocal answers exist, and that textually inscribed uncertainty in retronarratives must be amenable to resolution through inferencing, based upon a minute and exhaustive analysis of all textual information. The interminable debates about the "true" status of the ghosts in Henry James's *The Turn of the Screw* is a paradigmatic example of this rage for certainty. Let me add in parenthesis that many postmodern novels do portray worlds that are ontologically multiple or indeterminate, but in these novels the multiplicity or undecidability itself is presented as an irreducible fact, not as competing hypotheticals.

Indeterminacy may also be conveyed by means of narratorial hypothetical inferences, where the truth of the premise is unknown to the narrator. For example, "If she was there that morning, then she saw the accident happen" or "If she was there that morning, she may have seen the accident happen" or, finally, "If she was there that morning, she must have seen the accident happen." In all of these cases, the speaker is unable to assert the truthfulness of the antecedent, hence that of the consequent as well, and can only assert the logical relations between the two. But unlike counterfactuals, the speaker has no grounds to deny that what is asserted in the antecedent (being there that morning) did take place in the story world. Since here too the events are past with respect to narration time, the assumption once again is that there is a fact of the matter: she was there that morning or she was not, she saw the accident happen or she did not, only we cannot know for sure.

2.6 Let me now draw the balance of our discussion so far. In retrospective narration, the factive, represented by certain knowledge or unqualified truth claims, usually predominates, defining a stable framework of determinacy consisting of what was and was not the case, and of what was actually possible at a given moment. Relative to this framework, certain areas of indeterminacy can be defined, and some states and events are presented as things that may or may not have existed or occurred in the story world. The retrospective temporal location of the narrative act and the temporal closure of the story world further enable the narrator to configure the individual events into a macrostructure with global coherence, human significance, and a well defined narrative theme (Ryan 1988). Within such a macrostructure, events are not just described but defined as regards their relative prominence and significance, as well as their contribution to later phases of the action and to the sequence as a whole, from initial move or turning point to opportunity missed.

2.7 As we recall, modality is not just epistemic. In addition to knowledge, belief, and ignorance, speakers may also entertain wishes with respect to a domain, and can try to impose the actualization of certain states or events in it, typically by issuing orders or commands. In retronarration, the narrator may indeed formulate wishes or obligations with respect to the narrated domain, but such formulations are devoid of any possible impact on this domain. For after all, wishes and obligations concerning what has already come to pass can no longer be imposed or have any influence on the course of events in question.

3.

3.1 *Concurrent narration* ("present tense narration") in the diary-novel form has a long history, dating back to at least the eighteenth century (Martens 1985). In its non-diary form it has risen to prominence in contemporary literature, not least through the experimental novels of the French *nouveau roman* from the late 1950s onward (Fludernik 1996b, 399, note 45). As I have mentioned before, there is no full overlap between grammatical and semantic features, so it is only a subset of present-tense literary narratives that can be meaningfully recuperated as creating the illusion of concurrent narration. Conversely, although diary novels are mostly written in the past tense, the events they describe are usually still in progress at writing time. In this type of narration, a major shift occurs both in the temporal placement of the events relative to viewing time and in the internal structure of the narrating activity itself. The textual voice is now experiencing and reporting events and activities that are still in progress and that have not yet reached their completion or final stage as one views and speaks or writes. The narrative act is now perforce durative, not momentary in nature. In retrospective narrative, we have an implicit default clause to the effect that whenever the duration of the narrative act is not textually specified it is assumed to occupy a single dimensionless point in time and to constitute one macro speech act. This is especially true for retronarratives that emanate from a disembodied voice or speech position. The only decisive factor is that viewing time is later than event time and that the whole sequence of reported events has elapsed by speech time. Concurrent narration of more than a single, punctual event, on the other hand, cannot by definition be temporally dimensionless. It consists of a sequence of NOW intervals, stages, or phases that, put together, make up the durative or ongoing narrational process. The object of this process too is an unfolding sequence of concurrent temporal stages, phases, or intervals that, put together, make up the course of events being reported. By definition, the two sequences run in parallel and are coterminous (= possess the same initial and terminal temporal points). Stages of the narration are matched with stages of the narrated, and these matched pairs jointly define the overlapping NOWs of discourse and of reported situations. One hence reports or registers as one experiences, or, in Beckett's words, "I say it as I see it." It is this correlated, ongoing, stepwise passage of time on both levels (speech and events) that is the specific constitutive feature of concurrent narration. In other words, the inner temporal structure or constituency of the reported situations and of their viewing and reporting is the crucial factor here. This is precisely aspectuality as defined in the TAM model (Lyons 1995, 322).

3.2 Being viewed from within, and in the midst of the action, the narrated domain is inevitably represented as a succession of unconfigured particulars, while narration itself becomes the gradual figuring out of what is the case as it evolves. "Narration is now a record of what one sees, what is happening at the moment [of speech] and is the antithesis of the historian's narrative statements, which retrospectively invest acts and actions with meaning" (Fleischman 1990, 302). The fact that numerous events are of necessity presented as still being in progress at narration time has far-reaching implications for the factive dimension, that is, for what and how much can be reported as fact with certainty or full knowledge. Some ongoing conditions, activities, and dispositions can be reported as definitely occurring at a given moment, and the same holds for some, especially momentary, actions and events. But what about all those long-term actions that are directed to a certain goal, which involve success or failure, accomplishment of a task or lack thereof, achievement or inability to reach the terminal stage of a process? Many of these actions, especially multistage ones, have already begun, but have not yet reached their completion at any given moment of narration. Their results or outcomes simply do not exist as yet. We are thus faced with the (prior) onset or inception of a situation, but with no termination, with action but no result as yet. The same applies to the negation of many processes and complex actions, that is, the assertion that they have definitely not taken place or have failed to achieve their goal. In both cases, future projection or conjecture, which envisions alternative outcomes and weighs their relative probabilities, is the only narratorial option. But this is not all. Even the certain and complete reporting of moments, instants, or immediate scenes and the punctual actions and events that occur in them is often restricted to reporting them as mere doings or happenings, since they cannot yet be defined in terms of typification, motivation, human significance, and value judgment. (This has often been observed with respect to Robbe-Grillet.) A situation can thus be recorded as it takes place, but not yet interpreted as, say, an error or brilliant move, act of perfidy or of courageous defiance. The same applies to the function and role of an individual action or event within some larger whole, that is, its relational properties within a larger frame, its contextual significance, place, and relative importance in a pattern of earlier and later actions and events. Examples of such knowledge not available at reporting time could include the causal role a present event plays in a sequence (it was the beginning of, it led to), its relevance to earlier and later situations (it was a minor incident), its ultimate impact and effect, and its place in and contribution to a global course of events (climax, major turning point).

Since events are reported in concurrent narration as they occur, as a sequence of NOW moments, or as the immediate experiences of the reporting voice, the sequence as a whole may often have an additive, paratactical quality, with events being juxtaposed or strung together one after another. A striking example is J. M. Coetzee's *From the Heart of the Country* (1976), with its 266 numbered sections in 139 pages. Local cohesion between adjacent events can often be established, but not global coherence, since the series has not yet reached its terminal point (upper boundary) at any moment of narration. In most cases, such an upper boundary can be established only in retrospect. The narrator does not possess, by definition, any temporal distance from the actions and events, no external later point of vantage from which s/he could survey and define the structuredness of the reported sequence as one integrated whole, often in terms of its final phase (for example, heroic struggle crowned with success or heroic struggle with tragic failure). The narrated domain is a world in the process of becoming, progressively taking shape as it is being narrated, not a bounded whole. It is not yet possible, therefore, to elicit a pattern from the succession, describe it in terms of macro-coherence, plot, or narrative theme and suggest any "point of the story." As Monika Fludernik says, one cannot live a story and narrate it at the same time, or tell what one is currently experiencing as a story, as contrasted with ongoing reporting. The reason is that story schemas put a premium on narrative's explanatory force. Narratives retrodictively explain why things happened, and provide a consistent interpretation of the events in their entirety (Fludernik, 1996b, 252–53; see also Ryan 1993). Any pattern that seems to emerge up to a given point is temporary and tentative, because it may yet be undone or replaced by a different one as events proceed. In retronarration, an author may choose to forgo the narratorial privileges of defining actions in terms of their results, human significance, and overall role, and of presenting the series as patterned and having a point. But in literary retrospective narration these privileges are inherent, so forgoing them is a highly marked cognitive and aesthetic decision. In concurrent narration, on the other hand, such options are either not available or at best severely reduced.

3.3 As for the alternatives and possibilities that may exist at any given moment, the narrator cannot as yet tell which of them will be actualized, and even their very existence may be merely possible from his epistemic perspective. Uncertainty as to the nature or even very occurrence of some current events is an inevitable component of concurrent narration, as are hypothetical inferences from present situations whose very existence is uncertain to the speaker. Conversely, utterances expressing the narrator's wishes and hopes at any given moment regain at least part of their potential impact with respect to the narrated domain, especially as regards the outcomes of processes not yet completed. The deontic or imperative, too, has now its full force, since all commands are issued at the present, and are meant to be accepted by the addressee as commitments on his or her part as soon as they are being issued.

To conclude: concurrent narration is located on the cusp or borderline between factivity and indeterminacy, actuality and virtuality, ontic and purely epistemic possibilities in the narrated domain. It inevitably faces a curtailment in the type and scope of knowledge the narrator can claim, hence in the factive zone, and a corresponding rise in the weight and extent of the modal, be it epistemic (conjecture, asserting propositions as possibly true) or wish- and command-oriented. The major differences between it and retronarration are systematic and well accounted for in terms of the TAM underlying model.

4.

4.1 *Prospective narration* ("future tense narration") is a narrative of that which has not yet occurred at speech time: a prediction, prognosis, scenario, projection, conjecture, wish, plan, and the like. Here, the temporal *cum* modal, rather than the aspectual, is the decisive factor. In the given universe of discourse or base world there is as yet no fact of the matter, positive or negative, to be experienced and recounted. Prospection, construction, and prefiguring are now what the narrator or textual voice is engaged in. The story world is purely virtual: a mere potentiality or possibility being projected, entertained, and described, not a range of actual facts (actual within the story world that is) to be experienced and narrated. Everything can be presented as uncertain, potential, or hypothetical only, that is, as an object of mere belief. While the semantic distinctions between fact, negative fact, and possibility remain, propositions containing all three are unexceptionally subjected to the global "possibly" operator. Much is possible, but nothing has been decided as yet. The only fact in prospective narration is that a narrating voice in the NOW of narration time is engaged in an act of supposition, fabulation, or mental simulation. This act gives rise to a purely notional construct (a situation that does not yet exist), and a prospective narrative is in fact the verbal representation of this construct. In other words, we are witnessing the process of the semiotic construction of a not-yet situation. In retronarratives, as well as in concurrent ones, the governing constitutive convention is that a story world exists that is independent of the narrator, his knowledge and beliefs. For even if such a narrative is recuperated as a record of the narrator's hallucinations, the implicit assumption is that there are some things in the story world that are actual. This distinction no longer applies in prospective narration, where the ontological collapses into the epistemological. Both facts of the matter and counterfactuals are merely projected, not reported, while the narrator's intentions, wishes, and desires and his instructions regarding the projected future domain possess their full force.

Curiously enough, prospective and retrospective narration share the ability, severely curtailed in concurrent narration, to project a long and detailed course of events, endowed with global coherence and narrative significance, causal links and overall point. The reason for this is not hard to find, though. In both forms the speaker is located temporally outside the course of events being recounted or envisioned, so that s/he can view the whole series synoptically as a structured and completed whole, a thing clearly impossible when one is placed in the midst of an incomplete series. But the modal gulf between retrospective and prospective narration still remains.

4.2 The essential intertwining of the temporal and the modal in prospective narration (some would even argue that the future itself is essentially a modality) opens the door to a wide array of variously modalized narratives, all future-oriented and all opposed to the classical, factive prototype. Let me define them by means of a semi-serious phrase each, and then proceed to a fuller discussion and illustration: (1) The future possible simpliciter or "Once upon a time there will be"; (2) "This may happen to you/one if something else takes place"; (3) "May this happen to you"; (4) "Do this and trigger the ensuing course of events." The dominant modalities of these kinds of narrative can be arranged on a scale as follows. First, the doxastic, the speaker's belief that the following may take place. Second, the hypothetical, claiming that certain possibilities of action exist for one/whoever if a certain prerequisite condition is fulfilled. Third, the optative, the speaker's wish that such and such should befall his addressee. Finally, the deontic—understood in the wide, linguistic sense— the speaker imposing obligations on his/her addressee, instructing him/her to perform or initiate certain actions so that certain events could develop in the narrated domain. In terms of dominant mental faculties, the movement is from the cognitive via the emotive to the volitional. We are correspondingly moving from a scenario, in the sense of an outline of a potential course of events, through an intermediate stage to a script, in which the textual addressee is given instructions that need to be fulfilled in order for an envisioned project to be realized. While all four varieties are inherently opposed to the concept of narrative as a factive telling of what has already occurred, the report, as a description of temporal progression (that is, of a sequence of events, acts, activities, and processes), regardless of its ontic and epistemic status, still dominates future-oriented narratives. But as we move from 1 to 4 it gets framed by more and more different types of discourse: inferential-conditional, emotive, and imperative. The dominant type of illocutionary act moves correspondingly from the representative (constative), via the expressive (emotive), to the directive, in John Searle's terminology. The presence of a textually marked speaker or addressee is optional in future and conditional narratives, while it is built into the other two, the optative and imperative. In the last two, the addressee, as both recipient of the message and its topic entity, is naturally the essential constituent. The standard grammatical forms by which the dominant modalities of the four kinds of narrative are expressed are the future indicative, present conditional, present subjunctive, and the imperative, respectively. And now let us look at a few concrete examples from contemporary literature.

4.2.1 Suzanne Fleischman observes (Fleischman 1982, 30) that we can regard the future discourse as a temporal screen onto which human beings project a variety of modalized notions, such as possibility and uncertainty, rooted in the present time, as a projection of one's experiential present hopes and apprehensions, and not as an objective ontological category. This linguistic insight is beautifully borne out by Christine Brooke-Rose's novel *Amalgamemnon* (1984), a first-person narrative consisting of the diverse alternative scenarios constructed by the speaker as to her possible future life course following her impending forced early retirement from her university post due to cutbacks.

The only factive component of the narrative concerns the speaker's present state of anxiety and her ongoing activity of projection and speculation. All narrative propositions refer to nonrealized states and events: future or future conditional, expressed by verbs in the future tense or modal auxiliary (may, could, should, would, might). There are hence no grounds for including or excluding any particular projected sequence from the story world or for choosing between alternatives, the entire world of *Amalgamemnon* being left dangling in an ontological limbo (Brian McHale's term). The discourse of the characters, as distinct from that of the narrator, does include references to past and present events, but only in the interrogative or negative, thus, as Brooke-Rose herself says, preserving the notion that nothing can be said to have happened or be happening. Since the future is essentially indeterminate, several alternative probable branches are grown from the common present node, and the resultant canonic structure of the narrative is "possibly (a or b or c)." And now from future to conditional.

4.2.2 As we know, all open conditional sentences (if p, then q) consist of an antecedent and consequent (protasis and apodosis in traditional grammar). In the present context, we are concerned with cases where the antecedent proposition sets up explicitly a possible future situation or event, while the consequent one describes what may probably or likely follow from it. In other words, both p and q are entertained as mere future possibilities or suppositions, not as facts. The maximally conditional, hence minimally factive, would accordingly consist of a description of a merely possible future state of affairs, with what follows left completely open or unspecified, that is, a problematic supposition or premise with no conclusion, or, quite simply, "If p, then what?" This is precisely the case of the would-be story generated by the chapter headings of Calvino's *If on a winter's night a traveler* (1981[1979]): "If on a winter's night a traveler . . . leaning from a steep slope looks down in a network of leaves . . . what story down there awaits him?"

The reverse case, that of a deleted but easily recoverable initial assumption and a detailed description of what could probably/possibly follow, is provided by the Swiss-German author E. Y. Meyer's novel *In Trubschachen* (1973). The novel consists of a potential narrative, recounting on a day-by-day basis the activities of an anonymous traveler *man* (= indefinite singular pronoun, roughly equivalent to the French "on," that is, one/whoever) who could, might, or would spend a brief Christmas vacation (December 27–January 3) in this small village in the Emmental. The deleted premise is quite banal: "Should one go on vacation in Trubschachen in this time of year, then one would . . ." The activities of this *man*, from the inbound to the outbound train trip, are recorded almost entirely in the *Konjunktiv* form: "man würde" (one would); and so are the setting, circumstances, and coagents: "ein Wind wäre aufgezogen, der Himmel würde sich bedeckt haben" (a wind would/could rise, the sky would have become cloudy), or "die meisten der Reisenden würden den Zug rechtzeitig genug bestiegen haben" (most of the passengers would have boarded the train on time), and so on. While the activities *man* engages in range from the generic and typical, applicable to every traveler/whoever, such as carrying one's luggage, to the specific and unique, such as reading this particular passage of this specific book at this hour, their rendering is relentlessly hypothetical, as if saying "here is a description of a possible situation and course of events, of what one could do," and not a report or assertion of actualized, factive events. The total avoidance of direct speech, which requires that all speech be reported in the indirect mode, which in German is always in the *Konjunktiv,* further enhances the merely potential quality of the narrated. While the *man* pronoun itself may be recuperated as either first- or third-person narrative, the associated actions and situations cannot be naturalized into a traditional narrative form, since they are possibilities entertained, not facts asserted. Meyer has also judiciously chosen the *würde* form, which expresses a degree of probability in between the absolute *müsste* (must have) and the weaker *könnte* (could, could have).

Both "if" and "then" clauses regularly occur in Marguerite Duras's *La maladie de la mort* (1982). This would-be story is presented by a voice that invokes in the present conditional certain possibilities regarding an encounter between an unnamed "vous" (you—here singular masculine) and an "elle" (she) and the stages of their relationship, and then goes on to describe in the present tense scenes from this relationship, thus alternating repeatedly between *pouvoir-être* (envisaged possibility) and *assertion d'être* (what is), between "si" (if) and "ainsi" (thus). In other words, the phrases in the conditional set up certain possibilities or potentialities for action whose envisioned consequences are explored by scenes in the present tense. But the factive sections, and the text as a whole, are invariably framed by a conditional, thereby making the narratively actual conditional upon the realization of the open, hypothetical possibility. For example: "Vous devriez ne pas la connaître . . . vous pourriez l'avoir payeé" (you should not know her . . . you could/may have paid her), where the modal verbs and the conditional ending both convey the idea of hypotheticality, and, further on, "chaque jour elle viendrait . . . chaque jour elle vient" (each day she may come . . . each day she comes), etcetera. The use of *vous* + conditional can be construed, however, also as a set of cinematographic or scenic directions for an actor who is about to perform the male role, as a programme of staging, or as a script, as well as a story *sous condition.* Under this interpretation, the conditional nature of the events is linked to an anticipated creation of a ludic world or game of make-believe, described in the present-tense passages. Because of the possibility of the generalized *vous* being appropriated by actual male readers, a third, related interpretation is also conceivable: that the text is in fact a series of guidelines to the reader how to imagine from beginning to end a love affair with an unknown woman. On these last two readings, the doxastic clearly shades into or is even displaced by the deontic: by what "vous" ought to do to bring the story about in a make-believe domain of individual imagining or public staging.

4.2.3 The voice with whom a future-oriented narrative discourse originates may not only draw inferences with respect to potential situations and courses of events, but also express its attitude towards such imagined situations: hoping and wishing that they come about, wishing that a given individual be of a certain nature or do, experience, and say certain things. Insofar as the individual in question is personalized and specified as an addressee, we get a blend of the referential (the story being invoked), the affective (the speaker's attitude toward his/her projected reality), and the conative, as the very formulation of these propositions is meant to have an impact on the addressee's future destiny. While in Duras's case the deontic reading was optional, now we are clearly faced with a narrative that is inherently on the borderline between scenario and script. Jean-Michel Raynaud's *Pour un Perec lettré, chiffré* (1987) is a rare example of an extended text predicated upon the speaker's wishes with regard to his addressee: "que vous concluiez . . . que vous insistiez, que vous fassiez remarquer, que vous soyez, que l'université ait organisé cette conférence, que la nuit soit belle" (may you conclude . . . may you insist, may you remark that, may you be, may the university have organised this lecture, may the night be beautiful), and so on. The necessity, at least in French, of employing repeatedly not only the same verb form (subjunctive present), but also the same phraseological mold prevents us from being absorbed in the would-be reality, insisting on its purely wished-for rather than actual status. The projected or wished-for nature of the life story is also reflected in its very title, "Pour," toward. The text as a whole thus describes a project, not an accomplishment. As in standard narrative, here too the text is macrosemantically concerned with the progression of events. But it no longer possesses the logical form of standard narrative, that of a set of claims, assertions, or propositions to which a truth value (true, false, probable) or epistemic modality can be assigned.

4.2.4 It is only a small step from a narrative consisting of wishes with respect to the addressee to one in which s/he is put under obligation to perform certain acts and thereby give rise to the story in which s/he plays a/the major role. Narratives whose framing clause consists of imperatives are an obvious case in point, since they are by definition future-oriented, directed to an addressee, and express the speaker's desires with respect to the domain of reference. In six of the stories in Lorrie Moore's collection *Self-Help* (1985) a female character, teenager or adult, is instructed how to behave in situations involving a divorced mother, a lover, a husband, an intended literary career. The purpose of the behavior is the realization of specific states or the achievement of certain goals. The fulfillment of the initial instructions gives rise to the development of the corresponding personal interrelations, described in a series of scenes in the present or future tense, with further instructions being interspersed as the sequence of the projected events progresses. We thus have an intercalation of instructions and attendant projected action sequences, which, put together, yield a possible biography of the recipient of the instructions as regards those items of behavior that are either at issue in the instructions or that result from them. The repeated intercalation of imperative and indicative forms yields a hybrid text-type. While both forms are concerned contentwise with the progression of temporal situations involving the heroine, the imperative component is not truth-functional, while the indicative one is (see 4.2.3). Two more points about instructions are worth noting. First, instructions always look ahead to what is not yet there. The title of Moore's collection (*Self-Help*), as well as the titles of individual stories in it ("A Guide to . . . ," "How to . . ."), reminds us that the point of departure consists of a script yet to be performed, not a *fait accompli*. Second, their illocutionary force notwithstanding, instructions may or may not be carried out and, even if they are, may not yield the expected results. Any results expected from following a set of instructions are a conjecture, not a fact. And indeed, even though the "you" closely follows the textually inscribed instructions, all ensuing affairs and relations in Moore's stories inevitably end up in failure. Finally, it is worth noting that Moore further enhances the merely potential nature of the narrated by occasionally issuing instructions as clusters of alternatives, such as: "begin by meeting him in a class, in a bar, at a rummage sale."

5.

5.1 The existence of literary narratives embodying the full spectrum of temporal, modal, and aspectual options defined by the abstract system is a fact. But the system by itself does not privilege any of these permanently available possibilities, so that both the historical preponderance of retronarration and the contemporary rise of concurrent and prospective forms must be explained not by internal semantic factors but rather by contextual, cognitive, or pragmatic factors of a psychological, aesthetic, or general cultural nature. Any explanation one can offer here is speculative to some degree, since it is not based on extensive empirical research but on readerly intuitions. It seems to me then that the privileging of retronarration is motivated by a basic readerly desire for both closure and full disclosure, for certainty, totalizing significance, and global coherence, all of which can be attained only in fictional retrospective narration, preferably of the omniscient variety. In all such narratives one encounters two levels of time, knowledge, and awareness that are constantly being juxtaposed. On the framed or embedded level we watch the narrative agents lead their lives as an unfolding sequence of present moments or stages. At any stage, their knowledge and understanding of earlier events may be incomplete and/or erroneous. A large part of their mental activity is concerned with trying to formulate beliefs about what is happening to them at each moment and with making sense of it. No less effort is devoted to making projections about the future course of their lives. Narrative agents are also constantly forming plans, intentions, and expectations about their future destiny, and are trying to manipulate their human environment through the issuance of requests, orders, and interdictions. In a word, they exist in a basic mode of uncertainty, and sometimes also of error and ignorance. On the embedding or framing level, on the other hand, there is either a textual voice or a personalized narrator who can have certain, complete, and error-free knowledge about any of the narrative agents' situations, the outcomes of their acts, and the (non)realization of their expectations. For this voice or narrator the whole course of events is already past, completed, and seen from the outside. For him/her, temporal stages that are merely being projected or imagined by the narrative agents are already objects of recall. Retrospective reflection and commentary, assessing situations from the perspective of their end results, are both natural and well motivated for such a narrator. The *in situ* uncertainty of the narrative agents about the significance and subsequent implications of the situations in which they find themselves is replaced by the certain knowledge of the backward-looking narrator. Such constant tension and juxtaposition between two epistemic stances provide the reader of retrospective narratives with the best of both worlds. The reader can thus identify with a narrative agent's momentary situation or predicament, be concerned for this character and involved with his or her mindset at any given moment, and at same time be superior to the character or detached from it, being given by the narrating voice the full information, gained in hindsight, about this very situation and its future outcome ("how it will turn out in the end"). A paradigmatic example is provided by the opening sentence of Garcia Marquez's *One Hundred Years of Solitude* (1971[1967]): "Many years later . . . Colonel Aureliano Buendia was to remember that distant afternoon when . . ."

5.2 Concurrent narration is deprived by definition of this kind of privileged and superior narratorial perspective, hence readerly knowledge. The constant dual optics of on the spot AND in hindsight gives way to the singular optics of unfolding events and evolving, uncertain knowledge, devoid of the benefit of retrospective correction and completion. What motivation can one provide for this radical excision of fictional narrative's greatest prerogative? One can think of several reasons why contemporary artists have embraced this much more limiting mode. The first has to do with a view of reality itself, the object of knowing, as devoid of any underlying unifying macro patterns or overarching regularities, as consisting of nothing but more or less random sequences of momentary events and states, with at most local connections among them. Another motivating factor could be an epistemological or psychological assumption about the working of the human mind, about what and how much we can know and in what ways. The view then is that we are always in the midst of things, that our process of knowing is not only ongoing but also fragmentary, consisting of a succession of moments with their highly incomplete and often hypothetical information, and that this succession of partial glimpses cannot be cognitively integrated into a meaningful whole. We are thus always on our way to (*unterwegs zu,* in Heidegger's term) knowledge, but never there. What is more, this process goes on for as long as we are conscious, so any closure or upper bound imposed on it is purely artificial and arbitrary. Now, a most effective artistic procedure to convey such views is indeed concurrent narration, where there is no closure, either ontic or epistemic. Robbe-Grillet's insistence on "premier au présent" (= first-person present tense narration) as a more realistic or verisimilar narrative mode than the retrospective one can well be explained by the foregoing.

Motivation of a different kind could be provided by the influence of radio and TV reporting. In the last generation we have witnessed an enormous increase in the amount of on the spot, real-time reporting ("live coverage") of events in these two media, where the reporter literally says it as s/he sees it, with a near overlap of intervals of action and narration, and without any possibility of certain knowledge (versus projection and earlier plans) as to what will happen next. The dominance of TV in contemporary culture may well have modified the underlying aesthetic norms of readers as well concerning what is an effective, convincing, or even natural way of narrating. "Tell as you live" (breaking news story, live coverage) rather than "live now, tell later" is the emerging new norm or central convention of the media, which is then fed back from actual-world discourse to fictional narration. Finally, a general bias for "life as lived" forms as being more authentic, vivid, and immediate than "life as recalled" forms may also be at work here. (M.-L. Ryan, personal communication).

Concurrent narration may also be motivated by a view of literary narrative

as a communicative transaction that consists of activities of authorial production on the one hand and of readerly immersion on the other. The simultaneity of events and their reporting can serve as an analogue of the very process
of artistic world projection in the actual world. The author envisions, writes
down as he envisions, and the world envisioned comes into being concurrently. A good example is the beginning of Robert Coover's short story "The
Magic Poker" (1969): "I wander the island, inventing it." Literally speaking,
the narrated world always emerges in stages, in a series of now moments of inventing and expressing, and takes shape and substance simultaneously with its
verbalization.

The reader's (whether textually inscribed or actual) side of the "now" equation is somewhat more complex. The majority of literary narratives (obviously
excluding metafiction) seek to establish a game of make-believe in which the
reader makes it true within the game that certain events take place, that they
are being reported by a narrating voice, that s/he (the reader) can or even
should be "caught up in the story" by caring about the agents of these events
as well as their outcome, by being emotionally involved with the agents, and so
on. (For the concept of make-believe see Walton's classical study [1990].) One
could possibly argue that the depth and intensity of the reader's immersion,
involvement, and participation in the game of make-believe are enhanced by
doing away with retrospective global summation, and reporting the events instead in the mode of scenic immediacy, in the right here and now of their
occurrence. The reader as participant in the game can now imagine being then
and there as the events unfold, and not being able to find out until later how
things will turn out. Such scenic immediacy has always been a main source of
the immersive potential of the theater and of the feature film, which seldom
employ proleptic scenes. This is obviously a game only, since the reader can
always jump to the last page of the text, but as long as s/he is inside the game
and abiding by its rules, the reader's involvement and illusion of eyewitnessing
can only be enhanced by stage-by-stage concurrent narration.

While any totalizing claim about the superior immersive power of concurrent narration may be moot, there is at least one mode of narration where this
claim clearly holds, and this is second-person narration. Statistical evidence
indicates that the majority of second-person narratives are indeed written in
the concurrent mode (on this issue, see Fludernik 1994). Now "you" narrative
agents range from the generic "lettore" (male, singular) of Calvino's *If on a
winter's night,* who is compulsively engaged in reading activities, to the highly
individuated and named protagonist of Butor's *La modification* (1957). But the
point of all second-person narratives is that for the duration of the game of
make-believe the reader should take the position of the "you" not only as ad-

dressee of the current narrative activity but also as the protagonist of the course of events being narrated. It seems to be far easier and more natural to insert oneself into such a protagonist role when the events and actions themselves are being presented as concurrent with or unfolding alongside the ongoing processes of narration and reception. Issuing instructions to a generic, this time female, "you" as to what to do next and how to proceed — as in Lorrie Moore's *Self-Help* — further enhances the immediacy and urgency of the situation and may create the illusion that it is up to the reader as participant in the game of make-believe to decide what turn events will take next. The "you could" and "one might," the governing modes of Duras's and Meyer's narratives respectively, can also be construed as invitations to the reader to play imaginatively with the situations and activities described by these texts, to become the "you" or "one" in question. Stories in the imperative, or second-person optative and conditional modes, "exhort the reader to imagine the fictional scene, and cater to the reader's eventual identification with the protagonist" (Fludernik 1996b, 261). Moreover: in all these forms, a fictional scene is established by fiat, with its setting, situation, protagonist and story. The very process of invention, of positing a reality through words, is foregrounded in all three forms. The narrating voice's activity now *generates* the story, rather than reporting events that are presumed to be prior to and independent of linguistic creation (Fludernik 1996b, 262).

5.3 Instructions and successive choices lead us next to the as yet undecided or open alternatives, associated with prospective narration. The strongest motivation for future and conditional narratives is supplied by our culture's preoccupation, if not obsession, with the virtual. Projecting the future possible course of one's life story, speculating on what may happen simpliciter or if something else happens are ubiquitous human activities. In the contemporary world they are enhanced by popular versions of "the postmodern world" that model reality as a field of multiple alternative courses of events. Reality is thus envisioned as consisting essentially of a space of at least partially indeterminate potentialities existing around us, or in which we exist, at any given moment. The formulation and playing with alternative complex projections or future scenarios in all fields is the resultant pervasive contemporary preoccupation, supported by computer technology, where many options can be considered side by side simultaneously and where everything is quite literally virtual. The prognosticating hordes parodied in Brooke-Rose's *Amalgamemnon* (4.2.1) are upon us daily: futurologists, economic, social, political, military, and environmental forecasters, each with his own different version of the future. It seems that the production and consumption of such multiple future visions is becoming the main occupation in the here and now of an ever increasing number of people, aided and abetted by millenarian hysteria. Brooke-Rose's novel, then, is a clever artistic utilization of such wider modes of thought and of being.

6.

6.1 The time has come to formulate some of the wider theoretical implications of the preceding discussion. I believe to have shown that an integrated model of narrative varieties based on the linguistic TAM model is feasible, justified by both general theoretical considerations and actual literary practice, and capable of bringing a sense of order and unity, an inner logic to a wide range of phenomena, many of which could not be accounted for by the tools of classical narratology. The whole range of phenomena surveyed is presented as forming a coherent system, and the transition from retrospective narration first to concurrent narration and then to prospective narration can now be described as an inner-systemic shift of the dominant element from the factive and completed first to the unfolding and incomplete and then to the merely potential or possible. Technically speaking, the decisive operator shifts from temporal first to aspectual and then to modal. The narrative act inside the fictional sphere shifts accordingly from factive recounting and commenting on preexistent states and events first to immediate reporting of what the narrating voice is experiencing and then to world projection or mental simulation of possible situations. From configuring one moves to prefiguring via an intermediate stage of figuring out. The deontic and optative modalities, which are devoid of impact when the narrative act refers to past situations, gradually come to possess their full force, and may even be as important as the alethic or truth-functional one. The classical model of narrative, centered as it is on retronarration, and not considering aspectuality and modality as being among the defining factors of each and every narrative proposition, is thus a limiting case of the wider, conceptually richer and more powerful TAM-based model. Another advantage of this model is that it correlates considerations that have so far been relegated to two different areas of narratology, namely, possible-worlds semantics and the study of types of narration and of narrators. The need to correlate the two has recently been pointed out by David Herman in the more specialized context of hypothetical focalization (Herman 1994a). In the model proposed here, the specific nature of the temporal, aspectual, and modal operators that attach to every narrative proposition is shown to be a function of the narrating voice's epistemic position with respect to the narrated events.

6.2 Finally, what is literary narrative "all about"? In other words, what is its indispensable constitutive factor or element? Where does narrativity reside? The answers available in the professional literature tend to concentrate either on the telling or on the told. On the side of the telling we have, for example, Genette's insistence that the very act of narration, and not any specific kind of narrated, is the constitutive, essential element. The same view is arrived at independently and by an entirely different route by the philosopher Kendall Walton, who says: "Perhaps the fact that fictionally the narrator speaks or writes the words of the text is a primary fictional truth, one that depends on no others. It may even be the only one" (1990, 372–73). On the side of the told we have Gerald Prince's equally insistent claim that narrativity exists if and only if the text represents a temporal progression of discrete and specific situations and events (acts, activities, processes) that are conjoined or interrelated to some degree according to some principle of relevance (G. Prince 1982, chapter 5).

The model I have proposed puts a somewhat different spin on both foregoing views. Yes, all (or at least most, see below) literary narratives have both a telling voice (associated with a viewing position) and some temporal situations that form the topic of this voice's discourse. But the conjunction of a teller-viewer in time and of a temporal told also implies that literary narrative inevitably and essentially models the full complexity of the human experience of things in time, "of what is past, is passing, or to come" in Yeats's immortal phrase. In less metaphorical terms, one could argue that literary narrative models the basic cognitive factors involved in the mental representation or mapping of temporal situations, that is, temporal perspective and mental attitude (M. Turner 1996), and the different possible configurations of these factors. On this cognitivist view, literary narrative—and especially the narrating voice's discourse—offers us models of the human mind at work as it constructs different internal representations (cognitive maps) of dynamic situations. If literary texts in general are display texts, as Mary Louise Pratt argued long ago (Pratt 1977), then literary *narratives* display both these operations of construction and their diverse products. Following Jackendoff (Jackendoff 1996), one could say that the domain of dynamic situations is a major object of activities of cognitive structuring by humans. The products of these activities are various human conceptual structures or mental constructs that embody the different ways in which dynamic situations can exist for the human mind as regards their temporality and reality status. Fictional narrative is free from the constraints of actuality, and so forms the ideal locus for both exercising and studying the activities involved, and for examining the full range of their possible products. Now mental constructs are accessible only via semiotic means, including of course natural-language expressions. The varieties of textual Tense-Aspect-Modality configurations we have surveyed are one major way to access the mental models in question.

So far I have assumed that all narratives contain a narrating voice or speech position. But what happens if we accept the view of Chatman (1978, chapter 4), Banfield (1982), and others that there are also narrator-less narratives or "non-narrated stories" (Chatman's term)? It is significant to note that the processing, inner representation (temporal, aspectual, modal), and attempted interpretation of dynamic situations are key elements of *both* standard narratives and narrator-less ones, for example, those consisting entirely of the unframed, unmediated interior monologue(s) of one or more narrative agents or SELVES. Leutnant Gustl's mind, for example, in Arthur Schnitzler's story of the same name (1900), is occupied entirely with events of the recent past, the immediate situation in which Gustl finds himself, and the various possible alternatives for future action. In the TAM context, the opposition between the two kinds of narrative concerns only the source or anchoring of the highest-level temporal, aspectual, and modal specifications, while these specifications themselves play an equally crucial role in the constitution of both kinds of narrative.

Support for this view can be found in several areas. In cognitive psychology, we have Jerome Bruner's conclusion that: "the narrative mode leads to conclusions . . . about the varying perspectives that can be constructed to make experience comprehensible" (Bruner 1986, 37). From the side of linguistics, we have the recent works in cognitive linguistics of, among others, Langacker 1987 and 1991, Chafe 1994, M. Turner 1996, Fauconnier 1997 and the Lille school of Culioli and Joly (examples of their approach include Culioli 1978 and Joly 1987). Closer to home, one could draw on Monika Fludernik's recent comprehensive *Towards a 'Natural' Narratology*, with its basic claim that narrativity is the semiotic representation of experientiality, not of actions and events as such, and that experientiality itself is the mediating activity of individual human consciousness in a world and with respect to a world. If we focus on the narrating voice (or on the originator of the interior monologue) as an instance of mediating consciousness, and on temporality as one inalienable feature of this consciousness, of the world of events being processed by it, and of the relation between them, then the model proposed here is fully corroborated as a constituent of Fludernik's wider project.

"Speak, friend, and enter": Garden Paths, Artificial Intelligence, and Cognitive Narratology

Manfred Jahn

Classical narratology in the late sixties and seventies vitally relied on the benefits of structuralism—its graphic models, its crisp formalisms, its linguistics-inspired toolboxes—features that were generally appreciated by teachers and students alike. Unfortunately, the new-frontiers phase of classical narratology lasted only until deconstructionists and poststructuralists came along and radically pulled the rug out from under the common-sense axioms that narratology had so optimistically built on. In response, postclassical narratologists started a number of remedial and recuperative programs. Progressive trends in the late eighties and the early nineties produced a critical reassessment of narratological terms, a general broadening of scope, and an increasing interest in thematic aspects. Less spectacularly than before, narratology branched out into a feminist narratology, a historiographic narratology, a possible-worlds narratology, a "natural" narratology, even a postmodern narratology, to name only a small number of important diversifications.

Another adjustment suggested at a very early stage was a more detailed consideration of the reader's role in the grammar of narrative, and a suitable exploration of this subject was first presented in Sternberg's (1978) and Perry's (1979) investigations into the dynamics of reading. Pursuing these researchers' quest for a cognitive narratology, the present essay takes a "process turn" paralleling that already taken in cognitive linguistics, discourse analysis, and linguistic stylistics. My point of departure is the notorious "garden-path sentence"—a type of sentence that causes unexpected processing difficulty. As has been noted in the psycholinguistic literature, the garden-path phenomenon can also be found in certain kinds of jokes, riddles, and stories, apparently involving very similar error-recovery and reanalysis routines. I shall argue that these texts draw the researcher's attention to a number of interesting cognitive mechanisms that have largely remained hidden below both the reader's and the narratologist's thresholds of awareness.

When Todorov coined the term "narratology" in 1969, French *analyse structurale du récit* (structural analysis of narrative, also the title of a seminal 1966 special issue of *Communications*) had already divested itself of the ballast of early twentieth-century normative poetics (Lubbock 1963[1921], Beach 1932) and, following Saussurean and Jakobsonean precepts, had begun to isolate new basic units of narrative analysis, probed into syntagmatic and paradigmatic relations, and stratified and taxonomized the phenomenology of its object. During the seventies, many narrative theorists took an additional cue from Chomskyan generative grammar and, thinking in terms of "deep" and "surface structures," set as their goal no less than the formulation of a universal grammar of "narrative competence" (Greimas 1971, Füger 1972, Culler 1975, G. Prince 1982). Classical narratology's chief success came from the work of Gérard Genette (1980; 1988), though Genette considered his own use of grammatical terms as merely metaphorical. Unlike most of his colleagues, who were bent on distilling what was common to all narratives, and who intentionally avoided detailed analyses of specific works (Culler 1975, 120), Genette combined his theoretical exposition with a compelling "Proustology," as he called it (1988, 12). In fact, so convincing was Genette's two-in-one enterprise that his *Narrative Discourse* soon became a pilot study in "applied" narratology, and his terms were widely accepted as the discipline's tools of trade.

The new-frontiers phase of classical narratology did not last long, however. When deconstructionists and poststructuralists entered the scene in the early seventies, few of the seemingly common-sense concepts and premises of structuralism were allowed to stand. On the poststructuralists' view, the very idea of coherent structure sealed the critic in a golden cage, and every sensible person's first duty was to escape by whatever means possible—by favoring decentering over centering (Foucault 1972), dis-closure over closure (Spanos 1977), heterogeneity over homogeneity, and plays of meanings over an impoverished "correct" interpretation (Derrida 1972). In comparison, narratological methods and objectives seemed naive and inadequate, and many began to consider the discipline a "paleostructuralist relic" (Chatman 1993, 59). Yet the momentum of narratology was not spent, and its potent conceptual toolbox—a poststructuralist anathema if ever there was one—formed the basis of a number of excellent studies (for example, Nünning 1989 on George Eliot, Edmiston 1991 on the eighteenth-century French novel, Collier 1992 on Patrick White, and Stevenson 1992 on modernist fiction). The late eighties and the early nineties also saw a critical reassessment of terms and concepts (Chatman 1990), a general broadening of scope, especially as to the range of text types to be admitted (Pavel 1985b, Cohn 1990, Bal 1990, Branigan 1992), and an increasing interest in combining technical and thematic aspects. Since then, the discipline has branched out into a feminist narratology (Bal 1986, Warhol 1989, Lanser 1992), a historiographic narratology (Cohn 1990), a narratology of historiographic fiction (Nünning 1995), a possible-worlds narratology (Ryan 1991, Ronen 1994), a "natural" narratology (Fludernik 1996b), and a postmodern narratology (Hutcheon 1988, McHale 1987), to mark a few important diversifications. As to methodological advances, where classical narratology preferred an ahistorical/panchronic vantage, postclassical narratology today actively pursues historical/diachronic lines of inquiry; where many first-generation narratologists insisted on an elementarist (or analytic, or combinatorial, or "bottom-up") approach (Chatman 1975, 234; Lanser 1981, 35–36; Genette 1988, 129), postclassical narratology today welcomes the uses of synthetic and integrative views (Cohn 1981, Stanzel 1984); and, finally, where classical narratology assumed a holistic and retrospective stance, there is an increasing tendency today to pick up the thread of Sternberg's and Perry's explorations into the cognitive dynamics of the reading process.

Following up this latter line of inquiry, the present paper deliberately takes a "process turn" paralleling that taken in cognitive linguistics (Bever 1970), discourse analysis (Brown and Yule 1983, chapter 1.3.3), and linguistic stylistics (Fludernik 1996a). The crucial linguistic test case elucidating "discourse-as-process" as opposed to "text-as-product" (Brown and Yule 1983, 24) is the "garden-path sentence"—a type of sentence that traps the reader in a processing failure and requires an act of reanalysis to recuperate its actual structure and meaning. Interestingly, the cognitive mechanisms that trigger the garden-path effect are precisely those that allow effortless comprehension of ordinary sentences in the first place. The mechanisms involved are quite ubiquitous, and researchers like Hockett (1977a, 1977b) noted from early on that garden-path effects also occurred in jokes, riddles, and stories. The present paper will trace this widening circle of the garden-path phenomenon, first by looking at the cognitive research into garden-path sentences and introducing a set of basic concepts and models, then by discussing a couple of garden-path jokes and riddles, and finally, by analyzing two garden-path stories (James Thurber's "The Secret Life of Walter Mitty" and Ursula Le Guin's "Mazes"). The narratological conclusions that are drawn from this are almost entirely due to what is rapidly becoming a fruitful and promising interdisciplinary exchange between literary theory and Artificial Intelligence (Colomb and Turner 1989, Schank 1995, Ryan 1991, Cook 1994, Duchan et al. 1995, Herman 1997a, Jahn 1997).

1. The Linguistics of Garden-Path Sentences

Descriptive linguistics in the 1960s set itself the aim of capturing the system of a native speaker's linguistic competence. The production side—how speakers go about constructing sentences—and the cognition side—how hearers manage to understand sentences—were deliberately set aside as less relevant aspects of "performance." Competence grammar was grounded on a powerful testing procedure—an idealized native speaker's ability to decide whether a given sentence was grammatical or ungrammatical. Although it was acknowledged that sentences also submitted to "degrees of acceptability," these were again considered a largely negligible matter of performance (Chomsky 1965, section 2). When Bever (1970) finally initiated an investigation into "The Cognitive Basis for Linguistic Structures," however, he was able to present a number of sentences that elicited sharply contradictory grammaticality and acceptability judgments. Particularly striking was the following item, now usually cited as the classical "garden path":

(1)   The horse raced past the barn fell. (Bever 1970, 316)

In cursory (that is, *nota bene,* normal) reading, (1) appears ungrammatical, garbled, and incomprehensible. If one treats (1) like a piece of polymorphous wallpaper pattern, however, and simply stares at it for a while, then there is a good chance that it will miraculously "change structure" and become readable as *The horse THAT WAS raced past the barn fell,* that is, comply with the perfectly grammatical pattern of sentences like *The horse sent/ridden past the barn fell* (Bever 1970, 316). Of course, the very obvious cognitive difference is that (1) tricks the reader into a construction from which it is very difficult to recover.

Ever since Marcus (1980, chapter 9) used the term, garden-path sentences have become a popular subject in the cognitive sciences, especially in parsing theory and psycholinguistics.[1] Parsing theorists invent garden-path sentences to test their parsing algorithms, psycholinguists use them to investigate strengths and limits of cognitive strategies, and empirical researchers analyze eye movement and reading-time data. Across these different foci of interest, the general pattern of garden paths is considered to be basically identical. The main analytical concepts used to define the "problem space" (Minsky 1979, 22) of garden paths are best illustrated by comparing and contrasting (1) with the following item:

(2)   They told the boy that the girl met the story. (Fodor and Inoue 1994, 409)

Like (1), (2) begins with an unproblematical *initial region* (*They told the boy*). The initial region borders on a *locally* or *temporarily ambiguous region* (*that the girl met the*) which opens the door to the garden path—most readers wrongly assume that the sentence will continue as indirect speech. By no means all ambiguities induce the effect, however, so the ambiguous region is only a necessary condition (if that; see section 2). In fact, the reader only gets *garden-pathed* when he or she follows a *cognitive preference* for a specific reading of the ambiguous region which is later discarded in favor of the "correct" reading. In (2), it is the functional ambiguity of the word *that* (complementizer or relative pronoun) which is retrospectively identifiable as the *source* or *onset of error*. For the duration of the ambiguous region, however, there is no obvious indication that (2)'s syntax might be different from what it appears to be; in fact, the reader in all likelihood becomes increasingly *committed* to the incorrect indirect-speech reading chosen. Eventually, however, the realization comes that something has gone wrong: in (1), the word *fell* appears as a supernumerary and nonattributable constituent prohibiting syntactic and semantic closure; in (2), the reader is confronted with the semantic oddity of somebody "meeting a story." As (1) and (2) show, garden-path *symptoms* come in a variety of forms, and what makes the matter complicated is that, as a general rule, there is no obvious link between a garden path's symptom and its source of error.

Even though linguists are usually interested in inventing garden paths that are "virtually unprocessable" (Pritchett 1988, 540), not all garden-path sentences are in fact equally difficult. Empirical garden-path indices such as slow reading times and regressive eye movements vary considerably with sentence-internal and contextual factors.[2] Garden-pathing is usually felt to be more or less "severe" or "persistent," and recovery from it can be "easy" or "difficult" (Fodor and Inoue 1994, 411). For convenience, one might posit a rough and ready scale on which occasionally or potentially misleading sentences like (3a–b) fall on the low-difficulty end, mild garden paths like (4a–b) occupy a middle ground, and breakdown garden paths like (5a–b) congregate at the high-difficulty end. As is common practice in the psycholinguistic literature, I am using ellipses marks to indicate the symptom onset locations:

(3)   a. They knew the girl at the bakeshop . . . was hungry. (Fodor and Inoue 1994, 417)

        b. The old man's glasses were filled with . . . sherry. (Schank and Birnbaum 1984, 215)

(4)   a. After John had started the car . . . pulled up to the curb. (Hockett 1977b, 238)

        b. Without her contributions . . . failed to come in. (Pritchett 1988, 543)

(5) a. The horse raced past the barn . . . fell. (Bever 1970, 316)
    b. The daughter of Pharaoh's son is the . . . son of Pharaoh's daughter.
        (Fodor and Inoue 1994, 411)

Garden-pathing may take place momentarily in (3a–b), but recovery is more or less routine; in (4a–b), recovery is difficult but not impossible, and (5)'s sentences are such "dramatic garden paths" (Fodor and Inoue 1994, 411) that it is safe to predict that no ordinary reader will be able to make satisfactory sense of them quickly.[3] Despite the largely provisional and impressionistic nature of this scale, it appears that the difficult and "artificial" (Marcus 1980, 218) items normally singled out by linguists are just radical instances of a very common phenomenon. In fact, many naturally occurring garden-path items can probably be found in wastepaper baskets and first-version manuscripts.

Whether natural or artificial, easy or difficult, the items discussed so far clearly suffice to identify ambiguity, preferences, and symptoms as major features of the garden-path phenomenon as one encounters it in isolated sentences. I will now move on to the question of how these factors shape up in the cognitive models used in Artificial Intelligence research.

2. The Artificial Intelligence Approach: Frames, Scripts, Preferences

Artificial Intelligence research in natural-language comprehension can be divided into an engineering section and a cognitive science section. AI's cog-sci researchers focus on designing cognitive models, and AI's engineers attempt to implement computer programs that mimic efficient human cognitive capabilities. In the sixties, design and implementation of a computational natural-language processor (CNLP, for short) progressed well, raising very high hopes and collaring substantial grants. Early versions of CNLP were soon able to perform adequate syntactic parsing, and it was briefly believed that it needed only a bilingual dictionary and a set of suitable transfer rules to move on to more ambitious tasks like machine translation. As is well known, this proved to be illusory, mainly because everybody had underestimated the problem of ambiguity. The problem was not that CNLP was unable to handle ambiguity at all, but that it handled it too well. For instance, given a textbook favorite like *Time flies like an arrow*, a sixties-seventies vintage CNLP would reliably derive no less than three parses (Brainerd 1971, 211; Winograd 1983, 92),[4] a feat no ordinary human natural-language processor (of sound mind) would ever dream of. Embarrassingly, AI operators had to be advised in all seriousness to take CNLP's multiple parses to "the person who entered the input and to let her or him indicate which [alternative] was intended" (Winograd 1983, 368). For anything approaching a practical purpose, this was counterproductive. It became clear at this point that ambiguity was no isolated phenomenon that would go away of its own accord; what was worse, the designers of CNLP had to admit that they had not the faintest idea how to implement formally and explicitly what ordinary humans do automatically and unconsciously, namely *resolve* ambiguity and settle for a most likely reading.

It does not take much insight or introspection to recognize that ambiguity is normally resolved on the basis of situational and contextual knowledge. For instance, encyclopedic "world knowledge" tells us who or what is flying where in *I saw the Azores flying the Atlantic* (Johnson-Laird 1983, 235), and context tells us which meaning of the word *seal* is relevant in (i) *John goes to the zoo often; he is very fond of one particular seal* vs. (ii) *The royal proclamation was finally completed, and the king sent for his seal* (Lehnert 1979, 80). Hermeneuticists have always claimed that while each part X of a discourse tells us something about the whole, the whole also tells us something about X; in fact, they propose that it is the mutual reinforcement or "hermeneutic circle" of these processes that eventually produces understanding. Unfortunately, what the AI programmer encounters as soon as s/he attempts to implement a context-sensitive ambiguity resolution routine is mainly the hermeneutic circle's vicious twin—the *hermeneutic dilemma* that one knows neither function nor meaning of part X unless one knows the context, but that one cannot know the context (made up of parts more or less like X) unless one already knows X. Moreover, it is all very well to say that context (or "the whole") disambiguates the word *seal* in *The royal proclamation was finally completed, and the king sent for his seal*—but what if the king has a pet seal (Lehnert 1979, 80), in other words, what if local context is overridden by global context or various stages of widening context (Fish 1980, 281–92)? In order to overcome this notorious paradox of context, AI theorists realized that the vague notion of "context" had to be replaced by a more tangible construct.

In the mid-seventies, Marvin Minsky at M.I.T. and Roger C. Schank collaborating with Robert P. Abelson in New Haven began to experiment with computational data structures aiming at capturing a person's knowledge and expectations about standard situations like walking through a room, going to a restaurant, etcetera. Designing what they called "frames" (Minsky) and "scripts" (Schank and Abelson), these theorists soon hit on a number of cognitive intricacies that, owing to the seemingly obvious nature of things, had been ignored by previous researchers. For instance, given a standard "theater script," Schank and Abelson pointed out that "we need not ask why somebody wants to see our ticket when we enter a theater, or why one should be quiet, or how long it is appropriate to sit in one's seat. Knowledge of specific situations such as the-aters allows us to interpret the remarks that people make about theaters" (1977, 37). Similarly, when processing a restaurant story, the restaurant script enables us (and, ideally, CNLP, too) to "assume that what was ordered was what was eaten" (Schank 1995, 8), even if this is nowhere explicitly stated in the text itself.

For a closer glimpse into the theory of frames and scripts, it is instructive to note that the original central definitions overlap and complement each other in a number of relevant aspects:

(6) [A frame] is a remembered framework to be adapted to fit reality by changing details as necessary. We can think of a frame as a network of nodes and relations. The "top levels" of a frame are fixed, and represent things that are always true about the supposed situation. The lower levels have many terminals—"slots" that must be filled by specific instances or data. Each terminal can specify conditions its assignments must meet. (The assignments themselves are usually smaller "sub-frames.") ... Much of the phenomenological power of the theory hinges on the inclusion of expectations and other kinds of presumptions. A frame's terminals are normally already filled with "default" assignments. (Minsky 1979, 1-2)

(7) A script is a structure that describes appropriate sequences of events in a particular context. A script is made up of slots and requirements about what can fill these slots. The structure is an interconnected whole, and what is in one slot affects what can be in another. ... [A] script is a predetermined, stereotyped sequence of actions that defines a well-known situation. Understanding ... is a process by which people match what they see and hear to pre-stored groupings of actions that they have already experienced. New information is understood in terms of old in-formation. A human understander comes equipped with thousands of scripts. He uses these scripts almost without thinking. (Schank and Abel-son 1977, 41, 67)

In order to be able to utilize both definitions, AI theorists often stipulate that the scope of frames is wider than that of scripts, and that scripts are types of "frames designed for the specific task of natural language processing" (Lehnert 1979, 85). Extracts (6) and (7) above suggest that frames basically deal with *states and situations* (seeing a room, making a promise) while scripts cover *stereotypical action sequences* (playing a football game, going to a birthday party, eating in a restaurant (Minsky 1979, 7; Schank and Abelson 1977, 41). Since frames and scripts can occur at many different levels of complexity—hence the notion of subframes and subscripts—further conceptual integration allows frames to slot into scripts, and scripts to slot into frames. As I will argue in the following sections, the *frame of a narrative situation* (Jahn 1997) and the *genre-specific script of a narrative performance* will prove instrumental for a discussion of literary garden paths.

As detailed in (6) and (7), frames and scripts specify "defaults" to encode expectations, "nodes and relations" to capture categories and hierarchies, and "terminals" and "slots" to provide data integration points. The usual mode of frame or script structure visualization is the directed graph or tree diagram (Minsky 1979, 3; Schank and Abelson 1977, 43), a structure that is well manageable in computational terms. Frames and scripts are required to be "flexible" and adapt to "new and unusual situations," to deal with variants or "tracks" (Schank and Abelson 1977, 40), and to allow exceptions, "excuses" (Minsky 1979, 18), "interferences and distractions" (Schank and Abelson 1977, chapter 3.4). For both frames and scripts, the actual integration of lower level data is regulated by "conditions" and "requirements." Some of these are necessary conditions representing "things that are always true about the supposed situation" (Minsky), others are of a more probabilistic or modal nature, specifying ideal types or defaults, but also marginal cases, permissible exceptions, and so on.

Because frames and scripts must be flexible and adaptable, most of their cognitive power lies in the non-necessary conditions encapsulated in them. In the following, I will take up a suggestion by Ray Jackendoff and treat a frame's or a script's non-necessary conditions as *preference rules* — a doubly convenient term because it establishes a direct link to the subject of garden paths. Preference rules usually come in pairs, groups, and oppositions, and accumulate in complex *preference-rule systems* in which each rule is weighted and ranked according to a specific priority, confidence, or stability rating. A preference-rule system is a carefully calibrated operational model of a restricted area of cognitive decision-making (Jackendoff 1983, chapter 8; 1987, chapter 8.3). As Jackendoff (1983, 155) shows in more detail, preference-rule systems can be used to formalize cognitive decisions in such varied fields as visual and musical grouping, prototype images, categorization judgments, taxonomies, word meanings, markedness conventions, parsing heuristics, and pragmatic strategies. In fact, Jackendoff convincingly claims that "the characteristics of preference rule systems are found everywhere in the psychological process, all the way from low-level perceptual mechanisms to problems so prominent in our conscious life as to be of social and political concern" (1983, 156).

Many comprehension strategies discussed in the literature can be recast as preference rules using the formula *Prefer to assume that p, else prefer to assume that q, else . . .* (etc.). For instance, Bever (1970, 294) isolated a reading strategy to prefer *to assume that the first N . . . V . . . (N) clause is a main clause* — not quite coincidentally, this is the very low-level preference that opens the door to the garden path of (1), *The horse raced past the barn fell.* In similar manner, the context-sensitive "strict subcategorization" and "selection restriction" rules envisaged in Chomsky (1965) can be turned into preference rules in a cognitive context, and the same goes for the "theta grid" restrictions now assumed in more recent "government and binding" theory (Chomsky 1986). The perceived oddity of "the girl met the story" in garden-path item (2), above, is a consequence of violating a restriction of the verb "meet" according to which human agents usually meet other human agents. Some dictionaries specify default restrictions of this type by citing standard context patterns like "said of a person" or prototype sentences like "an attractive sister I want you to *meet*" (thus *Webster's Third* under "meet"). On higher levels of analysis, the speaker/hearer assumptions and felicity conditions of speech acts (Searle 1969), the principles of politeness and face-saving (Leech 1983, Brown and Levinson 1987), and the maxims of conversational cooperation (Grice 1975) are easily converted into hearer/reader-oriented preference rules (see Jackendoff 1983, 155).

Frames/scripts and data enter into a mutual dependency-and-reinforcement relationship which constitutes an operationally practicable version of the hermeneutic circle. On the one hand, frames and scripts offer slots within which the data accumulate and "make sense," and on the other, the data continually test the adequacy of whichever frames and scripts are active. Put simply, frames and scripts tell us what the data are, and the data tell us whether our choice of frame or script is appropriate. Functionally, frames, scripts, and preference rules disambiguate structural, lexical, referential, and illocutionary ambiguities, supply the defaults to fill the gaps in the discourse, and provide the presuppositions that enable one to understand what the discourse is about. In the final analysis, it is the degree of compatibility or competition among preferences that decides "whether a sequence of data is perceived as standard, stereotypical, new, unusual, indeterminate or persistently ambiguous" (Jackendoff 1987, 252).

Although the psychological correlatives of frames, scripts, and preference-rule systems are circumspect, efficient, and time-tested inference engines, they are definitely not fail-safe devices. It is in the nature of things that humans occasionally misconstrue and misunderstand, and this fact is nowhere more apparent than when one is led down a garden path. Put simply, a garden path triggers a preference-rule system failure that causes processing to be impeded or break down. Since preference rules are general and ubiquitous it follows—extending the definition given in section 1—that there are garden paths that do not depend on ambiguity at all. Consider the following enlightening item invented by Johnson-Laird:

(8)   The book fills a much needed gap. (1981, 122)

As Johnson-Laird points out, without explicitly using the term "garden path," there is a strong likelihood that readers will misconstrue (8). In fact, one normally has to re-read (8) a couple of times before one realizes "that it is the gap, not the book, that is needed" and that the sentence is not as "laudatory" as one thought (1981, 122). Since (8) leads the reader into an interpretation that in view of later evidence cannot be upheld, it is a garden path like all the other garden paths treated so far. It *differs* from the previous garden paths firstly because it cannot be tied down to any known type of lexical, structural, or referential ambiguity, and secondly because it does not show any obvious symptom. On the face of it, (8) says what it says, and it says it clearly, so it does not lead one astray by violating any known conversational maxims. What does lead one astray is one's anticipation of good sense, and this is itself a consequence of a human understander's unwillingness to consider nonsense, of a general horror of semantic emptiness, of a craving to make satisfactory sense of a discourse, in short, of preferring what makes more sense or even most sense (Lehnert 1979, 84–85). Evidently, the preference to read for maximum cognitive payoff ranks higher than the complementary preference to take an utterance to mean exactly and nothing but what it literally says. As (8) very clearly shows, the cognitive payoff preference initially dominates the text. It is only when the reader is forced to reprocess the sentence (repeatedly, if necessary) that the cognitive value of the first reading (a much-needed book filling some kind of a gap) degrades up to a point where the secondary preference gets the upper hand and recovers (8)'s other (textually more accurate, but less sensible) reading (tolerating the notion of a much-needed gap).[5] Luckily, the blinkeredness induced by (8) is not the rule. Notorious cases like *The postman bit the dog* (Marcus 1984, 259) or *Man Eats Lion* (an advert for a piece of confectionery) show that the cognitive payoff preference is not so dominant as to suppress all messages that run against normal sense and probability. Significantly, children around the age of three, accessing smaller knowledge bases and differently organized preference-rule systems, are prone to be garden-pathed by these cases (Bever 1970, 306–7).

Consider also how the cognitive payoff preference affects processing of the following item:

(9)   Police Say Detective Shot Man With Knife (*Private Eye* 1979, 29)

This is one of many examples of unintentional (or possibly intentional) headline humor and prepares the ground for material to be dealt with in the next section. (9) has only one probable reading, yet one also easily (almost eagerly) retains the improbable alternative suggested on low-level syntactic grounds. Considering that one is not at all tempted to do this sort of thing with a comparable case like the notorious *We saw the boy with the telescope,* it seems we are dealing with a type of material where it virtually pays not to disambiguate. Specifically, there seems to be a general impulse to deactivate ambiguity resolution if this helps to retain a reading that allows one to laugh at authority (in this case, the police), or speaking more generally, if this helps to instantiate a joke frame (see next section). In fact, items like (9) are collectibles, and the book from which it has been quoted also contains the similar "boob" *Police found drunk in shop window* (*Private Eye* 1979, 5). Aided by competing preferences and garden-path conditions, the cognitive payoff preference can be seen to maintain or even generate polyvalent readings that hold their own against the odds of probability.

Frames, scripts, and preference rules regulate the interfaces between data-driven ("bottom-up") and context- or knowledge-driven ("top-down") cognitive strategies. One of the main preferences is to read a text for maximum cognitive payoff. If this rule is not satisfied, then no appropriate sense can be made of the input, and the data will exhibit the very oddity that psycholinguists identify as a garden-path symptom. The garden path is confirmed if the symptom goes away on conscious or unconscious reanalysis, either by switching frames or scripts, or by reshuffling the preference rules. This is the standard scenario, but in view of the evidence of (8) and (9) one should also keep in mind that there are garden paths which are not attended by a symptom, as well as recovery procedures which maintain polyvalent readings for ulterior cognitive payoffs.

3. The Evidence of "Simple" Forms: Jokes and Riddles

In 1930, André Jolles published a path-breaking investigation into the *Simple Forms* of legends, sagas, myths, riddles, proverbs, anecdotes, fairy-tales, and jokes. The word "simple" is best put in scare quotes because, as Jolles noted, theoretical exposition of these genres is far from simple (Jolles 1965, v; see also the more recent exposition in Koch 1994). In the present context, "simple" may be taken to indicate that the performance of simple forms is stereotypically scripted. Specifically, a joke's communicative frame consists of a speaker/ narrator N and an audience R (R1, R2, . . .), and the text is expected to culminate in a punch line effecting a specific audience reaction, laughter. As was noted by Hockett, there is a class of jokes that turn on carefully crafted garden paths. In fact, Hockett distinguishes two types of garden-path jokes, exemplified by (10a–b), below:

(10) a. If you hit me I'll wax wroth, and then Roth will be all slippery.
          (Hockett 1977a, 266; quoted in Yamaguchi 1988, 324)
      b. Underneath that rugged exterior there beats a heart of . . . stone. (269)

According to Hockett, (10a) is a "punning garden path," and (10b) is a "nonpunning garden path." Both items are clearly similar to the sentoids constructed by psycholinguists: (10a) turns on a locally ambiguous (sound) sequence, and (10b) — like (8) — is based on a preferred (but misguided) anticipation of a fixed expression (*heart of gold*). According to Hancher's (1980), Raskin's (1985), and Raskin and Attardo's (1994) pragmatic models, jokes usually evoke two "opposed" scripts and generally tend to mislead by deceptively violating the maxims of cooperation of bona-fide communication (mainly those of relation, quantity, and quality). Taking up Hockett's examples, Yamaguchi (1988) defines a garden-path joke as

(11) [a] joke in which the context is potentially ambiguous in that it has potentially a first and a second reading, the former being replaced by the latter at the end of the joke. (Yamaguchi 1988, 325)

Clearly, however, (11) is too narrowly ambiguity-oriented and overlooks the evidence of items such as (8) and, in fact, (10b). More importantly, although (11) presupposes that a garden path can be the central element or "pivot" (Hockett 1977a, 267) of a joke, it does not address the question why some garden paths are funny and others are not. Consider, for instance:

(12) a. When Bill finally met John, he was wearing his gorilla costume. Gosh, I am impressed, John said.
      b. The airship was about to leave the airport. The last person to go up the gangway was Miss Hemming. Slowly her huge nose turned into the wind. Then, like some enormous beast, she crawled along the grass. (Crystal 1995, 233)

Both (12a) and (12b) hinge on an ambiguous pronominal reference. On the usual preference of proximal binding, "he" in (12a) and "her/she" in (12b) will initially be associated with John and Miss Hemming, respectively. Wider context indicates that this is wrong in both cases, so one generates the appropriate alternatives, reenacting the recovery process predicted by Yamaguchi, in (11). Yet while (12a) remains unfunny to the point of being boring, (12b) is funny enough to be quotable by Crystal, himself quoting from another source. Evidently, one cannot hope to approach the elusive causes of humor (Navon 1988) without including a psychological component. Paradoxically, psychological research into humor (especially the humor of dirty jokes) has unanimously found that what a joke's audience is laughing about is rarely a laughing matter. Under psychoanalysis, jokes simply aren't very pleasant: their players are aggressors and victims (or "butts"), and often enough a joke treats a traumatic subject. As soon as one asks *who or what one laughs at* it becomes plain that a "joke frame" provides role slots for aggressors and victims, usually to be instantiated by characters in the joke's story. As Legman (1973, 116) points out, the roles of aggressors and victims may also project to the outer levels of the joke frame. In garden-path jokes, specifically, it is the teller who acts as the aggressor, and the listener who assumes the role of the butt.

Hockett also noted that riddles tend to invoke the same patterns and frames as jokes. One of his examples is a classic of folk literature:[6]

(13)   As I was going to St. Ives
        I met a man with seven wives,
        Each wife had seven bags;
        Each bag had seven cats;
        Each cat had seven kits.
        Kits, cats, bags, wives,
        How many were there going to St. Ives?
                    (1977a, 273)

Employing the frame of a first-person (homodiegetic) narrative situation, (13) contains a minimal narrative, or perhaps it would be more adequate to say, following Chatman (1990, chapters 1 and 2), that both story and descriptive detail are "put in 'the service of'" the riddle. The story is clearly fictional; no one is asked to believe that the speaker ever actually went to St. Ives, or really saw what s/he says s/he saw. To use Bal's (1981, 45) formula, there is a narrator-speaker (N) who tells an audience that X ("I," the narrator's experiencing Self) sees what Y ("a man with seven wives") does. Despite its brevity, the story's tellability (Labov 1972) is high, largely owing to the exotic nature of the man's seven wives. Otherwise, the story is abortive; there is no development, no plot, no denouement. From line 6, the speaker simply abandons the narrative and concludes by putting the riddle's poser. The standard riddle script now requires the interaction of a member of the audience, R ([13] being a "nursery rhyme," R is most likely a child), who, as Hockett points out, "cannot normally guess the answer and is not really supposed to try" (1977a, 271). When R fulfils his/her part of the script by saying "Don't know," the speaker reveals the correct answer, "One."[7] Not surprisingly, the answer will strike R as symptomatically odd, and may well produce a "phenomenological shock" (Jackendoff 1987, 117) similar to that encountered in a garden-path sentence.

Again, like (8) and (10b), (13)'s garden path arises not from a linguistic ambiguity but from R's being artfully primed to expect a numerical calculation task of some sort or other. Even in the context of a riddle script, R will preferentially be inclined to assume that the speaker is speaking cooperatively and making his or her "contribution as informative as is required." Of course, it is the flouting of this maxim that eventually leads to R's misapprehension of the drift of the final question.

As Hockett further notes (1977a, 270–71), there is an obvious family resemblance between nursery rhyme riddles like (13) and genuine problems posed in a contest. The main points of difference are (a) that a bona-fide competitive problem is not literary (Ryan 1991, 2), and (b) that the answer is expected to be within reach of the contestant's capability. But, as (14), below, shows, it is certainly legitimate for the problem to involve a garden path:

(14)   You are rowing a boat upstream. The river flows at three miles per hour; your speed against the current is four and one-quarter. You lose your hat on the water. Forty-five minutes later you realize it is missing. . . . How long does it take to row back to your floating hat? (Gleick 1992, 33)

Although (14) poses as an algebraic problem, the difficulty is that it will take too long, under contest conditions, to do the necessary calculation. The feat actually required is to recognize that no calculation is needed at all. Here is how Richard P. Feynman, winner of the Nobel Prize in physics in 1965, reportedly solved (14) at age eighteen:

(15)   Given a few minutes, the algebra is routine. But a student whose head fills with 3s and 4¼'s, adding them or subtracting them, has already lost. This is a problem about reference frames. The river's motion is irrelevant. . . . In fact all the velocities are just so much foliage. Ignore them, place your point of reference at the floating hat — think of yourself floating like the hat, the water motionless about you, the banks an irrelevant blur — now watch the boat, and you see at once, as Feynman did, that it will return in the same forty-five minutes it spent rowing away. For all the best competitors, the goal was a mental flash, achieved somewhere below consciousness. In these ideal instants one did not strain toward the answer so much as to relax toward it. (Gleick 1992, 33)

Apparently, Feynman "simply" disabled the cooperative preference, correctly guessing that it was being flouted. Rather than becoming swamped by the discourse's "foliage," he imaginatively transposed to the story's scene of action where the answer was simply waiting to be picked up — interestingly enough, it is a strategy that would also crack (13), much, presumably, to the annoyance of everybody concerned. Feynman later realized that conducting innovative research was not much different from solving garden-path puzzles. New physical laws, he pointed out, were discovered by deliberately going against the grain of one's expectations: "[R]easonable things are where the trouble always is. . . . In general we look for a new law by the following process. First we guess it" (Feynman 1992, 156). The same creative problem-solving techniques were later popularized by de Bono (1983) under the label of "lateral thinking."[8]

What has, hopefully, become evident in this section is that the AI-enhanced conceptualizations introduced in sections 1 and 2 can be applied to good explicatory effect to the seemingly simple and minimally narrative forms of jokes and riddles. Let us widen the scope once more and consider two short stories which make particularly effective use of garden paths.

4. Two Garden-path Stories

James Thurber's famous "The Secret Life of Walter Mitty" juxtaposes an action line situated in the ordinary world of the Mittys (their shopping trip to Waterbury) with the wildly escapist daydreams of the henpecked husband. Although much energy has been expended on psychoanalyzing the protagonist of this unquestionable "masterpiece of associational psychology" (Hasley 1974, 506), very few critics discuss the narratological cruces of its dream episodes or the story's challenging garden-path beginning. Here are the story's first three paragraphs:

(16) [a] "We're going through!" The Commander's voice was like thin ice breaking. He wore his full-dress uniform, with the heavily braided white cap pulled down rakishly over one cold grey eye. "We can't make it, sir. It's spoiling for a hurricane, if you ask me." "I'm not asking you, Lieutenant Berg," said the Commander. "Throw on the power lights! Rev her up to 8,500! We're going through!" The pounding of the cylinders increased: ta-pocketa-pocketa-pocketa-*pocketa-pocketa*. The Commander stared at the ice forming on the pilot window. He walked over and twisted a row of complicated dials. "Switch on No. 8 auxiliary!" he shouted. "Switch on No. 8 auxiliary!" repeated Lieutenant Berg. "Full strength in No. 3 turret!" shouted the Commander. "Full strength in No. 3 turret!" The crew, bending to their various tasks in the huge, hurtling eight-engined Navy hydroplane, looked at

each other and grinned. "The Old Man will get us through," they said to one another. "The Old Man ain't afraid of Hell!"

[b] "Not so fast! You're driving too fast!" said Mrs. Mitty. "What are you driving so fast for?"

[c] "Hmm?" said Walter Mitty. He looked at his wife, in the seat beside him, with shocked astonishment. She seemed grossly unfamiliar, like a strange woman who had yelled at him in a crowd. "You were up to fifty-five," she said. "You know I don't like to go more than forty. You were up to fifty-five." Walter Mitty drove on toward Waterbury in silence, the roaring of the SN 202 through the worst storm in twenty years of Navy flying fading in the remote, intimate airways of his mind. (1973, 69)

Four more daydream episodes are interspersed in the further course of the story; all are presented in the easily recognizable style of (16a). In fact, the story not only begins but also ends with one of these episodes (when Mitty, now a prisoner of war, but "undefeated to the last," faces a firing squad). Despite this circular framing, ordinary world knowledge tells us that Mitty's dream existence (as Commander Mitty, Dr. Mitty, Captain Mitty, etcetera) ontologically presupposes his fictionally real existence (henpecked Mitty driving his car to Waterbury). Hence it is generally assumed that Mitty's daydreams are "embedded" in the story's representation of Mitty's real world. What is less clear is the exact narratological status of the embedded segments. According to Genette, dreams, daydreams, and recollections ("subjective analepses") are to be treated like "metadiegetic" narratives, in which intradiegetic narrators tell "second" (or third or fourth) narratives (Genette 1980, 231). In "Notes on Narrative Embedding," Bal (1981) has argued to use the prefix "hypo-" rather than "meta-" (a proposal that has been accepted by many narratologists); and she has also suggested that dreams should be treated as "hypofocalizations" rather than "hyponarrations" (a point on which most narratologists are notably reluctant to commit themselves). One may well ask which of these accounts captures the state of affairs presented in "Walter Mitty." Particularly relevant is the question whether the well-spoken narrator of the fictionally real sections (who can talk of the "intimate airways of [Mitty's] mind") is the same as the second-rate, bungling, cinematic narrator of the fantasy episodes (who lets his protagonist "twist a row of complicated dials"). Or is it Mitty himself who bungles the "complicated dials," becoming a metadiegetic narrator "by delegation," and turning (16a) into hyponarration as well as hypofocalization? Throwing these questions into sharp focus, Mitty's daydreams point up some troublesome narratological aporias (Jahn 1996, 248).

What is less problematic is the fact that "Walter Mitty" begins with an episode whose embeddedness (if one accepts it as such) is only recognizable when it is over, that is, when the narrator passes his remark about "the remote, intimate airways" of Mitty's mind in (16b). Adapting Genette's terms, one might say that (16a) is a "local" alteration, a case of paralipsis, of giving too little information at one point. But "local paralipsis" does not adequately cover the case because when one begins to read the story there is no background norm on which (16a) could be recognized as an alteration, whereas, from (16b) onward, the text is as informative as one could wish. Of course, no one can postpone interpretation until everything has been said, so, by the time the reader comes to (16b), the (faulty) frames and scripts under which (16a) makes some sort of initial sense are already instantiated and working. Since it is easy, subsequently, to recover from (16a)'s garden path, and instantiate more suitable replacement frames and scripts, the question naturally is why Thurber uses a garden path at all.

As Ryan (1991, 180–81) has shown, the popular Chinese-boxes visualization of embeddings, while accurate as a final state model, is neither very specific about the local states at which transitions from or into embedded elements occur, nor does it particularly bother about the transitional "edgework" (Segal 1995b, 74) that accomplishes the shifts from framing texts to embedded texts, and vice versa. As Ryan suggests, processual aspects such as these are better captured by a dynamic structure known as a "stack" in computer science. Stacks, like Chinese boxes, lend themselves well to visualization, and the bit of AI jargon that goes with them is quickly established. The particular type of stack most relevant for embedding scenarios is one called a "LIFO" (last-in, first-out) stack. A stack is either empty or contains any number of elements. Only one element, the one on top of the stack, is "visible." State changes are achieved by two simple operations: a new element becomes accessible by "pushing" it onto the top of the stack, and an old element (an element *in* the stack) becomes accessible by "popping" elements off the stack until it is the current one. Applied to meta- or hypodiegetic narratives, the narratological analogy is that when a story begins, it pushes its first narrative onto an (as yet empty) stack. Any metadiegetic second or third narratives are additionally pushed onto the (growing) stack (note the incidental fittingness of Genette's "meta" prefix in this context—see Genette 1988, 91). As soon as a metadiegetic story ends, it pops off the (diminishing) stack, returning the narrative to whichever level happens to lie below.

Recently, a number of "deictic shift theorists" (Duchan et al. 1995) have suggested that if one focuses on the reader's task of negotiating first and second "ontological realms" (rather than first and second narratives) then one is dealing with an ontological stack where the most usual pushes are from the ground level of the fiction's real or actual world into a character's perception of it (in standard narratological terms, this amounts to a shift from "objective" narration to "reflector mode" narrative), and from thence to the imaginary worlds of a character's recollections, visions, or dreams (Galbraith 1995, 47). Conversely, ontological pops variously return the reader from a character's dreams, visions, or recollections to the ground level of the story's actual world, or from thence to a narrator's commentary or description. Obviously, at the end of the story or novel, a final pop (or series of pops) clears off the fiction's ontological stack, returning the reader to his or her actual world. What is of particular interest in this account is that the life of a story's ontological stack becomes a scripted and preference-ruled process. Specifically, there is a default preference to assume that, at the beginning of a narrative, the story's ontological stack is loaded by pushing the narrative situation and the text's actual world. The reader will preferentially proceed on the assumption that any additional pushes and pops will be textually signaled. As a consequence, any text deviating from this pattern will present a garden path. For instance, at the beginning of *Alice in Wonderland* the text pushes from Alice's actual world into the world of her dream without letting the reader explicitly know (Ryan 1991, 188). A similar push occurs in another famous Thurber story, "The Lady on 142." Conversely, in *Crime and Punishment,* pops from Raskolnikov's dream world to the story's actual world are occasionally left unsignaled (Lethcoe 1969, 211). In *Alice in Wonderland* and *Crime and Punishment,* these garden paths are mild and local infractions only, and the necessary pushes or pops are more or less effortlessly performed on recognizing the dream quality of Alice's Wonderland, or on encountering a description of something Raskolnikov cannot possibly have seen. Conceivably, garden-pathing of this type can also be more radical, for instance, when an unsignaled push into a dream is maintained for over four hundred pages (as happens in Pelz von Felinau's *Tantalus*). Naturally, belatedly signaled pushes and pops can also serve the deliberate postmodernist strategy of "misleading the reader into regarding an embedded, secondary world as the primary, diegetic world" (McHale 1987, 115).

What happens at the beginning of "Walter Mitty" is that the story's ontological stack is already loaded beyond the default number of elements. Since first readers have no way of knowing this, they initially proceed on the preference to assume that (16a)'s action and setting, however unverisimilar it may appear, is situated in the ontological space of the story's real world. For a first reader, Thurber's story begins not as a daydream but as an action-packed military adventure. Symptomatically, setting, characters, and story line are immediately reminiscent of an old B movie, a mode of presentation not normally associated with an author like Thurber.[9] Things are even subtly and hilariously wrong from the beginning—the characters are overly clichéd, the "Commander" incongruously wears his "full-dress uniform" on a mission, the narrator can't be bothered with detail; most ludicrously of all, the sound of the airplane's engines is rendered onomatopoetically (and it is not the sound one expects from an eight-engined airplane). Yet these are dead giveaways retrospectively only; for the duration of (16a), the reader has *no* plausible ground for assuming that s/he has entered the world of Mitty's visions.[10] It is only when (16b) suddenly pops to an impossible second level of real action that the garden path's symptom manifests itself in full force. The reader now realizes, probably in "shocked astonishment" much like Mitty's (obviously, one of the garden path's fine functional effects), that the new story line—husband and wife in a car—is the one that constitutes the fiction's real world, whereas the one that was just popped off represented a phenomenological state; that is, Mitty's daydream. From here on, the "difference in flavour" (McHale 1987, 115) between the B-movie style of the dream episodes and the modernist reflector-mode style of Mitty's ordinary-life episodes are reliable indicators for all further pushes and pops.

Practically all of the foregoing points slip through the net of the holistic (final-state) view preferred in classical narratological analysis. The problem is not so much that the holistic model is inadequate but that it forgets, even represses, the (garden) paths it had to traverse in order to arrive at its final synthesis. Paradoxically, the foregoing processual analysis suggests not only that a garden path can be functional but that it actually leads somewhere. Moreover, as Perry has plausibly argued (1979, 41), in a second reading a story only unfolds its full luster when the readings rejected in earlier readings are at least partially resurrected. The initial garden path in "Walter Mitty" is functional not only because it forces us, at one point, to accept Mitty's ridiculous dream world as ground-level reality, but also because it makes us undertake the cognitive leap from seeing it as a bungling B-movie narrative to reinterpreting it as the wish-fulfillment "dreamwork" of a protagonist whose real life has become all but meaningless.

Let me turn to an even more effective garden-path case, a science-fiction short story by Ursula Le Guin. Very fittingly, it is entitled "Mazes."

Le Guin's story is told by a first-person (homodiegetic) narrator who is held captive by an alien who tortures and starves her.[11] The text appears in the form of a memo or personal briefing in which the narrator describes her present situation, recapitulates what she knows about the alien, tries to guess its motives, and to identify what has gone wrong. This may look like the beginning of a "problem-solving" script, but unfortunately nothing of the kind materializes. The only decisive reversal occurs when the reader abandons the garden path s/he is already on.

The narrator's main focus is naturally on the alien who basically instantiates an "evil" alien frame as found in science fiction and mythical monsters lore. The alien is "a giant" whose behavior is marked by an "elaborately perverse cruelty" (181). Not only does it provide inedible food, it forces on the narrator the Sisyphean task of (re-)running mazes of varying complexities (hence one meaning of the title). About halfway into the story, the narrator briefly describes the alien's physical features, and then expands on its lack of communicative intent or ability:

(17)   But it remains very hard to ascribe its behavior to ignorance.

After all, it is not blind. It has eyes, recognizable eyes. They are enough like our eyes that it must see somewhat as we do. It has a mouth, four legs, can move bipedally, has grasping hands, etc.; for all its gigantism and strange looks, it seems less fundamentally different from us, physically, than a fish. And yet, fish school and dance and, in their own stupid way, communicate!

The alien has never once attempted to talk with me. It has been with me, watched me, touched me, handled me, for days: but all its motions have been purposeful, not communicative. It is evidently a solitary creature, totally self-absorbed. This would go far to explain its cruelty. I noticed early that from time to time it would move its curious horizontal mouth in a series of fairly delicate, repetitive gestures, a little like someone eating. At first I thought it was jeering at me; then I wondered if it was trying to urge me to eat the indigestible fodder; then I wondered if it could be communicating *labially*. It seemed a limited and unhandy language for one so well provided with hands, feet, limbs, spine, and all; but that would be like the creature's perversity, I thought. (1986, 183–84)

However firmly the reader's alien frame may be in place, at this point it becomes symptomatically difficult to follow the narrator's reasoning. Much as one is inclined to empathize with the narrator's plight, one cannot help noticing now that her deliberations are predicated on a set of extremely unusual premises. Of course, like other science-fiction characters who live in a different time and world, the narrator will be granted a certain amount of exoticness. However, the number of "complaints" now generated by data not complying with important frame conditions, and more specifically, the number of "excuses" (Minsky 1979, 18) now needed to naturalize the narrator considerably weaken the present frame. Even as one continues to use the present frame, subattentive reasoning begins to argue somewhat along the following lines: If oral communication ("communicating labially") strikes the narrator as a strange thing[12] ...

but is natural to us as readers . . . then the story's alien is not as unfamiliar to us as it is to the narrator . . . add to this that a maze experiment is a common procedure for testing an animal's intelligence . . . add to this that descriptors like "is a giant" and "alien" are strictly relative terms . . . So . . . what if the story's alien isn't an alien but a human . . . in that case could the narrator be an animal? . . . No, animals don't tell this type of story (note, too, the narrator's remark about fish) . . . *So, what if the alien is a human and the narrator is an alien?*

Of course, this is indeed the replacement frame that undoes the garden path, successfully navigates the story's maze, and lets everything fall into place. Implicating the reader by offering a garden path and then letting him/her reason a way out of it, "Mazes" is a story about the limits of intelligence and mutual communicational failure. The story's human scientist certainly fails to pass his test of intelligence by blindly trusting his maze experiment. He should be forewarned, by the principle of uncertainty, that a measuring instrument may affect and distort the measurement. It should be in his intellectual grasp (especially since he cannot fail to realize that something is wrong) that a maze can be a piece of art as well as a piece of testing equipment. On the other hand, the narrator must be blamed for failing to see that her carefully choreographed dance through the maze is little more than an erratic failure when performed in the context of a "purposeful" intelligence test. (Repeating the maze tests, the scientist, far from intending to torture her, actually gives her a second chance.) The narrator should also realize that devouring the "indigestible fodder" she is given ("So I ate and ate, and starved," 181) can only be a wildly misleading signal.

In large measure, however, the protagonists' failures are also due to adverse circumstances. The worst of this is that both the narrator and the scientist are displaced from their natural habitats. The narrator's remarks about a "heavy foreign air" (181) and the "strange, smooth, curved wall" (182) of her prison are easily recognizable (in retrospect) as allusions to a spaceship manned by a single astronaut, himself "a solitary creature" (183). As a consequence, neither of the protagonists is able to observe the other in social contact or communication with his or her own kind, and all their tests and communicative gestures are doomed to remain ineffectual probings in the dark. When the narrator finally reads the scientist's body language, the message she gets is one of resignation and defeat:

(18)   There were no words, yet there was communication. I saw, as it stood watching me, a clear signification of angry sadness. . . . Never a word came clear, and yet it told me that it was filled with resentment, pity,

> impatience, and frustration. It told me it was sick of torturing me, and
> wanted me to help it. I am sure I understood it. (185–86)

But the narrator also knows that the "alien" cannot reciprocate even in this:
"No doubt it will come in to watch me die; but it will not understand the dance
I dance in dying" (186).

As can be imagined, this is a text that works well in a classroom. Navigating
into and recovering from its garden path is an exciting and rewarding experience. Exploiting the potential of ordinary preferences (narrators are human,
aliens are alien, texts are textual, etcetera), Le Guin manages to achieve the
coveted feat of depicting what it is like to be an alien. Throwing into relief the
narrato-logic of the reading process and releasing the energy of close and attentive reinterpretation, the story turns into an enlightening study of the problematics of alterity, epistemological limitations, and communicational failure.

5. Conclusion: The Uses of Garden Paths

One salutary effect of looking at garden paths in a range of text types, rather
than in contextless linguistic sentoids alone, was that a number of operational
linguistic concepts could be extended and modified to be used within the
larger cognitive models of frames and scripts. In the widened context it became
clear that garden-pathing is not always caused by local ambiguity, and that the
symptom, if present, translates not only into lack of cognitive payoff but into
the scenario of a frame or script on the point of breaking down. The literary
forms, especially, showed that a garden path's cure does not always involve
the wholesale rejection of the first reading. Although it has often been claimed
that garden paths are a mark of good literary texts (Perry 1979, 50, note 10),
even of literary discourse in general (Cook 1994, chapter 7), this hypothesis is
contradicted by the existence of garden-path headlines and garden-path jokes
which have little or no literary merit. However, whether dealing with contextless sentences, or with minimally narrative "simple" forms, or with more
sophisticated texts like the stories by Thurber and Le Guin—the garden-path
effect was always found to be tied to a dominant readerly preference. Following Jackendoff, such first preferences were placed within the framework of
larger preference-rule systems containing second, and third, and complementary preferences, and preference-rule systems were in turn seen as forming a
part of a frame/script configuration. Since each major preference can, given
an appropriate context, generate a garden path, occurrences of garden paths
in oral or written, fictional or factual, literary or nonliterary texts constitute a

rich source of material for further analysis and research. Genre-related frames/ scripts and preferences such as those discussed in sections 3 and 4 clearly merit more detailed attention as particularly productive generators of functional garden paths (see also Culler 1975, chapter 7). In addition, a number of worth-while projects would emerge from an investigation of the forms and uses (or mis-uses) of garden paths in philosophical, political, and juridical discourse; in indirect speech acts, irony, parody, equivocation, jokes, riddles, surprise stories, and shaggy-dog tales; in nonsense verse, detective novels, and unreli-able narratives; and, above all, in the work of authors like Henry James (Booth 1983, chapter 12), Ambrose Bierce, William Faulkner (Perry 1979; Andringa and Davis 1994), Vladimir Nabokov, Julio Cortázar (Mey 1991), Victor Borges, and Thomas Pynchon (McHale 1987, chapter 8) — to indicate what is clearly only the tip of an iceberg.

As was shown in section 1, a garden path's difficulty correlates with the time and energy it takes to find the reading that provides better cognitive pay-off. A closely related issue is what one might term a garden path's *vitality across a history of re-readings*. In a second or third reading, garden paths based on low-level preference rules seem to reactivate more fully than those based on high-level preferences. For instance, *The horse raced past the barn fell* is not only a very persistent and difficult garden path on first reading, it also deceives a reader repeatedly, though presumably not indefinitely. Whereas low-level preferences such as Bever's main-clause preference (see section 2) are largely beyond a reader's conscious control, many higher-level preferences are direct counterparts of overt convention and etiquette (maxims like "Be relevant," and so forth, Leech 1983, 8), and consequently are readily identified and remem-bered as a garden path's source of error. Still, as many commentators rightly point out, recalling a garden path and its error does not necessarily protect one from falling for it again (Perry 1979, 357; Jackendoff 1987, 244–45), especially in a context of art or play (that is, stories, jokes, and riddles), where it may have an important function.

This essay's attempt to marry AI and narratology brought out two main points of contact — a common focus of interest (stories, storytelling, story comprehension), and a common methodology (structuralism). Artificial Intel-ligence theorists have always been dedicated structuralists, and their models, unlike those of narratologists, were never sicklied o'er by the pale cast of post-structuralist thought. Because a dumb computer must have spelled out for it even the most trivial detail, AI programmers take nothing for granted, neither a self-adjusting hermeneutic circle nor automatic ambiguity resolution. The les-son to be learned from Artificial Intelligence is that one can use process models (like stacks and scripts) as well as state models (like frames) without losing the heuristics of structuralism; specifically, an enriched and flexible structuralism of this kind allows narratology to escape from its atomistic-holistic double-bind. Fortunately, postclassical narratology can also contribute its share to a fruitful exchange. For instance, when deictic-shift theorists assume that "[r]eal readers conceive of canonical fictional language (that is, narrative without a narrator) as self-constituting rather than emanating from a fictional teller" (Galbraith 1995, 32) then it is apparent that their approach could well profit from a dose of "natural" narratology (Fludernik 1996b).

The present author was never, for a moment, tempted to question the assumption that readers can be garden-pathed identically. Even a reader who happens not to be garden-pathed by a particular example will generally be able to appreciate its garden-pathing potential—copy editors do that all the time. For many of the items quoted in section 1 the garden-path effect is an empirically measurable fact, and for the other items it is a probable speculation which any reader of this essay can confirm or contradict on the spot. The matter cannot rest there, of course. If readers are garden-pathed identically then it is likely that they access identical preference-rule systems and come to identical cognitive decisions about a text—a nontrivial conclusion considering the postmodern truism that no two readers ever read alike. On the other hand, no evidence was found here to make the radical (and reactionary) counterclaim— that readers always and generally read identically, or always and generally work on identical preference-rule systems. Quite the contrary: many of the examples suggest that garden paths and preference-rule systems can differentiate as well as define what Stanley Fish (1980) has termed "interpretive communities." Getting garden-pathed by *The postman bit the dog* (section 2), children ostensibly use a different preference-rule system than adults. A linguist will not be garden-pathed by *The horse raced past the barn fell* in the same manner that an ordinary reader will (linguists smell this type of garden path a mile off). Following up this lead, it might be instructive to turn to comparative analyses of culturally determined preference-rule systems (Schank 1995, chapter 7) or the ongoing project of liberating and constructing the preferences for "reading as a woman" (Culler 1982; Morris 1993, chapter 1). Here and elsewhere, the methodological apparatus of frames, scripts, and preference-rule systems is bound to shed some interesting light on the commonalities of interpretive communities. As things stand, the circumspect cognitive critic will probably have to recognize a reading both in its potentially idiosyncratic character (where each reader is an island) and its dependence on commonly accepted interpretive moves and strategies of persuasion (where no reader is an island). As I have shown here, garden paths provide the most direct route into an individual's or an interpretive community's preference-rule systems. Moreover, because garden paths can be suspected and ultimately cured, they also lead somewhere in the sense that they show a way out of the theorist's dilemma of "situated-ness" — one's "proceeding in the context of innumerable beliefs which cannot be the object of my attention because they are the content of my attention," as Fish (1989, 326) puts it.

In ordinary communication, garden paths are a nuisance and an embarrassment, and the maxims of cooperation forbid them for good reason. Cognitive scientists deliberately invent vicious garden paths on the rationale that "if a mechanism is a sealed black box, the only way to determine how [it] works is to determine how it begins to fail" (Marcus 1980, 218). Narratologists turn to garden paths in order to investigate the narratorial manipulations that trigger and support them, and to assess their cognitive and aesthetic benefits. Perhaps in real life, too, one should welcome the day-to-day deceptions and misunderstandings for their ecological greater good; that is, for presenting an opportunity to exercise one's ability to recover from them. On second thought, perhaps one would not actually want to face a message like *In case of attack destroy documents and telephone,* where a misreading could be costly. Thankfully, it is quite sufficient, as well as more convenient, to "stage" such cognitive exercises in a riddle, or a joke, or in the virtual world of fiction (Iser 1993; Mey 1993, chapter 4.4.5).

Imagine that you are standing in front of a secret stone gate, and the powers of darkness are right at your heels. You know the gate opens on a password, and there is an instruction, chiseled into the stone, that says *Speak, friend, and enter.* Naturally you say something, anything, but nothing happens. Either the gate's mechanism is broken or your reading gets no results (not the required amount of cognitive payoff). Of course, as you may well suspect, the problem is an effect of your unconscious preferences, and when the solution finally hits you it is "absurdly simple, like most riddles when you see the answer."[13] Temptation and challenge, the garden path educates everyone, characters, readers, cognitive scientists, narratologists.

Notes

I want to thank Richard Aczel, Helmut Bonheim, Monika Fludernik, David Herman, and Ansgar Nünning for their very pertinent comments and suggestions.

1. The popularity of the subject can be gauged from the fact that a search on "garden path" in the 1981–97 MLA CD-ROM database produces thirty-two hits, twenty of which are indexed as dealing with garden-path sentences. An influential early parsing theory is the "garden path theory of sentence processing" (Frazier 1979; Clifton and

Ferreira 1989). Fodor and Inoue (1994, 408) report several monograph-sized garden-path studies in press.

2. See Altmann et al. (1992) and Rayner and Sereno (1994) for empirical evidence. As Marcus (1980, chap. 9.6) and Pritchett (1988, 543n.5) note, many garden-path sentences are less difficult, or even not at all difficult, when supplied with suitable punctuation marks or rendered in careful enunciation—consider, e.g., *The horse, raced past the barn, fell.*

3. Note that the quality of *satisfactory sense* is symptomatically lacking in the garden-path reading of (5b). Construing *[the daughter] [of Pharaoh's son]* will give the sentence a truth value of *false.* Construing *[the daughter of Pharaoh]'s [son]* will yield a more satisfactory truth value of *true,* but this construction is inordinately difficult to obtain. For an enlightening discussion of this item, see Fodor and Inoue (1994, 411–14). I will return to the crucial issue of satisfactory sense or "cognitive payoff" in the next section.

4. (i) *Time* (N) *flies* (V) *like an arrow* (PP); (ii) *Time* (V, imperative) *flies* (N) *like an arrow* (PP); (iii) *Time flies* (N) *like* (V) *an arrow* (N).

5. This is practically the same effect that occurs in the famous Necker cube experiment. First, one sees a cube (actually, an ambiguous wire-frame figure) from a preferred point of view, usually left-and-above. After a while, one subliminally asks, Is that all? Could there be a different interpretation? And bang, there is the cube seen from right-and-below. Jackendoff (1987, 116–17) discusses the Necker cube figure in the context of ambiguous sentences and garden-path items; Wenzel (1994, 123–25) relates it to a garden-path joke; and Jahn (1997) adapts it for a mental experiment illustrating the primacy-recency conflict. Jackendoff (1987, 117) further points out that subjects hearing the looped audio sequence *the see I sun the see I sun . . .* after a while tend to construe this as *ice on the sea ice on the sea . . .* Even more dramatic is the "repeating word" experiment reported by von Foerster (1990[1981], 42), in which the looped word *cogitate* induces hearers to construe a dramatic number of variant readings.

6. Opie and Opie (1977, 377) trace the earliest English version of (13) back to 1730. Hockett claims that a "prototype appears in the Rhind papyrus, from Egypt from about 1650 B.C." (1977a, 273).

7. As Opie and Opie point out, "The solution is 'one' or 'none' according to how the question is read. If the question is as plainly put as it was by a writer 200 years ago, 'Qu: How many Wives, Sacs, Cats and Kittens went to St. Ives?' the answer is clearly 'none'" (1977, 377).

8. De Bono himself illustrates lateral thinking by quoting two garden-path jokes (1983, 39). The notion of lateral thinking also comes up in Fodor and Inoue's discussion of their "repair model" of garden-path recovery (1994, 410).

9. Although the B-movie style of the daydream episodes is usually noted in passing, no one, to my knowledge, has done for "Walter Mitty" what Lowes (1978) did for "Kubla Khan." Ellis's "The Allusions in 'The Secret Life of Walter Mitty'" (1965) is basically just another psychoanalyzing approach, disdaining to even mention the influence of *Dawn Patrol* on the story's latter episodes. An "intermedial approach" (Wolf 1996)

accessing the story's actual filmic sources would certainly be of considerable narratological interest.

10. This lack of a dream quality distinguishes (16a) from the dream incipit of, for instance, Dickens's *Edwin Drood.* In retrospect, however, certain elements such as the sound of the car's engine, and "the ice forming on the . . . window" are recognizable as external stimuli reaching into Mitty's vision.

11. The narrator's sex is actually uncertain, but according to the sexing convention proposed by Lanser (1981, 166), when there is no indication to the contrary, a narrator may be assumed to have the same sex as the author. I am invoking Lanser's rule here merely in order to be able to use a pronoun; unlike in Cortázar's "Story with Spiders" (Mey 1991), the narrator's sex or gender has no bearing on the story's garden path.

12. As has been pointed out to me by one of my students, when the narrator compares physiological features, the one organ she misses is ears. In (17), she just sees the scientist's lips move, and on that basis guesses that he is trying to say something. From this, the student concluded that the narrator has neither ears nor a concept of auditory communication. In fact, since the narrator's code of communication is basically kinetic she does not need either. Belatedly, her own discourse, that is, the narrative we are reading, is identified as a mental dance: "I am dancing this, of course, in my mind" (185).

13. J. R. R. Tolkien, *The Lord of the Rings* (1991, 1:397). The password is *friend.*

PART THREE

Beyond Literary Narrative

7 | Narratives of Indeterminacy: Breaking the Medical Body into Its Discourses; Breaking the Discursive Body out of Postmodernism

Katharine Young

Stories offer an alternative locus in conversations for a presentation of self. Specifically, the stories patients tell about their lives during medical examinations release them from the constraints medicine puts on their bodies into a less constrained but disembodied domain. The body, even as it is inscribed into the realm of medicine, reinscribes itself elsewhere. On the one hand, this is a live performance of the postmodern disappearance of the body into its texts, but one in which the body's disappearance into narrative discourse is an act of resistance against its disappearance into medical discourse. On the other hand, it is the coercive staging of a split subjectivity. A woman in a gynecological examination is bound visually and verbally to the realm of the ordinary at the same time that she is bound tactually to the realm of medicine. Gynecological examinations are one of the sites for the postmodern production of multiple selves. In either instance, the body overflowing into narrative exceeds the boundaries of its modernist ascription as object.

1. Narratives of Indeterminacy

In conversations with doctors, patients appear to embark on storytellings. However, the stories they start to tell almost never get told. Technically speaking, patients fail to produce at least two necessarily sequenced clauses of which the second is consequential on the first. William Labov and Joshua Waletzky's work elaborates this minimal criterion as the core gesture of narrative (1967; Labov 1972; see Young 1987, 28–29.) Instead, patients produce what Erving Goffman calls "replays" (1974, 504), brief or ramifying recountings of things that have happened to them in everyday life which do not achieve closure, stories that do not come to an end, the sorts of stories Labov calls "so what" stories (1972, 366). In so-what stories, it's just one thing after another; in

classical narratives, one thing follows on from another. The difference is between events that are merely incidentally sequentially ordered and events that
are consequentially related (Young 1987, 206–9).

Consequentiality is what constitutes one of a series of narrative clauses the
end of the story. In effect, stories are constructed backward: tellers start with
the end and recoup the sequence of events that leads up to that end to arrive
at the beginning. "Beginnings do not so much imply ends as ends entail beginnings" (Young 1987, 29). By virtue of this entailment, stories achieve a kind
of redundancy that knits together a sequence of events in a relation hearers
take to be causal. As Paul Ricoeur writes, "By reading the end in the beginning and the beginning in the end, we learn also to read time itself backward,
as the recapitulating of the initial conditions of a course of action in its terminal consequences" (1980, 180). By virtue of this construction, the events in
stories appear to be causally connected. Consequentiality imparts a direction
to events, providing them with a temporal axis and a causal logic. The direct-
edness of events, which takes the appearance of temporal unfolding in tellings,
is in fact an effect of the atemporal enfolding of ends in beginnings. But in replays, there are no beginnings and ends, only, as it were, middles. Replays have
no temporal horizons in Maurice Natanson's sense of horizon as "the condition
for bounding what can be experienced" (1962, 89), the physical or metaphysical limits of its realm of events or taleworld.

The absence, lack, or failure of closure in the taleworld opens out into
another absence. Replays also fail to create an enclosure within the realm of
conversation for discourse of another ontological status, in this instance narrative discourse. In becoming patients, persons set aside some of their claims
as social interactants, among them the right to take an extended turn at talk in
order to tell a story. Instead, patients cede physicians exclusive rights to initiate
conversational sequences on the assumption that the resultant speech events
will suit the requisites of medical practice. This arrangement creates inequality
between physician and patient under the aegis of assuring the efficiency of the
examination.

Under the customary conversational arrangement, a turn at talk is protected, sealed off, in principle, from interruptions by prospective other
speakers. Narrative discourse forms an enclave of a different ontological status
within the realm of conversation, a storyrealm in which the storytelling transpires. The narrative frame does not preclude the interpolation of remarks
by other speakers; rather, it preserves the storyteller's claim to the floor despite these interpolations. Replays make no such claims to holding the floor.
Like stories, replays consist of sequentially ordered narrative clauses but, unlike stories, these clauses are not consequentially related. One clause does not

imply another, so each event recounted might be followed by a next event but, equally, it might not. Just as no next narrative clause completes a replay, that is, makes the replay into a story, so the replay is not incomplete without it. If all the narrative clauses that make up a story are entailed in a single turn at talk, despite interpolations by other speakers, each narrative clause of a replay, by contrast, constitutes a single turn at talk which is potentially complete. Replays remain open to remarks by other speakers which are therefore never interruptions. The storyrealm is open at the edges. Thus, the boundaries of both realms, the realm of the events the story is about, or taleworld, and the realm of narrative discourse within conversation, or storyrealm, remain pervious. Neither the event nor the story is sharply defined off as a separate reality.

Replays permit either the physician or the patient to break off the patient's narrative in the interests of the examination, without the break-off counting as an interruption. For this reason replays, rather than fully formed classical narratives, are prevalent in medical examinations as a situation type (cf. Gumperz 1982, 153–71).[1] The narrative to be examined here was told by a patient during a gynecological examination. It runs against the grain of the typical fragmentary forms that characterize conversations during medical procedures in that it has, on first blush, the aspect of a classical narrative, proceeding to an end that is a consequence of its beginning. As one of a handful of such narratives, in among hundreds of replays gleaned from forty-one tape-recordings of 117 medical examinations conducted at University Hospital between 1984 and 1987,[2] this narrative presented a little mystery, the mystery of how this patient managed to get such a developed narrative into the occasion and why it was still not quite a classical narrative. The solution turns out to be a little mystery itself. This would have been one of the rare instances of a patient telling a story during a gynecological examination except that in the middle of it, the patient decides not to reveal a dark secret. The part of the story she does tell provides a clue to what the secret is, but one I only caught onto years later when I was analyzing the transcription, and one the gynecologist never caught onto, or never let on he caught onto, at all. Our impercipience in the matter may perhaps be accounted for by the fact that the broken-off character of the narrative is disguised, like Edgar Allan Poe's purloined letter, by its occurrence among a lot of narrative replays, all of which are in a sense broken off.

Physicians characteristically treat storytelling as an interruption of, distraction from, or incursion into the realm of medicine, especially as displacing the patient's subjectivity from medicine to narrative—as the realm in which she is able to spin out a "presentation of self" (Goffman 1959)—can disrupt the dominance of medical discourse over what Elliot Mishler calls the "voice of the lifeworld" (1984, 128). But shifting the patient's attention from the realm of medicine to the realm of narrative can release the woman from some of the constraints of the examination. She can, as it were, disembody, relinquishing her body to medicine by locating her self in narrative. Embodiment elsewhere permits disembodiment here. Disembodiment supports the general medical project of objectification, which is especially requisite for the specific gyneco-logical attempt to ensure propriety.[3] This particular gynecologist, Dr. David Casaccio, invokes such an ontological shift in his patients as he initiates each phase of the gynecological examination: the breast examination, the abdomi-nal examination, and the internal examination. Most unusually, Dr. Casaccio invites his patients to tell stories. As he touches a patient's breast, for instance, Dr. Casaccio says, "How's your legal — battles." As he touches her abdomen, he says, "Still riding your horse?" And as he touches her vulva, he says, "When were you in South Africa?" (May 1, 1987, Lefkowitz transcript: 1, 2, 3. See ap-pendix 1 for transcription devices).[4] Despite these solicitations, the women Casaccio so addresses never, or almost never, tell stories. But on this occasion, the patient, Evie Jones, accepts Casaccio's invitation to tell the story of her legal battles.

The examination begins when Dr. Casaccio comes into the examination room and says, "Evie. What's going on." [5]

As is typical of medical examinations, the remark that might have been produced by the gynecologist as a greeting ritual, "What's going on," is treated by the patient as a medical inquiry, making it the pivot for shifting from the realm of the ordinary to the realm of medicine. I have spoken to Ms. Jones beforehand in order to get her consent to observe and tape-record her exami-nation,[6] and as I come in with Dr. Casaccio, she says, "Hi again," to me and then to him, "Um. Same old thing." [7]

Dr. Casaccio says, "Have your periods?"

"Yeah? — but="

"=they hurt like mad."

"Right."

By chiming in on the patient's response to his question, Dr. Casaccio shows an attention to the joint construction of the realm of medicine commensurate with the patient's transformation of Casaccio's opening remark. Chime-ins are one of a class of discourse phenomena Harvey Sacks refers to as "collaborative productions" or sometimes "joint productions" (1992, I, 321; II, 570). Like all such phenomena, they display the shared understandings that characterize a joint reality. It is perhaps this displayed mutuality that encourages Evie Jones to embark on a story.

Evie continues,[8] "This side right here hurts again."

Conversation lapses as Dr. Casaccio has Evie lie down, lifts her right arm over her head to rest on the cot, and moves her gown off her right breast preparatory to beginning his examination. At the moment he touches her breast for the first time, Dr. Casaccio says, "How's your legal — battles."

"Um, I don't know- we don't know if we'll have a house — anymore or not."
"Oh, yeah?"

Casaccio's inquiry licenses Jones to take an extended turn at talk in order to tell a story and this is what, initially, she appears to do. Jones's response, "I don't know- we don't know if we'll have a house anymore or not," is an abstract that could serve either as an answer to Casaccio's question or as a preface to the story. Casaccio's inflection of his attention marker, "Oh, yeah?" as a question, has the effect of turning Jones's abstract into the preface initiating a narrative sequence, rather than an answer that completes her turn.

Dr. Casaccio continues, "That's terrible."
"Tell me about it. But —"

These paired evaluations, his and hers, offer appreciations of the import of her abstract which could either mark closure or encourage continuation of the narrative (Sacks 1992, II, 125; Young 1987, 88). To tilt the balance toward continuation, the gynecologist offers a possible opening narrative clause in the form of a question.

"Lawyer came and assessed everything in your property?"

The trouble with questions is that they admit of answers which, of their nature, close the embedded interchange or "adjacency pair," in Sacks's terminology (Goffman 1981, 6). However, Ms. Jones takes the question as an invitation to continue her story. Since stories consist of at least two necessarily sequenced independent clauses, they take at least two sentences to complete. Conversationalists monitor speakers' talk for ends of sentences in order to know when to take up their turn. License to narrate sets aside the rule that speakers relinquish their turn at the completion of a sentence for the duration of the story. Instead of monitoring sentences for their completion, hearers monitor stories for their ends.

Evie continues her story, "The lawyer himself said he did- Ron was ready- Ron was — he was out there ready to- he was pointing his- Justin said, second time?, he goes, 'Oh I've had a death in my family I have to leave,' I said that's what you said last time."

With the phrase, "second time?," Jones clarifies that the lawyer, Justin, has been out before to look over her property. On this occasion he encounters Evie's husband, Ron. What Jones offers as a story turns out to be a replay in which the second narrative clause is sequential to but not consequential on the first; that is, what Justin does is not represented as a consequence of what Ron does. It's just what happened next. So it cannot constitute the end of the story. Saying something constitutes an act in the taleworld but what is said does not—with one exception, "performatives." A performative is an utterance that does something by saying something. It is, in fact, the notion J. L. Austin introduced in *How to Do Things with Words* (1962) as precisely a thing done with words; that is, an act accomplished by speaking in which, as John Searle puts it, "utterances are not sayings, but doings" (1969, 68). Instances of such doings with words are promising, oath-taking, giving verdicts, making contracts, cursing, bequeathing, wedding, warning, and the like (Austin 1965, 150–51). Such utterances are not merely locutionary acts, they are "illocutionary acts" (Austin 1965, 103); they have "illocutionary force" (Austin 1965, 149); that is, they do what they say. Searle once proposed the "hereby" test for performatives (Unpublished Lectures, U.C. Berkeley, 1963): if the word "hereby" could intelligibly be inserted into an utterance, as in "I hereby promise," the utterance is a performative. The consequence Evie's abstract leads hearers to expect is in fact a performative of the form, "I hereby seize your property."

But the lawyer does not do a performative; what he does is a replay. He says, "Had a death in my family I have to leave." It's a story within a story, or more precisely, a replay within a replay, in which the embedded taleworld has no effects on the taleworld in which it is, as Erving Goffman puts it, "laminated" (1974, 505). That is, the death, if there is one, has no consequences for the taleworld in which it is told. Of course, mentioning the death has: it constitutes the speech act of making an excuse. The lawyer's departure leaves Jones's story incomplete. It is neither the consequence of a previous clause nor the cause of a subsequent one. Instead of committing the illocutionary act of seizing of their goods, house, or lands, the lawyer says something quite unrelated to the legal situation and departs the scene.

In telling stories in conversation, narrators fairly commonly shift from the past tense to the present tense at the climax of their stories (Goffman 1974, 508), as if they become engaged in its events as a present reality. Thus the shift at this juncture of the laminator verb from "said" to "goes" proposes the lawyer's response as the point of the story. Instead, Jones truncates what promised to be the climax of her legal battle and turns it into the replay of an inconclusive encounter. In so doing, she substitutes a story within a story for the story she did not tell. Instead of resolving the action, the lawyer's departure delays resolution of the story to some subsequent episode.

Replays like these, following an argument of Mark Workman's about narratives within what he calls paradigms of indeterminacy (1993), I should like to call "narratives of indeterminacy." Such open-ended narratives are not to be regarded as flawed, either failed deliveries or failed receptions, but as intendedly incomplete. Their incompleteness is aimed in two directions. One is a strategic direction: the organization of the narrative to span a piece of interaction in the course of which or at the conclusion of which it can be abandoned or cut off without counting as having been interrupted. The other is a constructionist direction: the refusal of consequentiality as an organizing principle dismantles temporal unfolding and its underlying assumption of causality in narratives of indeterminacy. Mark Workman and others (Nicolaisen 1991, 9) have speculated that the recursive character of narratives of indeterminacy puts forward spatiality rather than temporality as the organizing principle of narrative. On the one hand, then, the realm of medicine constrains the production of narrative discourse and, on the other, the narratives produced in turn construe indeterminate realities.

2. Breaking the Medical Body into Its Discourses

This particular story is told during a gynecological examination which organizes the perceptual modalities of the body. Medicine translates me bodily from the realm of the ordinary in which I am a self into the realm of medicine in which I am an object.[9] It is to protect the social person from what would otherwise be the improprieties of the examination that the self is displaced from the body. The intimacies of an examination are in theory transacted on a mindless object. Propriety entails a strict discretion between the realm of medicine and the realm of the ordinary. In gynecological examinations, both realms are set up in the same region of space and conducted over the same span of time. These alternate realities are instantiated and sustained by the architectural organization of the examination room, the discursive practices of its inhabitants, and the disposition of the body. The space, the discourse, and the body are all cleaved in two. The boundary between them is partially reified in a material barrier: the gown and drape laid over the patient's body. Roughly, what transpires underneath these coverings lies in the realm of medicine; what transpires above them lies in the realm of the ordinary.

Realm discretion is strictest during the pelvic examination. For this, the patient is lying on her back with her legs bent double and her feet mounted in stirrups on either side of the examination table. The gynecologist sits on a low stool at the foot of the table. Between them, a drape is mounted up across the patient's abdomen and thighs, tucked along the sides of her legs and hung over the edges of the table. The drape provides what Erving Goffman calls an "evidential boundary" (1974, 215) that intervenes between the participants in the examination and their perception of each other. Visually, the drape prevents either the patient or the gynecologist from catching a glimpse of the other's face between her thighs. From the perspective of the woman, the upper frontal aspect of her body down to her knees appears as a series of mounds and hollows protruding through the horizontal blue-green surfaces of her gown and drape. From the perspective of the gynecologist, the drape frames the underside of the patient's haunches, which appear as a vertical surface rimmed by the forepart of her calves and feet and enclosing her vulva, its central fold extending downward to the anus. Woman and gynecologist visually substantiate different realms. For the woman, visuality substantiates the realm of the ordinary; for the gynecologist, visuality substantiates the realm of medicine.

The visual boundary creates an enclosure in the matrix of the gynecological examination for tactile perceptions. In both pain and pleasure, touch thematizes the body. Pain constrains me to my body. As Elaine Scarry suggests, the universe contracts to my skin or my body swells to fill the universe (1987, 35). The instrumental gestures of the gynecological examination cause pain, ranging from discomfort, a sort of eeriness of the interior, to exquisite torment.[10] Pain binds the woman to her body in the realm of medicine. To permit her to express it, however, is to permit her to reconstitute herself as a subjectivity in this realm and so to invite an impropriety. To prevent this, the gynecologist disregards pain. Expressions of pain, either in the physical form of flinches, winces, starts, grimaces, jerks, tightening or twitching the lip, arching the neck, throwing back the head, closing the eyes, blinking, or squinting, or in the audible form of inbreaths, whimpers, sighs, gasps, moans, groans, cries, or screams are either suppressed by the patient or disattended, in Erving Goffman's term (1974, 202), by the gynecologist. When the patient's pain disrupts the examination, the gynecologist may be obliged to deal with the pain but not to sympathize with the patient. To acknowledge pain as a subjective state would be to acknowledge the woman's presence in the flesh. Such an incursion threatens the objectified realm of medicine.

The parts of the patient's body to which the gynecologist has both visual and tactile access are within the enclosure bounded by the gown and drape. The woman, by contrast, has tactile experience of just those parts of her own body from which she is visually excluded. Within the enclosure, her body is thematized, brought to awareness by the touch of the gynecologist. Without the enclosure, her body is effaced. The primary perceptual modality which, according to Drew Leder (1990, 14–15), expands the sense of self out of the body, visuality, is focalized for her there. The perceptual modality which contracts her to her body, touch, is confined to a region to which she does not have visual access. Thus the woman is inveigled into substantiating two realities corporeally. One, a discourse of social subjectivity, mapped onto her upper outer body, engages her visually; the other, a discourse of medical objectivity, mounted on her lower inner body, engages her tactually. She is obliged to construct a split orientation: she is bound tactually to the realm from which she is visually excluded. Pain is occluded in the medical body.

Sounds travel unhindered between realms. The evidential boundaries thus effaced can be recouped by what Marie-Laure Ryan calls illocutionary boundaries which "delimit speech acts within a text or a conversation" (1991, 176). Forms of talk can thus be used to reconstitute ontological difference. Talk between the gynecologist and the nurse within the enclosure is earmarked by an "arcane medical terminology which," according to Candace West, "mystified their patients" (1984, 24). The intent of technical jargon is to inscribe objectivity on the body; its effect is to exclude the woman from the discourse. The inaccessibility thus iterated is reiterated by the gynecologist and the nurse by lowering their voices and directing them toward each other, using what Malcah Yeager calls "aside intonations" (1978, pers. comm.). As these locutions remain quite audible to the patient, they are delivered with respect to her as asides so that overhearing the doctor and the nurse takes on the aspect of eavesdropping. It is as if the patient were permitted to overhear remarks to which, as overhearings, she is not permitted to respond. Though the patient has auditory access to this technical talk, she does not have what Amy Shuman conceives as speaking rights in it (1986, 18).

The patient is invited to participate verbally in the realm of medicine by describing her pain. The gynecologist pitches inquiries about her interior and its history out of the enclosure to the patient. Occasionally he lifts his head up above the rim of the drape or tweaks it down between her knees to catch her eye. In response, she transforms the tactile into the verbal. In doing so, however, she has lifted the pain away from her body. Pain becomes an artifact of discourse to which the gynecologist attends, as it were, in translation. He regards pain, not as a sign of the presence of a self but as a clue to the condition of an object. Pain is mentionable but not expressible.

Articulating pain, even as it dematerializes the body (Scarry 1987, 223), materializes for the woman in pain another reality. Scarry writes, "*[E]xpressing physical pain eventually opens into the wider frame of invention*" (1987, 22). In speaking, the woman retrieves the contents of the world dismantled by pain, including her own body as a sentient presence in that world. We are witness to what Scarry calls the making of the world (1987, 23).

As he is palpating her abdomen, Dr. Casaccio asks Evie about a pain she mentioned.

"Where's this pain?"

"Right here but my whole abdomen's been cramping."

In doing so, Casaccio is not treating pain as a sign of the self but as a symptom of something else. He continues his examination.

"Something there. — I can feel the pulse in your artery but — that may-"

Dr. Casaccio breaks off and continues examining Evie's abdomen. After a considerable silence, he says, "I can't feel anything."

A shorter pause.

"I think it's just close to your backbone . . . feel your- — feel your heartbeat."

A very short pause.

"This is the artery."

Evie starts to say, "Well something's there but once in a while something's-" and at the same time Dr. Casaccio continues, "Let me check you (below) see how — you feel."

And Evie finishes, "-something's hard right there occasionally."

"Really?"

"But I don't know what- — It goes away."

Dr. Casaccio moves round to sit on his stool at the foot of the examination table and gloves himself. His nurse turns on the spotlight and aims it at the patient's vaginal opening.

"It's not like it stays there and it's anything to worry about," Evie continues. She pauses. "Least I don't think so."

Dr. Casaccio touches her vulva and says, "Still riding your horse?"

(The above interchange is from Lefkowitz transcript, May 1, 1987, 2.)

Uttered at the moment the gynecologist touches her body, this remark splits off the woman's attention from her embodiment on the occasion of the examination and redirects it to her embodiment elsewhere. The woman is poised to tell stories, to recount a world in which she is sovereign even as she is perceptually bound to a world in which she is, in Julia Kristeva's term, abject (1982). Thus the gynecologist occasions the creative act in which the woman can reconstitute herself narratively. Out of the pain that binds her to her body, the woman can fabricate the imaginative act that lifts her out of her body and into her self. Why does she so rarely do so?

The gynecologist's touch of the breast, the abdomen, or the vulva serves gesturally as the opening frame of each of the three phases of the physical examination. With each gesture, the gynecologist enters into an examination of the body. In doing so, he changes what Charles Goodwin refers to as the "engagement framework" of the interaction (1981, 10). Up to the first gesture, the gynecologist and the woman have displayed mutual orientation to their engagement. Once the physical phase of the examination begins, participants "move from a state of talk to a state of disengagement" in order to permit the exigencies of the examination to take precedence. As Goodwin points out, "After disengagement has been entered, talk is still possible, but this talk has both a different sequential organization at its boundaries and a different structure of coparticipation in its course than talk produced during full engagement." Nonetheless, he notes that "although during disengagement the participants are explicitly displaying nonorientation toward each other, each is in fact paying close attention to what the other is doing" (all quotes from Goodwin 1981, 10). The disengagement of talk of course sets up a framework for engaging the body. Thenceforth, talk is inserted into interstices in the physical examination.

In putting questions to the patient just as he touches her body, the gynecologist is opening the state of disengagement to the sort of loose talk Goodwin mentions. When the questions are about her lifeworld, the gynecologist proposes himself as what Goodwin calls an "unknowing recipient" of some proposed piece of talk (1981, 10). The woman is then expected to produce an utterance that imparts to him new information. For instance, when Dr. Casaccio asks Diana Reed, "What's CBS up to now," just as he touches her vulva, she corrects him, "NBC," and then answers, "Making money," continuing without a pause, "all they do is try to um — get you know with General Electric in, all they want is uh — make more more and more money=" (May 8, 1987). This timing of his question appears to be designed to assure that the woman is taken up with producing talk while the gynecologist attends to her body. To sustain her production, the gynecologist need only evidence hearership. Goodwin notes that "one way in which a nonspeaking party can indicate whether he is acting as a hearer is by gazing at the speaker" (1981, 9). But mutual gazing has been dismantled in this disengagement framework. "Hearership can of course be demonstrated in other ways" (1981, 9), such as attentive vocalizations, tag questions, comments, or evaluations. In this instance, Casaccio cuts in on her answer to ask, "GE owns it now?" When these are not forthcoming, the patient can suppose that the gynecologist has invoked the disengagement frame and turned his attention to the examination. Within this framework, the patient can always be recalled, tactually or verbally, to her own examination. So most responses to the invitation to narrate are replays. Embarking on a story risks interruption.

One solution to the problem of sustaining talk within the disengagement framework is to direct talk to the examination, the proposed primary focus of interaction. And indeed the gynecologist occasionally addresses the questions with which he opens different phases of the physical examination to the examination itself. Questions like "Are you having any problems?" as he touches the patient's breast (May 8, 1987, 31) or "Did you have any problems after the operation?" as he touches the site of the operation, the woman's vagina (May 8, 1987, 43), license the patient to participate in medical discourse. Throughout her pelvic examination, bracketed by the gynecologist's paired instructions, "Come on down," and "O.K., scoot back," Dr. Casaccio and Erika Christianson talk about her mastectomy.

Dr. Casaccio says, "Come on down."

The patient slides her recumbent body down the examination table. Over the course of the ensuing conversation, the gynecologist puts on gloves, inserts the speculum, and does a Pap smear.

Dr. Casaccio says, "What's it been now, two years?"

"No."

"One," says Dr. Casaccio, at the same that Ms. Christianson continues, "It was a year at Christmas. — Yes="

"O.K.="

"Mmhm."

A brief pause.

Dr. Casaccio says, "Well that's really a- a shock to — to go through that="

"I feel like I've — made a — good adjustment"

"Oh yeah well now it's getting="

She continues, "you know="

At the same time, Dr. Casaccio continues, "further away — and I think you feel a little bit more="

"Mmm.="

"secure. — But you know when it first happens — you know — your whole security is gone."

"Well I (had) to — have the uh pulmonary embolism at the same time. — It was," they both speak at once and then Dr. Casaccio says, "It wasn't easy."

The gynecologist has removed the speculum and, with this remark, inserts his hand into the patient's vagina to do the internal examination.

Ms. Christianson says, "It took me a good six months."

"Even the family probably had a hard time."

"We had a rough year." She chuckles.

A pause during which Dr. Casaccio inserts his finger in Ms. Christianson's anus, removes a trace of fecal matter, and wipes it on a slide.

He turns to his nurse. "Let me have a stool."

The nurse holds out a glass slide for the sample.

"O.K., scoot back." He tucks his hands under her buttocks to guide to sit up.

(The above interchange from Lefkowitz transcript, May 8, 1989, 23.)

Besides obliging the patient to translate tactile experiences into verbal modalities, a question about her present condition also obliges the woman to recount what has happened to her body historically rather than attuning to what is happening to it currently. Ms. Christianson's account is topically connected to her bodily experience but temporally disconnected. Permitting the patient to participate in medical discourse makes the gynecologist's gate-keeping job more difficult. The elaborate constructs designed to exclude her from that realm are set aside. In an instance in which the gynecologist provides the patient a minute-to-minute account of what he is doing in the examination, such as Dr. Casaccio's hunt for the source of the pain in Evie Jones's belly, he does tune his talk to her experience but keeps it under his control. Her descriptions provide signposts for his explorations. In contrast to medical discourse, in which the patient is proposed as unknowing recipient, in excursions into ordinary discourse the gynecologist proposes himself as unknowing recipient.

Some women embark on accounts of other medical experiences which apparently maintain topical relevance to the realm of medicine without intruding on their own examinations. This solution has the curious property of making the gynecologist the unknowing recipient of information about his own domain. In one instance in which a woman was recounting to Dr. Casaccio the story of the premature child of a friend of hers, this reversal apparently became so uncomfortable that, despite the gynecologist's attentive comments, in the middle of her story, she switched the gynecologist to knowing recipient. "But I- I- I hope- — Where did- — Doctor Casaccio — do you think the one that's in the hospital will be O.K.? — Will it ever be normal?" (May 1, 1987, Lefkowitz transcript, 21).

Persons proposed as knowing recipients participate in talk by telling the speaker what they know; persons proposed as unknowing recipients participate in talk by indicating attention to the speaker's talk. Since signs of hearership can be subtle or absent here, the patient transforms the gynecologist from unknowing to knowing recipient in order to assure his active participation.

Most of the questions Dr. Casaccio times to coincide with the moment he first touches the patient's breast, abdomen, or vulva direct her attention away from the occasion of the examination and toward the lifeworld in which she can be presumed to exercise her sovereignty. Some of these questions are designed to address what the gynecologist takes to be the woman's circumstances. These range from generic questions like "Anything happening?" (May 8, 1987, 28) to patients he does not know well, to such circumstantial questions as "Getting all ready for the summer?" (May 8, 1987, 47), "Where do you go to school now?" (May 8, 1987, 29), or "How's the family doing?" (May 8, 1987, 22) to patients he knows slightly. To patients he knows well, he addresses quite specific questions like "How's your legal battles?" (May 1, 1987, 1), "Go flying with your father at all?" (May 1, 1987, 30), or "What's CBS up to now?" (May 8, 1987, 10). These not only invite stories about the woman's lifeworld but also attest to the gynecologist's attention to such stories on prior occasions. The uses of narrativity are similar whether the gynecologist knows the patient well or not. The invitation to narrate keeps the patient from intervening in her own examination and at the same time offers her another footing for presenting a self.

The gynecologist's conversational moves toward storytelling rarely eventuate in patients' stories. Instead, many patients take these invitations as questions to which they make short answers, thus keeping the floor clear for proper medical inquiries. Those who do appear to embark on stories are often recalled to their corporeal circumstances either by a medical question or by a pain in their bodies. Because the beginnings of stories aim for their ends, the introduction of consequential relationships between narrative clauses lays the story open to interruption if the patient is recalled to the realm of medicine before its end. For this reason, patients characteristically produce narrative-like speech events or replays in the form of episodic accounts whose rambling structure could be broken off at any point without counting as interruptions.

Evie Jones's account of her legal battles closes with a replay whose last phase is the speech act that constitutes a leave-taking, "Justin said, second time?, he goes, 'Oh I've had a death in my family I have to leave.'" It is this event, the sudden departure of the lawyer, as it were, in the middle of the story, that makes this replay an episode in a prospective longer narrative rather than a story in itself. What made the lawyer leave? The replay elides the precipitating cause but provides clues from which, I think, we might detect it. "Ron was ready- Ron was — he was out there ready to- he was pointing his-." What do you suppose he was pointing? My guess is, a gun. Ron is standing melodramatically in the doorway, waving a gun at the evil lawyer who is threatening to attach their property to pay off some sort of debt. If Evie Jones had elucidated this fact, Justin's departure would have been a consequence of what preceded it. Instead of delaying resolution, it would have been the climax of a story it completed. Eliding the gun not only preserves Jones's presentation of herself as the lawyer's victim rather than he hers but also reduces the story to a replay. The lawyer's response, ignominious retreat, becomes intelligible under this interpretation. The description of Ron's gestures is not part of the sentence about Justin's visit but the beginning of a separate utterance that gets broken off in the middle. It's a false start that discloses a secret, not what the secret is—that's a speculation—but the fact that there is a secret. If she had stuck to her guns, so to speak, she would have managed one of the rare instances of storytelling during a gynecological examination. Without the gun, the lawyer's departure is not the conclusion of a course of action but the extension of that course into some future account. Indeed, the lawyer reappears in a subsequent episode of Jones's ongoing picaresque tale, one which likewise detours resolution and one from which she is recalled by a visceral twinge. I am tempted to argue that Casaccio's comment on Justin's death-in-the-family line is what Sacks calls a conversational pun (1971) that reveals, as obliquely as Jones conceals, that David Casaccio has caught onto the gun.[11]

He says, "That's a polite way of saying I do(hoho)n't want to stick — around — and face the heat?"

"Heater" is a slang term for "gun." But that's wildly speculative.

Evie responds with a heartfelt, "Ye:ah."

And Dr. Casaccio echoes in a whisper, "=Yeah."

A brief pause and then Evie continues, "Well I was pretty upse:t when — he came out and said Um — that he'd been on my property?"

"Yeah that was worth X amount of dollars."

At the same time Evie says, "Kind of="

And after a pause, Dr. Casaccio appends, "I don't know."

Dr. Casaccio is now palpating Evie Jones's abdomen. She directs her gaze straight ahead of her; his gaze is angled up under his eyebrow, abstracted. Neither looks at her body nor at the other.

After a moment, Evie says, "He's definitely different as a lawyer than he is as a — person= Ouch that's the pain."

(Lefkowitz transcript, May 1, 1987, 2.)

The indeterminate narrative becomes an episode in a presumably ongoing saga to which the teller adverts intermittently. Although events within each episode are sequentially ordered, the episodes are not necessarily sequentially ordered with respect to each other. It is rather as if the taleworld provides a spatial anchorage for various narrative presentations, over the course of an occasion or a number of occasions, of a self who is unfolding. The storyteller produces fragments for a history of the *postmodern* body, to adapt the title from *Zone* (Feher et al. 1989), an incomplete, discontinuous, metamorphic, ramifying body, appearing at disjunctive intervals in the same narrative space. This is the body dismantled into its discourses.

Since narratives of indeterminacy never come to an end, breaking off in the course of them cannot be construed as an interruption. These narratives are not closural but improvised flexibly to span the rhythm of the examination as it transpires in the realm of medicine. Such narratives are open-ended, episodic, ongoing, and either recursive or temporally indeterminate. Instead of a temporal unfolding, the narratives take up a spatial anchorage. So women solve the problem of the interruptibility of their narratives within the disengagement framework by traversing the space of a narrative realm, a taleworld, without fully inhabiting it, without being enclosed in it. Instead, they keep the taleworld open for quick visits, brief sorties which give them a foothold in another realm.

3. Breaking the Discursive Body out of Postmodernism

In gynecological examinations, the body is, as it were, lifted out onto different planes of reality, reconstituted in different universes of discourse. It materializes as the passive object of medical discourse; it appears as the active but etherealized subject of narrative discourse. But these are not instances of the postmodern disappearance of the body into its signs; this is the insistence of the body on its substance. When Evie Jones is recalled to her body by a visceral twinge, she transfers what Alfred Schutz calls "the accent of reality" from narrative to medicine, both as embodied practices (1973, 252). As N. Katherine Hayles remarks, "One belief from the present likely to stupefy future generations is the postmodern orthodoxy that the body is primarily, if not entirely, a linguistic and discursive construction. . . . [D]iscourse theory, . . . information theory, . . . information technologies . . . collaborate in creating the demateralization of embodiment that is one of the characteristic features of postmodern ideology" (1993, 147). The body does not so much dissolve into its signs, its discourses, into a virtual body, as it constitutes or discovers itself there. And it finds itself not as an essential modernist whole arising out of its own interiority but as a jagged, fragmentary, disjunctive, partial locus or figuration occasioned by circumstance. This is not the perverse postmodernist view that the props have been knocked out from under everything so that discourses of the body no longer have anchorages in the real, but its obverse, that the real has its anchorages in the body, that the real is fabricated out of the body.

Grant the postmodernist dictum that there is no foundational knowledge and arrive at Donna Haraway's "local knowledges," which are always bodily knowledges (1991, 194). Evie's narrative, struggling between the coherent and the fragmentary, the essentialist and the constructionist, the disembodied and the embodied, illustrates the struggle between modernism and postmodernism. The problem is how to actuate a self: by improvising one flexibly on the spot, inconsistent with alternate selves, or consistent with alternate pasts; or by spinning out a self-consistent persona which sustains the illusion of its roots in one history and one body. Instead of saying that postmodern narrative, or narrative in postmodern theory, has no footing in reality, it would come nearer to say that postmodern narrative, postmodern narrative theory, moves against the givenness of narrative's referential footing or against the givenness of the body. In each discourse, the body invents itself. Evie, flushed with shame, tweaked by pain, pricked with ire, experiences her narrative bodily. To express the matter with a social constructionist twist, narrative in the postmodern conception plays with its act of either constructing itself out of bits of reality or constructing that reality. Sometimes, narrative conceals or erases its constructedness to put itself forward as a transparency to reality: I am transported to Evie's farm, the ambiguous incident, the palpable but inarticulate tension of the situation. Sometimes it permits some of its junctures, seams, or fissures, where realities are hitched together, to become visible (or for theorists to materialize them): I am aware of Evie closing up seams made visible by their disappearance. This visibility, this materialization, makes narrative just another bit of reality, not its representation or fabrication. At the same time, the visible constructedness of postmodern reality makes claims for the givenness of the body suspect.

In fact, postmodernism is heavily dependent on modernism, against which it makes its gesture, and before that, on realism. Modernism makes reality primary and its representations secondary. What is at issue with respect to the relationship between them, according to Amy Shuman and Nan Johnson (1993), is whether or not they match. If they do not match, the representation is held to be deceptive; if they do, the representation is held to be superfluous or what Jacques Derrida calls "supplementary" (1973, 88). On a modernist view, Evie has told a lie, or more trivially, invented an alternate reality, a merely narrative realm, extraneous to the real. The postmodernist approach reverses this hierarchy. It privileges the representation, the construction, the supplement, but refuses to secure its anchorage in the real. We see that Evie constitutes herself bodily at her various discursive loci. She is being present to herself and to the gynecologist in a certain way. Her narrative proposes, not reality, but presence.

As a consequence of the postmodernist refusal, scholars have become exercised about whether or not our investigations are of the real at all. Postmodernism dismantles, as Shuman and Johnson remark, the supplement (1993). What it does not do, and it is difficult to put this quite clearly, what postmodern narrative[12] does not do is erase experience. It does not dematerialize, attenuate, or thin out everything, though on some accounts that seems to be its drift. In fact, those accounts, I would argue, move postmodernism toward its fatal end, solipsism. Rather, narratives, bodies, things, thoughts, acts, writings, all evanesce and recrudesce, recede and obtrude, in various "modalities of materiality," to borrow a phrase of Althusser's (1971, 169), refuse or elude any fixed ontological status or positioning or footing. Narrators—and I think this is the postmodern key—make it up as they go along. They take different holds, both on realities and on narratives, shift holds, get another, let go, free-fall a bit. But they do not take no holds. They do not produce free-floating, disembodied, unanchored discourses. They do not, heaven forfend, embrace solipsism.

It is this slippage between holds, where the new hold (and here my metaphor begins to fail me) is on the outcroppings of another reality, that marks the postmodern conception of narrative. When we perceive, uneasily, Evie quickly stitching up another world, when we notice the breach between realities and realize that neither anchors the other, we entertain a postmodern sensibility. Sometimes, that is to say, narratives flatten out, become part of the topography of the real; sometimes, they pull away onto a different plane of reality and show as representations. The interest of these narratives is the strategy of shifting holds, not the crumbling underpinnings of the holds taken, if indeed they are crumbling. What we attend to is how narrative hooks itself to realities and how it breaks itself off. My suspicion is that postmodernism, in eschewing all anchorages, has hollowed itself out too much. Its discourses are the dry shells, exoskeletons, carapaces of the fabulous, fat, thick, tacky, meaty realm of the modern.

Dismantling the body into its discourses does not dematerialize the body but rather has its footing in embodiment. Hayles writes,

> In contrast to the body, embodiment is contextual, enwebbed within the specifics of place, time, physiology and culture that together comprise enactment. Embodiment never coincides exactly with 'the body,' however that normalized concept is understood. Whereas the body is an idealized form that gestures toward a Platonic reality, embodiment is the specific instantiation generated from the noise of difference. Relative to the body, embodiment is other and elsewhere, at once excessive and deficient in its infinite variations, particularities, and abnormalities. (1993, 154–55)

Insofar as narrative fragments, tiny replays of the real, fall under postmodernist theory, they point to the constructedness of the real, the uncontainability of the body, the noncausality of phenomena. Narrative makes available alternate footholds in the real, alternate realities. Evie steps through but she never vanishes.

Appendix 1

Transcription Devices for Quoted Text*

| — | Pauses |
| , | Pause intonations |

Transcription Devices for Transcript*

Line ends	Pauses
=	Absence of obligatory end-pause
/	One beat pause
Capital letters	Start of utterance
.	Down intonation at end of utterance

?	Up intonation at end of utterance
-	Correction phenomena
( )	Doubtful hearings
(hehe)	Laughter
(( ))	Editorial comments
[[	Simultaneous speech
[ ]	Extent of simultaneity
.....	Elisions
:	Elongated sound

*Adapted by Malcah Yeager, from James Schenkein (1978).

Appendix 2

Evie Jones's Narrative

Dr: Evie.
      What's going on.
[[[   ]
EJ: Hi again. *((To the researcher.))* (Heh.)
      Um
      Same old thing. *((To the gynecologist.))*
Dr: Have your periods?
EJ: Yeah?
      but
Dr: =they hurt like mad.
EJ: Right.
      This side right here hurts again.
Dr: All right, let me take a look at you.
      ///
      ((During this pause, Dr. Casaccio has Ms. Jones lie down, lifts her right arm over her head to rest on the cot, and moves her gown aside to begin the breast examination. Over the course of their subsequent talk, he conducts the examination, moving from her right to her left breast, then to her abdomen. During this time the gynecologist looks intermittently at the patient's breast and belly; the woman turns her gaze to the ceiling. Just as he touches her breast for the first time, Dr. Casaccio asks a question.))
Dr: How's your legal
      battles.
EJ: Um,
      I don't know- we don't know if we'll have a house
      anymore or not.
[[[   ]
Dr: Oh yeah?

That's terrible.
EJ: Tell me about it.
But
Dr: Lawyer came an' assessed everything in your property?
EJ: The lawyer himself said he did- Ron was ready- Ron was
he was out there ready to-
he was pointing his- Justin said, second time?
((Ron is Evie's husband; Justin is the opposing lawyer.))
he goes,
"Oh I've had a death in my family I have to leave," I said that's what you said
last time.
Dr: (Hehehe) uh (he) ah ah.
EJ: He says the same thing every time when he gets in trouble?
and he has to leave quick?
"Had a death in my family I have to go."
All: *((All laugh.))*
(May 1, 1987, Lefkowitz transcript, 1.)

Notes

This essay is adapted from "Perceptual Modalities," in *Presence in the Flesh,* by Katharine Young. Copyright © 1997 by the President and Fellows of Harvard College. Reprinted by permission of Harvard University Press. My rewriting of this article has benefited from critical readings by Marie-Laure Ryan, David Herman, and the outside readers for the Ohio State University Press.

1. See also Young (1997), chaps. 1 and 2.
2. As one of the requisites for conducting research on human beings, the names of the patients, physicians, and the hospital itself are confidential. I use the pseudonym "University Hospital" to refer to the institution where I conducted my research.
3. In the practices I observed, issues of propriety appeared to arise not from the gender of the physician but from the gender of the patient in the circumstances of the examinations. Both male and female physicians treated male patients more casually and female patients more primly in similar circumstances. On sexual propriety, see Young (1997, especially 15–16); on the etiquette of touch, see Young (1997, 31–32).
4. Unless otherwise noted, Daniel Lefkowitz did the transcriptions of the gyneco-logical tapes. These texts are renderings of his originals.
5. See appendix 2 for a complete transcription of this interchange.
6. Another requisite of the university committee for research on human beings was that I give every participant in the study a written consent form. For the gynecology examinations, I submitted these forms to patients for their consideration during the nurse's intake procedure before the examination.

7. My effect on these occasions was unpredictable. After the first few examinations, or the first half-hour of a longer procedure, the physicians seemed to get used to me. Because this was a teaching hospital, they were accustomed to being followed about by apprentices, or even eminences, of various sorts. But for the patients, I was often a new wrinkle. They may, for instance, have behaved more properly in my presence. But this propriety can only have enhanced the etiquette of touch I was after. Some of the patients were themselves used to this sort of thing, and when I started to explain my research, they would say, "Oh, another one of those," and either wave me off or grab the consent form and sign it unceremoniously.

8. Although I address the patient, as a matter of professional practice, as Ms. Jones, and refer to her, as to him, according to academic practice, by the last name, I preserve in the transcription and description of their conversation the asymmetry of address between them: she calls him "Dr. Casaccio"; he calls her "Evie."

9. I deal with the objectification of the body by medical technologies, which is the problem of dehumanization, elsewhere (1997, chap. 1). Here I am concerned with the production of subjectivities despite or against the grain of this objectification.

10. Examinations include postsurgical bodies, currently infected bodies, and traumatized bodies; but also individuals vary in their perception of this disturbance of their interior as pain. Some bodies experience a kind of anesthesia just as others experience hyperesthesias. For more detailed descriptions of pain in gynecology, see Young (1997, 53–54, 57–59, 62–69).

11. Sacks argues in his lectures on storytelling that such puns, whether consciously constructed or not, disclose an understanding of the stories on which they comment (1971).

12. Marie-Laure Ryan prefers the phrase "the postmodern conception of narrative" here, reserving the term "postmodern narrative" for intendedly postmodern writings, because, as she argues, "we are all constructing a postmodern self through our narratives even if we think we are constrained by circumstances." Insofar as these narratives of indeterminacy achieve postmodernity, they, too, construct a self or a self-fragment whose anchorage is not the body but who is nonetheless not disembodied but otherwise embodied, in narrative. Ryan, pers. comm.

8 | Toward a Socionarratology: New Ways of Analyzing Natural-Language Narratives

David Herman

As an outgrowth of structuralism in France in the late 1960s, narratology in its classical version sought to elaborate the underlying code or langue *of individual narrative messages—the system of features and contrasts in terms of which story recipients are able to identify narrative discourse and interpret it as such. Modeling itself on the so-called pilot science of French structuralism (Dosse 1996, 59–66)—that is, structural linguistics—narratology was designed to focus not on* what *narratively organized sign systems mean but on* how *they mean, and more specifically on how they mean as narratives. Yet in making a distinction between system and message, the analyst must be careful not to relegate all aspects of the message, a priori, to the category of the nonsystemic and hence the nonsystematizable. Recontextualized as discourse strategies, narrative messages may begin to display new properties that can be systematically described and analyzed. From this perspective, stories will figure not as manifestations of a code that preexists all communicative contexts, but rather as an interactional achievement, negotiated by participants in the ongoing discourse.*

Reassessing the structuralist metaphors of narrative code and narrative message, my essay works toward integrating two traditions of narrative analysis that have evolved in parallel but without much cross-fertilization up to now. These are the sociolinguistic approach inspired by Labov and Waletzky (1967; also Labov 1972) and the narratological approach. In its classical formulations, narratology was hampered not only by its excessive reliance on Saussurean theories but also by its failure to accommodate developments being advanced by Anglo-American researchers, especially in the areas of pragmatics, discourse analysis, and (interactional) sociolinguistics. At the same time, the Labovian model can gain in both descriptive and explanatory adequacy if it is enriched with research tools developed at first under the auspices of narratology. Based on ghost stories elicited during a socio-linguistic interview, this essay focuses on two narratological ideas, both of them useful for analyzing how stories unfold as patterned sequences of referring expressions. The first idea is the distinction between story and discourse; the second is the redescription of certain entities in the story world as narrative actants. Placed in dialogue with the Labovian approach, these narratological ideas suggest that any analysis of narrative structure must be complemented by an account of narrative communication. If structuralist models throw light on aspects of narrative form, (socio)linguistic theories provide insight into storytelling as a mode of interaction. Accordingly, my essay outlines an integrated, "socionarratological" approach that situates stories in a constellation of linguistic, cognitive, and contextual factors.

1. Narrative Code and Narrative Message

Narratology, christened as such by Tzvetan Todorov (1969) in his "grammar" of Boccaccio's *Decameron,* originated as an outgrowth of structuralist literary theory in France. Though its roots extend as far back as Vladimir Propp's *Morphology of the Folktale* (1968[1928]) and the work of Russian Formalist literary theorists like Victor Sklovskij, classical narratology was profoundly shaped by French structuralism—both in the way it defined the object it analyzed and in the way it developed its method of analysis. In their attempts to develop a generalized science of the sign, the structuralists had adopted Saussure's emphasis on *la langue* over *la parole.* The priority was to discover the properties characterizing language viewed as a system, not those attaching to the individual speech acts made possible and intelligible by the linguistic system. Likewise, structuralist narratologists sought to elaborate the underlying code of individual narrative messages, the system of features and contrasts in terms of which story recipients are able to identify narratively organized discourse and interpret it as such. The object of narratological investigation, then, was narrative *langue;* it is on the basis of this supratextual system, presumably, that narrative units can be defined, their modes of combination specified, and various textual features and structures ranked as more or less narratively salient. Narratological method reflected—and was reflected in—the choice of narrative langue as the object of analysis. The difference between studying the code of narrative and studying specific narratives paralleled the difference between poetics and criticism, which had been clearly demarcated by Roman Jakobson in 1960. Narratology was not first and foremost a hermeneutic enterprise, let alone an evaluative one. Modeling itself on the so-called pilot science of French structuralism, that is, structural linguistics, narratology was designed to focus on *how* narratively organized sign systems mean, and—as stated above—more specifically on how they mean *as narratives*. The critic engages in serial readings of individual stories; the narratologist studies the network of conditions and conventions that allows certain sets of signs to be processed as stories in the first place. By the same token, the narratologist does not restrict his or her attention to great narrative works. In principle, narratology can go wherever stories are to be found, on the street as well as in the library, in everyday conversation as well as in famous (or not-so-famous) novels.

In practice, however, since its inception narratology has remained fundamentally a way of analyzing *literary* narratives. Though the structuralists purported to have developed a science of narrative, an approach whose descriptive adequacy made it applicable to all and only stories, for the most part classical narratology never really caught on outside of literature departments—with the possible exception of programs in film studies. Narratology's limited appeal can be traced back, again, to the way it defined its object of study and its techniques for studying it. Intuitively, at least, the distinction between narrative system and narrative message is a valid one: to reduce code to message or message to code is to traffic in two, equally pernicious forms of reductionism. Yet in making a distinction between system and message, the analyst must be careful not to relegate all aspects of the message, a priori, to the category of the nonsystemic and hence the nonsystematizable.[1] *La parole* is after all not the underachieving sibling of *la langue*. Indeed, rather than being consigned beforehand to the domain of the random and the unpredictable, facts about the production and processing of stories should be anchored in the actual practice of participants engaged in narrative communication. Put otherwise, by changing our methods for studying narrative, we may discover unexpected patterns in the way that stories are used to facilitate communication. Recontextualized as discourse strategies, narrative messages may begin to display new properties that can be systematically described and analyzed. In turn, accounting for such properties may compel us to redraw the lines between the narrative system and particular acts of storytelling—to rethink the whole relation between code and message, or at least the metaphors previously used to capture that relation. Narratologists may well need to redescribe code and message as aspects of two different modules of "narrative competence"—in much the same way that modern-day (post-Saussurean) linguistics conceives of syntax, semantics, and phonology, for example, as separate but interacting modules of grammatical competence (Garfield 1987; Jackendoff 1997). From this perspective, narrative code and message can be situated in discrete but complementary domains of cognitive and linguistic expertise; both domains are necessary for the design and interpretation of stories viewed as modes of social interaction.

2. Two Models for Narrative Analysis

Rethinking the relations between "narrative" and "narratives" requires that we reevaluate, too, the models developed during the 1960s, 1970s, and 1980s by narratologists—European, North American, Israeli—working in the structuralist tradition. More precisely, these models need to be enriched—synthesized—with ideas advanced by language theorists working outside the Saussurean paradigm. Martin Cortazzi (1993, 87–90) identifies five basic concerns shared by structuralist narratologists. First, structuralist models define narrative as an autonomous object of study, a level or mode of semantic organization with specifiable rules and determinate patterns (Barthes 1977b; Pavel 1985b; G. Prince 1973; Todorov 1968). Second, they postulate a distinction between story and discourse, between the *what* of a narrative and the *way* those basic story materials are presented or linearized in a given stretch of narrative discourse (Chatman 1978; Rimmon-Kenan 1983). Third, they distinguish between deep and surface narrative structures, sometimes from a transformational or quasi-transformational perspective (Pavel 1976; G. Prince 1973, 1980a). Fourth, they redescribe characters as narrative actants, agents that fill a limited, typifiable number of paradigmatic slots or participatory roles in the syntagmatic unfolding of a narrative (Barthes 1977b; Coste 1989; Greimas 1983 and 1987; cf. Kafalenos 1995, 1997). And finally they focus on larger sequences, combinations, and hierarchies of narrative units (Barthes 1977b; Todorov 1969). In all facets of this research program, the systematically describable properties of the narrative message remained underexplored. It is my purpose here, in part, to work toward reversing that trend. Based on ghost stories elicited during a sociolinguistic interview, my essay outlines a (socio)linguistically enriched model for narrative analysis. Along the way, I propose new research strategies for the study of narrative competence and its ingredients. My proposal entails not a jettisoning of all things narratological but a recontextualization of classical theories of narrative, an exploration of just what sorts of narrative phenomena the structuralist approach can and cannot help us describe and explain.

My overarching claim is that narratology was hampered not only by its excessive reliance on Saussurean theories but also by its failure to accommodate developments being advanced by Anglo-American researchers (Herman 1995; Pavel 1989), particularly in the areas of pragmatics, discourse analysis, and (for example, interactional) sociolinguistics. These subfields of linguistics are especially important when it comes to studying units of language beyond the sentence. What is more, because narratologists have devoted most of their attention to literary narratives up to now (see, however, Fludernik 1996b, 53–91), narratology has remained insufficiently grounded in natural-language data, the empirical methods designed to record and analyze such data (Milroy 1987), and the theoretical models used to interpret the data and integrate them with other sociocultural practices. Still tied to structuralist taxonomies, narratology has not yet come to terms with the communicative functions of stories in conversational and other discourse contexts. Nonetheless, it must also be pointed out that some of the ideas developed by narratologists can be integrated with (socio)linguistic models to provide new insights into the way stories facilitate communication.

Put briefly, the basic premise of the early narratologists—the premise that linguistics can throw light on narrative discourse—deserves further exploration. Note that the same insight informs a tradition of narrative analysis that is perhaps still more familiar to linguists than to narrative theorists at large. I am referring to William Labov and Joshua Waletzky's sociolinguistic model for narrative analysis. This model divides stories into a six-part structure. There is the Abstract, a brief preparatory statement encapsulating the point of the story. There is the Orientation, a section of the narrative in which the story's time, place, participants, and context are identified. There is the Complication, a section comprising the main body of narrative clauses, centering on some complicating action in the story. There is the Evaluation, which is not necessarily a discrete section of the story but rather "the means used by the narrator to indicate the point of the narrative, its raison d'être: why it was told, and what the narrator is getting at" (Labov 1972, 366). There is the Resolution, a section that describes what finally happened in the story. And lastly there is the Coda, a section found at the end of the story signaling that the narrative is in fact finished and "returning the verbal perspective to the present moment" (Labov and Waletzky 1967, 39). (See Labov 1972, 362–70; Labov and Waletzky 1967, 32–41, for further details.) This model has proven widely influential in the linguistic literature, as can be seen in the work of narrative analysts such as Nessa Wolfson (1982), Teun A. van Dijk (1988), Livia Polanyi (1989), Charlotte Linde (1993), and Deborah Schiffrin (1994). Arguably, though, what I shall call the Labovian model (for short) can gain in both descriptive and explanatory adequacy if it is enriched with research tools developed at first under the auspices of narratology.[2] I shall focus on two such methodological tools here, both of them useful for analyzing how stories unfold as patterned sequences of referring expressions (cf. Schiffrin 1994, 203–27). The first tool is the distinction between story and discourse; the second is the redescription of certain entities in the story world as narrative actants. Meanwhile, these narratological ideas need to be integrated with the linguistic and sociolinguistic traditions from which the Labovian model emerged. This merging of theories and methodologies suggests that any analysis of narrative structure must be complemented by an account of how storytellers communicate. If structuralist models throw light on aspects of narrative form, Labov's and other linguists' theories illuminate aspects of narrative functioning. At issue, in the latter instance, is the interactional work done by narrative messages yet neglected, up to now, by classical narratology.

Section 2.1 offers a somewhat more detailed review of the story/discourse distinction and the idea of narrative actants, and discusses some of the implications of the narratological concepts. In the following section, I first provide background information on two ghost stories elicited during a sociolinguistic interview with a resident of Robeson County, North Carolina. (A complete transcription of the two stories is given as an appendix.) I then (3.1) draw on ideas and methods taken from conversation analysis and interactional sociolinguistics to sketch a preliminary account of the discourse contexts embedding the ghost stories. Sections 4 and 5 use the story/discourse distinction and the idea of narrative actants, respectively, to analyze features of the two ghost stories themselves. Both of these sections discuss ways in which narratological ideas can help recontextualize and enhance the Labovian approach to narrative analysis. In turn, section 6 again draws on interactional sociolinguistics to reframe the structuralist approach to narrative analysis—to work toward a *socio*narratological characterization of stories as speech events both shaped by and shaping communicative practice. Socionarratology is construed here as one branch of narrative analysis in its postclassical setting, its life after structuralism. Section 7 concludes the paper by indicating how the research hypotheses outlined here might be used to isolate at least some of the ingredients of narrative competence. At stake are aspects of communicative competence required to create and understand stories in a variety of discourse contexts.

2.1 The two main narratological ideas under consideration, then, are the story/discourse distinction and the concept of narrative actants. Distinguishing between story and discourse, between the matter being told and the manner of its telling, suggests that a narrative can be modeled as a rich but finite set of referential options. Or rather, a story consists of a set of referring expressions whose members can take on, according to constraints that remain yet to be specified, different kinds of narrative patterning, as well as different sorts of phonological, morphosyntactic, syntactic, and lexical properties. The "same" story can be told in a variety of ways, the events narrated in alternative orders, told more or less repetitively and at a slower or faster pace. Put otherwise, a story can be variably instantiated through a range of linguistic features pertaining to narrative discourse. Thus, differentiating between story and discourse helps point up affinities between narrative analysis and variationist models in sociolinguistics, which likewise "try to discover patterns in the distribution of alternative ways of saying the same thing, i.e. the social and linguistic constraints on linguistic variation" (Schiffrin 1994, 287; cf. J. K. Chambers 1995, 30–32; Wolfram and Schilling-Estes 1998). What is more, redescribing members of the story world as actants helps account for speakers' intuitions about narrative as a particular genre of discourse (Virtanen 1992), as opposed to other discourse genres like lists, service encounters, syllogistic arguments, and so on. A narrative is not just a concatenation of discrete events; to be processed as narrative, event-strings must also involve a specific configuration of participants or actants whose doings conform to known behavioral paradigms. Such paradigms have been described by cognitive scientists as knowledge representations that store groupings of actions required to perform particular tasks. These representations allow processors to make predictions and inferences about emergent experiences in terms of experiences already undergone (Schank and Abelson 1977, 1–64; Tannen 1993; cf. Goffman 1974; Herman 1997a, unpubl. ms). My analysis suggests that, likewise, storytellers draw on actantial paradigms as a resource to promote inferences about entities populating the narrated world. In stories, strings of events are encoded in sequences of clauses or sentences. The idea of actants may generate a heuristic that explains how certain expressions are tagged as coreferential across such verbal sequences — and across the event-strings they encode. Minimally, actantial paradigms are devices used to establish and maintain discourse coherence in stories. More than this, though, studying inferences about actants may also help reveal just what stories *are*.

3. Two Ghost Stories: A Preliminary Analysis of Their Discourse Contexts

This essay constitutes part of an ongoing study of ghost stories told in three of the vernacular varieties of English found in North Carolina and associated with three distinct cultural regions of the state. The data for the present analysis are taken from an interview with an eighty-one-year-old female resident (hereafter identified as LL) of Robeson County, which is located in the coastal plains of North Carolina, and which contains zones of contact between language varieties spoken by African Americans, Anglo Americans and Lumbee Indians. (Other storytellers in the larger study include speakers of language varieties found in Appalachia, a region located in the mountainous western part of North Carolina, and in the Outer Banks region located in the state's eastern coastal area, in particular the quasi-isolated island community of Ocracoke Island.) Informants from all these regions sometimes told ghost stories during conversational interviews designed to gather data about their dialects; recordings and transcripts of the interviews are part of a larger collection of tape-recorded interviews housed at the William C. Friday Linguistics Lab at North Carolina State University.

The choice of this narrative subgenre for my study was not accidental. For one thing, focusing on ghost stories provides an analytic constant to measure the effects of language variation on a particular kind of story. At issue is the way linguistic variables bear on a story type that features certain recurrent topics, analogous settings, shared strategies for creating narrative suspense, and so on. As only one installment of a larger study, however, this essay will not directly address the problem of identifying ghost-story constants across language varieties.[3] More germane to the present analysis, ghost stories as a narrative subgenre yield insights into the way narrative in general unfolds as a sequence of referring expressions matched to strings of events in the story world. Because they orient themselves around highly fugitive experiences — because they are about entities and events that are by their very nature hard to locate, identify, and describe in the narrated world — ghost stories provide an important test case for understanding the referential strategies at work in narrative discourse at large.

3.1 In order to facilitate the subsequent analysis, I reproduce in the appendix to this essay two ghost stories told by LL during a sociolinguistic interview. The primary interviewer will be identified throughout as NSE; a second interviewer was present during the interview but did not play an active role during the segment of the interview under examination. (Transcription conventions, which are adapted from Deborah Tannen [1993], are also included in the appendix. For convenience of reference I have listed clauses of narratives 1 and 2 on separate lines and then used letters to label the lines.) At this point, conversation-analytic and interactional sociolinguistic models can be used to offer a preliminary description of the discourse contexts in which LL (collaboratively) produced the two ghost stories under study.

Note that both of the ghost stories were prompted by questions addressed to LL by the primary interviewer, NSE. In both cases, the initial question-answer adjacency pairs clear the way for an extended turn by LL. Narratives represent abnormally long turns at talk (Cortazzi 1993, 28) and the "pre-sequences" that initiate both stories can be seen as invitations to LL to occupy the floor as long as the telling of the ghost stories (or "sequences") requires. Even so, in the pre-sequence that leads up to the first narrative, notice that LL is careful to *propose* to tell the story (*let me tell you this*) before engaging in her extended narrative turn. By means of this narrative proposal, LL double-checks with her interlocutors whether she is in fact entitled to occupy the conversational floor for what will be a noticeably long turn. Even the best storytellers adhere to conversational protocol: they make sure a narratively organized turn is appropriate for a particular slot in the ongoing discourse. Then, at the beginning of the second story, LL uses the discourse marker *well* to initiate her extended narrative turn. Conversation analysts have observed that, as a turn-initiator, *well* reveals little about the construction and/or length of the turn it introduces (Schiffrin 1987, 102; Sacks, Schegloff and Jefferson 1974). Schiffrin (1987) has argued, however, that "*well* is a response marker which anchors its user in an interaction when an upcoming contribution is not fully consonant with prior coherence options" (102–3). In other words, respondents are apt to use *well* when unsure whether they can meet a conversational demand for a response; specifically, *well* marks a respondent's uncertainty over the ideational content of his or her response—whether it fits the response-options opened by a prior question (Schiffrin 1987, 114; cf. Schiffrin 1985). In this sense, LL's use of *well* again represents a more or less tentative proposal to take a (long) turn at talk—a turn whose relevance or appropriateness to the ongoing exchange she is not exactly convinced. But the tentativeness encoded in the discourse maker *well* is offset by what can be construed as a floor-clearing strategy: namely, the sentence-final intonation at the end of line (a) in narrative 2 (*there's one night here*). This discourse unit can be glossed as "I am going to tell you a story about what happened one night not too long ago, so listen up!"

Finally, note also that the interviewer's prompts in the narrative pre-sequences remove certain conversational burdens from LL. One such burden is the necessity of marking off events and details pertaining to the story world from those pertaining to the surrounding conversational context. More precisely, the interviewer and LL jointly facilitate what cognitive narrative theorists have termed a shift of deictic centers. Deictic terms such as *here* and *now* refer to a specific conceptual location; but in the case of narratives, "the deictic center often shifts from the environmental situation in which the [telling of the story] is encountered, to a locus within a mental model representing the world of the discourse [i.e., the story world]" (Segal 1995a, 15; cf. Ryan 1991, 13–30). The interviewer as much as LL sets the stage for the production of a tale about a not-immediately-accessible world filled with ghosts—a world located in the past, but displaying demonstrable (and potentially scary!) connections to the present. After all, even though LL distances the narrated world from the world of the present by remarking that *You don't hear /of/ boogers and things now, like you used to*,[4] it is LL, the present narrator, who experienced the supernatural occurrences recounted in her stories.

4. Referring Sequences, the Story/Discourse Distinction, and Iterative Narration

Given the precedent set by Labov and Waletzky, it is fairly noncontroversial to characterize stories as sequences of referring expressions. Thus Labov influentially defined narrative as "one method of recapitulating past experience by matching a verbal sequence of clauses to the sequence of events which (it is inferred) actually occurred" (1972, 359–60; cf. Labov and Waletzky 1967, 20–21). Yet Labov goes on to distinguish between two different functions of narrative: the referential and the evaluative function (Labov 1972, 370; Labov and Waletzky 1967, 13). *Prima facie,* at least, it seems that these two functions can be interdefined: any departure from the linear sequencing of events in a series of (independent) clauses constitutes not storytelling proper, but rather an evaluative comment on the story being told, an attempt to signal the "point" of the narrative itself (Labov 1972, 371ff.).[5] True, the basic underlying form of all stories is the primary sequence, which encodes temporal relationships of the sort *a*-then-*b*—as opposed to relationships such as "*a*-and at the same time-*b* or *a*-and now as I think back on it-*b*" (Labov and Waletzky 1967, 30–32). More technically, clauses can be categorized as *narrative* if and only if "a change in their order will result in a change in the temporal sequence of the original semantic interpretation" (Labov 1972, 360–61). Other kinds of clauses—differentiated by the breadth of their "displacement sets" (Labov and Waletzky 1967, 21–28) or the degree to which they can be transposed across stretches of the discourse—are to be categorized as *free* and *restricted* clauses instead. Yet a narrative consisting only of narrative clauses is atypical. More than that, a story "may carry out the referential function perfectly [by telling that first *a* and then *b* happened], and yet seem difficult to understand. Such a narrative lacks significance: it has no point. . . . A simple sequence of complication and result does not indicate to the listener the relative importance of [certain] events or help him distinguish complication from resolution. We also find that in narratives without a point it is difficult to distinguish the complicating action from the result" (Labov and Waletzky 1967, 33, 35).

This is where evaluation comes into play. If the *a*-then-*b* relationship is what makes a story a story, it does not suffice to make it an effective, a memorable, or even an intelligible story. *Evaluation* designates a class of features, ranging from the macrostructural organization of the narrative to the syntactic elaboration of individual clauses, by virtue of which storytellers purposely deviate from the order of the primary sequence. Such deviations signal the tellability of events, why they are worth narrating at all (Labov 1972, 370). In their 1967 essay, Labov and Waletzky focused mainly on "the placement of evaluative clauses in an 'evaluation section' which suspended the narrative at a crucial point"; in 1972 Labov broadened the investigation to include narrative syntax (Labov 1972, 355). The later analysis hinges on the assumption that "[s]ince syntactic complexity is relatively rare in narrative, it must have a marked effect when it does occur" (Labov 1972, 378). Specifically, by postulating that narrative syntax is inherently linear and simple, the analyst can label as evaluative rather than narrative a great many of the linguistic resources found in "ordinary conversation." These resources include modals, negatives, auxiliary verbs, and embedded constructions (Labov 1972, 377–78).[6]

Note, here, that there are two ways of looking at the relation between reference and evaluation in narrative, and that the Labovian approach tries to have it both ways. On the one hand, the evaluative function can be indexed to any feature (or structural unit) of the narrative that marks a departure from the primary sequence, which is used in turn to refer to events comprising the narrated world. We would then characterize non-indicative verbal moods, negatives, and other grammatical devices as means for evaluation *rather than* as ways of referring to the story world itself. Likewise the evaluation section of a story would mark the suspension of narrative reference proper. On the other hand, the evaluative function can be described as a kind of supersegmental feature of narrative discourse, somewhat like the intonational contours of sentences. From this perspective, evaluation is a property that can neither be located in nor dissociated from any one aspect or unit of narrative structure, but that intermittently fuses itself with narrative form to help signal the overall point of the story. We might then hold that "[t]he evaluation of the narrative forms a secondary structure which is concentrated in the evaluation section but may be found in various forms throughout the narrative. . . . [T]hat *penetration* is accomplished through the internal structure of narrative clauses as well as the ordering of those clauses" (Labov 1972, 369–70; my emphasis). On this latter view, evaluation may be present not just "as lexical or phrasal modification of a narrative clause," but may "itself [be] a narrative clause, or coincide with the last narrative clause" (Labov and Waletzky 1967, 37). But if evaluation can *be* a narrative clause, if the narrative clause itself is as suited for evaluation as it is for reference, then the supposed simplicity of narrative syntax cannot be used as a criterion for distinguishing between features with a referential function and those with an evaluative function. Indeed, we can no longer talk about *narrative* syntax at all, as if there were, by contrast, other kinds of syntactic structure that cannot be used to build up narrative reference but only to signal why such reference is worth building up.

From a narratological perspective, any attempt to segregate reference and evaluation is counterintuitive, for two, interrelated reasons. For one thing, it undermines the distinction, more or less axiomatic to narratology, between story and discourse — between the causally and chronologically ordered events of a story and the various discourse features that constitute strategies for (re)presenting those events.[7] In order to illustrate this first point, I shall focus in this section on LL's use of non-indicative verbal moods to construct (and not merely evaluate) the story worlds she evokes. Second, it is misguided to attempt to locate the property of "being a narrative" in a particular aspect of verbal structure — that is, the "narrative clause" — and then to assign to other formal features the property of "being an evaluation." Arguably, no linguistic feature or set of features is criterial for narrative (or for evaluation). What makes a story a story cannot be ascribed to narrative form alone, but rather arises from the interplay between the semantic content of the narrative; the formal features of the discourse through which such narrated content manifests itself; and the kinds of inferences promoted via this interplay of form and content in particular discourse contexts. I shall outline some research hypotheses for an integrated, socionarratological approach of this sort — an approach that situates stories within a constellation of cognitive, linguistic, and contextual factors — when I turn to the idea of narrative actants in section 5 and then discuss narrative as an interactional achievement in section 6.

4.1. First, though, there is the issue of non-indicative verbal moods as a resource for story-world construction. It is true that, by and large, narrative is factive in nature; non- or anti-factive constructions involving the subjunctive mood and encoding conditional or hypothetical propositions (Leech 1987, 112–29) seem to run against the grain of narrative as a discourse genre. Narratives characteristically describe, from a stance of certainty and authoritativeness, singular past states and events. There is however some evidence suggesting that certainty may be a necessary feature of certain story genres though not of others (Herman 1994a; Margolin's contribution to this volume; G. Prince 1988). A tale of the supernatural is perhaps less apt to consist of factive reports than your average news story. What is more, in this connection it is crucial to separate out the aspectual from the evidential (Chafe and Nichols 1986) functions of modals in stories. Modals can serve not just to encode degrees of certainty concerning narrated events, but also as sources of aspectual information, and in particular information about habitual and/or ongoing activities as opposed to discrete, punctual ones. As we shall see, to exclude the durative/imperfective aspect from the province of narrative, to consign it to the realm of evaluation, is not only narratologically suspect; it also contradicts the narrative practice of storytellers like LL. In what follows I shall examine LL's use of non-indicative verbal moods in lines (b), (p), (q), (r), and (s) of narrative 1, and again in lines (f), (g), (j), (k), (m), and (x) of narrative 2. From a narratological standpoint, even a brief analysis of these modal constructions suggests problems with Labov's proposition that "[c]lauses containing *used to, would,* and the *general present* [e.g., *That really makes you feel alive*] are not narrative clauses and cannot support a narrative" (1972, 361–62).

One of the more important consequences of the narratological distinction between story and discourse is that it shows how storytellers exploit different ratios between story time and discourse time. For example, a chronological sequence ABC can be told (through a flashback) as BAC or (through a flashforward) as ACB. Again, the discourse can proceed at a rate faster or slower than that of the story. A narrative summary, for instance, abbreviates happenings in the story world; by contrast, a narrative pause represents a hiatus in the action while the narrator comments on the narrated world, and in a narrative scene events are represented at a pace that iconically matches their "real time" speed. Or again—and more significant for the present analysis— events in the story world can be narrated with different sorts of *frequency.* Thus Gérard Genette (1980, 113–60; cf. Rimmon-Kenan 1983, 56–58) differentiates between three types of narrative frequency: singulative, or telling once what happened once; repetitive, or telling *n* times what happened once; and iterative, or telling once what happened *n* times. As LL's ghost stories suggest, modal constructions facilitate iterative reports of events in the narrated world. Thus LL uses modal constructions in both narratives 1 and 2 not primarily as evaluative devices but rather as a linguistic resource for iterative narration— for capsule, concise recountings of nonsingular states and durative events in the story world. Or rather, LL's use of iterative reports suggests a superimposition of referential and evaluative motives; evaluation is not a departure from reference to the story world but part of the very process by which referring sequences are narratively constructed.

For example, in line (b) of narrative 1, part of the narrative Abstract, LL uses a modal (*it'd*) to recount the repeated floatings-upward of the "jack-o-lanterns" in the past world that constitutes the deictic center of her story:

(b)   and ah, it'd go up..

It is difficult to see how this modal construction could be construed as exclusively or even primarily an evaluative device; rather, it *refers to* one segment of the event-string underlying the narrative as a whole: that segment composed of the not precisely calculable, eerily floating movements of these otherworldly creatures LL saw back before her sister Mandy died. Further, notice the highly strategic use of non-indicative moods in lines (p) through (s):

(p) There'd be so many to go up..

(q) and so many to come down.

(r) They'd go up..

(s) and some would come down.

Here a grammatical form encoding a durative aspectual type is paired with a mode of narration intermediate between the singulative[8] and the iterative. The modals (and, in line (q), the infinitive construction) indicate happenings that recur indefinitely many times in the narrated world — happenings that LL recounts, however, exactly twice. The events told in this section of narrative 1 constitute the crux of the narrative, its Complication. Given the importance of this narrative segment, the modals and repeated clauses perform *a jointly referential and evaluative function*. They help auditors identify iterated occurrences in the story world, and they also emphasize the proportionately greater significance of these occurrences vis-à-vis the rest of the narrative. Thus, whereas the Labovian model sometimes suggests that reference and evaluation in stories should be analyzed into discrete structures and functions, lines (p) through (s) of narrative 1 demonstrate that both aspects of stories are commonly layered or intertwined in narrative practice.

Along the same lines, consider the iterative reports found in narrative 2. For example, lines (f), (g), (k), and (m), part of the Orientation section of the narrative, contain non-indicative verbal moods that enable LL to narrate past, recurrent moonshining activities on the part of her (then) husband. These activities attach to the event-string that includes, later in the story (lines (t) through (aa)), Harvey Bullard's spooky but pretty whistling *in absentia*. The constructions at issue include a *used to* construction in line (f), combining a past tense marking and a nondiscrete aspectual type in a form technically known as usitative,[9] and three modals of the form *he'd*. Again, it is difficult to construe such grammatical devices, and the iterative reports they make possible, as exclusively or even mainly evaluative in nature. To the contrary: it is arguable that, subverting the received wisdom about narrative logic (cf. Polanyi 1989, 20–30), the *dominant* aspectual type found in narrative 2 is durative rather than discrete. True, lines (a) and (p) indicate that the narrated action took place on *one* moonshiny night; but throughout the story most of the narration is iterative, and in lines (x) through (aa), LL hesitates between an iterative and singulative report of the ghostly whistling itself. Even though her interlocutors are encouraged to assume that Harvey Bullard whistled only on this one occasion on this one night about four years ago (line (b)), LL begins line (x) as an iterative report implying indefinitely many occurrences of the whistling. It is as if LL, despite her stated storytelling intentions, has trouble identifying the supernatural whistling as a discrete event or finite group of events within the narrated world she is in the process of creating:

(x) It'd say.. had the whistlinest.. voice
(y) "I'll see you again.
(z) I'll see you again.
(aa) I'll see you again."

As with lines (p) through (s) of narrative 1, analyzed above, the repeated clauses combined with the modal construction in line (x) create a style of narration intermediate between the iterative and the singulative. Further, just as in narrative 1, in narrative 2 LL's recounting of supernatural activity exploits the capacity of narrative discourse to be jointly (and simultaneously) referential and evaluative. The story of the whistling combines an emphasis on the relative significance of the activity with a grammatical encoding of its elusiveness. LL's ambiguously iterative and/or singulative reports suggest the ghost's indefinite extension in both mental and physical space.

In this section, I have suggested that the narratological distinction between story and discourse—a distinction that yields a typology of narrative modes based on the criterion of frequency—gives analysts an alternative descriptive vocabulary. One of my overarching points has been that the different kinds of narrative frequency described by narratologists themselves carry different sorts of evaluative weighting. From a socionarratological standpoint, however, such evaluative effects are built into referring sequences in stories; they are not interruptions or disruptions of properly narrative sequences. For example, repetitive narration can reinforce the general significance or effect of an otherwise localized event (as in, say, a narrative about a past trauma), while iterative narration can highlight the interconnectedness of events otherwise perceived as noncontiguous or disanalogous. But by the same token, as LL's narratives show, modal constructions (among other grammatical devices enabling iterative reports) are far from being *just* evaluative devices, tacked on to the referring sequences proper. Rather, they facilitate the rapid but also nuanced construction of story worlds. Iterative reports allow narrative discourse to unfold at minimal "conversational cost"; telling once what happened n times means that the storyteller need not exert as much effort in holding the floor as would be required to narrate those same events in the singulative mode. At the same time, iterative narration may be an especially important resource for ghost stories as a narrative subgenre—a subgenre in which storytellers need to signal the recurrent but not easily described manifestations of supernatural agents and events. The uncertain contours and fluctuating occupants of the supernatural domain prove uniquely resistant to a single, definitive telling. (As LL puts it in line (x) of narrative 1, *we ain't supposed to know God's work.*) Eventually, then, a socionarratological approach may have to explore whether different story genres involve different distributions of referential and evaluative effects across particular classes of discourse features, including but not limited to non-indicative verbal moods.

5. Actants and Narrative Inferencing

As mentioned in the previous section, there is a second basic problem with the Labovian model—or at least with some of the ways in which that model has been formulated. This second problem is related to the first: that is, the overrestrictive inventory of the kinds of linguistic resources that can be used to build up referring sequences in stories. The second problem has to do with the attempt to make a particular aspect of verbal structure—namely, the "narrative clause"—criterial for narrative itself. By contrast, on the integrative approach being outlined here, what makes a story a story does not depend solely on particular discourse features of narratives. Rather, narrative must be situated at the intersection of cognitive, linguistic, and contextual factors. The hallmark of narratively organized discourse is that it promotes a structured set of inferences about a sequence of actions involving a specific configuration of characters or participants. Here a second narratological idea, the idea of narrative actants, can help recontextualize an approach too narrowly focused on the narrative clause as definitive of stories. For the purposes of the present analysis, my comments on this second narratological concept will have to be more exploratory than exhaustive.[10] But the advantage of talking about actants and actantial or behavioral paradigms is this: It enables the analyst to anchor stories in cognitive and sociocultural contexts (see below, section 6), rather than viewing narratives as formal structures that preexist the communicative situations in which they cue a variety of inferencing strategies.

In his attempt to obtain tape-recordings of extended, maximally casual speech, Labov (1972) focused on "*narratives of personal experience,* in which the speaker becomes deeply involved in rehearsing or even reliving events of his past" (354). Given this focus, it is all the more peculiar that the concept of narrative character or agent remains, in effect, a primitive, undefined term in the Labovian scheme. In the narratological tradition, by contrast, narrative agents have long been an object of inquiry. Structuralist narratologists, interested in formulating a "grammar" of narrative, wanted to shift attention from characters as "beings" to characters as regularly recurring, typifiable "participants" in the syntagmatic unfolding of the narrated action (Barthes 1977b, 106; cf. Herman, forthcoming). Thus Propp (1968[1928]) initially subsumed characters under spheres of action articulated into seven general roles, from villain and donor to hero and helper (Rimmon-Kenan 1983, 34). A.-J. Greimas (1983, 202–6) then went on to redescribe characters as actants. Actants can be categorized into the six possible general roles (sender, object, receiver, helper, subject, opponent) assumed by particular actors in a given narrative situation. On this model, an actant can be realized by several actors, and conversely an actor can encompass more than one actantial role (Coste 1989, 134–35; Rimmon-Kenan 1983, 35). For instance, in narrative 2, Harvey Bullard's whistling ghost is a sender and possibly also a helper (the whistling is the prettiest that LL has ever heard); but then again, as the "toten" of a policeman who has tried to crack down on moonshining, the ghost also represents an old opponent. In turn, the actantial role of opponent is arguably split between the ghost and LL's husband, whom LL describes somewhat contemptuously in line (f) as a person who *used to fool with liquor* and who therefore probably caused LL herself a lot of trouble.

Classical models for understanding narrative actants are not without problems of their own. For one thing, they fail to specify any uniformly reproducible procedure for matching actantial roles with this or that segment of narrative discourse (Hendricks 1967, 43ff.). Too much is left to the intuitions of the individual analyst. Yet the concept of actants has prompted later researchers to argue that characters in a narrative can be viewed as constructs modeled on processors' pre-stored expectations about human beings and human behavior (Fludernik 1996b, 44; Rimmon-Kenan 1983, 33; cf. Margolin 1986; Pavel 1985b; Ryan 1991, 201–232). Narrative actants, in other words, can be characterized as the output of inferences triggered by grammatical cues in stories; those inferences are grounded in behavioral paradigms that form part of the broader cognitive repertoire of storytellers and their audiences — of language-users generally.[11] A cognitive approach to narrative actants might prove especially fruitful in concert with an analysis of the information status (Firbas 1964; McKoon et al. 1993; E. Prince 1981, 1992) of discourse entities in stories.

Narrators encode assumptions about the information status of story referents by making choices between morphosyntactic features — definite versus indefinite noun phrases, pro-forms (and zero anaphora) versus noun phrases. The more accessible or "given" an entity, the more readily will it be referred to and updated by way of a pronoun as opposed to a noun phrase, or a definite as opposed to an indefinite article. Less accessible or "new" information will typically be introduced by way of indefinite articles and full noun phrases. Thus, in narrative 2, LL introduces Harvey Bullard as *a man* in line (d) and then, having established reference to this new discourse item with an indefinite article, she uses the pronoun *he* in line (e) to refer to the already given entity. The same pattern holds for lines (f) through (k), where LL picks out another new entity with the noun phrase *my..husband* and then gives additional information about this now accessible referent by way of seven constructions involving the pro-form *he:*

(f) Well../my ol'/.. my..husband he used to fool with liquor.
(g) And ah..he'd have it back yonder in there that old graveyard.
(h) Now he was a man
(i) he wasn't a-scared of a booger nor nobody else.
(j) And 'cause he'd..when he'd..runned his liquor
(k) He'd hide /it/ in that old graveyard back yonder.

In line (l), however, when LL wants to refocus her story on the actions of Harvey Bullard, she again refers to the policeman by his full name. This facilitates reference to a discourse entity whose relative accessibility had been compromised (or at least interrupted) by the extended account of LL's husband's activities in lines (f) through (k).

But now consider lines (t) through (x) and also lines (bb) through (jj):

(t) But anyway.. I's a-laying in my room that bright shiny night,
(u) and the baby was in his trailer out there.
(v) That was before Harvey died.
(w) And uh..Honey..I heared as pretty a whistling— as I ever heared in my life.
(x) It'd say..had the whistlinest..voice

....

(bb) And I got up
(cc) and I looked out of the window,
(dd) I didn't see a soul in the God Almighty's world.
(ee) And Harvey Bullard at that time he was in..at Lumberton in the hospital low down..
(ff) looking for the last of /it/.
(gg) And ah..that..that next evening come.
(hh) I heared about him ah..a-passing away.
(ii) And that was his..his voice—
(jj) that had been down yonder where my old man was a-making liquor

As this portion of the narrative sequence proceeds, it retroactively triggers a chain of inferences about which expressions in the sequence are coreferential. Arguably, although considerations of information status play a role in the fashioning of this inferential chain, such considerations do not suffice to explain how the inferencing works. Rather, LL draws on shared behavioral paradigms to tag the expressions as coreferential—to index them as a cumulative series of references to a single narrative actant, that is, Harvey Bullard.

In the sequence at issue, LL twice mentions Harvey Bullard by name, in lines (v) and (ee). Note how the first mention of the policeman is consistent with LL's attempt to create narrative suspense. LL's choice of an indefinite article for *a whistling* in line (w) introduces that whistling as a new discourse entity or actant, ostensibly dissociating the whistling from Harvey, mentioned in the previous line. (For all LL's listeners know at this point, the mention of Harvey's name in line (v) might have been a vehicle for narrative Orientation, helping establish the exact time line for the narrated events, as opposed to the first mention of an entity followed up by a sequence of next mentions.) As the sequence goes on, however, Harvey is reattached to the event-string from which LL has only temporarily distanced him, for purposes of suspense. In moving from line (dd) to line (ee), LL invites her auditors to infer that Harvey is the "soul" that she could not see but only hear; however, it is not until lines (hh) through (jj) that LL herself offers a solution to the enigma of the whistling totem. The use of pronoun *him* in line (hh) marks the return of Harvey to the main focus of the discourse; this shift in information status coincides with the retrospective interpretation (lines (ii) and (jj)) of Harvey as the ghostly actant responsible for the long-distance whistling. In fact, Harvey's whistling indicates that the arm of the law is very long indeed, stretching perhaps into the next world!

My larger point, however, is that the shifts in the information status of discourse entities, as encoded in the morphosyntactic profile of the sequence, do not suffice to attach the predicate "whistling" to the discourse item "Harvey Bullard." Only when that item is interpreted as an *actant* can the relevant predicate be attached to it. Put otherwise, only because of general, cognitively based background knowledge about human agency can listeners use grammatical cues to construct a discourse model (Webber 1979; cf. Grosz and Sidner 1986; McKoon et al. 1993) in which the expressions *a whistling* and *Harvey Bullard* pick out the same entity. If pronoun- and article-choices encode assumptions that storytellers make about the relative givenness or accessibility of story referents; and if these same features are used by story recipients to build a discourse model for understanding the narrative; nonetheless, other sorts of processing skills are needed to organize story referents into a narratively structured whole, involving participants in a sequence of causally and chronologically ordered actions. The ordered distribution of referring expressions in a discourse may allow listeners and interlocutors to track items being referred to. But inferences that some of those referents are in turn actants help constitute a stretch of discourse *as* a narrative in the first place.

Note, however, that part of the uniqueness of ghost stories as a narrative subgenre derives from their use of actantial paradigms whose relevance and applicability the stories simultaneously place in question. Ghostly behavior by definition does not exactly match general expectations about human behavior; that is one of the main reasons for telling supernatural tales. LL exploits this generic feature of ghost stories when she delays attributing the mysterious whistling to the policeman—or for that matter to any *soul in the God Almighty's world* (line dd). Interpreters are cognitively predisposed to ascribe the whistling to some sort of agent. LL uses that predisposition first as a means to build narrative suspense, and then to modify and enrich expectations about the world itself. For in constructing her story world, LL creates what some narrative theorists have called a stratified or "salient" ontology (Pavel 1986, 61–64), in which different sorts of things are possible in different domains of the world being recounted. In LL's narrated world—and by implication sometimes and in some regions of the world at large—it is possible for whistling to be heard even when the whistler is miles away, dying or already dead.

6. Narrative as an Interactional Achievement

Yet it is important to keep in mind that cognitive predispositions, and their manipulation by skillful storytellers such as LL, do not exist in a sociocultural vacuum. Rather, a third set of factors plays a crucial role in narrative communication. These factors explain how the form of a narrative can trigger inferential chains on the basis of actantial paradigms. Here socionarratology might gain inspiration from the field of interactional sociolinguistics, where this third set of factors has been studied by way of analytic constructs that include *contextualization cues, contextualization conventions,* and *conversational inferences* (Gumperz 1982, 130–71; cf. Scollon and Scollon 1995, 50–73; Tannen 1993). According to this research tradition, "Conversationalists . . . rely on indirect inferences which build on background assumptions about context, interactive goals and interpersonal relations to derive frames in terms of which they can interpret what is going on" (Gumperz 1982, 2). In consequence, communication is made possible by metacommunicative devices or "metamessages" (Scollon and Scollon 1995, 67), also called contextualization cues; such cues are used by discourse participants to signal what sorts of contextual knowledge should be drawn on to frame the ongoing conversational interaction. In cases of mis-communication, contextualization cues fail to elicit the sorts of background knowledge needed to support conversational inferences that a speaker intends his or her interlocutor(s) to make. In general, contextualization cues allow interlocutors to assimilate a given interaction to a particular *activity type;* in turn, the activity type, as "the basic socially significant unit of interaction in terms of which meaning is assessed," does not itself "determine meaning but simply constrains interpretations by channelling inferences so as to *foreground* or make relevant certain aspects of background knowledge and to underplay others" (Gumperz 1982, 130–31).

Crucially, a subset of activity types is the *speech event,* which can be defined as a unit of verbal behavior bounded in time and space; kinds of speech events, including those called stories, are labels for the complex sets of norms in terms of which interlocutors evaluate one another's verbal behavior (Gumperz 1982, 165). Thus LL's ghost stories are themselves bounded by another, overarching speech event — namely, the sociolinguistic interview. Interviews involve differ-ent sorts of turn-taking procedures, for example, than do speech events whose contextualization cues allow them to be identified as conversations between peers (cf. Milroy 1987, 41–51). Since the interview can embed other types of speech events, however, interviewers and interviewees constantly co-construct emergent interpretive frames for their ongoing verbal activity. Put otherwise, by means of multiple, sometimes overlapping contextualization cues, interview participants collaboratively shift from one sort of speech event to another — from the interview proper, to a joke, to some general comments about the weather or the corruption of politicians, to a ghost story or two. An integrative or socionarratological approach must therefore study a wide variety of contex-tualization cues; it must study, too, the ways in which these cues do or do not allow certain speech events to be labeled (and thus interpreted as) stories.

Of particular interest here are what might be called boundary cues. Such cues signal the termination of a non-narrative speech event and the initiation of a story (or vice versa). Indeed, using the ideas of speech events and con-textualization cues, I can now reformulate a point made in section 3.1 above. Earlier I said that the interviewer's prompts in the pre-sequences of narratives 1 and 2 remove some of the burden that falls on LL to demarcate her story world(s) from surrounding conversational contexts. But NSE's prompts can also be thought of as boundary cues of the sort just described: they help initi-ate a shift, negotiated by NSE and LL, from the current type of speech event (that is, the interview embedding narratives 1 and 2) to speech events governed by norms associated with stories in particular. LL does not immediately start in on her ghost stories. Rather, during the pre-sequences she seeks clarification on the kind of speech event 'that NSE is prompting her to co-create. For example, in the pre-sequence of narrative 1 LL at first adheres to turn-taking norms associated with the interview, producing a discourse unit that functions as a (positive) answer to NSE's question about totens:

> NSE: A ^toten~ Like do you know.. have you ever.. seen — a toten or heard..
> LL: Yeah Honey.. Lord yeah. ^Good Lord yeah.

Initially, that is, LL assumes that the current speech event will continue to be organized as a series of question-answer adjacency pairs, with first-turns being controlled by the interviewer. LL fashions a response that can be construed as fitting into the answer-slot of one question-answer adjacency pair among a series of such pairs. LL thus promotes the conversational inference that she is continuing to collaborate in the production of a speech event that can be labeled an interview and interpreted as such.

But note the repetitions marking LL's response to the question about totens. In effect, LL's repetitions provide at least two different sorts of contextualization cues at once. On the one hand, by repeating (versions of) the same phrase three times, LL gives NSE three chances to make the conversational inference that she is simply answering an interviewer's question and readying herself for NSE's next turn, which LL predicts to be another question. On the other hand, however, the intonational stress on the third repetition of her answer, phrased as ^*Good Lord yeah,* marks LL's response as a boundary cue. The stressed word that begins this clause signals that LL is proposing to initiate another type of speech event — specifically, a narrative — whose collaborative construction will be based on norms that differ from the ones underlying the sequencing of question-answer adjacency pairs in an interview. In other words, the intonational stress indicates that a new kind of speech event is possibly in the offing. A moment later, but before embarking on her story about jack-o-lanterns, LL asks NSE *Are you ever seen one^.* The heightened pitch of the last word of the clause, together with the syntax of the clause as a whole, marks this discourse unit as a question. And that question again furnishes overlapping contextualization cues. It gives NSE yet another chance to craft a response that would allow her to continue with the current, non- or prenarrative speech event; but it also serves as an additional boundary cue, allowing LL to monitor NSE's response to LL's proposal to initiate a different, properly narrative speech event.

In general, then, narratives can serve particular communicative purposes only on the basis of a process of negotiation between storytellers and their interlocutors. Such negotiation proceeds on the basis of contextualization cues, and especially boundary cues between different types of speech events. Like interactional sociolinguists, socionarratologists would do well to focus on discourse situations in which storytellers fail to provide the appropriate cues, as well as situations where those cues fail to generate the appropriate conversational inferences about narrative speech events in the making. (Though they introduce additional challenges for contextualizers, sociolinguistic interviews may be a convenient source of information about boundary cues in particular.) Stories, as we have seen, live on the strength of inferences of various sorts. The present section has suggested that analysts should ground these inferences not only in formal and cognitive factors, but also in factors associated with the use of narratives as a part of communicative practice. Viewed as an interactional achievement rather than manifestations of a code that preexists all communicative contexts, narrative messages must be studied as speech events that help shape the social interactions by which they are also shaped.

7. Conclusion: Ingredients of Narrative Competence

In this essay, I have argued that by synthesizing (socio)linguistic, narratological, and cognitive models, it is possible to overcome some of the limitations not only of the Labovian approach to stories, but also of classical narratological models oriented primarily around literary narratives. At the same time, the paper has attempted to isolate at least some of the ingredients of what might be termed narrative competence. At stake are three aspects of communicative competence (cf. Schiffrin 1994, 386–405) which are required to create and understand stories in a variety of discourse contexts. One crucial aspect of story design and comprehension is the ability to distinguish between singulative, repetitive, and iterative reports and the durative or discrete events and activities to which such reports are indexed in the narrated world. Consigning iterative narration to the realm of evaluation, and definitionally excluding evaluation from the narrative sequence proper, does not illuminate this aspect of story use and interpretation. Nor does it allow analysts to capture the way reference and evaluation are inextricably interlinked in the build-up of the narrative sequence itself. By contrast, by drawing on the narratological research tradition and in particular its hypothesis of a distinction between story and discourse, investigators can use narrative frequency as a tool for studying the jointly referential and evaluative properties of narrative discourse. They can also reconsider prevalent notions of narrative as the recounting of singular past states and events, broadening the investigative frame to include a wider range of aspectual types and the grammatical devices (for example, non-indicative verbal moods) that encode them.

A second, equally crucial dimension of story design and comprehension is the ability to interpret (and cause others to interpret) event-strings as sequences of actions performed by identifiable participants. The narratological concept of narrative actants, particularly if it is modified along lines suggested by cognitive science, can throw light on the way narratives promote patterned sets of inferences about story agents. More specifically, in concert with existing theories about information status in discourse, the idea of cognitively based actantial paradigms may generate a heuristic scheme that accounts for three interrelated facets of narrative inferencing. The first facet is the process by which storytellers tag certain referring expressions as coreferential; such tagging prompts story recipients to construct a discourse model in which the expressions pick out one and the same discourse item. The second facet involves the creation of inferential chains that confer on *some* discourse items the additional property of narrative agency—the ability both to affect and to be affected by other agentive as well as nonagentive entities populating the story world. These same inferential chains play a role in the third facet of narrative inferencing, too. By virtue of these chains, a variety of predicates (modes of action or being acted on) can be attached to a given narrative actant. Collectively these three facets of narrative inferencing go a long way toward explaining how story referents can be organized into a narratively structured whole. Through such inferencing, a series of sentences or clauses can produce a specific kind of mental representation: that is, that of an event-string involving participants engaged in a sequence of causally and chronologically ordered actions.

Finally, and of special importance for a *socio*narratological approach, types of narration and modes of narrative inferencing must be studied not only in terms of formal and cognitive structures, but also as part of a variably situated speech event rich in contextualization cues. As the tradition of interactional sociolinguistics teaches us, such cues are socioculturally sensitive, and miscommunication in intercultural exchanges can often be traced back to the failure of contextualization cues to elicit the appropriate conversational inferences. Stories, too, can fulfil very different roles in different sorts of cultures and communities. To typify, describe, and compare those roles—to explore the contextual, linguistic, and cognitive bases for narrative competence in a variety of cultural settings—constitutes the primary research task for a socionarratology.

Appendix

Transcription Conventions (adapted from Tannen 1993, 53):

...	represents a measurable pause, more than 0.1 seconds
..	represents a slight break in timing

. indicates sentence-final intonation

, indicates clause-final intonation ("more to come")

— indicates length of the preceding phoneme or syllable

Syllables with ~ were spoken with heightened pitch

Syllables with ^ were spoken with heightened loudness

/ / enclose transcriptions that are not certain

Narrative 1

[The pre-sequence, including the interviewer's prompts:]

NSE: [Break in the recording] some questions about some things [break in the recording] the words that we've heard people use~ And.. um.. like one of the words I was wondering about was.. um toten~

LL: How was that.. you..

NSE: A ^toten~ Like do you know.. have you ever.. seen —a toten or heard..

LL: Yeah Honey.. Lord yeah. ^Good Lord yeah. It's not.. um.. let me tell you this. You don't hear /of/ boogers and things now, like you used to. Used to.. why years ago.. you could learn..I could set here and seed 'em a many time and before I ever got married. You see them there.. ^Jack-o-lanterns~ Are you ever seen one~

NSE: uh uh.

[The sequence or story:]

LL: (a) Huh~ It's a great big ^light —..

(b) and ah, it'd go up..

(c) when I was a.. I seen.. the last ones I seen,

(d) that was I reckon..about ten year ago.

(e) I was at my mother's.

(f) Back that a-way in the woods,

(g) there was a house a-sittin way back that a-way.

(h) My oldest sister Mandy..that was before she died.

(i) She said "Louie you ever seen them jack-o"

(j) I says "I ain't seen one"

(k) I said "in I don't know how many years."

(l) [To dog in the room:] Come here.

(m) Moon was shining as pretty.

(n) I went out there

(o) and.. looked like there's ten of 'em.

(p) There'd be so many to go up..

(q) and so many to come down.

(r) They'd go up..

(s) and some would come down.

(t) And them was the first ones that I had ever seen..in God knows when.

(u) And there ain't nobody to^day— that knows..

     (v)   what them there lights represent.

     (w)   Why that..that's God's work.

     (x)   We..we ain't supposed to know God's work.

Narrative 2

[The pre-sequence, including the interviewer's prompts:]

NSE: Well..what is it called when you hear something..like a big sound, a loud sound before somebody dies, or something~

LL: Honey.. [To dog that jumped up into her lap:] I..I..I don't want any sugar. /Get down with you/ I can't..Hon..Honey..I couldn't tell you.

NSE: Uh huh. I just heard of some people having ^that happen to them. It wasn't..it was a ^sound~ that they heard..and not something that they saw~ You haven't..ever had that happen to you~

[The sequence or story:]

LL: (a)   ...Uh..well..there's one night here.

      (b)   I reckon it's been about four years ago..

      (c)   /it/ might been longer than that.

      (d)   Did you know a man named...Lord..I..

      (e)   He's a Bullard..Harvey Bullard~

      (f)   Well../my ol'/.. my..husband he used to fool with liquor.

      (g)   And ah..he'd have it back yonder in there that old graveyard.

      (h)   Now he was a man

      (i)   he wasn't a-scared of a booger nor nobody else.

      (j)   And 'cause he'd..when he'd..runned his liquor

      (k)   He'd hide /it/ in that old graveyard back yonder.

      (l)   And Harvey Bullard..he was the police at Pembroke.

      (m)   He'd come out here,

      (n)   and if the old man wasn't here,

      (o)   he knowed exactly where his still was and everything.

      (p)   So there's one moonshiny night..

      (q)   I's a-laying in the room there..

      (r)   and ah..I don't know what my..whether my old man was in there or no.

      (s)   I'm forgot now it's been so long.

      (t)   But anyway..I's a-laying in my room that bright shiny night,

      (u)   and the baby was in his trailer out there.

      (v)   That was before Harvey died.

      (w)   And uh..Honey..I heared as pretty a whistling— as I ever heared in my life.

      (x)   It'd say..had the whistlinest..voice

      (y)   "I'll see you again.

      (z)   I'll see you again.

(aa)   I'll see you again."
(bb)   And I got up
(cc)   and I looked out of the window,
(dd)   I didn't see a soul in the God Almighty's world.
(ee)   And Harvey Bullard at that time he was in..at Lumberton in the hospital low down..
(ff)   looking for the last of /it/.
(gg)   And ah..that..that next evening come.
(hh)   I heared about him ah..a-passing away.
(ii)   And that was his..his voice —
(jj)   that had been down yonder where my old man was a-making liquor
(kk)   and was on his way a-coming
(ll)   he parked his car out there in the yard.
(mm) And I looked
(nn)   and that was as pretty a whistling as I ever heared in my life.
(oo)   And it was his toten

Notes

This research was supported in part by NSF Grant SBR-9616331 (Walt Wolfram and Natalie Schilling-Estes, Co-Principal Investigators) and by a Faculty Research Grant from the College of the Humanities and Social Sciences at North Carolina State University. I am grateful to Peter Dixon, Manfred Jahn, Natalie Schilling-Estes, and Walt Wolfram for helpful feedback on earlier drafts of this essay.

1. In one of the central documents of French structuralism, "The Structural Study of Myth" (originally published in 1955), Claude Lévi-Strauss set an unfortunate precedent for narratologists. He polarized message and code by making a radical — and arguably, a counterintuitive — distinction between *telling* and *understanding* myths (1986, 813). To understand a myth, the analyst must reduce it to the synchronic system of contrasts and oppositions by virtue of which events in the myth take on meaning; if anything, this system tends to be obscured by the diachronic unfolding of the myth, the linear presentation of its constituent events during the process of telling. Lévi-Strauss's approach forestalls investigation into how different styles of telling can license different interpretations of the story being told (see below, section 4.1). His approach also discourages the study of stories as a particular type of speech event, recognizable *as* stories only because of cues embedded in particular acts of narrative communication (see below, section 6).

2. For other perspectives on the possibilities and limits of the Labovian model, see Cortazzi (1993, 48–49) and the references cited there.

3. A variationist approach might illuminate discourse features of stories in the fol-

lowing way. As will be discussed in section 5 below, storytellers regularly make choices between morphosyntactic options (e.g., full noun phrases versus pro-forms, definite versus indefinite pronouns) as they build up (and assist story recipients in building up) a "discourse model" (Webber 1979; cf. Grosz and Sidner 1986; McKoon et al. 1993) on the basis of which narrative referents can be tracked as the story proceeds. Given the crucial functions served by these linguistic features in narratives, it is important to examine ways in which the features are differently realized in different language varieties (cf. Sankoff 1988; Wolfram and Schilling-Estes 1998). In other words, in order to understand how pronoun and article selections function narratively, the analyst must be aware of the types of grammatical patterning associated with particular dialects. Thus in some language varieties *them* functions as a plural demonstrative pronoun (e.g., *I heard about them ghosts*), as well as a plural personal pronoun (e.g., *The ghosts haunted them*), as in standard English. Put briefly, in monitoring the information status of story referents (Emmott 1994 and 1997; see also section 5 below) — in charting the emergent profile of objects and inhabitants located in the story world — both storytellers and story recipients build up dialect-specific assumptions about the relative accessibility of the entities evoked through variable pronoun usage.

4. Note LL's use of a similar strategy at line (u) of narrative 1. The intonational stress on the second syllable of the word *today*, together with a noticeably lengthened production of the syllable itself, helps reinforce the contrast between the comparatively ghost-less present and the haunted past.

5. Schiffrin (1994, 11) offers a concise synopsis of the Labovian approach to narrative, reference, and evaluation, the latter construed as a "means by which narrators highlight different aspects of a reported experience as a way of revealing the point of the story." As Schiffrin puts it, "Although evaluations are sometimes separate sections of stories, they are also distributed throughout narrative and embedded within narrative clauses themselves. (Narrative clauses are typically event clauses that report 'what happened.') Embedded evaluations rely upon deviations from the simple syntactic structure typical of a narrative clause."

6. In this connection, Livia Polanyi (1989) develops a more flexible and narratologically sound account of evaluation as a process by which important information is foregrounded in storytelling. For Polanyi, evaluation is not indexed to a specific subset of linguistic features but rather includes any device used by storytellers to assign prominence to textual information that is meant to be construed as salient by story recipients. Thus, "there are no 'absolute' evaluative devices; any device available for evaluation can be used nonevaluatively as well or can be so over-used that it becomes a textual norm" (22).

7. Note that Labov and Waletzky (1967) make an analogous distinction between the surface structures and the semantic interpretation of stories: that is, the linear sequence of events presented by the narrator "may be considered the *surface structure* of the narrative; there are often many narratives with rather different surface structures, but with equivalent semantic interpretations. In the same way, there are many sentences with

different surface structures which correspond to the same underlying string of formatives in the original phrase structure of a grammar" (29–30).

8. As Rimmon-Kenan (1983, 57) notes, telling *n* times what happens *n* times is a special case of singulative narration. In lines (p) through (s), however, something that happened indefinitely many times is reported only twice, so this segment of the story does not exactly match the special variant of singulative narration that Rimmon-Kenan describes.

9. Whereas the usitative tense has formal markings associated with the indicative mood and past tense, functionally it implies past, habitual, and/or iterative activity.

10. For a fuller investigation of how actants can be used to analyze natural-language narratives, see Herman (unpubl. ms). There I further develop a cognitive-scientific approach to actants as mental representations of characters in stories. Such mental models make it possible for storytellers and their listeners to assign particular referents to the referring expressions associated with narrative agents.

11. Note that Greimas's (1987) early account of actants anticipates later, cognitively based approaches. In a paper first published in 1973, Greimas writes: "actantial models . . . constitute an attempt to account for instances and trajectories of meaning that generate discourse. But their importance is also pragmatic: They have to be considered as models of predictability, as hypotheses presented in the form of logical articulations, that, once projected onto texts, can enhance their readability" (113).

9 | Fictional and Historical Narrative: Meeting the Postmodernist Challenge

Lubomír Doležel

The classical narratology of French structuralism was centered on the story (récit). Stories are told in many media (sign systems) and discourse types. A "grammar" of récit is a universal model that does not register any of these differences, specifically the difference between fictional and historical narrative. Roland Barthes's essay, "Le discours de l'histoire" ("The Discourse of History"; 1967) is a turning point between structuralism and poststructuralism. Espousing a constructivist philosophy of language, Barthes explicitly denied the distinction between fiction and history. In North America, Hayden White's work is the best-known statement of the equation of fiction and history.

This paper attempts to formulate a new response to the poststructuralist, postmodernist challenge. It proposes to reexamine the relationship between fictional and historical narrative within the theoretical framework of possible worlds. Both fictional and historical constructs are possible worlds, but historical worlds are subject to restrictions that are not imposed on fictional worlds. Consequently, significant macro-structural differences between the two types of possible worlds can be discerned. Reasserting the opposition does not mean denying the diverse and persistent exchanges between fiction and history. The paper accepts the idea of an open boundary and sketches some of the narrative worlds that arise when the fictional penetrates into historical worlds and vice versa.

The corpus of "classical" narratology is constituted by the works of the French structuralists and their fellow travelers. The hero of this neo-formalist trend was the "récit." The complete theory of the récit consisted of three levels — the "deep structure" (A.-J. Greimas), the semantic structure (Roland Barthes, Tzvetan Todorov, Claude Bremond), and the discourse structure (Gérard Genette).

The influence of this narratology spread far beyond its original domain. Since the world's récits are countless ("innombrable," Barthes), the space of narratology is limitless. This narratological "imperialism" rolled over long-established boundaries between text types and genres. In particular, it erased the traditional boundary between fiction-making and historiography, between fictional and historical narrative. This is narratology's contribution to the self-destruction of French structuralism; this is the ammunition needed for launching the poststructuralist, postmodernist challenge to the integrity of history.

1. The Fatal Equation

The turning point is Roland Barthes's essay "The Discourse of History."[1] As the title indicates, Barthes proposes to look at historical writing as a form of discourse. He shows convincingly that in historical writing prominent discourse devices are present, both formal—such as "shifters"—and thematic units, classes and macrostructures of "content." The revelation of the discourse devices in historical writing is subservient to the main thrust of Barthes's essay; that is, the undermining of the opposition between historical and fictional narrative. At the very beginning, Barthes asks the crucial question: "Does the narrative of past events, which, in our culture from the time of the Greeks onwards, has generally been subject to the sanction of historical 'science,' bound to the unbending standard of the 'real' and justified by the principles of 'rational' exposition—does this form of narration really differ, in some specific trait, in some indubitably pertinent feature, from imaginary narrative, as we find it in the epic, the novel or the drama?" (7). At the end, Barthes provides an answer, and this answer is negative.

The negative outcome could have been anticipated. It is difficult to imagine historical discourse lacking shifters and thematic structures. In these aspects it does not differ from fictional discourse, or from journalistic prose or everyday conversation. Universal features of discourse cannot serve as distinctive features of discourse types. Barthes may have been aware that his discourse analysis is irrelevant for answering the crucial question. So in the last part of his essay he forgets about the discourse categories of "énonciation" and "énoncé," switches to "signification" and formulates a new argument. He claims that (for unspecified reasons) in "our civilization" "the historian is not so much a collector of facts as a collector and relator of signifiers; that is to say, he organizes them with the purpose of establishing positive meaning and filling the vacuum of the pure series" (16). The "pure unstructured series of notations" (chronologies and annals) are assigned meaning ("signification") by "ideological elaboration, or to put it more precisely, an *imaginary* elaboration, if we can take the imaginary to be the language through which the utterer of a discourse (a purely linguistic entity) 'fills out' the place of subject of the utterance (a psychological or ideological entity)" (16). It is amusing to observe that the mere mention of "language" (albeit metaphorical) drives Barthes toward a radical constructivist conclusion:

> From the moment that language intervenes (and when would it not intervene?), the fact can only be defined in a tautological fashion. . . . We thus arrive at the paradox which governs the entire question of the distinctiveness of historical discourse (in relation to other types of discourse). The fact can only have a linguistic existence (as a term of a discourse), and yet everything proceeds as if this existence were nothing but a pure and simple "copy" of another existence situated in the extrastructural domain, in the "real." This discourse is doubtless the only type in which the referent is aimed for as something external to the discourse, without it ever being possible to attain it outside this discourse. (16–17)

In other words, the discourse of history is caught in a confusion of its own making: mistaking the signified ("signifié") for the referent.

Historical discourse cannot reach the "real," so it cultivates "the reality effect" ("l'effet de réel"). It produces this effect by instituting (at least since the nineteenth century) narration as the privileged signifier of the real. Like the realistic novel, history "draws its 'truth' from the careful attention to narration, the architecture of articulations and the abundance of expansions (known, in this case, as 'concrete details')" (18). The "realistic" narrative history closes a paradoxical circle: "Narrative structure, which was originally developed within the cauldron of fiction (in myths and the first epics) becomes at once the sign and the proof of reality" (18).

I have quoted in some detail from the final section of Barthes's essay because the two-step argument developed here is the crux of the postmodernist challenge: (1) Language is incapable of referring to anything outside itself (the world, reality, the past); therefore, historiography has to resort to narrative in order to make its discourse meaningful and convincing. Narrative replaces, is a substitute for, the impotent language. And (2) history borrows narrative from fiction where it was developed; consequently, historical narrative becomes indistinguishable from fictional narrative.

Barthes is familiar with contemporary developments and knows that narrative history is not the last word in historiography. But he maintains that the "relative lack of prominence (if not complete disappearance) of narration in the historical science of the present day" (an obvious allusion to the *Annales* school) does not disprove, but rather confirms his argument: "Historical narration is dying because the sign of History from now on is no longer the real, but the intelligible" (18). In other words, when historiography gives up the ambition to represent the "real" it is free to throw away the crutch of narrative. Is non-narrative history as fictional as narrative history? Barthes does not say. The sentence just quoted is the last sentence of his essay.

Hayden White's *Metahistory* (1973) remains safely within the scope of nineteenth-century narrative history. White's theory of historical narrative is inspired by Barthes, but he has to be given credit for a systematic, logical ordering of the postmodernist challenge: "The elements in the historical field" (historical events) are arranged sequentially into a chronicle, the chronicle is transformed into a story, and the story is given a meaning (is "explained") by emplotment. The final step is the most important historiographic operation.[2] Explanation by emplotment is tantamount to encoding the story as a certain "kind of story"; that is, as Romance, Tragedy, Comedy, or Satire. Conveniently, the nineteenth-century historians studied by White represent severally the four modes of emplotment: "Michelet casts all of his histories in the Romantic mode, Ranke casts his in the Comic mode, Toqueville used the Tragic mode, and Burckhart used Satire" (1973, 8).

Proceeding further in Barthes's shadow, White crowns the postmodernist theory of history by embedding his narratology in a constructivist philosophy of language. Language operates by and through figuration. All thought, indeed all consciousness, is a tropological "processing of experience" (1973, 40). Consequently, the narration of the past is preceded by a hidden "precognitive and precritical" figuration. This stage is a *poetic* (we should rather say *poietic*) act in which the historian "both creates his object of analysis and predetermines the modality of the conceptual strategies he will use to explain it" (31). "If this is the case," White elaborates later, "then it may well be that the kind of emplotment that the historian decides to use to give meaning to a set of historical events is dictated by the dominant figurative mode of the language he has used to *describe* the elements of his account *prior* to his composition of a narrative. . . . The implication is that historians *constitute* their subjects as possible objects of narrative representation by the very language they use to describe them" (1978, 94, 95). It is the poetics of tropes that "provides us with a basis for classifying the deep structural forms of the historical imagination" (1973, 31).

It is noteworthy that in *Metahistory* White does not equate history and fiction; indeed, as far as I can tell, the term fiction does not appear anywhere in the book. Only in his next book, *Tropics of Discourse*, does White state the equation. It is instructive to observe how he arrived at it. He repeats that explanation in history is a matching of "a specific plot structure with the set of historical events that he [the historian] wishes to endow with a meaning of a particular kind." But then comes the surprising non sequitur: "This is essentially a literary, *that is to say* fiction-making, operation" (1978, 85; emphasis added). The double equation "plot structuring = literary operation = fiction-making" is arrived at not by analysis, but by a substitution of synonyms, or at least of terms that White considers to be synonymous. The equating of history and fiction is smuggled into the postmodernist paradigm by a tautology. Emplotment is a literary operation; therefore, history is tantamount to fiction-making.[3]

Barthes used the constructivist philosophy of language as the launching pad for the postmodernist challenge, White as its justification. Later, the double equation "historical narrative = literary narrative = fictional narrative" (often in a simplified form "history equals fiction") has become a dogma, repeated without any theoretical justification by a large postmodernist chorus. We can hear slight differences in formulations, but no new argument.[4] It is the *Zeitgeist* that speaks through the chorus.

2. Taking the Holocaust Test

The majority of practicing historians went about their business as usual, unaware of, or unconcerned about, the postmodernist challenge. A small group of theoretically minded historians and philosophers of history have recorded the threat to the epistemological foundations of historiography and have decided to react. The most serious response to the postmodernist challenge comes from those who ask a quite simple question: How would a theory based on the equation of fiction and history deal with the most traumatic events of the human past, such as the Holocaust? Saul Friedlander assembled articles by prominent scholars who were willing to tackle the question (Friedlander, ed., 1992). One of the contributors is Berel Lang, who had suggested earlier that the Nazi genocide is a test that has to be applied whenever the relationship between fiction and history is argued: "The fact of the Nazi genocide is a crux that separates historical discourse from the process of imaginative representation, perhaps not uniquely, but as certainly as any fact might be required or is able to do" (1990, 158). It is to Hayden White's credit that he agreed to take the Holocaust test. He had to face, finally, the problem of historical truth which his formalist and constructivist theory of history has evaded or eliminated. Under the pressure of the traumatic historical fact, White splits historical discourse into two levels. The first level is the "account[s] of events already established as facts"; on this level, " 'competing narratives' can be assessed, criticized, and ranked on the basis of their fidelity to the factual record, their comprehensiveness, and the coherence of whatever arguments they may contain." The second level is constituted by "poetic and rhetorical elements by which what would otherwise be a list of facts is transformed into a story. Among these elements are those generic story patterns we recognize as providing the 'plots.' . . . Here the conflict between 'competing narratives' has less to do with the facts of the matter in question than with the different story-meanings with which the facts can be endowed by emplotment" (1992, 38; see already 1987, 45).

Our expectation that White will deal with the first, "new" level of the discourse structure of historical writing, that he will tell us how, in his theoretical framework, "events" become established as "facts" and what would be the criteria of "fidelity," "comprehensiveness," and "coherence" of competing "historical narratives," is disappointed. Instead, he stays within the old frame of reference and makes the test easier: Are there any limits on the emplotment, any "unacceptable modes of emplotment" of such periods as the Nazi epoch and of such events as the Final Solution? Obviously, "we would be eminently justified" in removing the "comic" and the "pastoral" modes from the list of "competing narratives" about the events of the Third Reich.[5] More to the point, when defending Andreas Hillgruber's controversial emplotment of the defense of the eastern front by the Wehrmacht in the winter of 1944–45 as "tragedy," White for the first time admits that a mode of emplotment can be a distortion rather than an interpretation of history. It is worth our while to give a longer quotation of this remarkable admission:

> Hillgruber's suggestion . . . indicates how the choice of a mode of emplotment can justify certain kinds of events, agents, actions, agencies, and patients that may inhabit a given historical scene or its context. There is no place for any form of low or ignoble life in a tragedy; in tragedies even villains are noble or, rather, villainy can be shown to have its noble incarnations. Asked once why he had not included a treatment of Joan of Arc in his *Waning of the Middle Ages,* Huizinga is said to have replied: 'Because I did not want my story to have a heroine.' Hillgruber's recommendation to emplot the story of the Wehrmacht's defense of the eastern front as a tragedy indicates that he wants the story told about it to have a hero, to be heroic, and thereby to redeem at least a remnant of the Nazi epoch in the history of Germany. (1992, 43)

Admitting that "in tragedies even villains are noble," White admits that his theory of history fails the Holocaust test. By this way of reasoning, all it would take to make Hitler, Himmler, Heidrich, Eichmann, and others "noble" would be to emplot World War II and the Holocaust as *their* tragedy.

The failed test reveals most tellingly those fundamental weaknesses of White's theory which some of his critics had pointed out before: that in order to assess the "fidelity" of "competing narratives" a theory of history cannot expel the concept of historical fact and truth-valuation of historical representations; that to allow modes of emplotment to dictate the choice of historical events to be included in the representation means acquiescing to distortions of the past; last but not least, that a formalist theory of historical writing deprives historiography of any sociopolitical or ethical significance. In the postmodernist perspective, historiography is a web of more or less interesting stories, governed by narrative patterns and tropological shifts, but with only an incidental connection to the human past and present.

Justifiably, historians see the postmodernist challenge as the latest manifestation of historical relativism. Their response is then a restatement of the old argument against historical relativism: "Some claim to 'truth' appears particularly imperative" (Friedlander 1992, 3). The reassertion of the truth-functionality of historical narrative is welcome, but does not really meet the postmodernist challenge. It leaves intact the grounding claim of the challenge, namely that there is a necessary and unbridgeable gap between discourse (writing, representation, sign) and reality; that no sign, no representation can give us access to reality, can "hook onto reality." History, being discourse, suffers from this malaise of signs, from their inability to pass from meaning to the world. This paralysis of signification cannot be remedied by a reinterpretation of the concept of discourse but by a new understanding of the notion of world.

3. Possible Worlds

Let us imagine a language that would give us direct access to reality. Every utterance in that language would produce or recreate that portion of the world, that actual object or state of affairs that it signifies. If by uttering the word "child" you would produce and publicly display a child, nobody could deny that your language "hooks onto" reality. Alas, only a divine language, only a magic performative can produce such special effects. While awaiting a new Prometheus who would steal for us the divine language, we are confined to human language, a language with a weak performative power: it can bring about certain changes in our human affairs, but it cannot create the actual world that exists and goes on independently of language and any other representation. The only kind of worlds that human language is capable of creating or producing is *possible worlds*. To be helpful in any cognitive enterprise, philosophy of language has to proceed from this axiom. It is therefore mandatory for our task to present in a brief outline the conceptual system of possible worlds.

It is a concept with a venerable philosophical tradition. In the 1960s it was resurrected to provide a semantic interpretation of modal logic (Kripke 1963) and then it slowly penetrated into the theoretical discourse of natural, social, and human sciences (see Allén 1989).[6] In the process, the traditional concept had to be adjusted to its new tasks.

The first adjustment concerns the origin of possible worlds. In Leibniz's metaphysical conception, possible worlds have transcendental existence, they reside in the omniscient divine mind. Contemporary thinking about possible worlds is not metaphysical. Possible worlds do not await discovery in some transcendent depository; they are constructed by the creative activities of human minds and hands. This origin of possible worlds, which is in full accord with our above-stated axiom, was tersely expressed by Kripke: "Possible worlds are *stipulated,* not *discovered* by powerful telescopes" (1980, 44), and by Cresswell: "Possible worlds are things we can talk about or imagine, suppose, believe in or wish for" (1988, 4; see also Hintikka 1975, 28; Rescher 1975, 2–3; Adams 1979, 203–05; Bradley and Swartz 1979, 63–64; Stalnaker 1984, 50–51).

The second adjustment of the concept affects its extent. Possible worlds of logical semantics are "total" or "maximally comprehensive" states of affairs, "maximal cohesive mereological sum(s) of possibilia" (Kripke 1980, 18; Wolterstorff 1980, 131; Yagisawa 1988, 180). Robert M. Adams, following Rudolf Carnap, formulated criteria of "completely determinate" possible worlds: "(1) For every possible world, *w,* and every pair of contradictory propositions, one member of the pair is true in *w* and the other member is false in *w*. (2) Each possible world, if temporally ordered at all, is a complete world history and not a momentary stage of one. The actual world, therefore, includes what has actually existed or happened and what will actually exist or happen, as well as what now exists or happens" (1979, 191; see also Bradley and Swartz 1979, 4–5; Rescher and Brandom 1980, 2). The infinite size of complete worlds can be handled by logical formalisms, but is beyond the reach of empirical theories and research methods. Two heuristic moves have been suggested to overcome this problem: (1) choose as your universe of discourse a manageable subset of possible worlds, which is pertinent to your problem (Hintikka 1975, 75; Kripke 1980, 18); (2) design small worlds ("miniworlds") comprising a finite number of elements and determined by a limited number of parameters (Kripke 1980, 19; Cresswell 1988, 74; Hintikka 1989, 55).

Kripke's inconspicuous note is very important in assuring us that the concept of miniworld is logically compatible with the infinite possible world: "If we restrict the worlds to a narrower class of miniworlds, essentially all the issues regarding say, rigid designation, remain the same. So do the questions of modal semantics" (1980, 19, note 18). The concept of small worlds was taken up and developed by Umberto Eco. He also realized that the logicians' possible worlds—"*abstract* entities like numbers and propositions" (Bradley and Swartz 1979, 63–64)—have to be complemented by "furnished" worlds, possible worlds made up of "individuals endowed with properties" (1989a, 343;

1989b, 55; 1994, 85; see also Coste 1989, 113). From now on, when I speak of possible worlds I mean small worlds comprised of particular entities.

Possible worlds are not haphazard assemblies of constituents, but macro-structures formed by specific global restrictions. These restrictions determine the "general order" of the world, the conditions of existing and acting in that world. A typology of possible worlds is a project in the making, but the basic types are well established. I have in mind the distinction between physically possible and physically impossible worlds. A physically possible world is a world that "has the same natural laws as does the actual world"; in a physically impossible world "the natural laws are different from those in the actual world" (Bradley and Swartz 1979, 6–7; see also Rescher 1975, 144–49).[7] The conditions of existence and acting in a possible world are dependent on whether it is a physically possible or physically impossible world.

The idea of possible worlds is a forceful reminder of the contingency of cosmic and human existence. If the basic physical constants were only minutely different, a different universe or no universe would obtain (Rees 1989). Brutus might not have killed Caesar, Trotsky might have become the leader of the Soviet Union, Nixon could have been a car salesman. Brutus who did not kill Caesar, Trotsky the leader of the Soviet Union, Nixon the car salesman are possible counterparts of the historical Brutus, Trotsky, and Nixon, respectively. The relationship between counterparts, the transworld identity, is formally represented by Hintikka's individuation function: it "picks out from several possible worlds a member of their domain as the 'embodiment' of that individual in this possible world or perhaps rather as the role which that individual plays under a given course of events" (1975, 30).[8]

In logical semantics the possible-worlds model does not require ontological commitments. Pointing specifically to Hintikka's and Kripke's proposals, a Russian logician emphasized that they should be taken "simply as mathematical models of the corresponding logical calculi, without any philosophical interpretation" (Slinin 1967, 137). Outside formal logic, however, the notion cannot preserve ontological innocence. As recognized by Adams, it follows the fundamental split in ontology, becoming either *actualism* or *possibilism*. For possibilism, the actual world "does not have a different status" within the set of possible worlds, while for actualism the actual world is "a standpoint outside the system of possible worlds from which judgments of actuality which are not world-relative may be made" (1979, 194, 202; see also Lycan 1979). The actualist position is inscribed in Kripke's original model structure where set G (the actual world) is singled out from the set of sets K (all possible worlds) (1963, 804), and is accepted by Plantinga (1974, 45–51), Rescher (1975, 90–92), Stalnaker (1984), Nolt (1986), and Cresswell (1988, 1). Even David Lewis's "indexical" theory (1986), which relativizes the concept of actual world, is compatible with "modal realism" (see R. R. Miller 1990).[9]

4. Fictional and Historical Worlds

The relationships between possible worlds, their similarities and differences, are determined by comparing or contrasting their macromorphologies. Relocating the problem of fiction and history from the level of discourse to the level of world[10] means asking whether the possible worlds of history and fiction are homomorphous or whether they show some marked macrostructural differences. I believe that a number of such differences can be found, but I will consider only the most conspicuous ones:

1. The fiction maker is free to roam over the entire universe of possible worlds, to call into fictional existence a world of any type. This is eminently true about the basic types. Physically impossible worlds, called supernatural or fantastic, are as well represented in fiction of all periods as are physically possible worlds, called natural or realistic.[11] In contrast, historical worlds are restricted to the physically possible. The boundary between history and mythology lies precisely here. In mythology, supernatural beings (deities, devils, spirits, and so on) are part of the agential constellation and they make their actional contribution to the narrative. In historical worlds events cannot be assigned to divine agency (even if the historian is a believer). Human history is a history of natural agents.

When it comes to feats of imagination, nothing is more attractive than impossible worlds. It was Leibniz who circumscribed the universe of the possible by defining the impossible — the worlds that contain or imply logical contradictions. Fiction makers, especially of the postmodernist stripe, are fascinated by the challenge of constructing impossible worlds, just as mathematicians have been attracted to the impossible task of squaring the circle. In his *98.6* (1975) Ronald Sukenick constructs an Israel that looks like this: "Here in Israel the extraordinary is run-of-the-mill. We are capable of living in a state in which certain things that have happened have not. At the same time that they have. . . . The way you enter The State of Israel is through Psychosynthesis. In the processes of Psychosynthesis as in the subconscious as in the laws of physics there is no negation" (179). The construction of the impossible world is here displayed as a radical *logical* rupture, the replacement of standard (classical) logic by nonstandard logic where "there is no negation." It is difficult to imagine a historian who would consider constructing impossible worlds. Logical contradictions, explicit or implicit, would destroy the structure of the historical world.[12]

2. The cast of agents in the historical world is determined by the set of agents involved in the past event(s). If it is revealed (by new documents, say) that a person who did not actually exist or could not have participated in the event was included in a historical world, he or she has to be removed from the grouping. If, on the contrary, new evidence shows that a person who was not included in the historical world participated in the historical event, he or she has to be added to the grouping of agents. No such restriction applies to the constellation of agents in fictional worlds. Commonly, this set consists of persons who never existed and are assembled to act and interact by a decision of the fiction maker. This macrostructural opposition between fictional and historical worlds comes into sight most clearly when one considers a literary genre where fiction and history seem to overlap, that is historical fiction. It is a defining feature of the genre that fictional persons coexist and interact with counterparts of historical persons. Thus in E. L. Doctorow's *Ragtime* (1974) Emma Goldman, Teddy Roosevelt, Harry Houdini, Sigmund Freud, and others mingle with Father, the little boy, younger brother, Mameh, Tateh, the little girl, and so on. This feature gives Doctorow's novel its literary effect, but invalidates it as a history of the American society at the beginning of the twentieth century. A possible world where counterparts of historical persons cohabit with fictional persons is not a historical world.

3. Neither fictional nor historical worlds are inhabited by real, actual people, but by their possible counterparts. Yet there is a major difference between the fictional and the historical treatment of transworld identity. Fiction makers practice a radically nonessentialist semantics; they can alter even the individuating properties and life episodes of historical persons when transposing them into a fictional world. Verisimilitude is a requirement of a certain poetics of fiction, not a universal principle of fiction-making. It is essential for the historical Napoleon that he died at St. Helena. But according to a legend, quoted as a motto to Georg Kaiser's play *Napoleon in New Orleans* (1937), Napoleon was rescued from the island and taken to North America, where he died in New Orleans.[13] The persons of historical worlds — as well as their events, settings, etc. — have to bear documented properties. Historians are involved in a continuous refining of historical worlds in order to "supplement or rewrite narratives according to the state of the sources" (Baumgartner 1975, 61).

4. Both fictional and historical worlds are by necessity incomplete. To construct a complete possible world would require writing a text of infinite length — a task that is beyond human capability. If possible worlds of fiction and history are incomplete, then gaps are a universal feature of their macrostructure. Yet in the character, distribution, and manipulation of gaps, fiction and history show fundamental differences.

The fiction writer is free to vary the number, the extent and the functions of the gaps; his choices are determined by aesthetic (stylistic) and semantic factors. For instance, the radically incomplete physique of the romantic hero serves the semantic aims of romantic narrative: a physical detail surrounded by emptiness is brought into sharp focus and thus offered for symbolic reading (Doležel 1980, 1–7). Thomas Pavel, noting that "authors and cultures have the choice to minimize or maximize" the "unavoidable incompleteness" of fictional worlds, has suggested that cultures and periods of a "stable world view" tend to minimize incompleteness, whereas periods of "transition and conflict" tend to maximize it (1986, 108, 109). Marie-Laure Ryan used the degrees of incompleteness as a criterion for a triadic typology of fictional worlds, with realistic fiction striving for the highest degree of completeness, without ever being able to reach the ideal (1984, 121–39). Lucien Dällenbach has come independently to a similar conclusion: the reality-like completeness of realistic narratives is no more than an illusion "destined precisely to camouflage [their] blanks" (1984, 201). What applies to fiction in general applies to historical fiction in particular. The writer of historical novels or stories is free to include in his fictional world certain historical facts and omit others. Viktor Shklovsky investigated in detail the choices that L. N. Tolstoy made when writing *War and Peace.* Tolstoy omitted well-documented facts that did not suit his aesthetic and ideological purpose.[14]

Since fictional gaps are created in the act of world-making, they are ontological in nature. They are irrecoverable lacunae that cannot be filled by legitimate inference. Statements about fictional gaps are undecidable: it can never be decided whether Emma Bovary did or did not have a birthmark on her left shoulder.[15] Alluding to a *cause célèbre,* Nicholas Wolterstorff has succinctly explained the ontological character of fictional gaps: "We will never know how many children had Lady Macbeth in the worlds of Macbeth. That is not because to know this would require knowledge beyond the capacity of human beings. It is because there is nothing of the sort to know" (1980, 133; see also Rescher and Brandom 1980, 5).[16]

Historical worlds are incomplete in a different manner and their gaps are of a different kind. The gaps in historical worlds are epistemological, given by the limitations of human knowledge. Paul Veyne expressed this incompleteness in a grand metaphor: "History is a palace whose full extent we do not discover . . . and of which we do not see all the suites at once" (1984, 261). The first source of gaps is the historian's cognitive strategy, guided either by purely practical considerations (the scope of the investigation) or by a chosen "plot" structure, as Veyne and others would have it. Whatever the motivation, these gaps result from the historian's conscious selection,[17] and he or she must be ready to defend it. The other kind of gaps in historical worlds, the gaps that are due to lack of evidence, shows most clearly their epistemological character. They will be filled if new documents become available. This cognitive progress is a well-known feature of historiography.

Hugh Trevor-Roper's splendid study *A Hidden Life* (1976) is an instructive example of this progress. We are let into the historian's workshop watching him perform two roles: he is simultaneously a detective, who uncovers or is given documents about a mysterious person, and a writer who constructs a possible life of that person.[18] A major part of Trevor-Roper's detection work is to assess the veracity of the documents compiled by his subject. The historian's razor divides the documents into reliable evidence and "fabrication," "fantasy," "fiction," or "forgery." The construction of the historical world can proceed only from reliable evidence. If no such evidence is available, a gap is left in the world, a gap that Trevor-Roper clearly marks as epistemic: "Of Backhouse's duties and success in this post [as a professor of law and literature at the University of Peking], which he held for ten years, we know nothing; the documents of the university of Peking have disappeared from human, or at least from Western, sight" (1976, 37). If the documents of the University of Peking are opened for research, then, of course, this gap in Trevor-Roper's possible life of Edmund Backhouse might be filled.

Between the gaps and the historical facts there exists a broad spectrum of plausible conjectures. The conjectured events are not marked as certain facts, but are assigned a degree of probability. Trevor-Roper applies a rich vocabulary of expressions that assess the reliability of his conjectures, such as *perhaps, it is probable, it is possible, possibly not, conceivably, historically plausible, almost certain(ly), we may surmise, it may well be, we may suspect, we do not know exactly, all this is pure speculation,* and so on. The decision about the factuality of the conjectured events is, so to say, postponed. A critical historian cannot go any further.

Historical relativism sees in the inevitable incompleteness of historical worlds a necessary distortion of the past. While the selection of facts and gaps often reflects the historian's personal bias, this selection, as already mentioned, is subject to critical scrutiny within the community of historians. Only in totalitarian history is the procedure of gapping truly relativistic, enforced by the political power. The gaps are created by erasing every historical agent who became *persona non grata*. The two pictures shown here are a pathetic demonstration of this technique.[19] The photograph was taken when Yezhov was Stalin's most powerful henchman; it was deliberately retouched after he was arrested

Above, Voroshilov, Molotov, Stalin, and Yezhov at the Moscow-Volga Canal.
Below, the same photograph with Yezhov removed.

in 1939 and shot. Yezhov evaporated, and nothing is left of him, except a small indentation in the wall along which the leaders are walking. A hardly noticeable, but powerful sign: history can be gapped, but it necessarily leaves traces.

Totalitarian power creates gaps in historical worlds by erasing documented facts. It is like fiction-making in that it gives its gaps ontological status, projects them into the actual world. Totalitarian historiography is not so much a rewriting of history as an attempt to remake the past. Such, at least, is its expected impact within the space and time under its control. But outside its sphere of control it cannot achieve more than to create recoverable epistemic gaps by suppressing existing evidence. Ultimately, the efforts of totalitarian history are in vain, because the acquisition of historical knowledge proceeds in just the opposite direction: filling gaps in historical worlds, epistemological gaps, by searching for new evidence. Historians outside the reach of totalitarian power cannot and have not tolerated its distorted historical worlds.

The four distinctions in macrostructural properties of fictional and historical worlds that I have just briefly presented boil down to an often stated general contrast between the freedom of the fiction maker and the constraints imposed on the historian. It is the awareness of these constraints that leads scholars to the standard formulation that history is the *reconstruction* of the past. From the viewpoint of possible-worlds semantics, this formulation is unobjectionable as long as we understand that historical reconstruction does not recreate the past in actuality, but in represented possibility.

5. Worlds and Discourse

I have used the concept of possible worlds to counter the equation of history and fiction on a "higher" level. Now I will return to the level of discourse to probe the equation on its own grounds. If discourse is seen as a means of constructing possible worlds, then we can posit major distinctions between historical and fictional discourse in terms of truth conditions, illocutionary characteristics, and aims.

Possible worlds of fiction are products of *poiesis*. By writing a text the author creates a fictional world that had not been available prior to this act. The key to understanding poiesis is the truth conditions of fictional discourse. As Gottlob Frege already recognized by 1892,[20] fictional texts (sentences) lack truth value; that is, they are neither true nor false (1980, 62). It makes no sense to ask whether Gustav Flaubert was telling the truth or lied when he made Emma Bovary die by poisoning herself. There was no world, no life, no death of Emma prior to Flaubert's writing. But the exemption from truth-valuation is only the first step of our conception of poiesis; the second step is the recognition of a specific illocutionary character of fictional discourse. Fictional discourse is performative in that it calls a possible world into fictional existence.

The explanation of the world-constructing power of fictional discourse is stimulated by J. L. Austin's theory of performative speech acts (1962). Fictional discourse includes performatives carrying the force of authentication.[21] When authenticated by a felicitous performative, a possible is converted into a fictional existent. It is as authenticated possibles that unicorns and fairies, Odysseus and Raskolnikov, Brobdingnag and Chevengur exist objectively and readers can gain access to them, fear or feel pity for them, talk and argue about them at any time.

But does the reader's, interpreter's, literary historian's discourse appropriate the truth conditions of fictional discourse? Obviously not. It is meaningful, indeed necessary, to ask whether it is true to state that Emma Bovary died of tuberculosis. The sentences *about* the fictional world of *Emma Bovary* are constatives in Austin's sense (1971) and as such subject to truth valuation.[22] They are true or false in/of the fictional world that is available for inspection after it had been constructed by the author's writing.

Historical discourse is a discourse of constatives. It is meaningful, indeed necessary, to ask whether it is true that Napoleon died at St. Helena or in New Orleans. This is, of course, just a repetition of the traditional response to historical relativism. But the concept of historical world enables us to support this position by a new argument. Historical discourse has to be truth-functional in order to construct possible worlds that serve as *models* of the past. While fictional poiesis constructs a possible world that did not exist prior to the act of writing, historical noesis uses writing to construct models of the past that exists (existed) prior to the act of writing.

The modeling role of possible worlds in cognition has been noted in general terms by Eco: "We explore the plurality of *possibilia* to find out a suitable model for *realia*" (1989b, 57). The nuclear physicist J. S. Bell constructed "six possible worlds of quantum mechanics" as models of the dynamics of elementary quanta. His possible-worlds model incorporates quantum phenomena "into a coherent theoretical picture," rather than dealing with "the permissible variation of incidental detail." Having presented the extant possible worlds of quantum mechanics, Bell poses and answers a question that is crucial for our considerations: "To what extent are these possible worlds fictions? They are like literary fictions in that they are free inventions of the human mind. In theoretical physics sometimes the inventor knows from the beginning that the work is fiction, for example when it deals with a simplified world in which space has only one or two dimensions instead of three. More often it is not known till later, when the hypothesis has proved wrong, that fiction is involved. When being serious, when not exploring deliberately simplified models, the theoretical physicist differs from the novelist in thinking that maybe the story might be true" (1989, 359, 368).

The physicist's words bear directly on the difference between a Fregean and a constructivist philosophy of language. We proceed in the Fregean spirit when we recognize that the different aims of poiesis and noesis require two different kinds of discourse, one performative, with the attending lack of truth valuation; the other constative, with the attending truth-functionality. We are in the constructivist philosophy when we abolish this distinction and claim that all worlds depend for their existence on discourse and that all discourse is performative.

The first half of the axiom of constructivist philosophy was explicitly stated by Nelson Goodman: "We can have words without a world but no world without words or other symbols" (1978, 6).[23] The philosopher did not give any direction as where to find "words without a world." The direction is pointed out in the second half of the axiom, formulated by Roland Barthes: "Writing (in the sense of écriture) can no longer designate an operation of recording, notation, representation, 'depiction' (as the Classics would say); rather, it designates exactly what linguists, referring to Oxford philosophy, call a performative" (1977a, 145).[24]

It is performative writing that creates the world in which words exist. Yet the performatives of writing, if they are to perform anything, have to be actual words and as such they cannot exist anywhere else but in an actual world. Ultimately, the entire edifice of constructivist philosophy, on which the equation of fiction and history rests, either collapses onto itself or must be supported by a magic performative that constructs the world for its words.

6. An Open Boundary

Some historians join the postmodernist challenge but take a more moderate position. Suzanne Gearhardt is a good example because she explains her thinking in a lucidly written introduction to her book (1984). Siding with the postmodernist critique of all rigid oppositions and closed boundaries, she points out that "we are witnessing an increasing interdependence of theories of history and fiction" (8). Taking her cue from Mikhail Bakhtin (a quotation from Bakhtin serves as the book's motto), she declares the boundary between fiction and history "open": "The very domains it is supposed to separate and delimit continually cross over it" (4). She rejects the view of literature (*sic!*) and history as "sovereign, autonomous entities" and pleads instead for "a relationship in which the two terms are seen as formally similar because each borrows from the other and refuses in its own way to acknowledge that borrowing." But Gearhardt concludes the outline of her theoretical position by reaffirming the opposition: "For the same reasons that history and fiction are not sovereign, they never completely merge. The difference between the two constantly reasserts itself, for though they may be seen from a certain perspective as *formally* identical, their relationship is never purely formal" (28).

Gérard Genette is, I believe, close to this position. He recognizes that "narrative forms traverse easily the boundary between fiction and nonfiction" (1991, 93). Not surprisingly, his narratological model works well when applied to "factual *récit*." This leads him to the conclusion that we must "tone down strongly the hypothesis about an *a priori* difference in the narrative regime of fiction and nonfiction" (1991, 91). But Genette sticks to a "Solomon's judgment" and does not explicitly endorse the equation of fiction and history.

The main claim of this essay has been that the relationship between fiction and history "is never purely formal"; it is, primarily, a semantic and pragmatic opposition. In asserting the opposition we are not forced to deny various kinds of interpenetration. Possible-worlds semantics has no quarrel with the idea of open boundary, but it couples this acknowledgment with a curiosity to know what happens when the boundary is crossed. In other words, it asks what happens to the historical when it penetrates into fictional worlds and what happens to the fictional when it intrudes into historical worlds. Let us examine briefly three well-known instances of the crossing.

1. Historical fiction. Historical fiction, which has already been mentioned, shows that in this case the historical migrants adjust to the semantic and pragmatic conditions of the fictional environment. Historical persons transform into fictional counterparts, thus becoming participants of interaction and communication with fictional persons. As a result, the agential constellation of a historical novel or story is split into two subsets, one constituted by fictional persons having historical counterparts, the second consisting of fictional persons without such counterparts. The split creates a macrostructuring that is worth investigating, but that does not threaten the sovereignty of the fictional world.

Neither do intrusions in the opposite direction. The historical novel, from its very beginnings, exercised strong influence on the conception of historical worlds. Trevor-Roper restates the influence of Walter Scott on the Romantic historians by quoting Carlyle: "Scott's historical novels have taught all men this truth, which looks like truism, and yet was as good as unknown to writers of history and others, till so taught: that the bygone ages of the world were actually filled by living men, not by protocols, state-papers, controversies, and abstractions of men" (1969, 23–24). But we could venture further. If, as Carlo

Ginzburg claims, the "cognitive strategy" of the historian is "intrinsically individualizing (although the individual case may be a social group or an entire society)" (1990, 106), then it is not too far-fetched to suggest that fictional worlds, worlds of individualized particulars, serve as exemplars of historical worlds.[25] This is certainly true of such historical worlds as centre around the life of a person or group of persons. The present interest in the history of everyday life gave new impetus to these historical biographies. Ginzburg's *The Cheese and the Worms* (1980) and Natalie Zemon Davis's *The Return of Martin Guerre* (1983) are perhaps the best known among these life histories.

2. Counterfactual history. It is fair to say that a majority of historians subscribe to the view that "what happened was bound to happen" and that to consider counterfactual alternatives is just a "parlor-game" (E. H. Carr 1990, 44). But the parlor game has been passionately played at least since 1932 and quite a few contemporary historians believe that it is not a mere diversion.[26]

Human history is a massive complex of private and social actions and interactions carried out by numerous persons-agents; all the snarls and bends, all attempts, successes, and failures constituting the unavoidable contingency of acting, are deposited in history.[27] Since its inception in the work of Georg H. von Wright, modern action theory, formulated in the possible-worlds framework, has emphasized this contingency: from any given initial state the agent can proceed toward two or more possible end states. In order to know an agent's life history "we must know not only how the world actually changes, but also how it would have changed from one occasion to the next, had it not been for the agent" (1968, 43–44, 47).

Trevor-Roper characterizes history in words very much reminiscent of von Wright's description of human acting: "At any given moment in history there are real alternatives, and to dismiss them as unreal because they were not realized . . . is to take the reality out of the situation. How can we '*explain* what happened and *why*' if we only look at what happened and never consider the alternatives, the total pattern of forces whose pressure created the event?" (1980, 12–13). In a similar vein, Geoffrey Hawthorn, quoting Robert Nozick's epistemological principle, points out that we can understand history only by "locating an actual in a space of possibles" (1991, 17).[28] For a discussion of a particular case Hawthorn takes up Philip Guedalla's counterfactual history which could ensue if the battle at Lanjarón (1491) had been won by the Moors, not by the Catholic kings. Under one possible scenario, the Islamic kingdom of Granada would have become an empire of the twentieth century. The possible consequences of the Moorish victory reveal the crucial significance of the battle. Considering nonactualized possibilities also reveals that even at such moments when the fate of entire countries or continents is at stake, random factors might decide the outcome. Would the October Revolution have succeeded "if by chance Lenin had been killed in the summer of 1917" asks Howe, returning to Leon Trotsky's question. And he adds that Trotsky's answer was "a gingerly no, it probably would not have succeeded, so central was the role of *this* individual" (1978, 16). But if the October Revolution had not succeeded, the twentieth-century history of Russia and of the entire world would have been radically different.

The precariousness of certain historical situations comes to the fore only if counterfactual outcomes are taken into account. This cognitive gain of counterfactual history has been pointed out by Trevor-Roper: "I do not hesitate to say that in 1940–41 a mere accident, and one which might easily have occurred, could not only have reversed the outcome of the war, and transformed the subsequent shape of the world, but also have imposed upon the world a new synthesis of ideas and power, creating a new context for both politics and thought" (1980, 11). Certainly, for those who believe that history is a result of "iron laws," the Catholic kings' weakness, Lenin's being alive in October 1917, Franco's saying "no" to the invasion of Gibraltar at Hendaye are insignificant. But for those who perceive that history is the acting and interacting of human individuals and groups, the possible alternatives that might have happened owing to errors of judgment, impulse of passions and drives, accidents, good or bad luck, and all other "random" factors are indispensable dimensions of historical worlds.

Alexander Demandt weighs carefully the role of chance in history. He suggests that it has a different force depending on the stage of the historical process and on the "sector" of history. In a vivid metaphor Demandt shows that "numerous historical processes have a funnel structure. They begin with a wide-open situation, where all kinds of things are still possible, but become narrowed in the course of time and gain in speed in the same measure as they lose in freedom. . . . Then in the final stage it becomes tempting to look back on the chance events which made the whole thing possible or could have prevented it." When it comes to "sectors" of history, Demandt believes that the force of chance is in inverse proportion to the role personalities play in the historical process; it is very strong in the history of art, literature, and religion, but relatively weak in the history of science and technology (1993, 69–113, 27, 26–34).

Counterfactual history is a thought experiment: by changing or eliminating a factor of factual history it tests this factor's significance. For this reason, counterfactual history focuses on simple yes/no situations: win/lose a battle, war, election, a power struggle; a leader assassinated/not assassinated. As the "treelike structure" of possible history becomes an extended labyrinth of forking paths, the whole enterprise loses interpretive power and interest. An alternative history of *longue durée*—such as A. J. Toynbee's construct of world history starting from the premise that Alexander the Great did not die as young as he actually did—reads like a fantastic story.

Counterfactual history is thought experiment but it is not arbitrary; it can be critically evaluated. When the German historian Andreas Hillgruber suggested that the failure of the July 20, 1944, attempt to assassinate Hitler and the consequent continuation of the war saved millions of German lives that otherwise would have been lost, he was rightly contradicted by his German colleagues. Perry Anderson sums up this criticism: "If a counterfactual calculation is to be made, the overthrow of Hitler in July 1944, by shortening the war, would without question have saved far more lives than the continuation of the fighting hypothetically saved before Germany surrendered" (1992, 59). The weighing of alternatives is quite exact when they can be quantified. Clearly, computer calculations and projections will make counterfactual history still more attractive and precise.[29]

Trevor-Roper pointed out that the historian's construction of counterfactual history is an act of the imagination: "To restore to the past its lost uncertainties, to reopen, if only for an instant, the doors which the *fait accompli* has closed, this requires an effort of imagination" (1980, 16). The link to fiction-making is thus established. As already indicated, it is often difficult to decide whether the counterfactual historian is engaged in cognitive thought experiment or in the composition of a fantastic story. The link is even more intimate, owing to the existence of counterfactual historical fiction, such as H. Robert Harris's *Fatherland* (1992) or Carlos Fuentes's *Terra Nostra* (1975). Both *noesis* and *poiesis* are engaged in the construction of counterfactual worlds. But these exercises have different aims. The historian's counterfactual worlds are methodological aids; they do not question the factual historical worlds: the Moors were defeated in the battle of Lanjarón, Lenin did not die in the summer of 1917, Germany did not win the war against Britain in 1940–41. The fiction maker's counterfactual history is a parody of classic historical fiction; the historical past provides actors and the stage for its "carnivalization" (McHale 1987, 90).

3. Factual narrative. "Faction," "documentary fiction," "nonfiction novel," "literature of fact," and other labels have been applied to genres of writing or discourse types which are the most remarkable manifestation of the open boundary between fiction and history. I will use the descriptive phrase "factual narrative" as a general term for these genres. Factual narrative has been cultivated in the past (Daniel Defoe, Charles Dickens, Anton Chekhov, Viktor Shklovsky); it has grown in popularity after World War II as one manifestation of our culture's fascination with graphic documentation.

Like historical narrative, factual narrative provides, or at least claims to provide, a documented and accurate image; unlike historical narrative, it images the present. In other words, the possible worlds of factual narrative are models of witnessed present. In contrast, the discourse of factual narrative is fictional. Or so it seems to a critic or theorist who equates narrativization with fictionalization. In this paper, I have rejected this equation. Now, in its conclusion, I would like to demonstrate how in the framework here advocated the most notorious manifestation of postwar factual narrative, the writings of the so-called New Journalism, can be theoretically assessed.

It has been stated that New Journalism is unabashedly subjectivistic: the author puts himself or herself at the center of the world, constructed usually by first-person narrative. Smart goes so far as to link the prose of New Journalism with metafiction: "The nonfiction novel . . . is always metafictional. . . . As the writer argues for the validity of the novel, he also pleads for the identity and validity of his own experience and existence within it" (1985, 12). Hollowell contrasts this subjectivism with the established standards of journalism: "In sharp contrast to the 'objectivity' that the reporter strives for in the standard news article, the voice of the new journalist is frankly subjective; it bears the stamp of his personality" (1977, 22).

Tom Wolfe disputes this claim. He points out that in "most of the best work in the form" "the writer keep[s] himself absolutely invisible" (1973, 42). The main aspiration of the New Journalists is not to cultivate their own image, but to "wipe out" the contemporary novel. The place of the "retrograde" and socially irrelevant fiction is taken by a documentary prose as powerful as classical realistic narrative. To this end, the New Journalists import into journalistic prose devices typical for fictional narrative. According to Wolfe, the most important of them are "scene-by-scene construction," "dialogue," "third-person point of view," and details symbolic of "status life" (1973, 31–33). Wolfe believes that these devices originated with Gogol, Dickens, Balzac, Dostoevsky, and other nineteenth-century realists. But we recognize that some of the devices used, especially the shifting point of view and the interior monologue, are favorites of modernism. New Journalism thus updates what nineteenth-century narrative history was doing: taking over devices that were created and proved effective in fictional narrative. New Journalism is the most recent stage in the history of the "reality effect," created by the workhorses of fiction-making.

The massive use of devices borrowed from fictional narrative makes New Journalism's factuality suspect. Yet all of its representatives assure us again and again that their writing is a meticulously accurate record of what "*has actually happened*" (Wolfe 1973, 34). All the suspect features—verbatim dialogue, revelation of "other minds," intimate knowledge of character and setting—can be explained by one traditional journalistic practice: skillful and patient reporting. The historian's reconstruction issues from knowledge gained by a careful examination of archival documents. The present which the New Journalist investigates is accessible, so he or she constructs models from knowledge gained by close-up observation, careful listening, and faithful recording of interviews.[30] If it can be proved that the documentarist included in the world-construct invented persons or episodes, he or she is guilty of violating the norms of the genre and his or her work has to be reclassified, declared fictional.[31]

Conclusion

This essay is an attempt to respond to the postmodernist challenge and reassert a fundamental distinction between fictional and historical narrative. Its strategy is to shift the argument from the formal level (narrative and poetic devices) to the semantic and pragmatic levels, that is, from narrative and poetic devices to possible worlds and illocutionary characteristics. Nevertheless, the postmodernist challenge gave us food for thought by revealing two kinds of tension within historical (and factual) narrative. The first tension is between the paratext, where the work is claimed to be strictly factual,[32] and the text, which reads like literary fiction. The second tension is between the constructing text, which seems to function as a fictional performative, and the constructed world, which is offered as a reconstruction of past or present events. This dual tension creates uncertainty about the status of historical (and factual) narrative.[33] Postmodernist theory, trusting to a purely formalist analysis, resolves this uncertainty by tipping the balance in favor of fictionality: the claim of factuality is a culturally motivated illusion, covering up the fictionality of this narrative. Possible-worlds semantics restores the balance by emphasizing the semantic and pragmatic factors of discourse (writing): without denying the existence of domains of uncertainty, it posits firm semantic and pragmatic criteria for distinguishing between historical (factual) and fictional narrative.

The postmodernist challenge has raised new questions that cannot be answered by the old arguments against historical relativism. Possible-worlds semantics can provide such arguments because its thinking itself is a child of the contemporary age. "Metahistory" need not be an instrument of the demise of historiography. On the contrary, it can theoretically justify the practicing historian's search for historical truth and ordinary people's revulsion against distortions of known historical facts.

Notes

1. The English reader should be warned against Peter Wexler's unreliable translation (in Lane 1970). It is superseded by Stephen Bann's accurate and articulate rendering in *Comparative Criticism* (Barthes 1981). My page references are to this translation, although I take the liberty of modifying Bann's wording when it is warranted by a comparison with the original.

2. It has almost been forgotten that in *Metahistory* White considers, in addition to emplotment, two more traditional kinds of explanation of historical events, of assigning "meaning" to history (the quotation marks are his): by argument (logical explanation) and by ideology (ethical explanation). In later writings emplotment monopolized the stage.

3. The equation is supported by a push from the other side, a tendency to treat literary fiction as mimesis, as imitation or representation of reality: "The aim of the writer of a novel *must be* the same as that of the writer of a history. Both wish to provide a verbal image of 'reality'" (1978, 122; emphasis added). In this normative formulation, White installs the most naive view of fiction as the law of fiction-making.

4. Thus Natalie Zemon Davis arrives at the double equation by the simple procedure of synonym substitution. Her book is seductively titled *Fiction in the Archives* and its Introduction states: "Whenever I read these royal letters of pardon and remission . . . I marvel at the literary qualities of these texts, or, I might say, their 'fictional' qualities, by which I mean the extent to which their authors shape the events of a crime into a story. . . . I want to let the 'fictional' aspects of these documents be the center of analysis." She mitigates the damage by using the term fiction in its etymological, rather than common sense: "By 'fictional' I do not mean their [the documents'] feigned elements, but rather, using the other and broader sense of the root word *fingere,* their forming, shaping, and molding elements: the crafting of a narrative" (1987, 2–3). It should not escape our attention that Davis puts all the crucial words — "fictional," "historical," and "real" — in quotation marks. (The use of quotation marks around terms in postmodernist writing deserves a special study.) Davis aims at relativizing historiography at a deeper level: already the historian's cherished archival documents show features of fictionality. But we will be much less affected by this conclusion if we realize that Davis's documents are of a special kind — letters of remission, in which a convicted criminal, usually a murderer, asks the king for pardon. After all, such letters have to present a moving tale in order to influence favorably the only person who can save the supplicant's life.

5. These modes of emplotment may be, however, admitted if they "[have] been set forth in a pointedly ironic way," as in Art Spiegelman's comic book that represents the Holocaust "in a mode of bitter satire, with Germans portrayed as cats, Jews as mice, and Poles as pigs." We might question the tastefulness of such a representation, but we have to agree with White that it is not "conventional history" (1992, 40, 41). Spiegelman's comics are no "historical narrative" and therefore have no bearing on White's argument.

6. There is even an existential import to possible worlds, stated succinctly by Janet H. Murray: "To be alive in the 20th century is to be aware of the alternative pos-

sible selves, of alternative possible worlds, and of the limitless interacting stories of the actual world" (1997, x).

7. Using a different term, Kirkham proposes the same definition: "Of particular interest is the subset of *naturally* possible worlds, which is the subset of worlds having all and only the same laws of nature as the actual world" (1992, 15).

8. Lewis, emphasizing that "things in different worlds are *never* identical," links the various incarnations of one thing in different worlds by the "counterpart relation" that is "a relation of similarity"; thus he seems to assume that the counterparts (have to) share some essential properties. But his relationship of similarity is flexible enough to link the Hitler of history and a Hitler who led "a blameless life." In the end, Lewis disarms all those who might classify him as essentialist with a charming innocence: "The essences of things are settled only to the extent that the counterpart relation is, and the counterpart relation is not very settled at all" (1983, 27–29, 42).

9. Chisholm considers the term "actual" ambiguous and proposes instead "the world that obtains" or "the prevailing world" (1981, 129); this might be a useful terminological suggestion, but it only confirms the need for assigning to one possible world exclusive ontological status.

10. This tactic, like everything under the sun, is not entirely novel. R. G. Collingwood, trying to define the difference between fiction and history, resorted to the opposition between a multitude of worlds of fiction and one and only one world of history: "Purely imaginary worlds cannot clash and need not agree; each is a world to itself. But there is only one historical world, and everything in it must stand in some relation to everything else, even if that relation is only topographical and chronological" (1993, 246). W. B. Gallie perceived the difficulties of this position (1964, 57–62), but did not offer a possible-worlds alternative.

11. For a study of fantastic worlds in the period of realism, see Traill 1996; the world of the "modern myth" is reconstructed in Doležel 1998, 185–98.

12. Even in the domain of fiction, the construction of impossible worlds is achieved only at the price of ruining the entire enterprise of fiction-making (see Doležel 1998, 165).

13. With respect to fictional counterparts of actual places, the principle of verisimilitude has been rejected by Ronen: "a) it is impossible to demarcate essential properties of Paris which do (or should) recur in each of its literary constructions; b) diverse descriptive sets can be attributed to the same name in different fictional worlds and therefore descriptions that replace a name in one particular fictional world cannot be transferred or applied to other possible worlds" (1988, 503). Discussing the opposition of biography and fiction, Cohn emphasizes "the biographer's constraint and the novelist's freedom" (1989, 6).

14. Tolstoy thus was able to present the campaign of 1812 as a war where all classes of Russian society fought enthusiastically. He created a radical contrast between Napoleon, who "wants to control history, who is convinced that he controls history," and Kutuzov, who believes only in the force of the people. He employed the subtle narrative device of "making strange" to strengthen the contrast between the French and the Rus-

sian story line. Shklovsky comes to the conclusion that *War and Peace* "is not history," it is "canonization of a legend" (1970, 64, 72, 60, 71, 75).

15. Example borrowed from Heintz (1979, 94).

16. Let me emphasize that fictional semantics has to differentiate between gaps and implicit fictional facts; the former are irrecoverable, the latter are recovered by inference (for details see Doležel 1995, 201–14, and 1998, 169–77).

17. "Confronted with the great diversity of nonrepetitive individual or mass happenings, the historian must choose which 'facts' he considers important and which he must discard as 'irrelevant' " (Baron 1986, 15).

18. Trevor-Roper states the bond between discovering sources and writing history: "When I found myself in possession of these . . . major sources, I believed that I was in a position to reconstruct and perhaps explain the life of Backhouse" (1976, 9).

19. These photographs are reprinted from Volkogonov (1991).

20. Frege does not use the term "fiction," but his German "Dichtung" is as close as one could get to the English term.

21. For details see Doležel (1998, 145–68).

22. To distinguish the sentences of the fictional text from statements about the fictional world, Pavel designated the latter as *ersatz-sentences* (1975–76). John Woods dramatized the truth conditions of *ersatz-sentences* by calling them "bet-sensitive": one would win a bet on "Sherlock Holmes lived on Baker Street," but lose a bet on "Sherlock Holmes lived on Berczy Street" (1974, 13–14). Charles Crittenden supports the truth valuation of statements about fictional worlds by an argument that is especially relevant in the context of contemporary literary theory: "The contents of a story — its fictional world — have an independent status that can be learned by anyone who reads it. These contents are objective and independent of individual belief in this way: whether a certain character is in a story or whether a given state of affairs holds there are not matters of arbitrary belief; rather, these depend on what the sentences setting out the story say" (1991, 93).

23. For a criticism of the "semiotic idealism" of constructivist philosophy see Savan 1983 and Freudlieb 1988.

24. In "Le discours de l'histoire" Barthes applies the general idea of the performative character of writing to historical discourse: "Historical discourse is a rigged performative in which the seeming constative (descriptive) is no more than the signifier of a speech act as an act of authority" (17). Let us remark that Barthes, in fact, violates the spirit of "Oxford philosophy"; Austin exhibited the performative, but did not jettison the constative.

25. "The fundamental compass of narrative" is "a world of individuals." "Cervantes's Don Quijote is not basically a type or symbol, but an individual" (Martínez-Bonati 1981, 24).

26. I mention the year 1932 since that year saw the publication of *If It Had Happened Otherwise: Lapses into Imaginary History,* edited by J. C. Squire. The second expanded edition (1972) includes George Trevelyan's essay going back to 1907. A comprehensive treatment of the issues of counterfactual history is Alexander Demandt's book (1993);

but its theoretical value is severely impaired by the author's total ignoring or ignorance of the idea of possible worlds in contemporary scholarship. Just as I was finishing this paper, Niall Fergusson's collection (Fergusson 1997) came to my attention. I did not have a chance to study the counterfactual narratives of this book, nor the editor's long (ninety-page) introduction. The very existence of this book lends new credence to the "parlor-game" of counterfactual history.

27. It is, I believe, the contingency of history that makes all predictions about its future course very risky.

28. Nozick's original formulation should be pondered: "I am tempted to say that explanation locates something in actuality, showing its actual connections with other actual things, while *understanding* locates it in a network of possibility, showing the connections it would have to other nonactual things or processes" (1981, 12).

29. The cognitive significance of counterfactuals has increased considerably since they were legitimated by David Lewis's possible-worlds logic (1973). Contemporary cognitive research suggests that "to reason counterfactually and to deal, more generally, with imaginal possibilities, is an important component of intelligence" (Roese and Olson 1995, 5).

30. Wolfe is not deterred by what many take to be the most importunate question: "How could a journalist, writing nonfiction, accurately penetrate the thoughts of another person?" The answer is "marvelously simple": "interview him about his thoughts and emotions, along with everything else" (1973, 32).

31. This is what Smart does with Truman Capote's *In Cold Blood.* He points out "three significant passages in the novel which have been invented or altered" and other incidents that "are apparently less than completely accurate" (1985, 81–84).

32. Paratext has to be taken in the broadest sense: all appendices to the world-constructing text, whether they are within the work itself (subtitles, mottoes, prefaces), or found in the author's commentaries outside the work.

33. The sphere of highest indeterminacy in factual narrative is the impenetrable and untestable sphere of private experience. Leona Toker hints that the concept of "reader hesitation" might be helpful: "[T]he reader may hesitate between accepting the material as true or mendacious — or else as precise or approximate" (1997, 198). But there is no theoretical advantage gained in replacing a semantic concept with a pragmatic one. In order for the reader to hesitate, he or she has to hesitate about something. The object of the hesitation is inscribed at the semantic level, not at the pragmatic (psychological) level of hesitation. For a critique of Todorov's original notion of reader's hesitation see Traill 1996, 4–5.

PART FOUR

Narrative Media, Narrative Logics

10 | Essential Narrative: Tempics and the Return of Process
Gary Saul Morson

This essay proposes an alternative to traditional poetics. Schools of poetics, for all their variety, view the literary work as something graspable as a whole, whose well-wrought structure is visible at a glance when the work is over. Details in the work are entirely explicable in terms of each other, and earlier ones may be understood by how they lead to later ones. For this reason, the temporality of literary works as understood by poetics is radically different from that of life, because in life there is genuine contingency. In a literary work, the purely contingent is, from the structural point of view, a flaw. Moreover, in life time flows only forward; unless one believes in omens, there is nothing equivalent to foreshadowing.

But a number of narrative masterpieces are genuinely works of process, written without an advance or overall plan of the whole. Though a minority, these works are rife with contingency, and, often, open to events of the real world. Often published serially, they proceed only forward, and there is no possibility of altering earlier parts to make them fit with later ones. Sometimes this form of writing is undertaken deliberately to illustrate the openness of time, as Dostoevsky and Tolstoy insisted. Such processual works—which include The Idiot, The Possessed, War and Peace, Anna Karenina, Eugene Onegin, *and* Tristram Shandy—*demand a different aesthetics, which I call* tempics. *Any attempt to force a structure on such works leads to a misunderstanding of them and reflects the fact that critics have no alternative to poetics at their disposal.*

Tempics is also designed to offer an alternative to a rather different trend in modern Western thought: that form of rationalism that seeks to eliminate contingency from an understanding of life. My essay discusses some examples of this aspiration in the social sciences, insofar as they are afflicted with "physics envy." In seeking to eliminate contin-

gency, this form of social science—oddly enough—arrives by a different route at viewpoints similar to those of poetics. But a number of thinkers have taken steps toward a tempics that makes meaningful (and often aesthetic) sense of contingency. The most important of these, I think, is Darwin; in literary theory, Bakhtin. I call for the further development and generalization of their (and other) processual ideas.

Prologue: Contingency, Narrative, and Process

Where are the futurologies of yesteryear? Despite all pretensions to the contrary, we know by our own experience that the world contains unavoidable uncertainty. Contingency usually makes precise predictions impossible. But many models of life and society that have enjoyed the greatest prestige do their best to eliminate contingency. We may turn to literature to find the harmony that we miss in life—Aristotle tells us that one source of art is an inborn desire for harmony—but we know that perfect order marks a work as artificial.

In his classic study *The Growth of Philosophic Radicalism,* Elie Halévy refers to a style of thought he memorably calls "moral Newtonianism" (1955, 6). The term names an aspiration that has dominated European thought since the seventeenth century: just as Newton found universal and timeless laws of the natural world, so a social (or "moral") science may find such laws of the human world. These laws will be statable "geometrically," that is, as principles from which specific events and institutions may be deduced with (ideally) an iron-clad rigor. Crucially, all such models treat contingency as something to be overcome. To the extent that a discipline still needs to invoke the merely contingent to explain a set of events, it has not yet achieved its scientific aspirations. Or to put the point differently, so long as *narratives are essential* (rather than simply illustrative and dispensable) to a discipline's explanations, it is flawed.

To be sure, many thinkers have challenged this aspiration—Tolstoy called it a superstition—and have proposed models in which contingency, open-ended processes, and irreducible uncertainty have played a central role. These challengers have hardly been minor figures: they include Darwin, Clausewitz, Adam Smith, Mikhail Bakhtin, and Jane Jacobs. To use the terminology of another challenger, Sir Isaiah Berlin, these are "foxes," aware of many truths irreducible to systematic unity, who have dismissed as utopian the faith of their "hedgehog" opponents that uncertainty, plurality, and the need for narrative will surely turn out to be temporary obstacles.

Nevertheless, the foxes themselves have been, we might say, "hedgehog-ized." Clausewitz, who argued that military theory must take into account the sheer contingency and inevitable "friction" of battle, has been turned into a proponent of deductive laws; and a similar fate has overtaken Smith and Darwin. Bakhtin was first turned into a structuralist and then into a Marxist, despite his pronounced hostility to both movements. This common fate eloquently testifies to the power of hedgehogism over modern thought.

I believe that a reorientation of thought would be productive. Indeed, it is already under way. I look forward to a detailed enunciation of an alternative view exploring the role that contingency and open-ended processes play in diverse disciplines. We might then arrive not at a comprehensive *system* but at some flexible maxims for taking contingency seriously. Laws would still be sought where they are genuinely possible, but geometric thinking and moral Newtonianism would not be adopted by default, as if no other way of thinking were respectable. We would have to *choose* between Newtonianism and "Darwinism," and in each case give reasons for our choice.

When a foxy, Darwinian view proved in order, we would see the world in terms of *processes*. I use the term "process" here in a special sense, to refer to sequences of events that manifest some discernible continuity and integrity, but which cannot be described as a mere "unfolding" of something already given. As Bakhtin liked to observe, the chronotope of unfolding is only one of many possible chronotopes. Genuine process allows for more than one alternative at some or all moments. No conceivable model could tell us what *must* happen at any given moment, for the moment possesses what Bakhtin calls *eventness* (*sobitiinost'*). When time is open in this way, each moment contains a *field of possibilities*. Some possibilities are more likely to be actualized than others, but none is inevitable, even if external obstacles do not intervene. If the moment could be repeated—if the tape could be played over again—something else might happen. To understand a moment is to grasp not only what did happen but also what else *might have happened*. I call the style of thinking oriented towards this sort of processes *tempics*.[1]

When one thinks in terms of tempics, narrative and eventness cannot be thought away. Ironically enough, however, a great deal of the history of poetics, which has of course been centrally concerned with storytelling, has itself consisted in overcoming narrative. This tendency is most evident in structuralist narratology, which spatializes plots and offers us a pattern, if not a symmetrical diagram, of what has happened. The sequence of events thereby becomes the realization, or unfolding, of the design that has governed the whole. Clearly, no room exists for contingency.

Structuralism, which may be considered an extreme form of poetics, makes visible assumptions present in softer versions. From Aristotle to the present, numerous schools of poetics have found different reasons for calibrating the success of a work according to its capacity to embrace as much as possible into an all-encompassing design. For Aristotle, and for the tradition of poetics deriving from him, the harmony of art insures that everything fits. It makes a perfect "unity." Nothing is just *there,* as it is in life, but everything is there for a purpose.[2] Otherwise the artwork would be flawed. A perfect poem manifests perfect form—a term that in Aristotle's thought means something like an overall plan or formula—or as we might say today, control of information. When a work is properly composed, all the matter out of which it is made has been subject to its design, "the structural union of the parts being such that, if any one of them is displaced or removed, the whole will be disjointed and disturbed. For a thing whose presence or absence makes no visible difference, is not an organic part of the whole" (Aristotle, 52). In the well-made work, nothing is *contingent,* if by the contingent we mean, as Aristotle defines the term, something that can either be or not be.

The idea of the work as a *whole,* as a unity, as the product of an overall design of one sort or another, perhaps constitutes the most recurrent theme in poetics. Principles of unity vary considerably, and we have even seen models in which unity is in effect conspiratorial, with a hidden design discrediting a manifest one. Different genres have been described as aspiring to different kinds of unity. Like principles of unity, types of relevance to an overall design have also varied from school to school, genre to genre, movement to movement, and period to period. But the idea that in a successful work some sort of overall design ideally governs all has remained remarkably constant.

Contingency, the presence of something that does not fit the overall design, can therefore only be a lapse. To be sure, in practice, critics almost always realize that in a lengthy narrative, not everything will fit. But perfect fit remains the asymptotic ideal. In *Before Reading,* Peter Rabinowitz cites an impressive array of very different theorists who have argued for total relevance of all details: Roland Barthes claimed that "a narrative is made up solely of functions: everything, in one way or another, is significant. . . . There are no wasted units." E. M. Forster contended in *Aspects of the Novel* that "we expect him [the plot-maker] to leave no loose ends. Every action of word in a plot ought to count." More colorfully, William Wimsatt and Monroe Beardsley maintained that "poetry succeeds because all or most of what is said or implied is relevant; what is irrelevant has been excluded, like lumps from pudding and 'bugs' from machinery." And Jane Tompkins justifies an interpretation by saying that "it is able to account for portions of the text that have hitherto been seen as irrelevant." It would be hard to pick critics more divergent in their theoretical commitments, yet they all agree on a version of the same point: that, as Barthes says, "everything signifies something" (Rabinowitz 1987, 48).

Rabinowitz then defends a countertradition, to which an early book of mine belongs (1981). This countertradition allows that perfection is rarely reached. Moreover, it stresses that not all details are equally important. Martin Price makes the point effectively. He sees the "irrelevant detail" in a realistic novel as constantly challenging the boundaries of design, at once representing the threat of mere contingency and asserting the presence of form barely reaching to it. Such details

> are there and, being there, they demand a share in the structure of the book. . . . They may be reminiscent of that rougher texture at the lower part of the statue or the building, at once an element of the design and a vestige of the resistant materials from which the work was fashioned. They are not to be put by entirely; if they contribute to the condition of illusion or testify to the real, they also budge somewhat the inner meaning or structure of the work. It must be extended, however slightly, to admit their presence. So long as they have this power, the meaning always remains in process, the form always emerging. (36)

"Always emerging": Price here recognizes that reading is an activity that takes place over time. Some theorists have stressed this process as an alternative to the structure of structuralists and thereby returned temporality to the work. We see this move in reader reception and rhetorical theory from Stanley Fish and Wolfgang Iser on; reading is itself an event, a sort of second plot. James Phelan has eloquently objected to the structuralists' omission of "the temporal progression of reading." "The dynamics of a text's movement are as much a part of it as are the binary oppositions [Robert] Scholes makes central. Both are elements that must be inferred from the literal surface of the text" (Phelan 1989, 75).

Phelan, Rabinowitz, and Price bravely remind us of distortions produced by spatializing narrative. I would like to take their argument one step further and suggest that, in some cases, not just temporality but genuine eventness is written into "the literal surface of the text." Phelan clings to the inevitability of an "overall design" in a successful work (1989, 111). He does not so much do away with the concept of a spatialized structure as he doubles it to include both the plot of the characters and the plot of reading.

> On this account, the text contains not just the patterns of instabilities, tensions, and resolutions but also the authorial audience's responses to those patterns. In other words, the concept of progression assumes that the narrative text needs to be regarded as *the fusion of two structures:* (1) the narrative structure per se—essentially the structure that [Peter] Brooks describes in his model, or what I call the pattern of instabilities and tensions; and (2) the sequence of responses

to that structure that the text calls forth from the authorial audience. (1989, 115; my emphasis)

The fusion of two structures: though the Aristotelian concept of form has been enriched, it has not been transcended.

Aristotle contrasts art with life because life does genuinely display contingent events that do not "tend to a single result." Is it impossible for literature to imitate that aspect of life? I am not speaking here of a dadaist work that includes random events to make the point that events may be random; for in that case we can see an overarching, if paradoxical, design governing the whole. I mean to ask whether some successful works may not be characterized by genuine eventness, process, open time, and fields of possibility, in much the way life is. Phelan insists that only the "narrative audience" (which takes the narrator and his account to be real) but not the "authorial audience" can accept genuine contingency. "The authorial audience, meanwhile, will seek to uncover what synthetic purpose the signs of an allegedly unplanned development are actually serving."[3] Undoubtedly, that is usually so, but is it necessarily and always so?

I believe it is not. The exceptions, though a minority of works, include some of the world's greatest masterpieces, including Tolstoy's *War and Peace* and *Anna Karenina;* Dostoevsky's *The Possessed, A Writer's Diary,* and, especially, *The Idiot;* Sterne's *Tristram Shandy;* Byron's *Don Juan;* and Pushkin's *Eugene Onegin* (which borrows its aesthetic from Byron and Sterne). But because poetics pretty much gives us no tools for examining genuine process, this aspect of these masterpieces has either been ignored or thought away on a priori grounds. As the foxes have been hedgehogized, processual works have been poeticized. Poetics does indeed work for most masterpieces. But not for all, and so we need an alternative, a tempics, for the rest. In each case, the choice between poetics and tempics should be just that, a choice.

Moral Newtonianism and poetics both describe worlds in which contingency has been banished. They make remarkably similar assertions, at which they have arrived by different routes. But not entirely different. Both are intertwined with theological history, which is one reason that the poet and God have so often been compared. Both creators know everything that will happen in the world they have created. St. Augustine draws the analogy explicitly in the course of his famous discourse on time in the *Confessions.* For Augustine, God has established and foreseen each event to take place in the history of the world; all events are guided according to a providential design. God knows history whole, from outside, for "in the eternal nothing can pass away but the whole is present" (1960, 265). Crucially, God does not exist in time and did not create the world at any particular time; he created time along with the world and remains outside it. "Times are not co-eternal with you [God]" (303). If that were not so, then God could be affected by events, which would make him imperfect and unable fully to foresee the future. Only a single will, not a succession of wills, describes God's action.

So it is with our experience of verse. Augustine explains: I begin a line — *Deus creator omnium* — and at whatever point I am reciting I have the whole in mind. What we do with a psalm God does with our whole lives and with all of time. To the mind of God "are known all things past and future, just as I know one well-known psalm. . . . [W]hatever there is of ages past and of ages to come is no more hidden than there are hidden from me as I sing that psalm what and how much proceeded from its beginning and what and how much remains to the end" (303).

The idea that the world, like a poem, is perfectly designed means that the future is already given for us as it is for characters in an already written novel. But what if, as Bakhtin suggested, God is not outside history but an actor in it? What if we do not think away all those passages in Genesis where Yahvew repents of his anger, regrets he made man, or allows himself to be persuaded by Abraham? In that case, the world would not resemble a perfectly designed poem; it would proceed processually. And sometimes, literary narrative does, too.

I shall begin by describing more precisely the aspects of literary works that processual writers sought to overcome as they attempted to give a central role to real eventness and contingency (sections 1 and 2). I shall then draw, in some detail, comparisons with the understanding of contingency in nonliterary thinkers (sections 3 to 7). At the end of this essay, I shall briefly sketch out what a tempics of processual works might look like (section 8).

1. Pies

As readers, we are all prophets. When we are engaged in a well-made novel, we know in advance many things we could not know in life. Should the story be nearing its end, we rule out certain events as impossible because they would make the narrative incoherent. Incidents that would make no sense thematically will not occur. We look for loose ends to be tied up and outstanding mysteries to be resolved. The fact that the work has been designed provides something close to a guarantee that an overall pattern is being traced.

In life, we lack such guarantees. None of us, I imagine, would believe we are immune to harm in a dangerous situation because our life would then be pointless. We are not confident that old friends will reappear at crucial moments, or at all. Loose ends, missed opportunities, and mere accidents compose the very fabric of real life, as they do not in literature. Things do not all fit. That is because no one has designed our lives in advance, and we experience the world, with all its chanciness and surprises, moment to moment as a process tending nowhere in particular.

A character in Chekhov's play *The Three Sisters* wishes that the life we are leading now were merely a "rough draft," taking place in some purely hypothetical time, so that we might then correct it and live it over the right way in real time. Then, he says, I would not only wish for flowers, but would have them, and would act on the opportunities I have let pass. Authors can indeed go over their works until they manifest a perfect pattern, one where every detail contributes to the whole. But in life we live our rough drafts; they are all we have. As W. H. Auden writes, none of us is perfect like the fountains; "We live in freedom by necessity, / A mountain people dwelling among mountains."[4]

Thus, even the most realistic novel fails to capture the temporality of lived experience.[5] It is too neat where life is messy, too much of a finished product, too directed to a goal implicit from the start. Tolstoy and Dostoevsky were keenly aware of this fact, and engaged in radical experiments with novelistic form in order to capture the open-ended time of lived experience. The fact that so many people have felt, as Matthew Arnold did, that *Anna Karenina* is not a piece of art but a piece of life indicates that Tolstoy succeeded to a considerable extent. Readers of Dostoevsky have felt that his thrilling scenes, in which characters stand on the threshold of a momentous choice, possess something more than literary suspense, something closer to the real openness of life. But what readers see, critics explain away. Although *War and Peace* and *The Idiot* violate to great effect traditional critical rules, they are still interpreted according to those rules.

How, specifically, does the temporality of most great literary narratives differ from that of life? To begin with, well-made novels, dramas, and epics possess *closure* (or, as Phelan would say, completion).[6] As critics from Aristotle to the present have stressed, they do not just end but resolve everything into a pattern retrospectively visible at a glance. That is why there are, ideally, no loose ends, no events that occur for no particular reason. And so readers know that if something happens, it must fit a pattern still unfolding and eventually visible. The characters, of course, are unaware of this pattern; they live, as we do, into open time. "Rules of notice" and "rules of significance" used by the "authorial audience" lie outside their purview, because they are not reading a novel but living lives.[7] The reader therefore sees and evaluates events from a perspective fundamentally different from theirs. They are immersed in events, we contemplate them from outside.[8] What for the character may be a mere accident may be for the reader a sign. Countless forms of narrative irony depend on this divergence of perspective.

Consider that first of all literary devices to be taught in high schools, foreshadowing. The hero is feasting in triumph, but the author pauses to describe a storm on the horizon. This storm will not itself cause any damage; from the character's standpoint, it is simply a meteorological fact. But the reader recognizes the storm as a sign from the author that a catastrophe is coming. That is, the storm has meaning only because of the reader's awareness that the whole is designed to show a pattern, in which past, present, and future are all taken into account from the outset. In life, the present moment has special significance, because the past is fixed and the future is not; but for the reader of novels, presentness is nothing more than the page we happen to be on. The future is already given, literally inscribed, and actions are pulled forward from events that *will be* as much as they are pushed by those that have already been. Otherwise, signs from the future would be impossible. The same people who reject the existence of omens in life easily accept foreshadowing in a novel, because the temporality of the two are so different. In novels, causation works both ways, from the past and from the future. There is backward as well as forward causation. In this special sense, time is symmetrical, whereas in life it is asymmetrical.[9] In life, the future depends on what we do now; in novels, it is as fixed by a plan of the whole as is the past.

At the beginning of *Great Expectations,* Pip gives a pie to a convict, and the reader knows that this act will prove significant, as indeed it does. If the event led nowhere, the author would not have included it at all. Novels are filled with such "pies," and when we read Dickens, our pleasure derives in part from his superb pie-baking skill. Characters encountered apparently at random turn out to be mysteriously tied to other characters. In *Bleak House,* the woman who first raised Esther is discovered to be Boythorn's lost love and Lady Dedlock's sister. And so on. Almost everyone in *Bleak House* turns out to be related to someone else in one surprising way or another. Dickens's confectionery produces awe that contributes strongly to our pleasure and constitutes one reason for his greatness.

So strong is our confidence in the design of a well-made novel that we believe we have detected a flaw when a loose end is not tied up.[10] But in life we have no such expectations. We do not expect our daily donations to be Dickensian pies; we cast our bread upon the water, but are surprised if it is returned manyfold. It would be pathological, paranoid, to believe that every event of our lives must be significant or else it wouldn't have happened; which is another way of saying that, in reading literature, we properly engage in forms of interpretation characteristic in real life of madmen.[11]

And yet scholars do often interpret, if not their daily lives, then culture, society, and history this way. In former centuries, this practice made sense because it was assumed that the world did have a Designer guaranteeing the significance of each detail, if we could only find it. Strange meanings were found that to us seem rather whimsical, as in bestiaries. Cicero's *The Nature of the Gods* and *On Divination* offer a catalogue of systems finding meaning in the most haphazard of occurrences. Later, the whole tradition of natural philosophy was based on the idea that God had revealed himself in two books, Scripture and Nature.[12] In understanding the world, we are reading, however unsurely, the divine mind, who made nature as perfect as the best poem, or more so.

The movement often called cultural poetics, a kind of invasion of literary criticism into adjacent disciplines like history and sociology, also often presumes the meaningfulness of apparently remote cultural events, practices, and artifacts. Apparently inspired by Clifford Geertz and Michel Foucault, scholars with great ingenuity find connections between events that are not alleged to have any causal link. As in a poem, meaningfulness is there to be found. But is it, or are these connections arbitrary? Would they appear different if drawn between other things? Of course, events sharing nothing but simultaneity may turn out to be related in interesting ways, but unless there is some designer, how can such meaningful relations be presumed? One wants to ask: Who acted as artist of that culture, who made it all cohere? The whole idea of "the poetics of culture" implies a peculiar sort of Creationism.

In many nineteenth-century novels, like George Eliot's *Middlemarch* or Anthony Trollope's *Can You Forgive Her?*, we follow two or three plot lines, which are only loosely connected. We see these stories as reflecting on each other, detect parallels and significant variations, and are right to do so. Why else would the author have narrated them together in a single work? This whole method of writing and reading presumes a designer, that is, an outside perspective unavailable to the characters themselves. Lydgate and Dorothea do not make their choices in order to contribute to a significant story containing the both of them. When they do at last meet, they are unaware of the many parallels and telling divergences of their lives, and we experience a special thrill that comes from seeing the hand of the author exposing the always implicit fact of design.[13] But we do not read life this way. Whose lives would we connect? Anyone's? We may sometimes intimate a mystical connection between two unrelated people, but we do not suppose that any two people may be chosen for this kind of interpretation.

All these characteristics of novels, which distinguish them from life, may be subsumed under the term *structure*. A structure (or a double structure, including the reader's story) is, upon completion of the work, visible at a glance. When the novel is over, and the overall pattern revealed, we admire the way in which everything relates to everything else in a hierarchy of meaning. As we have seen, it is not that everything is equally important, since structure makes some less important details contribute to more important ones; and it is not that authors do not sometimes fail to achieve the ideal; but ideally nothing is absolutely irrelevant. Each detail we notice — and we notice more on each reading — "budges somewhat the inner meaning or structure of the work." Indeed, when a passage appears extraneous, or not to bear its weight in pages, critics almost habitually look for the significance that has been missed. Perhaps alluding to Wimsatt's and Beardsley's pudding, Stanley Fish refers to this process as "transmuting the lump." [14] It is very hard to refute the assumption of a masterpiece's design, because any seeming flaw constitutes a problem for critics to explain away. Apparent refutations are future dissertations.

2. Pure Process

In the acknowledged masterpieces I mentioned earlier, the assumption of a perfect structure or overarching design is unwarranted. *War and Peace, Anna Karenina, The Idiot, The Possessed, Tristram Shandy, Don Juan,* and *Eugene Onegin* manifestly have loose ends, which are visible from a reading of the work and often explicitly insisted upon by the author. When *War and Peace* was being serialized, for instance, Tolstoy wrote and separately published an essay ("Some Words about the Book *War and Peace*") about the ongoing work, in which he declared that there were bound to be loose ends because he was deliberately not planning the story in advance. After all, he argued, history and individual lives are filled with contingencies, which novels usually rule out. The truth demands that his story not guarantee the significance of events, that there be no foreshadowing, and that no overall plan of the whole should ensure the meaningfulness of earlier events in terms of later ones.

So that such spurious guarantees would be absent, Tolstoy wrote, he was publishing each section of the "book" (he refused to call *War and Peace* a novel because the action of novels is directed toward a dénouement) with no knowledge of what would happen to his characters later. In each section, he would simply develop some of the potentials of earlier sections; as in life, time would flow only forward, into an open future. There would be a succession of wills, which could not be added up to a single one. Necessarily, some potentials would not be exploited, and events that seemed rich in promise would sometimes lead nowhere. "I strove only so that each part of the work would have an independent interest, which would consist not in the development of events but in development itself," Tolstoy explained. "Development itself," pure process in open time: the temporality of *War and Peace* would resemble that of life as we live it and not as we usually read about it.[15]

From the perspective of poetics, such a declaration could only be spurious, directed to a narrative but not an authorial audience; but that is just the sort of thinking Tolstoy wanted to defy by his special method of creation and by publishing "Some Words" separately while *War and Peace* was being serialized. He was insisting that his book should be read differently: that as author, he was closer to the perspective of a character with no knowledge of how everything would turn out.

War and Peace argues at length that battles and history are shaped by the unpredictable and cannot be reduced to a plan. After battles are over, historians commit "the fallacy of retrospection" by treating everything that happens as the result of someone's plan, but this reasoning fits the facts only by "stencil work," that is, by focusing only on confirming evidence. If one reads *War and Peace* as reflecting a unified design, one commits the same fallacy that the book repeatedly exposes.

Like Tolstoy's adored *Tristram Shandy*, *War and Peace* does not have closure; it just breaks off. In fact, Tolstoy contemplated making *War and Peace* much longer. As we have it, it begins in 1805 and ends in the late 1810s, but according to "Some Words," Tolstoy once thought to continue the story through 1856 or beyond.[16] *War and Peace* is a mere preface to what it might have been. In principle, it is endless and would never have had closure no matter how long it had continued. *War and Peace* is not a very long book, but one of indeterminate length. The threads remain untied, projecting into a future unknown: as our lives are.

Of course, critics have endeavored to provide closure for *War and Peace* as they have for *Tristram Shandy*, but such efforts are always strained because they derive from the a priori assumption of structure and overall design. After the fact, one could always think process away because it is over. That, apparently, is one reason that, after critics assumed *Anna Karenina* had ended with its eponymous heroine's suicide at the end of part 7, Tolstoy published part 8. And, as George Steiner appropriately asks, why not parts 9 and 10?[17] If an end, as Aristotle and theorists of closure have argued, tolerates nothing after it because a design is completed, then *War and Peace* and *Anna Karenina* do not have ends. And can anyone really say that Sterne could not have produced another part of *Tristram Shandy?*

Dostoevsky began writing without an advance plan for a more prosaic reason. We may picture him as he long was, hiding in Western Europe where he had gone to escape debtor's prison, having pawned his wife's clothes and their wedding rings, unable to get further advances from his publishers, and compelled to produce something, anything. In these conditions, he wrote *The Idiot,* frantically composing sections between his epileptic seizures and having them published with no idea where the novel was going. As this compulsive gambler remarked in one letter, "I took a chance as at roulette. Maybe it will develop as I write it!"[18] When we wonder what a character will do in a moment of crisis, the author does, too, and we sense that in this novel suspense is more than a device. That is, Dostoevsky learned how to make a virtue of necessity and to transfer the excitement and openness of the creative process to the novel itself. He made a principle of writing processually, as he was later to do, with accompanying explanatory essays, in *A Writer's Diary.*

In fact, the processual nature of intentionality, discovery, and creativity— of life itself—became one of *The Idiot*'s main themes. Ippolit, a character who seems to come out of nowhere, occupies some forty pages with his mad reminiscences about his anticipated death from tuberculosis and the ways in which his experience of time has changed. A few days ago, he explains, he gave up studying Greek and threw the book down in disgust: "I will die before I get to the syntax." Perhaps the most famous passage of the book occurs when he literally globalizes his insights: "Oh, you may be sure that Columbus was happy not when he had discovered America, but when he was discovering it. . . . It's life that matters, nothing but life—the process of discovering, the everlasting and perpetual process, not the discovery itself, at all" (1962, 374–75).

The Idiot is itself pure process. Time flows only forward; there is no overall design of the whole that selects events. Dostoevsky repeatedly signals that this is the case. For example, he has characters comment on recent events in the press—they are all reading and quoting the newspapers—that had not happened when the initial parts of the novel were published and so (as the reader well knew) could not have been part of any design governing the opening sections. Accounts of just-breaking, sensational crimes occupy the characters, who wonder if they might themselves commit, or fall victim to, similar ones. Some do, and some don't. In the meantime, their periodical fears exist as pure potential, as *genuine* possibilities that might or might not take place, depending on how the novel happens to develop and on what else occurs in the real world beyond the author's control.[19]

Far from having an end in mind, toward which all events are flowing, Dos-

toevsky did not sketch out the final scene — surely one of the most powerful in
world literature — until he was finishing the third part of four; and even then,
the notebooks demonstrate, he continued to toy with very different alternatives. Of course, it is possible that a novelist writing without a plan might seize
on an idea because it retrospectively creates an overall design, but why must
this necessarily be the case? In fact, most loose ends are not tied up in this
novel, and a catalogue of the important ones would occupy many pages. One
example may give a taste of many. In part 1, Myshkin experiences a series of
conflicts with Ganya that seem to promise a major confrontation before the
novel's end. Ganya says he is sure they will either be great friends or great ene-
mies, and three times calls Myshkin ominously (and eponymously) an "idiot."
All the weight of the title, and many other rules of notice, seem to cry out that
the other shoe will drop. But this is a novel of monopedes, and Ganya turns
into a relatively minor character who never again confronts its hero. Is this a
flaw, or is this a novel created by methods that preclude an overall design? Is it
not possible that the authorial audience is expected not to assume such a design, but to read events with only forward causality? Is it not fallacious to focus
on the handful of cases where rules of notice do turn out to be justified and
ignore the myriad cases where they do not?

With so many loose ends, this novel is a glorious mess. We move from
scene to scene, with the main characters far from view, as the author evidently
pursues any chance motif promising something of interest. In the midst of his
great scandalous events, where characters seem to go *too far*, not only for their
own peace of mind but also for Dostoevsky's already wide limits of probability,
the author is obviously experimenting as he writes, seeing if he can come up
with one more brilliant action or insight to justify all the indecency of his prose.
Along the way, he introduces what might be called "embedded critics" who say
that things have just gone *too far*, that no one would believe what is happening,
just when the reader must be thinking the same thing.[20] At one point, Ganya —
amazed that the consumptive, Ippolit, is still around to annoy him long after
characters and readers have expected him gone — remarks: "He promised to die
in three weeks, and here he is getting fatter!" (450). Like its madmen, this book
is *out of control,* and yet it somehow seems to gain from all that thrashing about.

Critics almost universally concur on two things: the work is replete with
structural flaws and yet it somehow seems to rise above them. All of traditional
poetics indicates that *The Idiot* should be a failure, and yet it is an amazing success. Such a conclusion ought to prompt critics to evaluate their criteria, but
instead they typically find some way, however improbable, to impose a structure on this strange book. Even critics who have studied the notebooks, and
know perfectly well that the author never planned what would happen next,

detect foreshadowing! The best scholar of *The Idiot*, Robin Miller, wants to assert that Myshkin's stories of execution in part 1 "foreshadow" Ippolit's confession in part 3, even though, as she has pointed out, the very idea of Ippolit had not occurred to Dostoevsky when he wrote part 1. It is worth listening to how Miller handles this problem:

> Of course we know from the notebooks that Dostoevsky had not even planned the existence of Ippolit at the time he wrote Part I of the novel. But that does not mean that we cannot talk about unities of construction in this novel. As readers, after having read a work, we *inevitably* gauge its impact upon us as a whole. Prophecies and fulfillments exist within a work; one cannot deny them simply because the writer at the beginning of his undertaking did not himself know the shape that his work would assume. (1981, 276 n. 8, my emphasis)

Prophecies and fulfillments: but what about all those promises that are *not* fulfilled? The essence of this argument is (1) no matter how the work was written, it *is* a structure, because (2) that's all it can be, we "*inevitably*" read it that way. But is it inevitable? Or is this a critic's inevitability, produced by the habits of poetics? Usually this approach works, but why must it be assumed a priori?

Notice also the priority given in Miller's formulation to re-reading as opposed to reading. After a work is over, we can take it in at a glance, spatialize it, more easily make it into a synchronic structure. But to do that with this novel, or with *War and Peace* and *Tristram Shandy,* is to read out its very soul: its sheer processuality.

Critics do this, I think, because all the tools at their disposal are (in the broad sense) structural. Usually, the only alternative to structure they see is sheer chaos. But in life we often make sense of events, and derive real pleasure from their contemplation, even when they have no structure. Process, too, has its own beauty and needs its own aesthetics. In addition to poetics, we need a way of reading relatively haphazard processes: a *tempics*.

3. Moles' Eyes

Over the past few centuries, thinkers in many disciplines have been drawn to models that, in effect, turn the world into a perfect poem. Literary theorists can learn a good deal from their reasoning and from that of their opponents.

For the moral Newtonians, the chanciness of things, their capacity to develop in unpredictable and messy ways, has been regarded as something to overcome with the right theory. Their opponents maintain that the quest for such a theory is a wild goose chase. The world does not operate by unfolding a pregiven pattern. Rather, contingency reigns in a way that is genuinely surprising. Events possess "eventness." Perhaps the most brilliant thinker ever to develop a view of the world as eventful process irreducible to structure was Charles Darwin. *The Origin of Species* stresses the messiness, historicity, and timeliness (not timelessness) of things.

In popular renditions of Darwin, many of which have pervaded the social sciences, this aspect of his thinking is often missed. When economists or political scientists refer to forces as "Darwinian," they usually mean that the pressure of competition eliminates whatever is less perfect and so drives things toward a state of optimality. Like the invisible hand, Darwinism is often invoked as an impersonal agent insuring perfection (or something approaching it).[21] Without God, it does what God would do. Pushed to this extreme, this "perfectionist Darwinism" leads thinkers to assume that if an organ or social institution exists, it must serve a current function or natural selection would have eliminated it. Like a scene in a well-made novel, it must pay its way. But to read Darwin this way is to miss his central point.[22]

The Origin of Species argues repeatedly that organisms are always *im*perfect. That is because they have derived from a long, contingent process, which insures that at each stage forms are constrained by earlier stages. In this way, adaptability is severely limited by history. Upon inspection, organisms appear temporally layered. They contain forms that are hardly optimal, and at times useless or even harmful, that have been inherited from earlier times. An organism is an *agglomeration* of parts. There must be minimal structural coherence to insure survivability, but, often enough, little more is possible. In any case, the world itself is always changing. Perfection in one environment would spell extinction in another, and so a continual process of imperfect adaptation goes on, never tending anywhere in particular. To understand a species is to comprehend it not just structurally, not just how its parts fit together to make survival possible, but also temporally, with all the vestigial organs that do not pay their way but show the marks of a long, undirected succession of earlier changes. Biology requires narrative.

To illustrate his point, Darwin describes a certain species of mole that lives its entire life underground, never seeing the light of day, but that nevertheless has eyes (1964, 137–39). Even if the mole should go above ground, its eyes would be useless because they are covered with a thick membrane. No analysis in terms of current function could adequately explain those occluded eyes.[23] Darwin also mentions a species of inland geese that copes with webbed feet, which do it no good. He insists on the significance of this incongruency, which has been wrought by time and invites interpretation as an instance of temporal layering:

He who believes that each being has been created as we now see it, must occasionally have felt surprise when he has met with an animal having habits and structure not at all in agreement. What can be plainer than that the webbed feet of ducks and geese are formed for swimming? yet there are upland geese with webbed feet which rarely or never go near the water. . . . In such cases, and many others could be given, habits have changed without a corresponding change of structure. The webbed feet of the upland goose may be said to have become rudimentary in function, though not in structure. (1964, 185)

Habits and structure not in agreement testify to the contingencies of histories. In the sense Aristotle uses when he describes poems as "organic," organisms themselves are not organic. Later in Darwin's book, we learn that the tail of a giraffe, for all the energy necessary to sustain it, serves merely as a poor fly-swatter, surely not reason enough for it to have evolved. It does not pay its way, and so little accords either with divine creation or perfectionist natural selection. In all these cases, Darwin argues, only history, by which he means processes that are shaped by contingencies and do not tend to perfection, can explain what we observe. The mole has eyes because its ancestors lived above-ground, and the inland geese have webbed feet because their ancestors lived by the water, not because these organs serve a present function in a perfectly integrated structure. The mystery of that uneconomical giraffe tail is that "organs now of trifling importance have probably in some cases been of high importance to an early progenitor, and, after having been slowly perfected at a former period, have been transmitted in nearly the same state, although now become of very slight use" (1964, 185–86). Life is a palimpsest. We need a story.

For Darwin, this point was crucial because it proved evolution by descent. Had species been created by a divine Designer, adapting them to their environment in *a single intentional expression*, they would be perfect structures. Perfection marks a unified intention, imperfection haphazard changes over time. That is why Darwin, in contrast to natural philosophers, stressed all the ways that animals are *ill*-adapted. He also observed that in similar environments around the world, animals occupying the same niche nevertheless differ, because the concept of perfect fit with surroundings, which could have been designed instantaneously, ignores history. In each locale, evolution is constrained by the materials at hand, which are themselves the contingent product of earlier times, and times layered on times. The origin of species demands explanation not by design but by narrative. To read natural selection from a perfectionist standpoint is to return, by a peculiar route, to divine creation. *The Origin of Species* imagines a world of constant small adjustments accumulating without plan, of adaptations tripping over earlier adaptations, and of unforeseeable circumstances forcing new directions again and again. It may be regarded as the best illustration of life viewed as tempics.

4. Crustaceans and Sufficient Reason

Poetics may be the oldest model of perfection we have, but it is not, I think, the most influential over the past few hundred years. Much more important in understanding the tenacious hold of perfectionist thinking is the prestige of rationalism and science, especially physics. Social sciences have been afflicted, as they say, with physics envy, as if the respectability of a discipline depended on its resemblance to Newtonian mechanics. The history of anthropology and the history of sociology contain numerous invocations to rationality and science understood in this way. Had the chosen model been geology or biology, especially evolutionary biology understood as Darwin did (and geology as Lyell did), the results might have been quite different.[24]

In *Cosmopolis,* the philosopher Stephen Toulmin chronicles a change in philosophy that took place in the time of Leibniz and Descartes. For most of Western history, and right up to Montaigne, what Aristotle called *phronesis,* or practical reasoning, was regarded as an essential part of philosophy. But the terrible experience of religious wars led philosophers to seek for timeless rules by which disputes could be arbitrated in some objective and rational manner. From this point on, properly philosophical ideas had to be concerned with the timeless, the universal, the purely theoretical, and the abstract. Ethics, for example, would be reconceived as the derivation of timeless rules that could be applied to particular instances, rather than the sensitive response to particular cases. Casuistry was out, syllogisms were in. One must reason down, not up, and truths that applied only in some cases, and which required some unformalizable experience to use, were no truths at all.

The world may appear as messy, chancy, and fortuitous, but behind all those odd shapes and random events there lies a hidden order conformable to precise, ideally mathematical, formulation: this was the faith (or superstition) that was to shape much Western thought. We see it in the nineteenth-century attempt to derive laws of history guaranteeing progress, a belief once so self-evidently correct that dissenters appeared to be mere obscurantists or curmudgeons. Had not life evolved from inanimate matter to higher and higher forms culminating in Man, and had not Man developed from the primitive cultures still existing in remote places into modern Englishmen? And why should such a process stop? Surely it was governed by laws that we may discover.

To all such reasoning, to "Buckle and Hegel," Dostoevsky's underground man replies: "[O]ne may say anything about the history of the world—anything that might enter the most disordered imagination. The only thing one cannot say is that it is rational. The very word sticks in one's throat" (1960, 27). Empirical facts, on which science supposedly relies, everywhere refute the concept of history as governed by laws and as manifesting a pattern we can descry. "But man is so fond of systems and abstract deductions that he is ready to distort the truth intentionally, he is ready to deny what he can see and hear to justify his logic" (21).

Tolstoy, known in his time as a "nyetovshchik" (one who says "nyet" to what everyone else believes), insisted that laws of history can only be discovered by imposing a template on events to make invisible everything lawless (*War and Peace* 1968, 1432). By such a method, "to subordinate history to the idea of progress is just as easy as to the idea of regress, or to any other historical fantasy that you like. I will say more: I see no necessity whatsoever to seek out general laws of history, not to mention the impossibility of doing so." The Hegelian "stencil" eliminates disconfirming evidence by ruling it out as "nonhistorical." "Progress is the general law for mankind, they say, with the sole exception of Asia, Africa, America, Australia, with the exception of one billion people. . . . To say that progress is the law of humanity is just as unfounded as to say that all people are blond with the exception of those with dark hair."[25]

Why, then, is such a belief so seductive? Because, Tolstoy answers, it is "natural and agreeable" for intellectuals to believe in laws accessible only to intellectuals, who therefore may be asked to govern the affairs of mankind.[26] Such a faith in intellectuals is sheer folly, Tolstoy asserts, just as Levin's attempts to rationalize farming in *Anna Karenina* inevitably lead to less productivity, not to mention suffering for the helpless peasants.[27] History, like battle in *War and Peace,* is made not by laws but by "a hundred million diverse chances, which will be decided on the instant by whether we run or they run, whether this man or that man is killed" (1968, 930). "On the instant": events are determined by considerations that no timeless design could take into account.

Famously, the underground man disputes the theory that individual people act rationally by choosing what is most advantageous to them according to their preferences. Dostoevsky had in mind the utilitarians, but the model is still with us, sometimes combined with game theory, in much "rational choice" theory, and, especially, in the model of rational economic man that appears in textbooks on microeconomics. In response, the underground man presents dazzling images of people who deliberately act against their preferences, for no particular reason or because, like himself, they simply do not want to be predictable. They refuse to be so many "piano keys" or "organ stops" played upon by social and psychological laws. After all, people are not atomic particles, because they can know the laws supposedly governing them and deliberately violate them.

Nothing essential to the underground man's argument would change if psychological laws included the irrational, as they do with Freud, so long as those laws supposedly reveal an iron logic the investigator can trace. The greatest psychologist in world literature, Dostoevsky declared that he was not a psychologist at all, if that term suggests the belief in laws allowing pre-diction.[28] Predictability destroys the essence of choice itself, which includes what Bakhtin called "surprisingness" and "unfinalizability." Developing Dos-toevsky's thought, which he believes to be implicit in the novel as a genre, Bakhtin insisted that we all possess a "surplus of humanness":

> An individual cannot be completely incarnated into the flesh of existing socio-historical categories. There is no mere form that would be able to incarnate once and forever all of his human possibilities and needs, no form in which he could exhaust himself down to the last word. . . . There always remains an un-realized surplus of humanness; there always remains a need for the future, and a place for this future must be found. . . . Reality as we have it in the novel is only one of many possible realities; it is not inevitable . . . it bears within itself other possibilities. (1981c, 37)

Contrast this view with that of Leibniz, the philosopher who perhaps most of all presents a picture of the world as utterly rational. To know a person is for Leibniz to know everything about him, for what he will do is given at the out-set. God has insured that we live in the best of all possible worlds, which means that at any given moment, one and only one thing can happen, for otherwise something less than the optimal would take place. Optimality and determin-ism go hand in hand. For everything that happens, according to Leibniz, there must be a "sufficient reason." Here we see how rationalism and poetics come to similar conclusions. In the well-made poem, every detail (ideally) also has a sufficient reason for being there, which it is the critic's business to discover. Lit-erary criticism has offered us countless versions of theodicy, all of which justify the ways of poets to men and prove, or rather assume, the poet to be the best of all possible makers.

While facing torture and burning at the stake, Candide asks, if this is the best of all possible worlds, what are the others like? Voltaire, I think, did not much exaggerate the implications of Leibniz's approach. Leibniz actually criti-cized Newton for not going far *enough* in creating an image of a world governed by mathematical laws. Halévy would perhaps have done better to refer to moral Leibnizians. In his well-known correspondence with Clarke, who represented

Newton's point of view, Leibniz contended that Newton's theory was flawed because, unable to show the stability of the solar system, he suggested that God occasionally intervened to maintain equilibrium. For Leibniz, such a view, which did not show the perfection of the world as God had created it, turned God into an inferior watchmaker. There can be no accidents, no instability, no need for the occasional miracle in a world designed by a perfect Being.[29]

Leibniz's assumptions about the world—equilibrium, optimality, a sufficient reason for every last thing and event, the givenness of the future—all have an exact parallel in our ideas about great poems. They have also left their mark on much, though by no means all, of social science. Social science has also often reflected Leibniz's Euclidean belief that the nature of things can often be deduced from a priori principles. Leibniz insisted to Clarke that such principles proved that no vacuums could exist (for a plenum is better than a vacuum). Clarke replied that Torricelli had in fact made a vacuum in a tube, but Leibniz was not impressed.

Newton's celestial mechanics, perfected by Laplace to show stability, eventually seemed to have achieved what Leibniz had demanded, and the impressive power of the theory became the model for numerous attempts to show that the social world might someday have its own Newton.[30] Culture and culture's laws lie hid in night; come Newton Two, and all will soon be light. Closer to our own time, Claude Lévi-Strauss insisted that social anthropology must be mathematicized to become a true science, like physics. Modern economics looks down on other social sciences because they have not been successfully mathematicized and cannot promise (as economics supposedly can) valid predictions. Those lesser disciplines still tell stories. It is therefore not surprising that over the past few decades doctoral programs in economics have taught and required less and less economic history.[31]

Heavily influenced by Russian Formalist linguistics, with its idea of language as a system, Lévi-Strauss wrote enthusiastically that modern linguistics was truly a science, in the hard sense, and that anthropology could also become one by imitating it. His "science" made a culture a perfect Formalist poem. All anthropology had to do was to find a way to study culture according to some "laws of combination" analogous to those of the (Jakobsonian) linguist or perhaps the game theorist. Lévi-Strauss was entranced by the idea that social scientists could formulate a table of human possibilities "that would be comparable to the table of elements which Mendeleieff introduced into modern chemistry." Looking at such a table, we could "discover the place of languages that have disappeared or are unknown, yet to come, or simply possible" (1963, 58). That "yet to come" is not uttered casually. Lévi-Strauss believed that with the right science one could theoretically predict that chanciest of all things, human fashion:

Some of the researches of [A. L.] Kroeber appear to be of the greatest importance . . . particularly his work on changes in the styles of women's dress. . . .
Kroeber has demonstrated that this seemingly arbitrary evolution follows definite laws . . . [that] result from measuring some basic relationships among the
various elements of costume. The relationship thus obtained can be expressed
in terms of mathematical functions, whose values, calculated at a given moment, make prediction possible. (1963, 58)[32]

Then why aren't anthropologists rich? Fashion almost stands for whimsy and
chanciness, and for Lévi-Strauss, what is crucial is that chancy things appearing
to elude systematization may in fact be subject to it: "Kroeber has thus shown
how even such a highly arbitrary aspect of human behavior is susceptible of
scientific study. His method may be usefully compared not only with that of
structural linguistics, but also with that of the natural sciences. There is a remarkable analogy between these researches and those of a contemporary biolo-
gist, G. Teissier, on the growth of the organs of certain crustaceans" (1963, 59).[33]

5. Survivals and Social Contracts

Earlier than Lévi-Strauss, the great anthropologist A. R. Radcliffe-Brown, in
the closing paragraph of his article "On the Concept of Function in Social Science," indignantly dismissed objections that anthropological laws either did
not exist or could never be found. "Argument against such a contention is un-
profitable or indeed impossible" (1935, 402), his article concludes, as if the
very questioning of laws and models based on the hard sciences were absurd
on the face of it. Radcliffe-Brown also insisted that culture is tightly organized,
that almost everything serves a function, and that order is the rule. Thus he
finds palpably absurd the anthropologist Robert Lowie's description of civilization as "that planless hodge-podge, that thing of shreds and patches" (cited
by Radcliffe-Brown, 401), and, writing in 1935, assures us that Ruth Benedict
herself would no longer accept what she wrote in 1923: "It is, as far as we can
see, an ultimate fact of human nature that man builds up his culture out of
disparate elements, combining and recombining them; and until we have abandoned the superstition that the result is an organism functionally interrelated,
we shall be unable to see our cultural life objectively or to control its manifestations."[34] It is noteworthy that Benedict clings to the idea of the social scientist
as someone to help us "control" culture even as she rejects the hypothesis of
a functionally integrated organism sometimes invoked to underwrite that ambition. Radcliffe-Brown sees Benedict's view as the consequence of diffusionist
thinking, which "tends to produce a conception of culture as a collection of
disparate entities . . . brought together by pure historical accident and having

only accidental relations to one another," as if the only alternative to pure system were pure randomness (1935, 401). He proceeds to reject her formulation as "in direct conflict with the hypothesis of the functional unity of social systems" (402). Neither Radcliffe-Brown nor Lévi-Strauss seem to be aware that, as Darwin insisted, even biological organisms do not manifest such functional unity.

Bronislaw Malinowski went even further than Radcliffe-Brown in insisting on total functional unity. Concerned to make anthropology a science, he rejected all notions of unformalizable humanistic insights as mystical and dismissed out of hand any approach that gave a role to "adventitious and fortuitous happenings" (1944, 5). Like Radcliffe-Brown and Lévi-Strauss, he, too, is appalled by the image of culture as "a patchwork of shreds and patches" (38). It is worth reflecting on the degree of hostility the "shreds and patches" view has occasioned. For Malinowski, that view is fatal to the discipline's aspirations, which include the ability, once truly scientific laws have been discovered, "for prediction of the future" (8). Again, to the extent that a narrative involving real contingency and process is required by a discipline, to that extent the discipline is felt to fall short of its scientific potential. (In practice, Malinowski proceeded much less systematically than his theoretical statements would imply.)

Malinowski's discipline also aspires to what he innocently calls "social engineering" (13), and he contends that, even before much scientific progress has been made, anthropologists should help determine the post–World War II settlement.[35] Contemplating such statements, one wonders whether these ambitions to power are themselves dictating the discipline's theories. After all, it is a poor, and hardly scientific, reason to reject a theory because its implications might diminish the prestige of the discipline adhering to it. Tolstoy's "natural and agreeable" description of how intellectuals choose ideas comes to mind. One wonders how often other social sciences, like economics and sociology, have placed the cart before the horse this way.

Malinowski pioneered the "functional" theory of culture. According to his version of this theory, every single aspect of a culture may be understood by the way it contributes to its overall functioning, by which Malinowski (in a view broadened by later anthropologists) meant the assurance of biological survival. Culture, we might say, is like a poem: everything fits. Or like Leibniz's universe: everything has a sufficient reason. There is nothing accidental, and above all, nothing that has simply persisted from earlier periods—no mere vestiges or "survivals." Malinowski, responding to the historical schools, was categorical on this point. Whatever is, is needed, or it would not be there.

A survival is "a cultural feature which does not fit with its cultural medium. It persists rather than functions, or its function somehow does not harmonize with the surrounding culture."[36] Malinowski refers to this idea as the "antiscientific concept of 'dead-weights' or cultural fossils in human culture" (27–28). In his view, closer examination always reveals that *any* apparent survival, for example the presence of horse-drawn carriages in an automobile age, has in fact acquired a new function (romantic rides). As in the study of poetry: ideas in a writer's notebooks only survive into the final text if they serve a function in the organic whole. Critics of many schools have come to look with suspicion on studies of the creative process, and Malinowski dismisses the historical, if by historical one means the "adventitious" or merely persistent. Both Malinowski and these critics reject what has come to be known as "the genetic fallacy," the idea that one understands something by seeing how it came to be. Nothing could be further from Darwin's parable of the moles' eyes.

The evidence of contingency is imperfection. Literary critics have much more right than social scientists to speak of a "genetic fallacy," because poets can go over their works to make everything fit. But what insures perfect or near-perfect coherence in a society? To answer this question, functionalist and other synchronic thinkers resort not only to versions of the invisible hand or perfectionist Darwinism, but also to myths of origin. At a given moment, things were set up in this perfectly organized way and have persisted. Malinowski speaks of institutions having an implicit "charter" oriented entirely to fulfilling specific functions to which all activities contribute (1944, 48). That is, they have "something which corresponds to Rousseau's *contrat social*" (43). Lévi-Strauss also cites Rousseau on this point (1963, 277). Of course, neither Malinowski nor Lévi-Strauss believed that there was a single moment of design, in which an intention was fully embodied, any more than Rousseau regarded the signing of a social contract as a historical event. But Malinowski did believe that cultures behave "as if" there were such a moment. He needed to see culture as if a poet, a god, or a wholly rational agent had imagined and executed it, or else there would be heterogeneous parts that "science" (as he conceived it) could not explain.

By contrast, suppose that instead of a single moment of design, a process of constant tinkering had gone on. At each moment, people did not optimize but "satisficed" (to use Herbert Simon's term) and made do, more or less, with the materials at hand.[37] Malinowski asserted that cultures only change when needs force them to, but that then they engage in a "complete remolding" of their institutions (1944, 41).[38] This activity again insures that everything fits, only in a new way. But what if there is a period of transition when things do not yet fit? And what if such "transition" is all there ever is? Unexpected events are always intervening and anyone who really spent the time and energy to remold completely would not only find his work outdated before it was finished but would also have specialized too much to adapt to a new, unforeseen situation.

In a world of uncertainty, which is the world we live in, imperfection is bound to occur and, indeed, may sometimes (however paradoxically) be better than perfection. The charter was never finished and is under endless revision, while the invisible hand is palsied.

6. "Diachrony"

The fact of change (which we usually cannot predict) is too obvious for even the most dedicated synchronic thinkers to overlook, and so they have developed ways to domesticate it. Sometimes, relying on Ferdinand de Saussure, they have regarded the world of events—where laws are "instantiated," mistakes are made and chances intervene—as outside the realm of scientific inquiry. Unfortunately, once these not entirely systematic events are set aside, their significance and effectiveness are often underestimated.

More often, the synchronic model is adapted to explain change in terms of the synchronic system itself. Here the pioneering work belongs to the Russian Formalists Roman Jakobson and Yuri Tynyanov, who contended that each "cultural series" is a system, but that systems possess imbalances that they correct over time, thus giving rise to new systems with new imbalances, and so on. Moreover, systems interact with neighboring systems, and so what seems a chance event to one cultural series may in fact be a wholly systematic expression of another. Much arbitrariness can be eliminated if we treat culture as a "system of systems." Taken together, Tynyanov and Jakobson assert, these insights allow history, purged as much as possible of the fortuitous, to be treated in structural terms:

> At the present moment, the achievements of the synchronic concept force us to reconsider the principles of diachrony as well. The idea of the mechanical agglomeration of material, having been replaced by the concept of system or structure in the realm of synchronic study, underwent a corresponding replacement in the realm of diachronic study as well. *The history of a system is in turn a system*. . . . The opposition between synchrony and diachrony was an opposition between the concept of system and the concept of evolution; thus it loses its importance in principle as soon as we recognize that every system necessarily exists as an evolution, whereas . . . evolution is inescapably of a systemic nature. (1971, 79–80)

Lévi-Strauss, whose obeisance to the Russian Formalists is impressive, adopted this model. "Evolution is inescapably of a systemic nature": nothing could be further from Darwin's view, which allowed for "agglomerations" at each present moment and haphazard events over time. The term "diachrony," as a supposedly neutral synonym for events over time, should always make us suspicious, because it so often smuggles into the argument the idea that synchronic systems explain change. As "praxis" is the theoretician's notion of practice, so diachrony is the synchronist's notion of time.

Other methods for speaking of change without admitting eventness or chanciness abound. Foucault treated periods as entirely homogeneous and as completely disconnected from subsequent periods, so that history became a series of synchronic slices. And of course, the influence of Marxism and other theories has led thinkers to detect a master story to history itself. When this procedure is used, history can be spatialized like a novel; we are in the middle of a plot tending to a goal. All these methods and more take as their primary objective the exclusion of contingency, eventness, or the open future. If narratives are invoked, they lack eventness; they are *unnecessary* narratives. Whether influenced by poetry or a Newtonian view of science, such thinkers view the messiness of life as a threat to be conjured away.

7. The Aesthetics of Process

When the spirit of poetry combines with rationalism, utopianism often results. Harmony beckons. Once it is believed that laws of society exist, and that we can know them by scientific (or imaginative) methods, then salvationist schemes are likely to appear. Those who formulate them are ready to see themselves as humanity's benefactors. In Russia, the intelligentsia lurched from one "scientifically" based utopia to another until, at last, the Bolsheviks with their scientific socialism seized power. Dostoevsky's anti-utopian analyses, his war against a mistaken poetics and a scientific view of humanity, were quite explicitly formulated as a reaction to the intelligentsia's aspirations. He objected in particular to the tendency of utopians to reach for perfection, which must be a finished product, whereas the essence of life is processual. Forecasting with uncanny accuracy the details of what we have come to call totalitarianism, he saw the ideal of harmony as a prescription for death.

Less apocalyptic thinkers than Dostoevsky have also understood the shortcoming of thinking in terms of finished products. City planning and design derive from the great utopias, which often included maps of their symmetrical spaces reflecting a single, rational idea. The first city actually to be built according to these ideas, St. Petersburg, was in fact designed by the will of a single autocrat with absolute power, Peter the Great, who was able to force his plan on recalcitrant nature and resisting people. Built on a swamp, the inhospitable capital for most of its history had a death rate higher than its birth rate, owing to disease and floods as well as to more prosaic urban dangers. From

Pushkin's "Bronze Horseman" to Bely's *Petersburg,* the city became a symbol of utopianism and life according to a rational plan. Dostoevsky's underground man complains of the "misfortune to inhabit Petersburg, the most abstract and intentional city in the whole world. (There are intentional and unintentional cities.)" (1960, 6). Intentionality here refers broadly to the idea that life can be designed like a poem or a sketch. It contrasts cities like Moscow or London, which were built by a series of accretions and continuous adaptations to contingent circumstances changing with the years, to those like Petersburg that reflected a single, overall design planned at once. As with all utopians, such designers regard the hodgepodge of past times as so much debris to be cleared away in the pursuit of order, harmony, and perfection.

That is precisely how Le Corbusier, the designer of Chandigarh (capital of the Punjab), inspirer of Brasilia, and inventor of plans for numerous unbuilt cities, regarded the "mess" of unintentional cities. "We must refuse to afford even the slightest concession to what is: to the mess we are in now," he declared.[39] On the one hand, Corbusier appealed to a *science* of planning, the sign of which is perfect, "geometric" (a term he used often) harmony. He proposed a beneficent despotism:

> The despot is not a man. It is the *Plan. The correct, realistic, exact plan,* the one that will provide your solution once the problem has been posited clearly, in its entirety, in its indispensable harmony. . . . It has been drawn up by serene and lucid minds. . . . It has ignored all current regulations, all existing usages, and channels. It has not considered whether it could be carried out by the constitution now in force. (Scott 1998, 112; his emphases)

On the other hand, this plan is also supported on purely *aesthetic* grounds. As much as anyone, Corbusier sees where poetics and Newtonianism come together, in the idea of an overall design and a single intentional expression. "The lack of order to be found everywhere in them [existing cities] offends us. . . . Why should not the town be . . . a source of poetry? Geometry is the means. . . . It is also the material basis on which we build those symbols which represent to us perfection and the divine. It brings with it the noble joys of mathematics" (1971, 1). Poetry, mathematics, and the divine: they are all the same in manifesting perfection and excluding the contingent.

In her celebrated book *The Death and Life of Great American Cities,* Jane Jacobs explores the disastrous consequence of utopian city planning, and of the more limited plans manifesting its spirit, from Ebenezer Howard's Garden City to Le Corbusier's Radiant City and David Burnham's City Beautiful. Taught in schools and encouraged by legislatures, the amalgam of these ideals ruined urban areas for reasons Dostoevsky would have understood. Cities (Dostoevsky would have said societies) work precisely because of the *diversity* of their purposes and agents, which any single-minded plan must suppress. They can work, that is, when to describe them one must resort not only to geometry but also to narrative.

As Jacobs observes, Howard, like so many planners after him, insisted that, "as in all Utopias, the right to have plans of any significance belonged only to the planners in charge. . . . He conceived of good planning as a series of static acts; in each case the plan must anticipate all that is needed and be protected, after it is built, against any but the most minor subsequent changes" (1992[1961], 17–19). For utopians, cities must be insured against contingency, process, and necessary narrative.

But cities thrive only with an incalculable variety of purposes. They need not only new but also old buildings, designed according to different fashions, styles, concepts of space, and technologies, so as to serve a mixture of needs. Projects laid down at a moment never prove adaptable to changing conditions because the very integrity of their design creates homogeneity. For the same reason, Jacobs insists that "gradual" influxes of capital are preferable to "cataclysmic" ones. Doing too much at once destroys the temporal layering necessary for diversity of purposes. After all, one cannot suddenly decide to build old buildings; they are created by time or, rather, times.

If by art we mean a design under the control of an artist realizing a prior intention, then, Jacobs insists, "*A city cannot be a work of art.* . . . To approach a city . . . as if it were a larger architectural problem, capable of being given order by converting it into a disciplined work of art, is to make the mistake of trying to substitute art for life. . . . All this is a life-killing (and art-killing) misuse of art" (1992[1961], 372–73; her emphasis). Cities can be beautiful, but not as a result of utopian artistic design.

It is diversity, rather than homogeneity, that creates urban aesthetic interest. When a city is attractive it is not because everything fits but because the eye traces a variety of patterns that yield to others in an ever-fascinating kaleidoscope of partially realized ideas and possibilities. We actively guess at stories and histories, while noting the contingencies or rival stories that arose with no advance design. There is a special aesthetics of such active viewing of life in its agglomerations and dissipations, structurings and unstructurings, with their ever-evolving energies tending to no goal. This is the aesthetics not of product but of process, not of utopian dreams but of Darwinian organisms. A beauty that cannot be reduced to a single design or intention, it is guided by no invisible hand or primordial contract.

In *How Buildings Learn*, Stewart Brand applies to architecture the perspective that Jacobs brought to cities. The problem with the credo that "form follows function" is that it presumes the initial designer knows what functions the building will serve over time. But no one knows that: "All buildings are predictions. All predictions are wrong" (Brand 1994, 178). For a building to last, it must be adaptable, as much as possible, to the unforeseeable. It must be designed with the idea that a story, unknowable in advance and never fitting a symmetrical pattern, will be told about it.

Besides, a special beauty may be visible in old buildings that have gone through layers of uses and adaptations. Contemplating them, we notice parts repeatedly modified and bearing the traces of successive uses; vestigial organs produced at many stages; a succession of processes tending nowhere in particular, each with its own integrity never dominating everything. Our mind makes such space *narrative,* as Richard Sennett likes to say, and we become involved with the tracing of partial patterns arising from each other.[40]

8. More to Come

> We are not and can never be completely without a forwardly directed grasp.
> — Husserl

I do not want to suggest that synchronic aesthetics or systems of knowledge have no place. They surely do, when we encounter artifacts in which perfect or near-perfect structure is manifest. Meaning is a function of structure and history, and when structure is ideal, history is usually irrelevant. In such cases, to understand the place of an element in a perfect design, one need only look at other elements.

That is really why, as numerous theorists have argued, the creative process is irrelevant to understanding a well-designed work. The intention is manifest in the design, and the creative process can at best tell us how the design came to be and so shed light on it only indirectly. Or to put the point differently: those who deny the relevance of the creative process, or regard it as merely an adjunct to understanding, themselves presume a certain theory of the creative process: one that, by whatever steps, leads to a design that makes that process irrelevant. But what happens when the creative process is not of that sort? What happens when we have a design that does not erase its traces or make them irrelevant — when we have a design that is itself in process and by its nature processual? Can we assume a priori that never is processual in this way?

Some artworks, and most of the rest of the social world, do not manifest a harmonious overall harmony and design. In such cases, we need a principled way of understanding that recognizes contingency and process without regarding them as simply so much arbitrary dross resistant to understanding. Rationalism and poetics have their place, but they should not be adopted by default or because of some theoretical or pseudo-scientific prejudice. To complement them, we need a way to read processes meaningfully; we need, for art and life, a tempics.

We may say of the cities Jacobs admires and the buildings Brand praises that they resemble *The Idiot* and *War and Peace*. Each manifests "unnecessary" parts resulting from a process of creation with no predetermined outcome. From the point of view of traditional poetics, these novels have numerous structural flaws; but *structural flaws exist only if one insists on reading in terms of structure*. How else might we read, if not in terms of structure?

I would like, all too briefly, to sketch out some of the characteristics of processual works and indicate how they might be read.

(1) The first and most important concept needed for understanding such works is that of *processual intentionality*. Processual intentionality is a difficult idea, contrary to our usual habits of thoughts. Tolstoy and Dostoevsky directed a great deal of their fire against those habits.

In the *Essay Concerning Human Understanding*, John Locke voices the common-sense view that intentions precede actions. Intentions may of course be changed, and we may "hold our wills undetermined till we have examined" the relevant circumstances. But if we are to act at all, at some point we must arrive at an intention. If no external obstacles intervene, "what follows after that, follows in a chain of consequences, linked one to another, all depending on the last determination of the judgment" (1959, p. 349).

For Dostoevsky, such a view is naive. Some intentions are genuinely processual and always incomplete. In *A Writer's Diary*, Dostoevsky discusses at length the trial of a woman, Kairova, who discovered that her lover and his wife were back together and attacked the wife when she was asleep, only to be restrained when the couple suddenly awoke. The jury at Kairova's trial was asked to determine what her prior, premeditated intention was — whether she intended to kill the wife. Dostoevsky argues that the question is quite unanswerable, because most likely there was *never* a moment when Kairova formulated an intention. Her intention was constantly incomplete and, at every moment, allowed for many possible actions at the next moment. The actions she took did not follow from a prior intention but were part of the process by which an incomplete intention continued to evolve.

If the identical situation could be repeated, and no external obstacles intervened, each time the result might be different. Dostoevsky sketches out some possibilities: Kairova might have passed the razor over her rival's throat, shuddered and run away; or she might have turned the razor on herself; or she might have flown into a frenzy "and not only murdered Velikanova but even begin to abuse the body, cutting off the head, the nose, the lips; and only later, suddenly, when someone took that head away from her, realized what she had done" (1994, p. 477). All these possibilities are consistent with her developing and processual intention, which was never complete at any moment.

In this model, nothing is inevitable. Kairova's many possible actions all "could have happened and could have been done by this very same woman and sprung from the very same soul, in the very same mood and under the very same circumstances" (477). If identical circumstances can lead to different outcomes, then time must be open. The past affects but does not exhaustively determine the present and future.

Processual literary works are deliberately created by an intention of this sort. They work in a way closely resembling the phenomenology of everyday life. Hayden White notwithstanding, narrative is not imposed on non-narrative experience but on experience that always already contains an essential narrative element, as David Carr insists. Every action we take derives from an immediate past and projects into an immediate future at which we guess; action would be impossible otherwise.[41] In a larger time frame, our sense of self involves open-ended stories of a lengthy past. From the midst of experience, we are always formulating tentative autobiographies that more or less make order of our lives. These stories differ from those of most literary works precisely because they are composed from within; they lack what Bakhtin calls outsideness, perspective on the whole. Narrating our selves from within, we can never make complete order or tie up all loose ends; we know that future events may alter the story and the significance of particular past events. We are aware that each of our stories revises an earlier one and is itself subject to revision. Processual art operates in time of this sort, where a future that may revise the past is always possible.

(2) In creating this kind of temporal experience, processual works therefore lack *closure*. Rather, they have what might be called *aperture*, the temporary and partial making of sense that is never complete and always subject to revision. That is the only story we can tell about our own lives because we cannot be outside them to view them as whole. The same is true of processual works. Their stopping point is simply the last moment at which we can perform an act of aperture. Each section of the work may create a kind of relative closure, a story more or less adequate to what has happened so far; and the last section possesses only this relative closure as it anticipates more sections that *could* be.

Aperture must not be confused with what is sometimes called anti-closure, the use of a device that asserts openness in a way that, paradoxically, achieves perfect closure. When a poem about the fleetingness of inspiration suddenly ends (as in the romantic form of the "fragment"), or a work about a character who cannot find a solution is broken off by an editor (as in *Notes from Underground*), the declaration of incompletion itself completes a structure that could not end otherwise. In Phelan's and Rabinowitz's terms, incompleteness is perceived by the narrative audience, completeness by the authorial audience. When aperture is used, the authorial audience itself experiences only partial completeness. The work could certainly be continued, and, indeed, sometimes authors of processual works do continue them at surprising moments.

(3) Thus, the position of the author changes. Like Yahvew in Genesis, he or she is in the world, not outside it. We sense the author in the act of looking for solutions, trying out plausible continuations, wondering what characters will do, perhaps regretting earlier choices that now cannot be changed. The work as we read it reflects not a unified will or design but a succession of wills and a shifting design.

(4) For these reasons, processual works employ only forward, not backward causation. There is no possibility of foreshadowing, since the ending is not there to send signs backward. That is not to say that later events do not echo earlier events; they certainly do, much as in life the same old habits can produce a recognizable pattern. But we must read these echoes precisely as later events repeating earlier ones, not earlier ones anticipating later ones. In life it would be mistaken to say that a child stole a candy because he was *going* to become a crooked politician; only the opposite may be the case, that the habit of stealing acquired in childhood carried over into adult life. But in a poetic work either statement is true. Processual works in this respect resemble life, which is, I think, one reason that so many people have found Tolstoy's novels so lifelike. Their *temporality,* which moves only forward, is closer to time as we experience it.

(5) Processual works necessarily contain loose ends. Each section of the work develops some potentials of earlier sections, and leaves some undeveloped. In a sort of temporal *relay,* the second section develops some potentials of the first while leaving others undeveloped; the third develops some from either or both earlier ones, whereas others of either and both are dropped. Some patterns arise, evolve, and are lost, while others, of which there was no previous hint, occupy our attention for more or less time and then yield to still others. If Tolstoy had continued *War and Peace* at the same number of pages per represented year for another few decades, as he once hoped to do, what would have been the status of Prince Andrei, who now dies at about page 1100? The work not only allows but demands that we ask such questions, which would be gratuitous or perverse when asked of a poetic work.

(6) Typically, the processual work is published serially or in separate parts

over a period of years. As Tolstoy indicates, the fact that each part is fixed before the next is created makes it evidently impossible to adjust its details to prepare for what will happen next. Contingencies are assured. The converse is not true: Not all serial works are processual: one can have an advanced design and simply publish in parts, as Dickens and George Eliot often did. But if one wishes to create a processual work, serialization may be profitably exploited.

(7) Often, serial publication allows the author to take advantage of real events that take place between installments. As we have seen, the events in *The Idiot* are shaped in part by actual crimes that took place after the opening sections of the novel had been published and which therefore *could not* be part of any original design. Time, in a sense, becomes co-author of the work. Today's readers usually miss the fact that part 8 of *Anna Karenina* centers on the Eastern War, which had not begun when the opening parts of the novel were published. The life of the author, as it has gone on since the opening part was published, manifestly affects *Eugene Onegin*. Moreover, the Decembrist revolt of 1825 haunts *Eugene Onegin*, whose opening chapter appeared in 1823. The extraordinary success of part 1 of *Tristram Shandy* becomes a topic of subsequent parts. Readers' responses, explicitly remarked upon, may also play a role.[42]

(8) The relative significance of reading, as opposed to re-reading, changes. In poetic works, *re*-reading occupies a privileged position, for it is only after one has completed a first reading that the overall design (including the story of the reader's experience) is apparent. Indeed, for experienced readers even a first reading takes on many of the characteristics of an anticipated re-reading—some professionals can in a sense *only* re-read a book—as we imagine the significance of each event in the design already completed and to be revealed. In processual works, reading enjoys greater privilege, because the processuality of that experience more closely matches the processual aesthetic of the work. In such cases, anticipated re-reading misleads because there is no clock, no pre-established harmony, synchronizing events and drawing them to a conclusion. Presentness is real. To apply the techniques of re-reading and poetics to such works is to Leibnizize them.

(9) Processual works ask to be read in terms of *potentials*, both wasted and exploited, developing unexpectedly into other potentials; and so on. Their narrativity exceeds structure and so is *necessary*. The power of Tolstoy's novels depends not only on their incredible realism, but also on the fact that they reward with special generosity a habit we practice every day, the reading of processes and the contemplation of present moments in flux toward nowhere. Undoubtedly, there are many ways of viewing such processes as beautiful and meaningful, many genres of processual art and perception.

(10) Most important, perhaps, is the sense of time that results from all

these techniques. We sense that the story as it develops is one of many possible stories; that if it were possible to play the tape over again, there are many points where something else might have happened. As in the real world: each of us is capable of leading more lives than one, and each moment contains the possibility of many futures. Time is a field of possibilities, and at every given moment more than one thing can happen. Process literature encourages us to see the field, not just the event that actually happens, and so we experience the genuine possibility of what did not happen. For to understand a moment is to grasp not only what did but also what might have happened. In the world of poetics, in the world of Leibniz, there is no "might have." Such works abide beyond regret, beyond hope, and beyond the counterfactual, which they sacrifice for order and harmony. By contrast, the literature of process takes us beyond providence, beyond structure, and beyond harmony into a world where things can either be or not be.

Notes

1. For more on Bakhtin from this point of view, see Morson 1994.

2. For an interesting recent study about the attempt to represent chance in novels, see Monk 1993. Monk concludes that "chance *always* takes on a necessarily fateful quality once it is represented in narrative" (2; his emphasis), a conclusion that follows from the assumptions of poetics and which does apply to works created according to poetics. Wallace Martin observes, "In the best realist narratives . . . we would never have imagined the revelation that came just after we turned the page, but after it appears, we realize that it was inevitable" (1986, 58).

3. Phelan 1989 (93). Phelan is here persuasively describing what happens in John Fowles's *The French Lieutenant's Woman*. I mean not to quarrel with that reading, but to suggest that the principle enunciated by Phelan does not necessarily apply universally.

4. W. H. Auden, closing lines of "In Time of War: A Sonnet Sequence with a Verse Commentary" (1945, 334).

5. For more on these points and examples, see Morson 1994.

6. Phelan (1989, 17–18). The term closure in this sense derives from Barbara Herrnstein Smith's *Poetic Closure*.

7. For an extensive discussion of these concepts, see Rabinowitz 1987.

8. This is the essential idea behind Mikhail Bakhtin's concept of "outsideness." See Bakhtin 1990 and Morson and Emerson 1990.

9. On symmetrical and asymmetrical time, see Paul Horwich 1987. I extend Horwich's ideas to literary time in *Narrative and Freedom*. For different reasons, Jonathan Culler argues that in narrative effects cause causes. See Culler 1981 (169–87).

10. See the chapter on *Bleak House* in Marianna Torgovnick's *Closure in the Novel*, which (not implausibly, in fact) faults the novel for not being symmetrical enough.

11. Rabinowitz observes: "[S]uperstition can perhaps be defined as the application of literary rules of configuration in reality" (Rabinowitz 1987, 118).

12. As Sir Thomas Browne observes in his *Religio Medici,* "There are two Books from whence I collect my Divinity, besides that written one of God, another of His servant Nature, that universal and public Manuscript that lies expans'd unto the Eyes of all: those that never saw Him in the one, have discovered him in the other." Cited in Basil Willey 1953 (58).

13. Phelan refers to this as the "synthetic" (as opposed to the "mimetic") element of the narrative (1989, 2).

14. In his essay of that title, Fish tells the story of how books XI and XII of *Paradise Lost,* which C. S. Lewis had faulted as "an untransmuted lump of futurity," came to be regarded as the center of the poem and its design.

15. See Tolstoy's "Drafts for an Introduction to *War and Peace*" and "Some Words about *War and Peace*" in the Norton Critical Edition of the novel (1966, 1362–74). For the quotation about development, see L. N. Tolstoi, *Polnoe sobranie sochinenii* [*Complete Works*—henceforth referred to as Jubilee], vol. 13, p. 55. For a gloss on these passages, see Morson 1987 (173–89).

16. In addition, drafts exist for where the novel was once to begin, with the return of the hero and heroine from Siberian exile in 1856.

17. Steiner 1996 (105). Steiner adds that Tolstoy aims at "the lack of a final curtain. . . . the effect being that of a live continuum in which the individual narrative had marked a brief and artificial segment." In thinking about process literature and its "continuous present," I have long been inspired by Northrop Frye's "Towards Defining an Age of Sensibility."

18. Cited in Frank (1995, 271). For a detailed account of how Dostoevsky wrote this novel, see Frank and the account in Edward Wasiolek's edition of Dostoevsky's *The Notebooks for "The Idiot."*

19. For more details on citing stories from the ongoing press, see the Wasiolek edition of the notebooks and Morson 1997.

20. My thanks to Julie Lasky for pointing out the "embedded critics" in the novel.

21. For that matter, Adam Smith, as a reading of *The Wealth of Nations* will demonstrate, did not mean the idea of the "invisible hand" as a mechanism that insures perfection. He, too, has been Newtonized.

22. My reading of Darwin leads me to accept, indeed to extend further, Stephen Jay Gould's interpretation. For the relation of my views to his on perfectionism and related topics, see Morson 1994.

23. Darwin's discussion of this mole repeats and elaborates on observation he made earlier in *The Voyage of the Beagle* on the tucutuco (or tuco-tuco), which does have eyes that can see. But these eyes are so ill-constructed that they frequently become infected, leaving numerous animals blind. In the earlier work, Darwin wonders: "[I]t appears strange that any animal should possess an organ constantly subject to injury." That is, he noticed imperfection and saw how such a fact little harmonized with divine creation.

In *Origin,* he mentions the tucutuco just before discussing the mole who cannot see at all. See Darwin 1989 (80) and 1964 (137).

24. Ernst Mayr retells the story of Darwin's confrontation with physicist Lord Kelvin, who asserted that Darwin must be wrong about the age of the earth, which, given the physics of the time, could not be as old as Darwin and the geologists assumed. Mayr observes: "It is rather amusing with what assurance Kelvin assumed the correctness of his own and the error of the naturalists' age determination. Since biology was an inferior science, there could be no question where the error was" — until the discovery of radioactivity showed that, in fact, Darwin had been right. See Mayr 1982 (42). It is amusing to ask social scientists invoking Darwinism how many tables and formulae are to be found in *The Origin of Species:* the answer is none. Though we sometimes turn to geology for warnings, the science is ineluctably historical.

25. Citations from "Progress i opredelenie obrazovaniia" [Progress and the Definition of Education], Jubilee, vol. 8, 332–33.

26. The idea of "natural and agreeable" is central to Tolstoy's understanding of intellectuals' ideas. In *War and Peace,* he writes that "history is written by learned men and so it is natural and agreeable for them to think that the activity of their class is the basis for the movement of all humanity, just as it would be natural and agreeable for merchants, agriculturalists, and soldiers to entertain such a belief (if they do not express it is only because merchants and soldiers do not write history)" (1968, 1419–20).

27. Tolstoy's insights have been repeatedly verified by the sad results of rationalist schemes for agriculture in the twentieth century, from Soviet collectivization to Tanzania's ujaama villages, and many plans funded by international agencies. See Scott 1998.

28. Bakhtin stresses this point in *Problems of Dostoevsky's Poetics* (1984, 60).

29. See *The Leibniz-Clarke Correspondence,* edited by H. G. Alexander.

30. I say "seemed," because in fact the solar system has still not been shown to be stable; the n-body problem remains unsolvable. See Peterson 1993.

31. See the essays discussing this issue in Parker 1986.

32. For Kroeber's remarkable (co-authored) article, complete with tables and graphs, see Jane Richardson and A. L. Kroeber, "Three Centuries of Women's Dress Fashions: A Quantitative Analysis" (1940–47). The article begins: "This study is an attempt to define stylistic changes in an objective and quantitative manner." In an appendix to the article, in which he responds to criticism of his thesis, Kroeber argues that such contingent factors as the invention of rayon, "the social position of women, sports, mode of dancing, cost of materials, and such," along with all psychological explanations, are at best secondary factors, if effective at all. He attributes resistance to his theory to an old-fashioned desire to believe in free will, once the province of theologians but now of social reformers who want to bend reality to their will.

Responding to criticisms that his position should allow for prediction — the very possibility Lévi-Strauss embraces so enthusiastically — Kroeber insists that such was not his intention. His approach was merely a "natural science" one.

The appendix ends with a self-congratulatory embrace of determinism, even if others, clinging to doctrines of freedom or chance, should be offended by this scientific advance: "I realize that any interpretation which diminishes the range of free personality and enlarges the effectiveness of superpersonal, cultural influences is likely to be unpalatable. It will irritate many and it will elicit rejections. But I am compelled to adhere to it — no doubt by the strand of culture of which I am part" (153). We have here a marvelous sample of the rhetorical stance invoked by believers in social science in a hard sense. Like Freud and many others, Kroeber relies on a charge of sentimentality. Curiously, he allows that determinism has "compelled" him to adopt his own views, without realizing that such an admission diminishes his appeal to evidence. For why couldn't the social forces here, as with women's fashion, have nothing to do with rationality or the reasons that have supposedly motivated him?

33. Lévi-Strauss continues: "Teissier has shown that, in order to formulate laws of this growth, it is necessary to consider the relative dimensions of the component parts of the claws, and not the exterior forms of these organs. . . . The object of a scientific zoology, in these terms, is thus not ultimately concerned with the forms of animals and their organs as they are usually perceived, but with the establishment of certain abstract and measureable relationships. . . . An analogous method has been followed in studying certain features of social organization, particularly marriage rules and kinship systems. . . . Proceeding from this hypothesis, it would only be necessary to make a mathematical study of every possible type of exchange between n partners to enable one almost automatically to arrive at every type of marriage rule actually operating in living societies and, eventually, to discover rules that are merely possible" (1963, 59–60).

34. Cited by Radcliffe-Brown (1935, 401n 9). After citing this comment, Radcliffe-Brown observes: "I think that probably neither Professor Lowie nor Dr. Benedict would, at the present time, maintain this view of the nature of culture."

35. This point is argued in detail in the essay "Whither Anthropology?" which appears in Malinowski 1944 (211–21). Malinowski's scientific conclusions would startle a modern readership: they include, to be sure, "equal treatment for all" and "full cultural independence for every group or nation," but also "no political sovereignty for any tribe" (220). Rather than sovereignty, anthropology advises Indirect Rule, "as this has recently been introduced in the British colonies. Indirect rule means self-government by any tribe or nation in cultural matters, under the advisory control of the ruling power" (219).

36. Malinowski (28) borrows this definition from A. A. Goldenweiser.

37. See Simon 1979 (3–19). Simon begins by assuming that "human thinking powers are very modest when compared with the complexities of environments in which human beings live. If computational powers were unlimited, a person would simply consult his or her preferences (utility functions) and choose the course of action that would yield maximum utility under the given circumstances. That, of course, is just what the 'rational man' of classical economic theory does. But real human beings, of bounded rationality, cannot follow this procedure. Faced with complexity and uncertainty, lacking the wits to optimize, they must be content to satisfice — to find 'good enough' solutions

to their problems and 'good enough' courses of action" (3). If choices are presented in sequential order, and one picks the first that is "good enough," one may well wind up with less than the optimum.

Societies also lack infinite capacity for information and time for decisions; they may well satisfice. Darwinian evolution may involve a structural homology to satisficing, as the organism evolves not the best conceivable forms but those that are good enough to allow it to survive in its current milieu.

38. Malinowski continues: "[N]o invention, no revolution, no social or intellectual change ever occurs except when new needs are created" (41). Note the categorical language here as contingency is excluded and functional explanation offered as exhaustive.

39. As cited in Scott (1998, 106). Scott offers an excellent discussion of Le Corbusier's thinking.

40. See Sennett 1990.

41. Our sense of present action always involves what the phenomenologists call retention and protension, an immediate past that is the beginning of an action and a projected future or futures that would be its continuation. See David Carr 1991. For Carr's discussion of White, see pp. 7–17. Carr, however, does not sufficiently appreciate the role of outsideness and the radical difference between storytelling by people in the midst of things and storytelling from a point radically outside lived temporality.

42. This may happen with works that do have an advance design but are published serially; the author may then change his design. It would perhaps therefore be more accurate to speak of processuality as a matter of degree.

11 | # New Directions in Voice-Narrated Cinema
Seymour Chatman

In its formative stage, narratology made much of the autonomy of narrative structure, of its independence from any medium. It was common to assert, as did Claude Bremond, that every narrative contains a "layer of autonomous significance, endowed with a structure that can be isolated from the whole of the message: the story [récit]. So any sort of narrative message . . . may be transposed from one to another medium without losing its essential properties: the subject of a story may serve as argument for a ballet, that of a novel can be transposed to stage or screen, one can recount in words a film to someone who has not seen it. These are words we read, images we see, gestures we decipher, but through them, it is a story that we follow; and this can be the same story" (1964, 4).

But critics of the narratological enterprise like Barbara Herrnstein Smith (1980) vigorously challenged the notion that the story *was the same. Every retelling, she claimed, even those in the same medium, was a different* version. *Latterly, some narratologists have come to agree with her. A necessary task of second-stage or "postclassical" narratology is to analyze the complicating effect of the medium on the narrative text.*

This essay attempts to assess the differences between literary and cinematic narratives arising from the capabilities and limitations characteristic of each medium. In particular, it is concerned with cinema's access to not one but two information tracks — sight and sound — especially when these work not redundantly but distinctly from each other. It concludes that the film medium could in theory facilitate a greater degree of narrative richness and complexity than commercial cinema allows, especially in the use of the human voice as a narrator cotemporal with visuals of the story.

For a while after the advent of sound in cinema, the use of the human voice as narrator was deprecated; some critics even condemned it. As late as 1938, Rudolf Arnheim, for example, said that sound "adulterated [films] by a hostile principle."[1] His purism was inspired by Lessing's argument in "Laocoön" (1766) against the mixing of genres—for example, the use of long descriptive passages in poetry. Fortunately, Arnheim's insistence on the sanctity of "pure visuals" had no impact on film production. Once introduced, sound was here to stay, and in the hands of directors like John Ford and Orson Welles, it enriched cinema greatly. Some recent films have even given preference to sound, treating the visual track as a mere frame for verbal text. Louis Malle's *My Dinner with André* (1981), Robert Altman's *Secret Honor* (1984), and Jonathan Demme's *Swimming to Cambodia* (1987) show how unreasonably limited Arnheim's stricture was. Alain Resnais seemed closer to the truth when he joked that sound is the more crucial track because the audience can easily shut its eyes but has trouble stopping its ears.[2]

The public's original excitement about sound was, of course, the novelty of "talkies," the synchronization of actors' voices with the images of their moving lips. But early on, the possibilities of other uses of sound clearly suggested themselves. From the narrative point of view, the most interesting has been "voice-over" narration, a device immediately recognized as a replacement for intertitles printed on the screen, which interrupted the image track to convey the characters' dialogue, expository background, moral commentary, and so on. Voice-over narration flourished exuberantly in Hollywood in the forties and fifties, for example, in such brilliant films as Joseph Mankiewicz's *A Letter to Three Wives* (1949) and *All about Eve* (1950). Later, its popularity tapered off somewhat, perhaps because filmmakers (at least in Hollywood) thought it minimized dramatic impact and represented a failure to visualize story material adequately. As recently as 1993, Martin Scorsese and his screenwriter Jay Cocks were criticized for using Joanne Woodward's voice-over to narrate certain moments in their adaptation of Edith Wharton's *The Age of Innocence*. Still, the best directors—Scorsese, Allen, Coppola, Kubrick, Malick, Alan Pakula, Ridley Scott among others—have used voice-over narration to excellent effect. The technique is even more popular in French cinema, where it occurs with considerable narrative sophistication. There is no reasonable question of the legitimacy of voice-over narration and its usefulness for certain kinds of films, particularly those that aspire to the complexity and psychological depth of the modern novel.

The place of voice-over narration in cinema requires a brief discussion of narrative's general surface manifestation or actualization. Literary narratology, argues Shlomith Rimmon-Kenan, has for too long neglected the enabling medium, natural language (1989). This neglect is ironic, since narratology is a historical offshoot of linguistics. But linguistics was used as the model for finding (or inventing) narrative structure, not as an explanation of its surfaces. Core narrative elements like event and character were often explained as extensions of grammatical predicates and subjects and objects: "[T]he ['monstrous'] development . . . given to a *verbal* form, in the grammatical sense of the term: the expansion of a verb. *I walk, Pierre has come* are . . . minimal forms of narrative, and inversely the *Odyssey* or the *Recherche* is only, in a certain way, an amplification (in the rhetorical sense) of statements such as *Ulysses comes home to Ithaca* or *Marcel becomes a writer*" (Genette 1980, 30). With the exception of specialized features (like indirect free style), the linguistic actualization of literary narrative has been little studied. Rimmon-Kenan argues that instead of "relegating language to a position external or irrelevant to narrative structure, we may perhaps reverse the perspective and consider it the determining factor of that structure" (1989, 160). Calling it *the* determinant seems too strong, but certainly it is *a* determinant. How language both enables and constrains narrative texts deserves careful study.

The scholarship on cinematic narrative has done more justice to the medium. Because of its technical novelty and complexity, especially in the sound era, scholars have vigorously investigated its ways of presenting narratives. Useful books by Bruce Kawin, David Bordwell, Edward Branigan, Sarah Kozloff, among others, analyze how the medium affects the way films show, and sometimes tell, stories.[3]

The usual term for "narrative film" is "movie" or "feature film." Of course, not all films are fictional and not all are narrative. A film like the recent *Microcosmos,* for example, is a factual exposition and description of the life of insects, not a narrative about them. My concern here is solely with movies—narrative fiction films that are exhibited in commercial theaters.

There are two ways of thinking about movies. One is to consider them, along with stage plays, as "mimetic," in Plato's original sense, revived by Gérard Genette. In semiotic terms, the signifieds of drama are represented by highly iconic signifiers: characters by human actors functioning as signs that "resemble" them, and settings and objects by imitative stage sets and props. Genette sets drama—plays and movies—off from epic and its modern descendants—novel, tale, short story—which are said to be "diegetic." In diegesis, according to Plato, the poet "himself is the speaker and does not even attempt to suggest to us that anyone but himself is speaking." Plato called the latter "pure" narrative. The basic epic mode is the report of a mediating agent—the narrator—speaking or writing in his own voice.

But epics can also include mimesis, or, more accurately, as Genette points out, the *illusion* of mimesis. The narrator may communicate "as if he were someone else," namely, a character. In literary narrative, the mimetic dimension is evident in directly quoted dialogue, and, more figuratively, in some descriptions — "word-paintings" — which may be said to work as verbal equivalents of visual representations. Genette evidently considers films and stage plays as performances, and it is this mode of presentation that distinguishes them from novels. Hence drama and film are excluded from consideration in his *Discours du récit.*

Other theorists, however, favor the view that the similarities between dramas and epics, movies and novels are no less important than their differences, and that looking at these similarities gives different and equally useful insights. Not only epic but drama too is a subclass of the Narrative text-type. At the structural level, stage plays, novels, movies, puppet shows, and the like share a characteristic that distinguishes them from texts whose structure is descriptive or argumentative.[4] They all turn on plots — events in a series — whereas arguments and descriptions turn on propositions or depictions of states of affairs. All texts unfold temporally, but narratives alone possess a double chronology — the chronology of story (or *fabula*), and the chronology of discourse (or *sjuzhet*). The chronology of story is formed by the events performed or experienced by the characters. The chronology of discourse is formed by the sequence of narrative acts, conveyed by written sentences in literature or movements or speeches by actors on stage or screen. At the deepest structural level, then, the traditional view that drama differs radically in *kind* from epic is difficult to sustain. The method of presentation, whether on stage or screen or television or in print, seems a secondary — precisely, a surface — issue. Further, just as novels may also contain passages of mimetic "showing" (in quoted dialogue, descriptions of states of affairs, and so on), plays and movies may include diegetic passages vocalized by a narrator.

Literary narratives (except for trivial cases like illustrated novels) are actualized by a single "track" — print; film is the more complex medium by virtue of its *two* information tracks. Once the technology of recording sound on film was perfected in the late twenties, cinema became a multimedia art. Sound could be used both in support of the visual image and independently of it. The first developments were obvious — the "talkies." Not only could actors' lips move, but these movements could be synchronized with speech sounds. Synchronized sound is often called "sound-on." The history of the talkies has been extensively documented, and its early problems hilariously parodied in such films as Stanley Donen's *Singin' in the Rain* (1952).

But the technical expansion of sound films did not immediately result in a greater artistic complexity or richness. Most early sound films were crude affairs, in which the sound track simply duplicated the image track. More sophisticated possibilities were soon recognized, however, most notably by cinema's greatest theoretician and practitioner, Sergei Eisenstein. In a manifesto cosigned by Pudovkin and Alexandrov in the magazine *Zhizn Iskusstva,* August 5, 1928, Eisenstein argued that though "talking pictures" were now possible, they were also aesthetically shallow. The film artist could use sound, he felt, for profounder purposes "ALONG THE LINE OF ITS DISTINCT NON-SYNCHRONIZATION WITH THE VISUAL IMAGES. And only such an attack will give the necessary palpability which will later lead to the creation of an ORCHESTRAL COUNTERPOINT of visual and aural images."[5]

Synchronized sound, or "sound-on," correlates with what we see on the screen. We hear a character say "Oh!" as we see her lips round and open; we hear a car crash as we see the car collide with something; we hear a piano as we see fingers move on the keys. Sound-on is sometimes called "diegetic sound," since it emanates from the story world (in this sense, "diegetic" means not "told" but "pertaining to the story," as opposed to "discoursive," or "pertaining to the discourse," the structure by which the story is told or shown).

Among the nonsynchronous uses of sound that Eisenstein anticipated, two have developed: "sound-*off*" and "sound-*over*." "Sound-off" refers to voices, music, and noises that are also in the diegetic or story world, but whose sources are not visible because they are outside the camera's range and therefore not projected on the screen. If we see nothing but the close-up of the faces of two dancers in a ballroom, we infer that the music they dance to is coming from somewhere nearby. The orchestra is just offscreen, within earshot. If a character is sitting in a living room and hears a car crash, we assume that the noise is coming from outside on the road (as in Joseph Losey's movie *Accident,* 1967).

"Sound-over," on the other hand, issues neither from a visible image in the story world nor from off-frame. The absence of the source, visible or implied, suggests one of two possibilities, which we select according to contextual clues. One is that the sound is diegetic; for example, if the voice is that of the character whose mouth is closed, we may infer that it conveys his current thoughts, his memory of what he said on a prior occasion, or the like. An early example occurs in Hitchcock's *Murder* (1930), when Sir John (Herbert Marshall), in service as a juror, wonders while shaving whether the accused woman is guilty or innocent. If the sound is someone else's voice, or music, or a noise that cannot emanate from offscreen, we interpret it as a memory, or a conjecture, or, especially if music or noise, symbolic of a feeling that cannot be put in words (just as comic strips use visual symbols, like a light-bulb to show a sudden mental illumination). In such cases, the voice is in and of the story world; it is diegetic (not discoursive) sound-over, since the sounds are the signs of a *character's*—

not the narrator's — thought activity. The character's thoughts, like other story events, can be occurring only in the story world.

Sometimes a character's voice is both "off" and "over." For example, in the first scene of Woody Allen's *Hannah and Her Sisters* (1986), a male voice, which we recognize as Michael Caine's, says about Hannah's sister Lee (Barbara Hershey), "God, she's beautiful. She's got the prettiest eyes, and she looks so sexy in that sweater." At this moment in the shot we cannot tell if this is voice-off or -over. The voice continues, berating itself: "Stop it, you idiot. She's your wife's sister. But I can't help it." And then, as the voice says, "I hear myself mooning over you, and it's disgusting," the camera, which has been prowling the room, picks up the figure of Elliott (Michael Caine). Of the actual conversation Elliott is having with another man we hear nothing. Though the lips of the two men move, what we hear is Elliott's voice-over saying ". . . when she squeezed past me in the doorway and I smelled that perfume on the back of her neck, Jesus, I, I thought I was gonna swoon! Easy . . ." We understand that we have been privy to the thoughts of Elliott, that what we might have considered an actually uttered remark, voice-off, is really a voice-over representation of Elliott's musing as the camera moves him from offscreen to onscreen and then off again.

The other possible interpretation of voice-over is that the sound derives not from the story world but from the discourse world, that it is a communication directed to a narratee, whether another character in the framing discourse or the theater audience. In such cases, the voice- or other sound-over is an alternative or supplement to the stream of images. In a broad sense, sound-over *comments* on the transpiring event. The most familiar example is mood music: a couple embrace in the middle of the Sahara, and through the "magic of the movies" we hear strains played by a full symphony orchestra. We know that the orchestra is not offscreen, sitting on the sand. Noise-over can also comment: for example, the ominous low-pitched thumping portending a hero's death in many films, such as Francesco Rosi's *The Mattei Affair* (1972), or the electronic buzz that comments on the psychological distress of the heroine of Antonioni's *Red Desert* (1964), Giuliana (Monica Vitti).

Human sounds detached from language can also function commentatively. True to its title, Ingmar Bergman's *Cries and Whispers* (1972) uses unintelligible, barely audible whispering and crying as commentative noise over extreme close-up shots of the faces of each of two characters assisting at their sister's deathbed. These serve as sound bridges accompanying flashbacks to scandalous or terrible moments in their lives, functioning both as social responses to and synecdoches for the characters' secrets and miseries — the adultery of Maria (Liv Ullmann) with the Doctor (Erland Josephson), which provokes her husband into attempting suicide; and the loathing of Karin (Ingrid

Thulin) for her husband, a loathing that prompts her to commit an unspeakable act of self-mutilation, smearing her mouth with her own blood as she mockingly invites him to bed.

This sort of music- or noise- or voice-over is sometimes called "nondiegetic," but that term seems too empty of content; a better one is "commentative."[6] Commentative signifiers work more as connotations than as denotations. They can either corroborate the visuals or undercut them ironically (for example, music inappropriate to the situation, as in the song "We'll meet again, don't know where, don't know when" over the image of a pilot riding his atomic bomb down into the USSR in the last scene of Kubrick's *Dr. Strangelove*, 1961). Or the signifier can stay neutral, as if it belonged to another story, or had an independent existence.

When the sound-over is vocal, our assumption is usually that it belongs to a narrator. He or she may be either a character-narrator, sometimes called a "first person" or "homodiegetic" narrator, or a person external to the story, a "third-person" or "heterodiegetic" narrator. This vocal narrator is either an additional tool used by the general cinematic narrator to supplement the showing of the story, or a narrator who "takes over" the generation of the visual images; that is, makes them the visual equivalent of what he or she is "saying"[7] (even if the latter is a lie: the classic example here is Hitchcock's *Stage Fright*, 1951, in which a murderer tells a story that "shows" that someone else committed the murder). The voice-over may be first heard and then associated with a person who appears onscreen, or vice versa. A transition can even be done in a single shot. For example, in Edward Dmytryk's *Murder My Sweet* (1945), we see the private eye, Philip Marlowe (played by Dick Powell), blindfolded and forced to talk, explaining why he returned to his office so late: "I'm a homing pigeon. I always come back to the stinking coop no matter how late it is." The camera then pans left and in the same shot, we see an establishing image of the space in the story he is about to recount (the street in which his office is located).

The conventions of sound-on and sound-off and sound-over are, of course, not set in stone, and gifted filmmakers sometimes play with them. For instance, sound-on may issue not from the story but from the discourse, as when an actor faces the camera, and hence the audience, and performs as narrator rather than character. The opening of Ingmar Bergman's *Autumn Sonata* (1978) reveals the protagonist Eva in medium-long shot, seated at her writing desk. A male voice says: "Sometimes I stand looking at my wife without her knowing I'm here. The first time she stepped into that room she said 'Oh, how nice. This is where I want to be.'" At this point, we cannot know whether the voice is sound-off or -over: it could be the husband standing nearby, that is, in the story world established by the beginning of the shot, visibly looking at his wife, his eyes turned inward into the set she occupies. In this case, the character-narrator would be speaking voice-off. Or the husband could be "nowhere" in the story world at this particular moment, but only a disembodied voice introducing the story (as in, say, *Sunset Boulevard,* in which the voice of William Holden, though he is deceased, begins the story of his relation with the mad ex-movie star). In *Autumn Sonata,* the question is resolved by the end of the shot: as the voice continues, the camera pans right to reveal the figure of Eva's husband. He is facing the camera, that is, speaking to "us"; and at this angle, of course, he cannot see Eva. He continues: "We had known each other only a few days. There was a bishops' convention in Trondheim, and Eva had come as a representative for a church journal." The doorway to Eva's study functions as a proscenium arch, framing her seated at her desk. We interpret the fact that the husband speaks directly into the camera to mean that he is at this moment *telling* the story rather than performing as a character in it. His visual image is so strongly marked as being in the set that many viewers would say that he *is* a character. Yes, he is a character in the larger context; but at this particular moment he is performing as narrator. That's precisely what a character-narrator is: sometimes a narrator and sometimes a character. Like the homodiegetic narrator of a novel, the cinematic character-narrator at times functions as a narrative voice, not as a participant in the action. In this mode, no matter how loudly the husband might speak, we know that Eva cannot hear him. His communication is solely with his narratees. This is not contradicted by the fact that he speaks from a point just outside the room. Visually he occupies that space, but narratively he occupies a space in the film's discourse. Bergman uses the spatial fluidity of the cinema to toy with the distinction between story and discourse.

Direct onscreen narration is used to humorous effect by Woody Allen, for example at the beginning and ending of *Annie Hall* (1977). Still another example of this fluid effect occurs in Lewis Gilbert's *Alfie* (1966), in which the protagonist, a Cockney man-about-town (played by Michael Caine), periodically faces the camera and conveys to us his philosophy of life, confessing his inability to know "what it's all about" (a motif reinforced by the movie's theme song). We know that his confessional words are addressed to the narratee alone, that none of the other characters can hear them.

One can make a rough distinction between movies that use voice-over briefly and expositorily and those that assign it a broader structural role. In the casual case, the narrative voice-over accompanies the initial sequence of images, explaining them and launching the plot, but then gives way completely to the visuals. A classic example is Carol Reed's *The Third Man* (1950). This movie is particularly interesting because it was released in two versions. In one, the voice-over is that of Holly Martins, played by Joseph Cotten, who functions both as character-narrator and protagonist. In the other, the voice-over is that of an unidentified ex-black-marketeer, actually the voice of Carol Reed himself, who was unable to locate Cotten for postproduction dubbing and needed to come up with a print for the film's release. Reed's unidentified voice functions as an external or heterodiegetic narrator, since no one with that voice ever shows up as a character in the film. The lines of both narrators are identical except for one telltale word: referring to the black-marketeer's activities, Cotten's voice-over says "*They'd* run anything" but the unidentified voice says "*We'd* run anything," the first person marking the speaker as a minor gangster not important enough to appear.

Especially in Hollywood productions, this casual, expository use of voice-over is most common, and usually occurs briefly in the opening moments of the movie. But some films use voice-over narration throughout. A famous example is John Ford's adaptation of Richard Lewellyn's novel *How Green Was My Valley* (1941). The movie is narrated at great length by Huw, who had been a young boy as character, but now speaks the narration as an old man. The occasion of the narration is his departure, after all these years, from his Welsh coal-mining village. The sustained voice-over keeps the nostalgia of reminiscence uppermost in the audience's mind.[8]

In most movies, however, the voice of the character and the narrator are identical, the period between the story events and the moment of narration being relatively short. Then we need context to understand whether the voice-over conveys the speech of a narrator out in the discourse or his thinking as character inside the story. For example, in Stanley Kubrick's *Lolita* (1962), Humbert Humbert (James Mason) narrates, but we also hear his inner voice as character, as when he writes his entries in his journal. (Another famous example of the vocalization of a journal is Robert Bresson's *Diary of a Country Priest*, 1950.) The extensive use of Humbert's voice-over narration was as necessary to the movie as was Nabokov's decision to make him homodiegetic narrator of the novel. Humbert is no *mere* child molester: he is an elegant European whose taste and culture help to mitigate, if ever so slightly, his unfortunate sexual proclivities. Like the novel, the movie's project includes a satire on American mores, and what better way to satirize them than through a cultivated voice like James Mason's? Other famous examples of extended voice-over narration are Billy Wilder's *Double Indemnity* (1944) and Orson Welles's *Lady from Shanghai* (1948).

Most Hollywood voice-over narrators, from *Wuthering Heights* (1939) to *The Usual Suspects* (1995) are homodiegetic, either protagonists or other characters who tell the protagonists' stories. Sarah Kozloff (1988, 53–71) has done so extensive an analysis of two famous homodiegetically narrated Hollywood films, *How Green Was My Valley* and *All About Eve,* that little need be added to her account. She also discusses the use of odd and problematic narrators: a corpse (*Sunset Boulevard*), a person not yet born (à la *Tristram Shandy*: Frank Tashlin's *The First Time,* 1952), and an Oscar statuette (*Susan Slept Here,* Tashlin, 1954).

But there have been more substantively innovative uses of homodiegetic narration in recent American cinema, for example, in Terrence Malick's *Badlands* (1973), whose discoursive structure achieves something of the profundity of *Huckleberry Finn*'s. The story, "a half-understood legend of fame pursued by boys watching James Dean and girls steeped in romantic magazines" (David Thomson 1994, 470), concerns a twenty-five-year-old drifter, Kit (Martin Sheen), who decides that he must elope with the fifteen-year-old Holly (Sissy Spacek) even if he has to kill her father, orphaning her, to do so. With the legendary energy and know-how of an American countryboy, he takes off for the West, building a rope and timber hideaway for Holly, shooting four state troopers in pursuit, and then bumping across the badlands of Montana in his low-rider sedan until he is finally captured. The movie features a brilliantly conceived and executed voice-over narration by Holly, who is a Midwestern equivalent of James Joyce's Gerty McDowell. Shots moving through a sleepy Dakota town and the surrounding countryside are interrupted by acts of sudden, blankly perpetrated violence. Tying it all together is Holly's affectless voice recounting the story of her romance with Kit. Her prose is so gooily adolescent that, in comparison, a Harlequin romance sounds like an Edith Wharton novel. For instance, as Kit collects garbage and Holly twirls batons in front of her home, her voice-over says "Little did I realize that what began in the alley and backways of this little town would end in the badlands of Montana." (In an interesting effect, Malick mixes Holly's voice-over with her childish voice-*on* whispering a poem or song as she moves about rhythmically.) As the affair progresses, Holly's voice-over continues with gems like "He said I was grand though he never met a fifteen-year-old girl who behaved more like a grownup," or "Our time with each other was limited and each lived for the precious hours when he or she could be with the other, away from the cares of all the world" — these over shots of her seated on the lawn in front of her high school and of Kit feeding penned cows after being fired from his garbage-truck job. Holly recalls, "In the stench and slime of the feedlot, he remembered how I looked the evening before," and over a shot of the two embracing, she says "He wanted to die with me and I dreamed of being lost forever in his arms." Holly's singsong reminiscence contrasts strikingly with the flat homeliness of her onscreen conversations with Kit. After their first sexual experience, she asks

"Did it go the way it's supposed to?"
[Kit nods without emotion.]
"Is that all there is to it?"
"Yep."
"Gosh, what was everybody talkin' about?"
"Don't ask me."

Then her voice-over tells of a balloon he launched in her honor: "Kit made a solemn vow that he would always stand beside me. . . . His heart was filled with longin' as he watched it drift off. . . . Somethin' must a told him that we'd never live these days of happiness again."

Kozloff limits her discussion to the American cinema, but voice-over narration has been more developed and sophisticated in European, particularly French, movies. Going beyond the usual tasks of Hollywood narration — summarizing events, epitomizing characters, filling in exposition, and the like — French films have been enriched by unusually imaginative uses of voice-over. A good example is Eric Rohmer's *L'amour l'après-midi* (1972, Englished as *Chloe in the Afternoon*). This is arguably the best of Rohmer's six-film project of *contes moreaux*. A most articulate expositor of his own thematics and craft, Rohmer defines these as follows: "not a tale with a moral, but a story which deals less with what people do than with what is going on in their minds while they are doing it." David Thomson characterizes them as "semiformal, literary inquiries into the sensibilities and thoughts of a group of people gathered round some modest action — so modest, indeed that an outsider might not notice it. . . . The films have a subtle and absorbing tension between the intellectual inflexibility (or resolve) of the characters and the evanescence of the situations in which they act" (647). *Chloe in the Afternoon* is the tale of a businessman, Frederic (played by Bernard Verley), who, though happily married, indulges in a vigorous but purely vicarious fantasy life about other women, whom he ogles on the commuter train and in the streets and bars of Paris. Or at least it is vicarious until he befriends an attractive young hippie, Chloe (played by Zouzou), and begins to meet her regularly in the afternoon. His intentions are platonic, but she proves sexually aggressive and quite determined to sleep with him. She cares nothing about his marital status but simply wants to make love and have a child. This poses quite a challenge to Frederic, but he resists "manfully," and the affair goes unconsummated.

Voice-over is the perfect vehicle for conveying Frederic's elaborate ruminations. What makes the film technically as well as thematically interesting is that it presents his thinking but leaves the *moment* of its articulation unclear. We're never quite sure whether we are hearing his thoughts as character, at the moment in the story that he thinks them, or a homodiegetic account of them after the fact — in other words, a more general commentary or contemplation, at some indeterminate time and place out in the discourse. We fall back on the assumption that his voice-over states a general position or personal philosophy. In a sense, the voice-over is not so much characteral or narratorial as essayistic, a meditation on the private moral issues that typically preoccupy Rohmer's characters — "relationships between men and women . . . friendship, love, desire . . . happiness, boredom, work, leisure" (Thomson 1994, 647). Rohmer has said that his "work is closer to the novel — to a certain classic style of novel that the cinema is now taking over — than to other forms of entertainment, like the theatre." "Classic," perhaps, in the sense of "philosophical," or "filled with extensive commentary and moral observation."

A similar blurring between narratorial and characteral voice-over occurs at the beginning of Francis Ford Coppola's *Apocalypse Now* (1979), but to quite different effect. The protagonist, Captain Willard (played by Martin Sheen), is a modern-day Marlow in search of Kurtz (a maverick colonel, played by Marlon Brando, gone off to fight his own war). In keeping with the evil of the Vietnam War, Willard's mission is not to rescue Colonel Kurtz, but to murder him. In the first scene of the film, we see Willard in a hotel room in Saigon, just back from one of the political assassinations that are his speciality. His voice speaks over the visuals, but presents an interesting narrative ambiguity. We cannot be sure whether the words are the thoughts of Willard-as-character or the narration of Willard-as-narrator. At first they seem to be the character's thoughts as he lies drunk, half-remembering, half-dreaming of helicopters flying over the burning jungle, their choppy noises blurring with that of an overhead fan in his hotel room. His first words are "Saigon — shit. I'm still only in Saigon." Note the present tense, usually the mark of a character's filtered thoughts. Though the present tense continues, Willard's voice then becomes more explanatory, like a narrator's: "I'm here a week now, waiting for a mission" — not the kind of thought that someone would need to say to himself. But it is also not clearly retrospective, since Willard has not yet heard about the mission to assassinate Colonel Kurtz, which is the subject of the rest of the movie. Suddenly, in mid-sentence, the voice-over shifts from present to past tense: "Every minute I *stay* [my emphasis] in this room I get weaker; and while Charlie squats in the bush, he gets stronger. Each time I *looked* [my emphasis] around, the walls moved in a little tighter." Then he goes slightly crazy, performing some strange mixture of dance and martial arts, breaking a mirror with his fist. Superimposed are more shots of helicopters and the burning jungle. Then a flashforward to a shot of his painted face as he advances to kill Kurtz (anticipating the symbolic matching of his face with the stone face of an idol at the end of the film). As he goes off to army headquarters at Nha Trang to meet the general who will give him his grisly mission, his voice-over completes the shift to full retrospection: "I wanted a mission. For my sins they gave me one. It was a real choice mission, and when it was over, I never wanted another." From then on, Willard's voice-over is used only for retrospective narration.

Just as in novels, homodiegetic voice-over narrators directly address an audience intrinsic to the discourse, the narratee, the recipient of the story. Sometime, as in Welles's *Lady from Shanghai* or Wilder's *Sunset Boulevard*, the narratee is simply equivalent to the viewer of the movie. But in embedded narratives—stories within stories—a framed narratee may appear in the framing narrative. For instance, in Ernst Lubitsch's *Heaven Can Wait* (1943), the character-narrator, the just-deceased Henry Van Cleve (played by Don Ameche), presents himself at the reception office to Hell (because he is sure he cannot get into Heaven), and tells the story of his life over flashbacks, to a narratee—the Devil himself (Laird Cregar). In *Double Indemnity*, the homodiegetic narrator, dying insurance agent Walter Neff (Fred MacMurray), having killed a woman's husband in order to share her love and a large death benefit, tells his story to a dictaphone, and through it to his friend, the security officer Keyes (Edward G. Robinson). The dictaphone proves unnecessary, since Keyes is standing just offscreen listening.

A framing story need not be merely skeletal, nor need the narratee be a completely passive ear. In Alain Resnais's *Hiroshima, mon amour* (1959), the frame story concerns the termination of a love affair between a movie actress (Emmanuele Riva) shooting a film about the bombing and a Japanese architect (Eiji Okada); the architect rejects her claims to have seen everything in Hiroshima: he is a reluctant or disbelieving narratee. Both voices speak at times over the visual track.

Heterodiegetic or external narrators are rarer in cinema, and it is interesting to consider why that is so. Ever since Fielding's *Tom Jones*, external voices have been used to narrate novels. The printed medium, being exclusively verbal, allows heterodiegetic narrators to address "reader" narratees directly, facilitating a full range of rapports, from distant and formal to warmly intimate. With the book in their hands, readers can easily adjust to whatever distance the author wishes to establish. But, by its nature, film entails a different interchange. The audience is not in control—we cannot put the movie down as if it were a book. Further, the visual dimension is so powerfully verisimilar that it dominates—indeed we often speak of the "viewer" rather than "the audience." Here, as elsewhere, seeing "fleshed-out bodies" seems more conducive to unquestioning belief than does reading print, which entails a double, not a single remove from reality. Some readers, psychologists say, don't do much mental imaging when they read. At the movies, however, it is impossible not to watch. So, language in films, whether spoken or written (as in intertitles), usually plays second fiddle. (The exceptions, like *Swimming to Cambodia* or *My Dinner with André* are rare and, as it were, deliberately "countermedial.") Synchronized dialogue usually complements the immediacy of the visuals, rather than the other way around. We accept that those characters are saying those words less because of the words themselves than because we see their lips moving. Indeed, the simple *fact* of lip movement seems more important than even synchronization itself. If an American actor "speaks" Italian in an Italian movie, no one leaves the theater in a huff because the actor obviously doesn't know the language. We simply accept the convention of dubbing. We might not even notice the absence of real synchronization, that the actor's visible mouth movements do not match those that would actually correspond to the spoken Italian.

Heterodiegetic voice-over narration obviously evolves from the written titles, or "intertitles," of silent movies. Intertitles usually wrapped the words spoken by characters in the silent film in quotation marks to distinguish them from heterodiegetic narration—explanations of events, summaries, moral commentary, and the like. Intertitles were kept brief because of their inherently static and unphotogenic quality: audiences obviously did not go to the silent movies to read. Though intertitles continued to appear during the thirties (and even in more recent films like *Mean Streets* (1973) and *Star Wars* (1977), they became increasingly abbreviated, doing less explaining than simply naming—introducing a character, a city, the date or amount of time elapsed, or whatever. The voice-over convention was able to expand considerably on the content of verbal narration.

There is an important difference between heterodiegetic narration in novel and film: the narrator of a novel tells the whole story, mediating everything we read. Even as we plow through long passages of dialogue, or direct or indirect quotations of a character's thoughts, we assume the continuing presence of the narrator. But in films, the narrator's presence is only salient at the moment he or she speaks. Otherwise, the combined force of the diegetic visual and sound images dominate, giving the impression that things are happening right there before us. It is easy to forget by the end of the film that it was begun by a voice-over narrator. The difference seems obvious: in written discourse, a source, once identified, continues by inertia until a new source is indicated, for example, by some graphic indication, like quotation marks. While reading novels we don't assume a change of source unless there is some strong indication of a change in context. But in films, seeing and hearing "the events themselves" in their total immediacy makes us forget that some external voice has told us about those events.

The heterodiegetic voice-over narrator tends to be even more expositional than the homodiegetic. This is so much the convention that Kozloff, staunch defender of voice-over narration that she is, criticizes Bergman's *Cries and Whispers* for introducing a heterodiegetic narrator "too late." The film, she complains,

> has been running some ten or fifteen minutes before an anonymous voice breaks in with narration. It is difficult to accept this tardy speaker as the teller of a film that has already been unfolding for quite a while, so even though this voice is not obviously diegetic, I think of him not as teller, but as told, perhaps a parody of typical narrators' certainties, part of the whispering torment of the three sisters. . . . [I]n order to accept the voice-over as primary, as the teller of the whole film the voice must speak at the very beginning. (1988, 77)

The suggestion that heterodiegetic narration (or any other convention) must follow certain rules is troubling. The phrase "the teller of a film" implies that there are films in which the voice-over *totally* controls the visual track. Perhaps so, but he or she would have to talk continually in order to deprive the visuals of their autonomy. And what does it mean to say that the voice-over narrator himself is "told"? If he is not a character in the story, how can he be told? As for "parody," it is hard to imagine that Bergman was making fun of the device, since all the voice-over says is a few words of exposition setting the scenes that illustrate the troubled lives of the two sisters. My own feeling is that the "late" appearance of the narrator is well motivated by the design of the movie. The early shots—of Agnes's (Harriet Andersson) pain as she dies of cancer, of the two other sisters, Karin (Ingrid Thulin) and Maria (Liv Ullmann), and the maid, Anna (Kari Sylwan)—are virtually silent. An intense atmosphere of hushed depression builds up, intensified visually by the reds of the walls and furnishings of the living room in which Agnes suffers her passion, reds freed of their attachment to objects by periodic fade-outs to a blank red screen (instead of to the usual black). At the beginning, the only sound is that of ornate clocks ticking Agnes's life away.

Dialogue of the most meager sort arrives with the visit of the Doctor (Erland Josephson). He has had an affair with Maria, which she keenly desires to resume. He refuses. The "late" sound of the voice-over heterodiegetic narrator occurs in the flashback transition to an earlier stage of their affair: over a shot of Maria, her face pensive and half-shadowed, whispers can be heard. These are not diegetic, but rather symbolic noise-over representations of the scandal in which her husband tried to stab himself. The voice-over simply, quickly, and efficiently moves us back to the moment when Maria, under the pretext of asking the Doctor to attend Anna's daughter, persuades him to stay overnight in her husband's absence. The neutrality of this voice is crucial: no character could have fulfilled the function homodiegetically.

Recent American cinema has largely rejected the use of heterodiegetic narration — presumably as "too literary" and "uncinematic." But the French have continued a tradition that is unabashedly literary; they have no problems making films that have to be read a bit like novels. One among many, Bernard Tavernier's *Un dimanche à la campagne* ("A Sunday in the Country," 1984) exemplifies how heterodiegetic voice-over narration can thicken and enrich a relatively simple and "eventless" story. Like a Balzac novel, the film presents explicit narration full of exposition, summary and explanation or clarification of events, direct character epitomizations and reports of thoughts and nonvocal feelings, statements of counterfactuals or unperformed but possible events, and so on. This enrichment, effected by an omniscient voice-over narrator, permits the visual appearances to stay rigorously noncommittal, to reflect the family's difficulty in communicating in the absence of the mother. The narrator gives us a full sense of what is going on just under the characters' surfaces.

M. Ladmiral (Louis Ducreux), an old painter of some eminence and wealth, receives his two children on Sundays at his country house. One is a son whom Ladmiral calls "Gonzagues" (Michel Aumont) but who is addressed as "Eduard" by his intensely bourgeois wife. The other is a daughter, Irène (Sabine Azéma), a beautiful and successful Parisian businesswoman. Irène plays exuberantly with her young nephews, teases her brother, and expresses deep affection for her father. But her gaiety covers the sorrow of a difficult love affair, about which we get no information except for her side of a phone conversation with her lover. She leaves abruptly, and a bit later so do Gonzagues and family. After walking them to the train station, the old painter sadly returns to his lonely home. But his art saves him from depression: he puts aside a painting that Irène did not like, and places a fresh canvas on the easel. He smiles in anticipation of the new work to come.

What makes this minimally plotted movie so rich is the psychological intricacy introduced by the heterodiegetic narration. The camera records the inspirational beauty of the environment — the rich furnishings, gardens, country roads, and open-air *bals musettes,* images so enchanting to the Impressionists. These attest to the exquisiteness of the painter's taste, but do not communicate the states of his soul, the sadness faced by an aging man of great talent, especially his inability to help his loved ones lead happier lives. The dialogue is filled (as it must be) with the triviality and banality of family life, totally unrevelatory of insight into the real psychodynamics. It is left to the voice-over to communicate what is really going in the family drama. The movie achieves its fine tensions by matching physical beauty with a vocal explanation of the old man's loneliness and his suppressed disappointment and sorrow about his children's fate. Since he is too gentle and sensitive to admit to the feeling even to himself, it would have been impossible to convey the delicacies of the situation by relying totally on the actors' gestures and dialogue.

The minor characters are epitomized quickly and neatly by the voice-over: as we watch Ladmiral's daughter-in-law, Marie-Thèrése, fuss around the parlor, the voice-over says: "Marie-Thèrése had all the virtues, all hidden. She was happy, certainly, ploddingly, but dedicated and placid. . . . She relished the pleasure of not working. Her family was far more work than she'd ever had at the office. But she didn't know it. She had settled into that marvelous cozy sloth of a hard-working housewife." Marie-Thèrése's feelings—of happiness, of placidity—are authoritatively stapled to her image in an instant, as is her all-encompassing bourgeois insensitivity and intellectual laziness (she asks the painter the philistine question why he didn't include a cat in his painting of the sofa). The heterodiegetic narrator has total moral and psychological authority. He is a judge whose sentence, which cannot be gainsaid, cuts beneath the surfaces to the soul of the world. Gonzagues's character is revealed in a more mimetic way. This seems appropriate, since he must be understood as a failure, but a failure highly conscious of his own shortcomings, his inability to achieve or even to try to imitate his father's artistry. Still, he has inherited some of his father's sensitivity. So the movie allows his failures to emerge in his own words, in dialogue, as he confides to his wife why he could not continue his own painting and has drifted into work that is too humdrum even to merit mention.

The voice-over plumbs the depths of the painter's feelings about his family, especially about his daughter, his darling, whose approval means so much to him. He could not himself articulate these feelings: they would have no verbal shape in his mind. The voice-over narrator can fill in the painter's silent sublimation: "The old man was preoccupied; he looked at his canvases and searched for the secrets in the redness of a cushion or a fold with an intensity that made him feel young, and a total and bitter certainty that he'd find nothing; this made him feel very old." He sublimates his feelings in his work as he has probably done all his life, but the old trick no longer works very well. "Secrets" here means not only the secrets of his art but those of his inner being. The intensity with which he seeks them doubtless absorbs and distracts him from worry about his children and his children's inability to provide the love and attention he once received from his wife. His sense of loss is so keen that his dead wife's figure materializes, not as a supernatural phenomenon, but as a remembered image in his mindscreen. This is more effective than a conventional flashback marked by editing: the contemporary "presence" of the dead woman seems perfectly appropriate given the man's longings and visual orientation. The voice-over also directly quotes the words passing through the painter's mind, but they too pass into a sublimation, or at least a self-distraction: "M. Ladmiral suddenly felt heartsick. He thought: 'My heart is heavy: it's giving out.' He saw already too clearly the moment when Irène would be leaving: so he stared hard at the landscape and thought of nothing but the colors of things."

As for Irène, whom we see reading her niece's palm, the voice-narrator explains her belief "in palm-reading as much as in insane love, romantic hero-ines, and story influences." The voice-over's interpretation of her philosophy of life is cleverly spoken over a scene of her affectionately romping with her nephews: "Irène wanted to live alone. Not so much free as alone. Those two words define girls who leave home." An interesting tension arises between what we hear and what we see: Is this the ultimate truth, or does her evident plea-sure in playing with the boys suggest that at some unconscious level she might like to have her own children? The only person who actually challenges her life style is her mother, reincarnated for her, as for M. Ladmiral, as a communi-cating force, not just a presence. Mme. Ladmiral asks Irène bluntly when she'll stop demanding so much of life.

> But for M. Ladmiral's part [the narrator goes on to explain], he had accepted Irène's departure with a courage so strong it couldn't be hidden. Only when her visits became rare did he ponder the ingratitude of children. Gonzagues visited him faithfully. When he left, Ladmiral wasn't sad but it reminded him that Irène had not come. In his adieu to Gonzagues he sensed his regret that the visitor hadn't been Irène. There were days when he went upstairs like a rejected lover.

M. Ladmiral avoids questions about Irène's personal life. His thoughts are quoted in indirect style by the voice-over. Note again the Balzacian self-assurance of the sentence "Did Irène have a lover? He never asked the question directly and he never intended to. It seemed apparent. But against those truths that hurt, men have one sure defense, denial." And still another generalization, underlined by the phrase "like all men. . .": "Had he known she had a lover, he'd have been unhappy. Like all men, he put a high price on the virginity of girls dear to him." On her side, "Irène was as discreet as her father when he had insisted on remaining ignorant of her first affair. This afternoon, however, amid the old shawls, he was sure that she had a lover, but that she'd never tell him and that he'd never ask and that they were both right to lie." The delicacy of this arrangement, worthy of Henry James, is in some ways the crux of the story and would be immensely difficult if not impossible to convey in a strictly scenic way (remember James's failure in the theater). It seems really only ar-ticulable through the medium of an authoritative outside voice.

A slyly characterizing note is struck in the next to last voice-over narration. Irène finds a shawl in the attic that she feels will gather a fine price in her antique shop. Her father tells her to take it, but Gonzagues wonders why she shouldn't pay for it (hints of a coming struggle between the heirs?). Irène insists on doing so. Whereupon the voice-over says: "M. Ladmiral resolved to buy gifts for his grandchildren with this money while vaguely suspecting that he wouldn't." Then the final voice-over narration sums up the full reality of the family relationship: "Irène was ready to go, already gone. Her cool authority had given way to hasty flight [to her lover]. M. Ladmiral who wanted so much to have her stay was ready to force her to: her need to leave was that strong." The film ends with a touching image—this time a flashback—of a younger Ladmiral and his dear wife laying a tablecloth on the lawn for a picnic. Gonzagues and Irène, preadolescents, come running from the house to join them.[9]

Another exemplary use of voice-over narration—this time homodiegetic—occurs in Alain Resnais's masterpiece *Providence* (1977). This film is much more experimental and requires the audience to figure out the exact relevance of the voice-over commentary to the visible action unrolling on the screen. After a shot of the sign "Providence" in front of a country mansion, the camera tracks into a bedroom, to a closeup of a hand attached to a red sleeve knocking over a glass and then pounding on a table. A voice clearly -off (not -over), which some may recognize as John Gielgud's, says "Damn, Damn, Damn." Then, with no clear reference to the hand and the voice, there begins a grim sequence in which an unnaturally hairy old man is chased by soldiers through a forest. In response to the old man's begging, a compassionate soldier, Kevin (played by David Warner), shoots him. Intercut with these events are flashforwards to the trial of Kevin as he is cross-examined for murder by the public prosecutor, Claud Langham (Dirk Bogarde). The story of the mercy killing of the old man turned werewolf is interrupted by a close-up shot of the same hand, attached to the same red sleeve, pouring another glass of wine; the pourer's face remains out of the frame, and this time his voice is not heard. Cut to the steps of a law court, from which a crowd exits, including a striking woman (Ellen Burstyn). The voice-over, addressing her as "Sonya," asks why she ever married the prosecutor, Claud, whom he identifies as his son. The voice-over says, "It'll have to be rewritten. And so little time." As the camera frames another member of the exiting crowd, the voice-over says, "Oh shit, it's Mark Eddington"; and then, evidently addressing Eddington, says "I'll make you a friend of Claud's."

How are we to interpret this sequence? By convention, we assume that the voice-over is commenting on the visual images of the unfolding story. But how is its relation to these images to be understood? Is the owner of the voice watching a film or videotape of real events, identifying people, and commenting on his relationship to them? Is this fictional footage that he has shot? Or is thinking of shooting? Or is he a writer, looking in his mind's eye at visual images of what he wants to write? Whether a film or novel, the remarks "I'll make you a friend of Claud's" and "It'll have to be rewritten, and so little time" suggest a story that is in the *process* of being created. And, it seems, the story is in some ways in control of itself: for instance, unwanted characters like Dr. Eddington intrude. The artist is not in full control. The voice-over asks, "But what are you in my scheme of things, Eddington? A jolly old, bloody old doctor character?" The voice-over seems as much subject to as creator of the visual images.

But it is clear that the voice is apprehensive — images occur later to confirm that his vision is obsessed with death and dying. Over images of a stadium filled with political prisoners awaiting execution, it says, "Oh, hell! These places are becoming almost *de rigueur* as fear symbols." Then it makes a remark that helps explain the source of the visual images: "Well, if one has led a fatuous life, one might as well have fatuous nightmares." But how can one who is awake — indeed, who seems *unable* to sleep — engage in a running commentary on his own nightmares? Is he speaking of literal or figurative nightmares, fantasies of a waking mind? Is "nightmare" being used in a loose sense for "unwanted" fantasy? Why do they contain such obsessive images of death and human misery? There is a growing association between the man's process of composition and his fears, from which artistic work does not liberate him.

The images turn more to his liking as Sonya invites Kevin home, presumably for an amorous interlude. The voice-over says, "Let that all commence," and then a line of explanatory significance: "Bang on, Clive Langham, get it all down." This remark explains a great deal: the name Clive has not been associated with anyone on the screen, so we surmise that he is speaking to himself. And the surname "Langham" is the same as that of Claud and his wife, Sonya. Further, the remark "Bang on. . . . Get that all down" suggests rather clearly that he is a writer, not a filmmaker. "Bang on" seems literally to mean "type," but the connotation is sexual, as if he vicariously lusts for Sonya. This impression is, however, rejected by a professional writer's second thoughts about how to handle the scene: "No, stop, it could seem vulgar."

At this point, then, the overall narrative structure is relatively crystallized: though we haven't yet seen the face of the protagonist, Clive Langham, in his own bedroom (the discourse space), creating but also being manipulated by characters and events transpiring in a story world under construction. That world is phantasmagoric, inhabited by werewolves, old men dying in the streets, grisly autopsies, pugnacious law proceedings, military occupation and repression, insurgency. Its protagonists are a cold-blooded prosecuting attorney, his disaffected wife, a gentle, spiritually inclined soldier, and an old mistress of the attorney who bears a striking resemblance to his mother.

Narratively, then, the movie is quite odd. Unlike most heterodiegetic narrators, Clive does not know how things will ultimately turn out. He does not seem to be telling the story retrospectively, but rather inventing it as it goes along, over its own resistance, so to speak. He cannot control the fantasies completely, and to that extent he is a kind of narrator-manqué. The visual track insists on keeping some of its autonomy. For example, Kevin does not make the appropriate amatory move toward Sonya as she unbuttons her dress. Clive's response is an onlooker's, not an author's, as he says "My God, he doesn't look like it's urgent though." Attempting to regain diegetic control, he asks where the husband, Claud, would be during all this. And we immediately cut to Claud in his office, dictating a nasty letter to his father. "Okay," says the voice-over, "in his office then." But again there is conflict between character and narrator. As Claud dictates in high, unfilial dudgeon, his voice fades out and that of Clive fades in, protesting vehemently about how his son reviles him. Again it seems as if the story is partly telling itself *to* him. (This is a state of affairs that many actual authors attest to when asked about how their works get written.)

Clive asks himself how he should introduce Claud's mistress. The matter is handled with a flourish seemingly calculated to demonstrate the artist's pure freedom, his ability to invent, to pick characters out of thin air, a freedom underscored by Clive's suddenly striking up a drinking song, "Hi-diddle-dee-dee," as if to say "See how easily I do this, as if with one hand." We see an airplane, passengers descending the ramp, among them one particularly attractive woman. Clive's voice-over says "Damned if I'm giving *you* to the dreaded Claud." Instead he picks an older woman (played by Elaine Strich) still on the plane: "Yes, you'll do. . . . Quick, quick, first name into the mind: Helen Wiener . . ." This insouciant and self-consciously arbitrary choice, however, proves not as innocently unmotivated as it appears, for the woman exactly resembles and is later symbolically identified with Clive's dead wife, Molly, shown in photograph and flashback. Thereby begins one of the Oedipal tangles of the film. (The other we only discover at the end, when it becomes clear that Kevin is also Clive's son.) Nor is it an accident that for the first time the face of the heretofore unseen narrator, Clive Langham, appears onscreen as the camera moves with the glass of wine up to his face. Clearly this visual facsimile of the dead wife whom he both loved and neglected gives him pause—a pause that must be *shown* since Clive's reaction is silent.

Clive's now full appearance in the discourse space changes neither the basic strategy nor the problematic of the narrative. The two spaces, of discourse and of story, remain clearly separate. And Clive continues to have trouble controlling the images. As the fey Kevin maunders on about astronauts, Clive's irritation with the character finds direct expression in a cinematic trick: his own voice, synchronized with Sonya's lip movements, says "Kevin, why are you so fucking obsessed by the bloody astronauts?" The line must be cleaned up for public consumption, presumably, so Sonya's correctly synchronized voice modifies it to "Why do you go on about the astronauts?" Later, an even more outrageous breach of narrative etiquette occurs, again showing how the story persists in following its own bent in defiance of Clive's discourse. Claud is on his way to his long-lost mistress, Helen; we see him entering her hotel, then the inside of her room; the door opens, and we expect him to enter. But instead of Claud, in walks Kevin! Whereupon the narrator protests and orders Kevin, who looks slightly confused, to leave, so that the proper characters can make their appearance. There are several other examples of the tension between how the story goes and how Clive wants it to go. Clive tries to get Claud to temper his accusations against him, but Claud adds a vicious wish that his father should die in terrible pain. So Claud is made to repeat the lines in a softer voice and a different setting, and the vicious line is deleted. In another place, Clive (always, of course, in the discourse) finds himself experiencing, of all things, an erection; he attributes it to Kevin, a creature of the story he is trying to create. But Kevin is discomfited: he denies that it is *his* erection. Once again a character is recalcitrant, denying a feeling his creator would assign to him.

In short, what the visual track shows sometimes exists by or under the control of the voice-over (and later voice-on) narrator—the author Clive Langham—and sometimes independently of him, even at odds with his intentions. In the latter case, he has to accommodate himself to what is happening visually of its own accord. Clearly, the novel that Clive is trying to write is not going very well. But that points up the theme of the film, namely the artist's struggle to create art out of raw fantasy, fantasy that has its roots deep within his psyche, teeming as it is with all the complexities, conscious and unconscious, that Freud has taught us to find there.

The dénouement is surprising but confirmatory of this hypothesis: we meet the originals of the characters of Clive's embryonic novel, and they are quite different from what the novelist has led us to believe. Claud *is* a lawyer but a quite gentle one, seemingly committed to honor and compassion, and desperately yearning to make contact with his father. Sonya is happy with her husband, clearly loves him, and is distressed to see how his father rejects him. There is not the slightest indication that Sonya has anything other than a sister-in-law's affection for Kevin. Far from being the fey dreamer whom Clive's fantasies had projected, Kevin, now identified as Clive's bastard but better-loved son, is an important astrophysicist based in Geneva. So everything that has happened in the fantasies and a-borning novel are the products of Clive's unconscious or conscious wishes, products that speak more to the tensions in his own psyche than to the realities of the family relationships as we see them for ourselves. For Clive, Kevin has been the fantasy vehicle of his remaining sexual lust—but also, more interestingly, of the kind of idealism that Clive in his cynical old age will no longer admit to and has severely repressed. This repression is the basis of his difficulty in dealing with the fictional Kevin in the previous night's struggles. A conscious side of Clive's psyche remains and longs for frank sensuality; another, repressed and unconscious, side is otherworldly, fey. The latter, even against Clive's conscious will, gets embodied in Kevin. Clive struggles with it, even to the point of endowing Kevin with an erection that he does not want. In a wonderful irony, the real Kevin presents his father with a brass telescope as a birthday present—which Clive, of course, promptly extends at a priapic angle from his groin. Sonya too seems to understand Clive's need for phallic reassurance by giving him a hunting knife purportedly owned by Hemingway. He holds that, too, at a sexual angle and then hands it to Claud, upon whom he has projected his aggression and cynicism, especially his cynical attitude toward sex.

Clive deals with the less easy relation, with his legitimate son, in a quite different way. In Clive's fantasy, the fictional Claud, the Claud he projects, is an implacable judge, hating his father, condemning him for his loose way of life, a way of life, which Claud argues caused his mother's suicide. Clearly, the fictional Claud is Clive's projection of his own sense of guilt, a guilt he will not consciously recognize and even now, suffering from terminal cancer, tries to drown in cold white wine and fantasies of women. As he projects this onto Claud, his work-in-progress punishes his son by tying him to an incestuous relation with his mother. Pathetically, the real Claud, still trying to win his father's love after all these years of rejection, still struggling to morally connect with Clive, gives his father a book of poetry. But even upon this Clive vents his cynicism, rejecting Claud once again. Only unconsciously, in fantasy, can Clive acknowledge idealistic and poetic feelings, and then only by projecting them, even as he derides them, onto his better-loved illegitimate son.

The film, then, concerns the plight and glory of being an artist, a person whose gift it is to turn fantasies into art. It is less concerned with the final product of Clive's struggle than with the agonies and riches of the artistic spirit in action, even at an advanced age. This theme encourages a rich panoply of cinematic effects and provides a good example of the great possibilities available to film as high art. And much of the film's success is due to the imaginative use of voice-over and voice-on narration, a narration that enables it to problematize the relation of discourse to story, of narrator to narrated, of imagination to reality.

Notes

1. In "The New Laocoön," as quoted by Sarah Kozloff, *Invisible Storytellers: Voice-Over Narration in American Fiction Film* (1988, 9). Kozloff surveys the aversion to voice-over narration among film theorists and practitioners in her first chapter, "The Prejudices against Voice-Over Narration." My essay relies heavily on her work, attempting to add a few insights and to extend the discussion to recent Hollywood and foreign films that exhibit innovative usages of the technique.

2. As paraphrased by Paul Coates, "The Sense of an Ending" (1996–97, 20).

3. Bruce Kawin, *Mindscreen: Bergman, Godard, and First-Person Film* (1978); Edward Branigan, *Point of View in the Cinema: A Theory of Narration and Subjectivity in Classical Film* (1984); David Bordwell, *Narration in the Fiction Film* (1985). The French have also been very productive in narrative-film theory: see particularly the work of François Jost, André Gaudreault, Jacques Aumont, Marc Vernet, and Roger Odin.

4. See the discussion of text-types in my *Coming to Terms* (1990), chaps. 1–4.

5. "A Statement," republished in Eisenstein 1957, 256–60.

6. The convention is highly susceptible to parody: in *Bananas* (1971), for example, the Woody Allen character, searching for his girlfriend in a Central American country, is told by a messenger to his hotel room that the President wants to see him. As he repeats "The President!" in rapt astonishment, we hear a harp glissando. Woody suspiciously opens the door of his closet to discover a harpist excusing himself for practicing there.

7. Kozloff explains this effect well: "[I]n many cases the voice-over narrator is so inscribed in the film as to seem as if he or she has generated not only what he is saying but also what we are seeing. In other words, films often create the sense of character-narration so strongly that one accepts the voice-over narrator as if he or she were the mouthpiece of the image-maker either for the whole film or for the duration of his or her embedded story. We put our faith in the voice not as created but as creator" (1988, 45). I agree in principle with this representation, except perhaps for calling this image-generating narrator the "mouthpiece" of the image maker. Isn't it better to say that the film medium allows an embedded narrator to both tell and (literally) show his story? In *Stage Fright* (1950), the cinematic narrator (or "image maker") generates the story of Jonathan (Richard Todd), who tells/shows a false version of the story, a version that later gets undercut by the cinematic narrator's truthful version, which is totally "shown," that is, "presented solely in visual imagery accompanied by story-dialogue and other sound." As to "putting our faith in the voice not as created but as creator," this very example of unreliable narration illustrates that we may retract our faith in a narrator even as we come to understand that he is at once creator of his own, embedded narrative and creature of the ultimate cinematic narrator or image maker.

8. Kozloff notes that the studio was so anxious to identify the voice-over with the boy Huw (played by Roddy McDowell) that it failed to give a screen credit to the adult actor whose voice was used, Irving Pichel.

9. It would be absurd to ignore a cinema that can represent the dynamics of family life so delicately. As long as Hollywood remains slave to an insistence on "visual purity,"

it forgoes such possibilities to its own artistic detriment. By the same token, one cannot criticize genuinely creative attempts to transform the various functions of omniscient narration into visual or partially visual forms. There have been some breathtaking film adaptations of novels, like that of *The French Lieutenant's Woman* (1981). In this most successful dramatization of a novel's discourse, the screenwriter (Harold Pinter) has transformed the modernist perspective of the novel's narrator into a modern story of the love affair of the two actors playing Sarah and Charles, the novel's protagonists. See my *Coming to Terms,* chapter 10.

12

Guilty Cravings: What Feminist Narratology Can Do for Cultural Studies

Robyn R. Warhol

Feminist narratologists analyze narrative forms with an eye to gender. Depending on the project, this might mean attending to the gender of a character, an author, a narrator, a reader, or some combination of these figures. The field originated in the observation that many structuralist narratologists had excluded female-written texts from their purportedly objective studies. Feminist narratology borrows the feminist-epistemological critique of objectivity to question the "either/or" reasoning of classical narratology. As a poststructuralist movement in criticism, feminist narratology attempts to consider texts within their historical contexts, understanding narrative forms as necessarily related to the era, class, gender, sexual orientation, and racial and ethnic circumstances of their producers and audiences. Nevertheless, feminist narratology maintains structuralism's focus on identifying patterns among narrative forms of story and discourse. Generally speaking, feminist narratologists have demonstrated more interest in elucidating the meanings of particular texts than have classical narratologists, who have tended to draw more sweeping generalizations than an anti-essentialist feminist stance can endorse.

Early projects in feminist narratology focusing on the function and positioning of female characters in narrative include Nancy K. Miller's enormously influential analysis of the eighteenth- and nineteenth-century British and French feminocentric novel, The Heroine's Text *(1980), and Mieke Bal's study of women in biblical narratives,* Lethal Love *(1987). Susan R. Suleiman's* Authoritarian Fictions *(1983) does not concentrate on gender, but serves as an early model of how structuralist methods for analyzing story and discourse can be reconciled with the study of political and cultural contexts. Studies of the impact of authors' and narrators' gender on the way stories get told include Rachel Blau DuPlessis's* Writing beyond the Ending *(1985) and*

340

my own Gendered Interventions *(1989). The most celebrated and influential statement of the movement's principles is Susan Sniader Lanser's essay, "Toward a Feminist Narratology" (1991[1986]); it has often been reprinted, and its revision of the structuralist theory of "voice" is the central concern of Lanser's important book* Fictions of Authority *(1992). Recent work in feminist narratology, such as Sally Robinson's* Engendering the Subject *(1991), shifts attention from the gender of the author, characters, and narrator to the ways narrative works to structure gender within culture. My contribution to this volume uses this latter approach in thinking about a popular-cultural narrative form, soap opera.*

> I adore simple pleasures. They are the last refuge of the complex.
> — Oscar Wilde

Feminism is supposed to be a defensive posture. In the popular imagination, at least, feminists are supposed to be humorless upholders of p.c. principles, devoid of playfulness or irony, incapable of understanding the punch line to the classic 1980s joke: "Question: How many feminists does it take to change a light bulb? Answer: That isn't funny!" Poststructuralist feminist theory, of course, revels in humor, in play, even in self-parody; one of its strongest contributions to academia, as far as I'm concerned, is the license it has granted to feminists everywhere to stop being so defensive, not just about feminism but about femininity as well. For me, feminism carves out a space in the academy where I can speak seriously about subjects the academy cannot or does not take seriously, topics that have never been or are no longer, academically speaking, *comme il faut.* I may feel guilty about the pleasure I take in such apparently antifeminist pursuits as the ultrafeminine activity of watching daytime television soap operas or the ultramasculine practice of narratology, but feminism — ironically enough — enables me to pursue them anyway, and even to transform the indulgence of those cravings into something I regard as politically useful work. My guilty cravings for "feminine" emotional excess, on the one hand, and for "masculine" orderly categorization, on the other, come together in feminist narratology. If there is something seemingly "simple" about daytime soaps and about narratology, the confluence of the two brings out complexities that must always emerge when we are speaking about gender, complexities that serve to destabilize received notions about what "femininity" and "masculinity" are supposed to be.

While the combination of "feminism" with "narratology" may no longer seem odd or unnatural, and the practice of "feminist narratology" may now be taken for granted as one among many possible approaches within narrative theory, this was not always so. Ten years ago a feminist had to feel guilty about being a narratologist; feminist narratologists faced serious challenges from both sides of their theoretical affiliation. Kathy Mezei has highlighted the awkward origins of "this hybrid of an *ology* (the science of narratives) and an *ism* (the action of being a feminist)" (1996, 2); as her formulation suggests, the link between "science" and "activism" implied in the phrase "feminist narratology" was neither obvious nor simple to make. Broadly speaking, "narratology" stood for objectivity and abstraction, "feminism" for historically grounded political commitment and subjective experience; "narratology" for general observations about texts, "feminism" for analysis of their meanings; "narratology" for the neat binaries of structuralist analysis, "feminism" for a poststructuralist inclination to mess those categories up.[1] What "narratology" suggested to feminist critics was not the original structuralist project of mapping out every possible configuration of story and discourse, as the great originators of narratology had tried to do. Feminists were on the vanguard of what Seymour Chatman was in 1990 to call "Contextualist Narratology," departing from classical narratology by taking "into account the actual setting in which literature is situated" (309).[2] In practice, this meant reading texts closely in relation to particular contexts, rather than making broad generalizations intended to cover any and all cases of narrative utterance.

Though structuralist narratology, in actual practice, offers brilliant passages of close textual analysis to illustrate its broader points (Gérard Genette or Gerald Prince can always be counted upon to tease as much meaning out of a phrase as the most subtle deconstructionist, after all),[3] it was never really about "close reading." Classical narratology claimed to describe systems of literary meaning, not to interpret the meanings of individual literary texts. "What does it mean?" was never the question for structuralist narratology; "*How* does it mean?" was the point. And the answer to that question was supposed to be deduced more or less objectively.

Feminists interested in narrative theory borrowed the feminist-epistemological critique of objectivity from the social and natural sciences to object that systems of meaning are never neutral, and that they bear the (gendered) marks of their originators and their receivers. Furthermore, feminists have always been interested in *significance,* in both the linguistic and historical senses of that word. Hence, feminist narratologists never tried to replace the structuralists' systems with alternative macrosystems of their own. Instead, feminist narratology focused on two kinds of projects that relied more on *both* close reading *and* historical context than structuralism ever did. These were: (1) finding examples of narrative written by women that posed challenges to the categories of classic narratology, and referring to historical context to account for (the significance of) the gendered differences they observed; and (2) "reading in detail," as Naomi Schor memorably called it, applying the analytic categories narratology made available to scrutinize texts very closely and arrive at gender-conscious interpretations of narratives. More recently, feminist narratology has begun to focus on gender not as a predetermined condition of the production of texts, but as a textual effect. As Sally Robinson puts it, "I am concerned with how gender is produced *through* narrative processes, not prior to them" (1991, 198, note 23). In other words, for feminist narratology in the 1990s, the first question is not so much "Was this text (really) written by a man or a woman?" as "How does this text construct masculinity or femininity in and for its reader?" Any attempt at a complete answer for such a question requires a close reading of that text. As far as feminist narratologists are concerned, "close reading" is still very much a "going concern" as we approach the turn of the century—though I confess a twinge of anxiety about the unfashionableness of the project in the larger context of literary and cultural studies, much like the penchant we academic feminists share for rather predictably wearing black, as it *was* indeed stylish to do a decade ago.

Contemporary cultural studies, as a field, is not in principle opposed to close reading, but its major theoretical statements have sought to establish a distance between cultural studies and "formalism," the movement in literary criticism most closely associated with close readings of texts. I am arguing that the kind of "close reading" feminist narratologists do is distinct from the "close reading" associated with the kind of new-critical formalism cultural studies theorists eschew, but I think that cultural studies' abhorrence of decontextualized formalism can partly explain the avoidance of close reading I see in much feminist film and television criticism. Richard Johnson's influential 1987 essay, "What Is Cultural Studies Anyway?," identifies what he rather dramatically labels "an opposition to abstract categories and a terror of formalism" (60) among practitioners of British cultural studies in the 1980s, and counters it by citing Roland Barthes's observation "that a little formalism turns one away from History, but that a lot brings one back to it" (60). For Johnson, critical practices seeking to identify the forms behind cultural processes are a problem only when they are conceived as narrowly "literary" pursuits. In his model of cultural studies, formal analysis of text is crucially important, as long as the text is decentered "as an object of study." Johnson elaborates:

> "The text" is no longer studied for its own sake, nor even for the social effects it may be thought to produce, but rather for the subjective or cultural forms which it realises and makes available. The text is only a *means* in cultural study; strictly, perhaps, it is a raw material from which certain forms (e.g. of narrative, ideological problematic, mode of address, subject position, etc.) may be abstracted. It may also form *part* of a larger discursive field or *combination* of forms occurring in other social spaces with some regularity. But the ultimate object of cultural studies is not, in my view, the text, but *the social life of subjective forms* at each moment of their circulation, including their textual embodiments. This is a long way from a literary valuing of texts for themselves. (62)

Reading texts closely to distinguish the forms that structure them is not, for Johnson at least, antithetical to cultural studies' larger goals.

Even so, British and American cultural studies focusing on the mass media have continued over the past ten years to demonstrate an aversion to close reading that is particularly distinct in feminist film theory. Film theorists tend to equate close reading of texts with what they call "formalism," a movement perceived as doggedly apolitical and ideologically naive, standing for a past moment in media studies that is, thankfully, over. "Formalism" is invariably set in opposition against a culturally situated criticism in histories of feminist film theory. The recent collection *Multiple Voices in Feminist Film Criticism* offers no defense of formalism, but supplies a range of arguments against it. For example, Patrice Petro, in an article that was originally published in *Camera Obscura* in 1990, identifies "two historicities" in film studies, "best described as the difference between a *formal* history of filmic conventions and institutions and a *cultural* history of film reception and spectatorship. Whereas formal film histories are characterized by an attempt to discern developments within institutional constraints and generic conventions, for example, cultural film histories aim to locate films within the history of larger cultural forces, such as consumerism, censorship, or reform. Given these alternatives, it is no coincidence that feminists have chosen to pursue issues in cultural history" (1994, 66–67). Given these oppositions, we might say it is no coincidence that detailed formal analysis has not played as strong a role in feminist cultural studies as it could. Christine Gledhill summarizes the move within film criticism from formalism to neo-Marxian semiotics as a shift from an undertheorized humanism to a more politically responsible and rigorous framework, "demanding that before a film's content is assessed closer attention be paid to the specificities of cinematic production and particularly to how character is produced by textual operations such as narration, plot and mise-en-scène. But it also implied investigation of a different order of meaning" (1994, 112). In practice, this shift of attention has meant less critical attention to details of narrative form, because the complexities of ideological analysis require such extensive contextualization and such exhaustive historical and theoretical work. Feminist film theorists writing in the 1990s continue to distance themselves from the practice of "formalism." Janet Staiger warns feminist film critics against falling "into a fallacy of reducing formal characteristics to a progressive ideological effect" (1994, 201); Jane Gaines concurs, saying, "While I would not want to argue that form is ideologically neutral, I would suggest that we have overemphasized the ideological function of 'signifying practice' at the expense of considering other ideological implications of the conflicting meanings in the text" (1994, 185). The necessary and invigorating move to diversify academic feminisms in the 1990s, to include consideration of a broader range of genders, sexes, sexualities, races, nationalities, (dis)abilities, and ages — as well as the spectrum of social classes a neo-Marxian perspective automatically brings into focus — has meant there is simply not enough time in the day, not enough space on the page, for feminist cultural critics to devote themselves to close analysis of texts' formal properties.

Yet even if we put aside its troubling history as the alleged opposite of culturally engaged, historicist analysis, the kind of "close reading" associated with formalist criticism also presents at least two logistical obstacles for the scholar interested in popular culture: First, which text(s) should the scholar try to read closely, when popular cultural texts are — in marked contrast to "literary" texts — ephemeral? In doing a reading of, for instance, a scene from a soap opera, the critic cannot assume an audience's familiarity with that particular text, or even that the audience could retrieve the text if they wanted to check their own impressions against the reading. In this respect, close formal analysis of popular culture has to be different from the kind of work that feminist narratologists have done, in that they have generally assumed an audience that knows their texts, even when those texts are not, strictly speaking, canonical. The critic must offer a more thorough description of the object being analyzed, while at the same time resisting the temptation to be swept away by the details of a summary for a plot no one needs or cares to know about. Also, the details under scrutiny will be different from those of the traditional close reading. Instead of teasing out the ironies and ambiguities inherent in well-wrought figures of speech, the feminist narratologist closely reads a cultural example in its broader contexts to find the multiple meanings it can carry for various audiences.

The question of canonicity raises the second difficulty for close readings of popular texts, one that Peter J. Rabinowitz has set forth very clearly. As he has argued, "close reading" was invented as a means of evaluating and interpreting canonical texts, and it favors texts that are written according to its premises. "The schools in vogue may change, but we still assign value to what fits our prior conceptions of reading," Rabinowitz explains, "and the academically sanctioned canon consequently consists largely of texts that respond well to close reading. . . . Not only do we reject many works that don't fit; more damaging, we also twist many others until they *do* fit" (1988, 219). Jane Tompkins has made a very similar observation in *Sensational Designs*. A "closely read" popular text — something that operates highly conventionally, as does detective fiction or television soap opera — can only end up looking bad. Based on the canon, the method of course reinforces the canon. But as I have mentioned, the kind of feminist-narratological close reading I am advocating would not do close readings for the purpose of evaluating or even interpreting texts (as canonical close reading was supposed to do), but rather to describe their formal operations for various audiences. As a feminist narratologist, I seek meaning not in the texts themselves, but in their interactions with and actions upon readers and viewers.

To be sure, this is nothing new for cultural studies. As I. Q. Hunter and Heidi Kaye have recently put it, "The most vibrant current research is committed to taking audiences and their pleasures seriously. Going beyond either castigating them for poor taste or worrying obsessively about the effects of popular culture, it asks instead what real, unruly, socially situated readers and viewers *do* with texts. Audiences are no longer envisaged as passive consumers but as active producers of popular culture" (1997, 1). And yet, the cultural-studies critic is faced with a methodological dilemma in trying to study "audiences" *per se*. If we ask what "real, unruly, socially situated readers and viewers *do*," we might borrow methods of surveying and ethnography from the social sciences, or we might borrow the electrodes and wires of certain branches of the behavioral sciences, or we might apply prefabricated models of desire from psychoanalysis. To use these methods in the absence of something like "close reading," however, is to neglect the role that formal properties and operations of popular texts play in structuring the very audience response we seek to study.

By advocating "close reading," I do not mean to invoke the old new-critical method for conquering ambiguity and paradox to arrive at a unified meaning for a (great) text. I am talking instead about a close analysis of form, a semiotics of how popular cultural texts convey meaning, rather than of what they mean to say. In the study of television drama, perhaps more than of film, reader-response theory and semiotics have sometimes combined to form an approach that closely resembles narratology. Recently, such excellent feminist analyses of television form as Jane Feuer's *Seeing through the Eighties* (1995), Lynne Joyrich's *Re-Viewing Reception: Television, Gender, and Postmodern Culture* (1996), and Laura Stempel Mumford's *Love and Ideology in the Afternoon: Soap Opera, Women, and Television Genre* (1995) have offered hypotheses about how narrative forms operate to make meanings on television. To date, the most compelling and original example of this critical genre is still Robert C. Allen's virtuoso chapter, "A Reader-Oriented Poetics of the Soap Opera," in his 1985 book, *Speaking of Soap Operas*. With a careful ear for feminist concerns, Allen encircles his narratology of soap-opera forms with detailed histories of the institutional production and the actual reception of soap operas, as well as with a culturally attuned study of the soap opera as "commodity and commodifier": no one could dismiss his formal analysis of soap opera's structures as detached from historically and ideologically significant contexts. In that formal analysis, Allen distinguishes between the "syntagmatic" and "paradigmatic" narrative structures in soap operas, explaining that only the "experienced viewer" of a given soap can go beyond the syntagmatic string of events (the seemingly random barrage of loosely related incidents and coincidences that typify a soap's short-term story line) to read paradigmatic significance in the long-term plot's repetitions of certain motifs. Allen lists "the variety of soap opera codes," offering "stylistic," "generic," "textual," "intertextual," and "ideological" codes as signs that seasoned soap-opera viewers read in order to make sense of the text. Allen proceeds in the spirit of narratology, drawing his poetics with broad strokes and giving cursory illustrations from what seems to be an extensive knowledge of certain soap-opera plots of the early 1980s. Except for the fact that he does not offer close readings of the texts he cites, Allen could be understood as doing feminist narratology, because he very carefully posits a "female reader" as the ideal addressee of the soap-opera text. According to Allen, "the Model Reader of *Guiding Light* is more likely to be a working-class woman than a male literary critic" (83).

For Allen, as for the feminist narratologists working a decade ago, gender is a category that preexists the text, an entity that shapes the text's production and reception. Allen follows the early work of Tania Modleski and Ellen Seiter in asserting that "the female reader" (as he calls soap opera's typical and ideal audience) may have a different relation to texts in general from that established by the male critical norm. As Allen explains, "The soap opera has been illegible as an aesthetic object partly because the terms by which it could be aesthetically engaged seemed foreign to most men. Feminist criticism of the past decade has raised the possibility that the narrative strategies and central stylistic features of 'mainstream' fiction and film are sexually loaded, that a male reader/spectator is 'inscribed' in the text. This does not mean that a female reader cannot enjoy such texts, but rather that her response is mediated by her difference from the text's implied reader. If this is the case, then the values that critics privilege in such works are likely to be sexually loaded as well" (93). The soap opera, Allen argues, "represents an alternative basis for narrative aesthetic pleasure in general—one that values complexity, repetition, and speech over simplicity, telos, and action" (95). Allen imagines the reader who can appreciate that alternative aesthetic as female—that is, as someone physically occupying a woman's body; his formulation posits the woman's feminine "gender" as a given.

The feminist narratology that was developing while Allen was writing his book also tends to treat gender as a "prior category," focusing on women writers and women readers. Kathy Mezei's current edited collection, *Ambiguous Discourse: Feminist Narratology and British Women Writers* (1996), demonstrates in its very parameters this same assumption, that writing about gender necessarily has something to do with women's writing—or, as in Allen's book, women's reading. A more progressive version of feminist narratology would focus not on the sex of author or reader (since that entails drawing certain stereotypical and essentializing assumptions about what "a woman" does or likes or thinks or feels), and would not assume a direct correspondence between a reader's sex and his or her gender; a feminist narratology for the 1990s must reflect an awareness—as does Susan Lanser's essay on Winterson ("Queering Narratology," 1996)—of the potential pitfalls inherent in making assumptions about the necessary links between a subject's sex, gender, and sexuality. The goal of the new feminist narratologies is, to quote Robinson once again, to study "how gender is produced *through* narrative processes, not prior to them." I believe that feminist narratology's great strength is its ability to ground its observations about gender and narrative in the evidence of close reading. To circumvent feminist cultural studies's prejudice against "formalism," to perform close readings of the narrative components of popular texts, and to do this in the service of understanding how popular cultural narrative forms work to produce gender (rather than to reflect or represent it) would be to bring feminist narratology and cultural studies together in a new and potentially productive meeting of methodologies.

In my own current work, I have been arguing that one of the things "readers and viewers *do* with texts" is to use them as a sort of exercise equipment for developing the affective muscles that constitute gender. In the spirit of 1990s poststructuralist feminism, I see gender not as an essential property of male and female bodies, but rather as the set of gestures, stances, inflections, postures, and feelings associated in a given culture with masculinity and femininity. Popular cultural texts can be understood as technologies for producing and reproducing fairly predictable patterns of feeling that partly constitute masculinity and femininity for their fans. Soap opera, perhaps the most powerfully gendered of popular cultural genres, puts its viewers through the paces of *feeling* femininity, on a daily and weekly basis, for months or years or even decades of a devoted fan's life. In order to get more specific about what femininity "feels like" in contemporary United States mainstream culture, I use the tools of feminist narratology to do "close readings" of individual episodes within a typical series, the CBS–Proctor and Gamble soap, "As the World Turns." The readings draw upon over forty years of "backstory" to show that more meanings inhere in a scene than would be evident to the uninitiated reader, but the meanings of that scene itself are secondary to the larger purpose of doing the close reading: uncovering the formal elements that signal the scene's participation in a gendered cultural form. The "reader" I posit is not a "female" reader, but rather a "feminine" one, a man or woman who participates in reinforcing feminine feeling by continually watching the soap.

For the purposes of illustration, then, I offer a feminist-narratological (as opposed to a formalist/new-critical) close reading of a thirty-second sequence from the end of a Wednesday episode of "As the World Turns," broadcast on August 6, 1997. I did not choose the scene entirely at random, because I wanted to dissect a sequence that drew upon long-term resonances within the soap opera's plot; it is not, however, an exceptional scene in any sense. On the contrary, it is arguably "typical" of this particular soap in this specific era of its forty-two-year history on the air. My reading is informed by Allen's five categories of soap-opera "codes," but I will complicate his already very subtle narratology of soap-opera poetics by inserting gender into my analysis, not as a prior category ("Is the viewer male or female?"), but rather as a process or effect of the text ("How does the scene structure feminine feelings in its audience?"). When I think about how a soap-opera scene makes meaning, I can only think in terms of the information various viewers might bring to bear on reading the scene. Depending on the amount of backstory the viewer has access to while watching the scene, the representation is relatively empty or overwhelmingly replete with meanings. For the initiated, informed viewer, the scene carries complicated narrative information, but—more importantly—it also inspires a powerful affective response. I am arguing that the diurnal repetition of that response, over days, weeks, months, years, and decades of a viewer's life, is part of what constitutes "femininity" in this culture.

The scene lasts for just thirty seconds. The literate soap-opera viewer (that is, the reader who understands the stylistic and generic codes of the genre of daytime soap) who has never watched "As the World Turns" and who tunes the television to CBS just for these thirty seconds would glean the following information from the scene: A man and a woman, both in their late twenties (signified by her Jennifer Aniston haircut and his long wet-look locks; her black silk sleeveless, short-skirted shift with bright asymmetrical floral print and his black polo shirt and black jeans; her tiny figure, shapely legs and arms and his broad shoulders and sculpted biceps) are standing together at the front

of a church apparently set up for a wedding, decorated with white floral bouquets and tapered, burning candles. A white-cassocked priest faces the couple,
as the young man says "Father, there isn't going to be a wedding. Not . . . not
for me and Lily." The priest responds, "But you sounded so sure when you
called me, Damian. What happened?" Damian replies, "Lily's going to marry
someone else, the man she—really belongs with. His name is Holden Snyder."
Lily, speaking as though choked with emotion, says to Damian, "Thank you."
Lily places her hand on Damian's face as she speaks. The camera backs up, so
that the perspective frames Lily and Damian as though from the church's en-
trance, with the priest off-center and out of focus in front of them. Lily's hand
drops from Damian's face to take his hand, and they caress each other's hands
and forearms as they look into each other's eyes, with evident gratitude on her
part and benevolence on his. The music on the soundtrack, gentle flutes and
strings, signifies peaceful reconciliation.

Into the frame comes part of a man's back, very close to the camera; we see
his elbow as we participate in his gaze at the couple at the front of the church.
Generic codes instantly tell the viewer that this is "Holden Snyder"; they also
indicate that he will misunderstand what he is seeing in the church. Cymbals
strike on the soundtrack, which rises in an electronic tremolo indicating emotional stress. The camera shifts to show Holden standing in the doorway with
a young woman behind him in shadow. The shot-reverse shot shows Holden's
shocked expression, then again in close-up the tableau of Lily and Damian
seemingly at the altar, Lily again touching Damian's face, then Holden's reaction. The stylistic codes require that the camera register the key character's
reaction to a surprising situation, especially when it comes, as this scene does,
at the end of an episode; ordinarily, the reaction is ambiguous (the character
registers shock, but not the emotion succeeding shock—usually, the viewer has
to wait for the next installment to know the action that will follow the reaction).
This reaction shot departs from that convention, as Holden gasps and raises
his hands to cover his mouth in a classically melodramatic gesture of horror.

This much the literate soap-opera viewer could glean in thirty seconds.
From here, a properly formalist close reading might get even closer, looking
frame-by-frame at the details that carry the meanings I have sketched. Such a
close reading achieves its effects by de-familiarizing the text; to do so, the critic
must take it as far out of context as possible, to see it as a detached artifact.
The kind of feminist-narratological close reading I am advocating moves in the
opposite direction from a formalist method of that kind, teasing the meanings
out of the scene that inhere not in the details of its composition, but rather
in the context of its reception. If the meanings I have sketched out are there
for the viewer who has encountered "As the World Turns" for only thirty sec-

onds, what would be the meanings for the viewer who has followed it for three days? or for three weeks? or three years? or, for that matter, thirteen years or even thirty? Depending on the amount of backstory — or what Allen calls "textual codes" — and of outside information from fan magazines and the internet (Allen's "intertextual codes") a given reader can draw upon, the meanings of the scene and its emotional resonances are increasingly complex.

To pursue, then, a few feminist-narratological "close readings" (different in nature from what formalist close readings would be) from the perspective of these different readerly contexts: a viewer who has watched "As the World Turns" for just three days knows that Damian and Lily have just weathered an extremely emotional passage, in which he has begged her, with tears running down his cheeks, to relinquish Holden and recommit herself to her marriage to Damian. During these three episodes his pleas have escalated into actions Lily says are "hurting and scaring" her, including holding her arm and blocking her exit from the bell tower of the church, where the scene takes place. He has admitted to lying to her and scheming to manipulate her into the bell tower by leaving her a false message to meet Holden there. Lily has been frightened and upset, and has argued vehemently that what Damian is demonstrating is not love for her, but just a desire to control her. In the context of these very emotional scenes, the later scene in the church carries extra resonances of relief, as Lily seems to have escaped from the threat of Damian's emotional dominance.

Watching for three days, the viewer would also know that Holden has been frantically trying to find Lily all this time (because he plans to elope with her on this night) and that the young woman in the doorway behind Holden is Molly, who has been claiming to believe that Lily is faithful to Holden while planting hints in Holden's mind to make him believe that Lily wants to reunite with Damian. Molly's role is clearer to the viewer who has watched for three weeks: she is a former girlfriend of Holden's, who bore him a child twelve years ago, but left Oakdale to keep her pregnancy a secret and never let Holden know he was a father. Molly is obsessed with finding the child she gave up for adoption, and with the passion for Holden she never got over. Holden and Molly have been pursuing the search for their child, even while Holden has been agonizing over Lily's choice between remaining married to Damian and marrying Holden instead. Indeed, during these three weeks, Damian has returned from the dead, having been presumed to have perished in a plane crash a year and a half ago, but having survived and suffered from amnesia until now. Damian has returned to Oakdale to see his wife, Lily, and their little boy, and, seeing them, has realized that he desperately wants to reunite with them, even though Lily has committed herself to Holden in Damian's absence. Molly and Damian have conspired to keep Lily and Holden apart on this crucial day, when Holden has planned to elope with Lily. The viewer of three weeks' standing has seen numerous romantic scenes between Lily and Damian, in which Lily has shown a strong inclination to succumb to Damian's appeals; to this viewer, Lily's repeated assurances to Holden that she wants to be with him could look disingenuous, as her actions with Damian have contradicted her words to Holden. This viewer might see Holden's desire for Lily as a mistake, and might wish for Molly's and Damian's desires to prevail. For this viewer, Holden's horrified reaction to the vision of Damian and Lily's apparent remarriage is an error he should "get over" and then he should turn to Molly for comfort.

The viewer who has watched for three years, however, would read the circumstances differently. For one thing, the character of Molly did not exist three years ago; this viewer knows her only as a recent interpolation into the long-term plot. This viewer has witnessed Damian and Lily's marriage, complete with Damian's proto-abusive behavior and Lily's continuous willingness to forgive him; the viewer of three years has also seen Lily's grief over Damian's apparent death, the dramatic results of her attempting to avenge the sabotage she believes has killed him (which landed her in jail on a murder charge), and Holden's active role in getting the case against Lily dropped. This viewer knows, too, that Lily slept with Holden once while she was married to Damian (in the very bell tower where Damian and Lily now are arguing), and (having been kidnapped by a terrorist and held captive with Holden) had planned to leave Damian for Holden; her plan fell through when the terrorist shot Damian during a heroic rescue attempt, and she stayed married to Damian out of guilt and concern over his wound. For this viewer, Lily's inclination to give way to Damian's desires is part of her long-standing pattern of self-defeating behavior. This viewer understands Holden's horror at the tableau he sees at the front of the church in the scene I am analyzing: Lily has chosen Damian over Holden before, and he believes he sees history repeating itself.

The longer-term viewer, who has watched "As the World Turns" for, say, thirty years, knows the whole story of Lily and Holden's romance, dating back to the early 1980s in "real time" (identified as "eleven years ago" in these scenes set in 1997). Lily and Holden met as young teenagers, and have shared a tempestuous romance ever since. They have been married to each other and to other people; they have been separated by amnesia (Holden, like Damian, was at one time alienated from Lily by this very common soap-opera affliction) and by individual decision (spurred, in most instances, by the actors' desire to pursue career opportunities outside the boundaries of the soap opera); they have taken turns, over the last decade and a half, desperately pursuing each other's love. With only a brief recasting of Lily during the early 1990s, they have been played by the same actors for as long as they have been part of the story. Viewers' feelings about Lily, Holden, and Damian run strong: As discussions of the "As the World Turns" plot on the internet show, many viewers of three years', thirteen years', or even thirty years' standing prefer Damian over Holden, while others find Holden more attractive (having known him, after all, since he was fifteen years old); many love Lily, who has been on the soap intermittently since she was little more than a child, while others find the character spoiled and annoying. There is no single, received reading of the situation presented by the tableau of Lily and Damian at the front of the church: different readers, even those with access to the same amount of backstory, feel differently about these characters and their pasts and futures.

For my part, I like all three of these characters, and I like the generic conventions that make this situation possible, including the back-from-the-dead return of Paolo Sagenti as Damian (who had left the soap for a time in hopes of becoming a movie star); the coincidence of Lily's having had not one, but two husbands whose amnesia interrupted their marriages; the suggestion that a quite ordinary but plucky young woman — Lily, as played by Martha Byrne — could command the undying passion of two improbably gorgeous men; and my intimate familiarity with such diurnally repeated details as the way Jon Hensley as Holden uses his hands when he speaks and hooks them in his armpits with his arms crossed when he is at rest, the way Sagenti's Italian accent mangles his readings of English lines, the way the twentysomething Byrne widens and rolls her eyes like a silent-film diva of a much older generation. The conventionality, the formulaic nature, the predictability — the very familiarity of all these things and of the feelings they invoke constitute the pleasure of watching. Having followed this story (or rather the soap's larger context for this particular subplot) for over forty years, I don't feel strongly about how it should resolve itself; my strongest desire is for the story just to keep going, as it has kept going, for as long as I can remember watching television. In feeling this way I am, of course, participating in a phenomenon many commentators on soap opera have observed: the devotée of serial fiction is less interested in a story's resolution or closure than in its indefinite open-endedness: climax and resolution are not the goal (as they are in the distinctly masculine narrative trajectory of a model like the one Peter Brooks employs in *Reading for the Plot* [1984]); instead, the long-term soap viewer experiences narrative climax after narrative climax as the multiple story lines continue, deferring forever the story's ultimate end. The stereotypical association of such a model of narrative reception with so-called female sexuality is perhaps too obvious even to mention; as a feminist narratologist, I would argue that the feminine connotations of such pleasure are not intrinsic to female bodies or even to women's sexual experience *per se,* but that the genre of soap opera itself — a subset of the cultural form of serial fiction — structures this model of pleasure into the feminine subjects who repeatedly rehearse it by watching their soaps day in, day out, sometimes over a lifetime.

The feminist narratology I am modeling here uses close reading, then, not to elucidate a given meaning for a piece of the soap-opera text by examining its formal properties out of context, but rather to understand that the meanings of the popular cultural text are various, contradictory, and immensely complex, depending on the readerly context in which they are received. While a resort to ethnographic research on individual readers' reactions to the scene offers important information, it can only give part of the picture. What matters to me is not the meaning or even the value of any particular scene to any individual reader or class of readers, but the scene's participation in the larger patterns of feeling the soap opera sets up. Whether the individual viewer sympathizes with Holden, Damian, Lily, Molly, or none of these characters, if he or she participates daily in experiencing the text, its complexities will ultimately inspire some feelings in that viewer. I have argued elsewhere that the soap-opera form structures feelings in a continuous "wave" pattern, building to emotional climaxes that never quite resolve themselves, as the undertow of reaction carries the story forward.[4] This wave pattern — resembling, as I have said, stereotypical notions of female sexuality — structures feminine emotional experience for the regular soap-opera viewer, be that viewer a woman or a man. Soap opera is one of those cultural forms that serve as what Teresa de Lauretis has called "technologies of gender," not just representing but producing and reproducing the affective patterns associated with femininity and masculinity in this culture.

I said at the outset of this article that one of the goals of feminist narratology was to "mess up" the neatness of structuralism's binary systems. I know that my argument exemplifies a certain messiness, and that I have not proposed a neat system by which soap-opera texts could be analyzed or categorized. If I have a guilty craving for binary neatness, I am capable also of feeling guilty about making a mess; my guilty craving for the "simple pleasure" of watching "As the World Turns" comes into conflict with my guilty desire to complicate the viewing experience by writing about it. These are the conflicting pleasures of feminism in turn-of-the-century academia: if there is nothing simple about them, they are at least simply calculated to complicate the terms in which we think about narrative in cultural forms.

Notes

1. Generally speaking, feminists were less troubled by the apparent conflicts between the projects of feminist criticism and narratology than were hard-core structural-

ist narratologists. See the notoriously rancorous critique of Lanser published by Nilli Diengott and Lanser's response in *Style*.

2. Quoted by Mezei (1996, 4).

3. See, for instance, Genette's brilliant exegesis of Proust's *Remembrance of Things Past* in *Narrative Discourse: An Essay in Method* (1980) or Prince's witty and rich readings between narratorial lines in "Introduction to the Study of the Narratee" (1980b).

4. In an essay in *Genders* which is also a chapter of my book in progress on gender and popular cultural forms.

Works Cited

Adams, Robert M. "Theories of Actuality." In *The Possible and the Actual: Readings in the Metaphysics of Modality,* edited by Michael J. Loux, 190–209. Ithaca: Cornell University Press, 1979.

Albers, Josef. *Interaction of Color.* New Haven: Yale University Press, 1963.

Alexander, H. G., editor. *The Leibniz-Clarke Correspondence.* Manchester: University of Manchester Press, 1956.

Allen, Robert C. *Speaking of Soap Operas.* Chapel Hill and London: University of North Carolina Press, 1985.

Allén, Sture, editor. *Possible Worlds in Humanities, Arts and Sciences: Proceedings of Nobel Symposium 65.* Berlin: de Gruyter, 1989.

Allende, Isabel. *Eva Luna.* New York: Bantam Books, 1989.

Althusser, Louis. *Lenin and Philosophy and Other Essays,* translated by Ben Brewster. New York: Monthly Review Press, 1971.

Altmann, Gerry T., Alan Garnham, and Yvette Dennis. "Avoiding the Garden Path: Eye Movements in Context." *Journal of Memory and Language* 31 (1992): 685–712.

Anderson, Perry. "On Emplotment: Two Kinds of Ruin." In *Probing the Limits of Representation: Nazism and the Final Solution,* edited by Saul Friedlander, 54–65. Cambridge: Harvard University Press, 1992.

Andringa, Els, and Sara Davis. "Literary Narrative and Mental Representation or How Readers Deal with 'A Rose for Emily.' " In *Naturalist Text Comprehension,* edited by Hesse van Oostendorp and Ralf A. Zwaan, 247–68. Norwood, NJ: Ablex, 1994.

Antrim, Donald. *The Hundred Brothers.* New York: Crown, 1997.

Auden, W. H. "In Time of War: A Sonnet Sequence with a Verse Commentary." In *The Collected Poetry of W. H. Auden,* 317–47. New York: Random House, 1945.

Aristotle. *Poetics.* In *Critical Theory since Plato,* edited by Hazard Adams, 47–66. New York: Harcourt Brace, 1971.

Augustine. *The Confessions of St. Augustine,* translated by John K. Ryan. Garden City, NY: Doubleday, 1960.

Austin, J. L. *How to Do Things with Words.* Cambridge: Harvard University Press, 1962.

———. *How to Do Things with Words.* New York: Oxford University Press, 1965.

———. "Performative-Constative." In *The Philosophy of Language,* edited by John R. Searle, 13–22. Oxford: Oxford University Press, 1971.

Bakhtin, M. M. "Author and Hero in Aesthetic Activity." In *Art and Answerability: Early Philosophical Essays by M. M. Bakhtin,* edited by Michael Holquist and Vadim Liapunov, 4–256. Austin: University of Texas Press, 1990.

———. *The Dialogic Imagination,* edited by Michael Holquist, translated by Caryl Emerson and Michael Holquist. Austin: University of Texas Press, 1981a.

———. "Discourse in the Novel." In *The Dialogic Imagination,* edited by Michael Holquist, translated by Caryl Emerson and Michael Holquist, 259–422. Austin: University of Texas Press, 1981b.

———. "Epic and Novel." In *The Dialogic Imagination,* edited by Michael Holquist, translated by Caryl Emerson and Michael Holquist, 3–40. Austin: University of Texas Press, 1981c.

———. "Forms of Time and of the Chronotope in the Novel: Notes toward a Historical Poetics." In *The Dialogic Imagination,* edited by Michael Holquist, translated by Caryl Emerson and Michael Holquist, 84–258. Austin: University of Texas Press, 1981d.

———. *Problems of Dostoevsky's Poetics,* edited and translated by Caryl Emerson. Minneapolis: University of Minnesota Press, 1984.

Bal, Mieke. *Femmes imaginaires: L'ancien testament au risque d'une narratologie critique.* Paris: Nizet, 1986.

———. *Lethal Love: Feminist Literary Readings of Biblical Love Stories.* Bloomington: Indiana University Press, 1987.

———. "Notes on Narrative Embedding." *Poetics Today* 2 (1981): 41–59.

———. "The Point of Narratology." *Poetics Today* 11 (1990): 727–53.

Balzac, Honoré de. *Sarrasine.* In Roland Barthes, *S/Z: An Essay,* translated by Richard Miller, 221–54. New York: Hill and Wang, 1974.

Banfield, Ann. *Unspeakable Sentences: Narration and Representation in the Language of Fiction.* London: Routledge and Kegan Paul, 1982.

Baron, Salo W. *The Contemporary Relevance of History: A Study in Approaches and Methods.* New York: Columbia University Press, 1986.

Barthes, Roland. "The Death of the Author." In *Image Music Text,* edited and translated by Stephen Heath, 142–48. New York: Hill and Wang, 1977a.

———. "The Discourse of History." In *Comparative Criticism: A Yearbook,* vol. 3, edited by E. S. Shaffer, translated by Stephen Bann, 7–20. Cambridge: Cambridge University Press, 1981.

———. "From Work to Text." In *Textual Strategies: Perspectives in Post-Structuralist Criticism,* edited by Josue V. Harari, 73–81. Ithaca: Cornell University Press, 1979.

———. "Introduction to the Structural Analysis of Narratives." In *Image Music Text,* edited and translated by Stephen Heath, 79–124. New York: Hill and Wang, 1977b.

———. *S/Z: An Essay,* translated by Richard Miller. New York: Hill and Wang, 1974.

Baumgartner, Hans Michael. "Narrative Struktur und Objectivität. Wahrheitskriterien im historischen Wissen." In *Historische Objektivität: Aufsätze zur Geschichtstheorie,* edited by Jörn Rüsen, 48–67. Göttingen: Vandenhoeck and Ruprecht, 1975.

Beach, Joseph Warren. *The Twentieth-Century Novel: Studies in Technique.* New Haven: Yale University Press, 1932.

Beidler, Peter G. "A Critical History of *The Turn of the Screw.*" In Henry James, *The Turn of the Screw,* edited by Peter G. Beidler, 127–51. Boston: St. Martin's Press, 1995.

Bell, Allan. "Language Style as Audience Design." *Language in Society* 13 (1984): 145–204.

Bell, John S. "Six Possible Worlds of Quantum Mechanics." In *Possible Worlds in Humanities, Arts and Sciences: Proceedings of Nobel Symposium 65,* edited by Sture Allén, 359–73. Berlin: de Gruyter, 1989.

Berkhofer, Robert F., Jr. *Beyond the Great Story: History as Text and Discourse.* Cambridge: Belknap Press, 1995.

Bever, Thomas G. "The Cognitive Basis for Linguistic Structures." In *Cognition and the Development of Language,* edited by John R. Hayes, 279–361. London: Wiley, 1970.

Booth, Wayne C. *The Company We Keep.* Berkeley: University of California Press, 1988.

———. *The Rhetoric of Fiction,* 2nd edition. Chicago: University of Chicago Press, 1983 (originally published 1961).

Bordwell, David. *Narration in the Fiction Film.* Madison: University of Wisconsin Press, 1985.

Bordwell, David, and Kristin Thompson. *Film Art: An Introduction,* 4th edition. New York: McGraw-Hill, Inc., 1993.

Borges, Jorge Luis. "Pierre Menard, Author of the *Quixote.*" In *Labyrinths: Selected Stories and Other Writings,* translated by James E. Irby, 36–44. New York: New Directions, 1964.

Bower, Bruce. "All that Jazz." *The New Criterion* 10 (1992): 10–17.

Bradley, Raymond, and Norman Swartz. *Possible Worlds: An Introduction to Logic and Its Philosophy.* Oxford: Blackwell, 1979.

Brainerd, Barron. *Introduction to the Mathematics of Language Study.* New York: Elsevier, 1971.

Brand, Stewart. *How Buildings Learn.* New York: Penguin, 1994.

Branigan, Edward. *Narrative Comprehension and Film.* London: Routledge, 1992.

———. *Point of View in the Cinema: A Theory of Narration and Subjectivity in Classical Film.* Berlin: Mouton, 1984.

Bremond, Claude. *Logique du récit.* Paris: Seuil, 1973.

———. "Le message narratif." *Communications* 4 (1964): 4–32.

Brooke-Rose, Christine. *Amalgamemnon.* Manchester: Carcanet Press, 1984.

———. "The Surface Structures in *The Turn of the Screw.*" In *Rhetoric of the Unreal,* 188–229. Cambridge: Cambridge University Press, 1981.

Brooks, Peter. *Reading for the Plot: Design and Intention in Narrative.* New York: Random House, 1984.

Brown, Gillian, and George Yule. *Discourse Analysis.* Cambridge: Cambridge University Press, 1983.

Brown, Penelope, and Stephen Levinson. *Politeness Universals in Language Use.* Cambridge: Cambridge University Press, 1987.

Bruner, Jerome. *Actual Minds, Possible Worlds.* Cambridge: Harvard University Press, 1986.

Burke, Peter. "History of Events and the Revival of Narrative." In *New Perspectives on Historical Writing,* edited by Peter Burke, 233–48. University Park: Pennsylvania State University Press, 1992.

Burke, Sean. *The Death and Return of the Author.* Edinburgh: Edinburgh University Press, 1992.

Butor, Michel. *La modification.* Paris: Les Editions de minuit, 1957.

Bybee, Joan, Revere Perkins, and William Pagliuca, editors. *The Evolution of Grammar: Tense, Aspect, and Modality in the Languages of the World.* Chicago: University of Chicago Press, 1994.

Bybee, Joan, and Suzanne Fleischman, editors. *Modality in Grammar and Discourse.* Amsterdam and Philadelphia: John Benjamins, 1995.

Calvino, Italo. *If on a winter's night a traveler,* translated by William Weaver. San Diego: Harcourt, Brace and Co., 1981.

Capra, Fritjof. *The Tao of Physics.* Berkeley: Shambala, 1975.

Carr, David. *Time, Narrative and History.* Bloomington: Indiana University Press, 1991.

Carr, Edward Hallett. *What Is History?,* 2nd edition. London: Penguin, 1990.

Carson, Diane, Linda Dittmar, and Janice R. Welsch, editors. *Multiple Voices in Feminist Film Criticism.* Minneapolis: University of Minnesota Press, 1994.

Chadwick-Joshua, Jocelyn. "Metonymy and Synecdoche: The Rhetoric of the City in Toni Morrison's *Jazz.*" In *The City in African American Literature,* edited by Hakutani-Yoshinobu and Robert Butler, 168–80. Madison: Fairleigh Dickinson University Press, 1995.

Chafe, Wallace. *Discourse, Consciousness and Time.* Chicago: University of Chicago Press, 1994.

Chafe, Wallace, and Johanna Nichols, editors. *Evidentiality: The Linguistic Coding of Epistemology.* Norwood, NJ: Ablex, 1986.

Chambers, Jack K. *Sociolinguistic Theory.* Oxford: Basil Blackwell, 1995.

Chambers, Ross. "*Sarrasine* and the Impact of Art." *French Forum* 5 (1980): 218–38.

Chatman, Seymour. *Coming to Terms: The Rhetoric of Narrative in Fiction and Film.* Ithaca: Cornell University Press, 1990.

———. "Narratological Empowerment." *Narrative* 1 (1993): 59–65.

———. *Story and Discourse: Narrative Structure in Fiction and Film.* Ithaca: Cornell University Press, 1978.

———. "The Structure of Narrative Transmission." In *Style and Structure in Narrative: Essays in the New Stylistics,* edited by Roger Fowler, 213–57. Oxford: Blackwell, 1975.

Chisholm, Roderick M. *The First Person: An Essay on Reference and Intentionality.* Brighton: Harvester Press, 1981.

Chomsky, Noam. *Aspects of the Theory of Syntax.* Cambridge: MIT Press, 1965.

———. *Knowledge of Language, Its Nature, Origin, and Use.* New York: Praeger, 1986.

Chung, Sandra, and Alan Timberlake. "Tense, Aspect, and Mood." In *Language Typology and Syntactic Description, 2: Grammatical Categories and the Lexicon,* edited by Timothy Shopen, 202–258. Cambridge: Cambridge University Press, 1985.

Clark, Katerina, and Michael Holquist. *Mikhail Bakhtin.* Cambridge: Harvard University Press, 1984.

Clifton, Charles, Jr., and Fernanda Ferreira. "Ambiguity in Context." *Language and Cognitive Processes* 4 (1989): 77–103.

Coates, Paul. "The Sense of an Ending: Reflections on Kieslowski's Trilogy." *Film Quarterly* 50 (Winter 1996–1997): 19–26.

Coetzee, J. M. *From the Heart of the Country.* New York: Harper and Row, 1976.

Cohn, Dorrit. "The Encirclement of Narrative: On Franz Stanzel's *Theorie des Erzählens.*" *Poetics Today* 2 (1981): 157–82.

———. "Fictional versus Historical Lives: Borderlines and Borderline Cases." *Journal of Narrative Technique* 19 (1989): 3–24.

———. "Signposts of Fictionality: A Narratological Perspective." *Poetics Today* 11 (1990): 775–804.

Collier, Gordon. *The Rocks and Sticks of Words: Style, Discourse and Narrative Structure in the Fiction of Patrick White.* Amsterdam: Rodopi, 1992.

Collingwood, Robin George. *The Idea of History,* edited by Jan van der Dussen. Oxford: Clarendon Press, 1993.

Colomb, Gregory G., and Mark Turner. "Computers, Literary Theory, and Theory of Meaning." In *The Future of Literary Theory,* edited by Ralph Cohen, 386–410. London: Routledge, 1989.

Cook, Guy. *Discourse and Literature: The Interplay of Form and Mind.* Oxford: Oxford University Press, 1994.

Coover, Robert. "The Magic Poker." In *Pricksongs and Descants,* 20–45. New York: New American Library, 1969.

Cortazzi, Martin. *Narrative Analysis.* London: Falmer Press, 1993.

Coste, Didier. *Narrative as Communication.* Minneapolis: University of Minnesota Press, 1989.

Cresswell, M. J. *Semantical Essays: Possible Worlds and Their Rivals.* Dordrecht: Kluwer, 1988.

Crittenden, Charles. *Unreality: The Metaphysics of Fictional Objects.* Ithaca: Cornell University Press, 1991.

Crystal, David. *The Cambridge Encyclopedia of the English Language.* Cambridge: Cambridge University Press, 1995.

Culioli, Antoine. "Valeurs modales et opérations énonciatives." *Le français moderne* 46 (1978): 300–317.

Culler, Jonathan. "Reading as a Woman." In *On Deconstruction: Theory and Criticism after Structuralism,* 43–64. Ithaca: Cornell University Press, 1982.

———. "Story and Discourse in the Analysis of Narrative." In *The Pursuit of Signs: Semiotics, Literature, Deconstruction,* 169–87. Ithaca: Cornell University Press, 1981.

———. *Structuralist Poetics: Structuralism, Linguistics and the Study of Literature.* London: Routledge, 1975.

Dahl, Osten. *Tense and Aspect Systems.* Oxford: Basil Blackwell, 1985.

Dällenbach, Lucien. "Reading as Suture (Problems of Reception of the Fragmentary Text: Balzac and Claude Simon)." *Style* 18 (1984): 196–206.

Danto, Arthur C. *Narration and Knowledge.* New York: Columbia University Press, 1985.

Darwin, Charles. *The Origin of Species: A Facsimile of the First Edition.* Cambridge: Harvard University Press, 1964.

———. *The Voyage of the Beagle,* edited by Janet Browne and Michael Neve. London: Penguin, 1989.

Davis, Natalie Zemon. *Fiction in the Archives: Pardon Tales and Their Tellers in Sixteenth-Century France.* Stanford: Stanford University Press, 1987.

———. *The Return of Martin Guerre.* Cambridge: Harvard University Press, 1983.

De Beaugrande, Robert. *Text, Discourse, and Process.* Norwood, NJ: Ablex, 1981.

De Bono, Edward. *Lateral Thinking for Management: A Handbook.* Harmondsworth: Penguin, 1983.

De Lauretis, Teresa. *Technologies of Gender.* Bloomington: Indiana University Press, 1987.

Demandt, Alexander. *History That Never Happened,* translated by Colin D. Thomson. Jefferson, NC: McFarland, 1993.

Derrida, Jacques. *Speech and Phenomena and Other Essays on Husserl's Theory of Signs,* translated by David B. Allison. Evanston: Northwestern University Press, 1973.

———. "Structure, Sign, and Play in the Discourse of the Human Sciences." In *The Structuralist Controversy: The Languages of Criticism and the Sciences of Man,* edited by Richard Macksey and Eugenio Donato, 247–72. Baltimore: Johns Hopkins University Press, 1972.

Diengott, Nilli. "Narratology and Feminism." *Style* 22 (1988): 42–51.

Dijk, Teun A. van. *News as Discourse.* Hillsdale, NJ: Lawrence Erlbaum, 1988.

Dinesen, Isak (Karen Blixen). "The Supper at Elsinore." In *Seven Gothic Tales,* 217–70. New York: Vintage Books, 1972.

Dixon, Peter, and Marisa Bortolussi. "Prolegomena for a Science of Psychonarratology." Manuscript under review.

Doležel, Lubomír. "Fictional Worlds: Density, Gaps, and Inference." *Style* 29 (1995): 201–14.

———. *Heterocosmica: Fiction and Possible Worlds.* Baltimore: Johns Hopkins University Press, 1998.

———. *Occidental Poetics: Tradition and Progress.* Lincoln: University of Nebraska Press, 1990.

———. "Possible Worlds and Literary Fictions." In *Possible Worlds in Humanities, Arts and Sciences: Proceedings of Nobel Symposium 65,* edited by Sture Allén, 221–42. Berlin: de Gruyter, 1989.

———. "A Short Note on a Long Subject: Literary Style." In *Voz'mi na radost': To Hon-*

our Jeanne van der Eng-Liedmeier, edited by B. J. Amsenga, J. Pama, and W. G. Weststeijn, 1–7. Amsterdam: Slavic Seminar, 1980.

Dosse, François. *History of Structuralism, Vol. 1: The Rising Sign, 1945–1966,* translated by Deborah Glassman. Minneapolis: University of Minnesota Press, 1996.

Dostoevsky, Fyodor. *The Idiot,* translated by Constance Garnett. New York: Modern Library, 1962.

———. *The Notebooks for "The Idiot,"* edited by Edward Wasiolek, translated by Katharine Strelsky. Chicago: University of Chicago Press, 1967.

———. *Notes from Underground and the Grand Inquisitor,* translated by Ralph E. Matlaw. New York: Dutton, 1960.

———. *A Writer's Diary,* vol. 1, translated by Kenneth Lantz. Evanston: Northwestern University Press, 1994.

Duchan, Judith F., Gail A. Bruder, and Lynne E. Hewitt, editors. *Deixis in Narrative: A Cognitive Science Perspective.* Hillsdale, N.J.: Lawrence Erlbaum, 1995.

DuPlessis, Rachel Blau. *Writing beyond the Ending: Narrative Strategies of Twentieth-Century Women Writers.* Bloomington: Indiana University Press, 1985.

Duras, Marguerite. *La maladie de la mort.* Paris: Les Editions de Minuit, 1982.

Eco, Umberto. "Possible Worlds and Text Pragmatics: 'Un Drame bien parisien.'" In *The Role of the Reader: Explorations in the Semiotics of Texts,* 200–260. Bloomington: Indiana University Press, 1979.

———. "Report on Session 3: Literature and Arts." In *Possible Worlds in Humanities, Arts and Sciences: Proceedings of Nobel Symposium 65,* edited by Sture Allén, 343–55. Berlin: de Gruyter, 1989a.

———. *Six Walks in the Fictional Woods.* Cambridge: Harvard University Press, 1994.

———. "Small Worlds." *VS. Versus* 52/53 (1989b): 53–70.

Edmiston, William F. *Hindsight and Insight: Focalization in Four Eighteenth-Century French Novels.* University Park: Pennsylvania State University Press, 1991.

Eisenstein, Sergei. *Film Form: Essays in Film Theory.* Cleveland: Meridian, 1957.

Ellis, James. "The Allusions in 'The Secret Life of Walter Mitty.'" *English Journal* 54 (1965): 310–13.

Emmott, Catherine. "Frames of Reference: Contextual Monitoring and the Interpretation of Narrative Discourse." In *Advances in Written Text Analysis,* edited by Malcolm Coulthard, 157–66. London: Routledge, 1994.

———. *Narrative Comprehension: A Discourse Perspective.* Oxford: Oxford University Press, 1997.

Fauconnier, Gilles. *Mappings in Thought and Language.* Cambridge: Cambridge University Press, 1997.

Feher, Michel, with Ramona Naddoff and Nadia Tazia, editors. *Zone: Fragments for a History of the Human Body, 1, 2, and 3.* New York: Urzone, 1989.

Fehn, Ann, Ingeborg Hoesterey, and Maria Tatar, editors. *Neverending Stories: Toward a Critical Narratology.* Princeton: Princeton University Press, 1992.

Fergusson, Niall, editor. *Virtual History: Alternatives and Counterfactuals.* London: Picador, 1997.

Feuer, Jane. *Seeing through the Eighties: Television and Reaganism.* Durham and London: Duke University Press, 1995.

Feynman, Richard P. *The Character of Physical Law.* London: Penguin, 1992.

Firbas, Jan. "On Defining the Theme in Functional Sentence Analysis." *Travaux linguistiques de Prague* 1 (1964): 267–80.

Fish, Stanley. *Doing What Comes Naturally: Change, Rhetoric, and the Practice of Theory in Literary and Legal Studies.* Oxford: Oxford University Press, 1989.

———. *Is There a Text in This Class? The Authority of Interpretive Communities.* Cambridge: Harvard University Press, 1980.

———. "Transmuting the Lump: Paradise Lost, 1942–82." In *Literature and History: Theoretical Problems and Russian Case Studies,* edited by Gary Saul Morson, 33–56. Stanford: Stanford University Press, 1986.

Flaubert, Gustave. *Madame Bovary,* translated by Geoffrey Wall. London: Penguin Books, 1992.

Fleischman, Suzanne. *The Future in Thought and Language.* Cambridge: Cambridge University Press, 1982.

———. *Tense and Narrativity.* Austin: University of Texas Press, 1990.

Fludernik, Monika. *The Fictions of Language and the Languages of Fiction.* London and New York: Routledge, 1993.

———. "Linguistics and Literature: Prospects and Horizons in the Study of Prose." *Journal of Pragmatics* 26 (1996a): 583–611.

———. "Narratology in Context." *Poetics Today* 14 (1993): 729–61.

———. *Towards a 'Natural' Narratology.* London and New York: Routledge, 1996b.

Fludernik, Monika, editor. *Second-Person Narrative. Style* 28 (1994) [special issue].

Fodor, Janet Dean, and Atsu Inoue. "The Diagnosis and Cure of Garden Paths." *Journal of Psycholinguistic Research* 23 (1994): 407–34.

Foerster, Heinz von. "Das Konstruieren einer Wirklichkeit." In *Die erfundene Wirklichkeit,* edited by Paul Watzlawick, 39–60. München: Piper, 1990.

Foucault, Michel. *Language, Counter-Memory, Practice: Selected Essays and Interviews,* edited by Donald F. Bouchard. Ithaca: Cornell University Press, 1972.

———. "What Is an Author?" In *The Foucault Reader,* edited by Paul Rabinow, 101–21. New York: Pantheon, 1984.

Fowles, John. *The French Lieutenant's Woman.* Chicago: Signet Books, 1969.

Frank, Joseph. *Dostoevsky: The Miraculous Years, 1865–1871.* Princeton: Princeton: University Press, 1995.

Frawley, William. *Linguistic Semantics.* Hillsdale, NJ: Lawrence Erlbaum, 1992.

Frazier, Lyn. *On Comprehending Sentences: Syntactic Parsing Strategies.* Bloomington: Indiana University Linguistics Club, 1979.

Frege, Gottlob. "On Sense and Reference." In *Translations from the Philosophical Writings of Gottlob Frege,* edited by Peter Geach and Max Black, 56–78. Oxford: Basil Blackwell, 1980.

Freundlieb, Dieter. "Semiotic Idealism." *Poetics Today* 9 (1988): 807–41.

Friedlander, Saul. Introduction to *Probing the Limits of Representation: Nazism and "the*

Final Solution," edited by Saul Friedlander, 1–21. Cambridge: Harvard University Press, 1992a.

Friedlander, Saul, editor. *Probing the Limits of Representation: Nazism and "the Final Solution."* Cambridge: Harvard University Press, 1992b.

Frye, Northrop. "Towards Defining an Age of Sensibility." In *Eighteenth-Century English Literature: Modern Essays in Criticism,* edited by James L. Clifford, 311–18. New York: Oxford University Press, 1959.

Füger, Wilhelm. "Zur Tiefenstruktur des Narrativen." *Poetica* 5 (1972): 268–92.

Gaines, Jane. "White Privilege and Looking Relations: Race and Gender in Feminist Film Theory." In *Multiple Voices in Feminist Film Criticism,* edited by Diane Carson, Linda Dittmar, and Janice R. Welsch, 176–90. Minneapolis: University of Minnesota Press, 1994.

Galbraith, Mary. "Deictic Shift Theory and the Poetics of Involvement in Narrative." In *Deixis in Narrative: A Cognitive Science Perspective,* edited by Judith F. Duchan, Gail A. Bruder, and Lynne E. Hewitt, 19–60. Hillsdale, NJ: Lawrence Erlbaum, 1995.

Gallie, Walter Bryce. *Philosophy and Historical Understanding.* London: Chatto and Windus, 1964.

Garcia Marquez, Gabriel. *One Hundred Years of Solitude,* translated by Gregory Rabassa. New York: Avon Books, 1971.

Gardiner, Michael. *The Dialogics of Critique: M. M. Bakhtin and the Theory of Ideology.* London and New York: Routledge, 1992.

Garfield, Jay L., editor. *Modularity in Knowledge Representation and Natural-Language Understanding.* Cambridge: MIT Press, 1987.

Gaudreault, André. *Du littéraire au filmique: Système du récit.* Paris: Klincksieck, 1988.

Gearhardt, Suzanne. *The Open Boundary of History and Fiction: A Critical Approach to the French Enlightenment.* Princeton: Princeton University Press, 1984.

Genette, Gérard. *Fiction et diction.* Paris: Seuil, 1991.

———. *Narrative Discourse: An Essay in Method,* translated by Jane E. Lewin. Ithaca: Cornell University Press, 1980.

———. *Narrative Discourse Revisited,* translated by Jane E. Lewin. Ithaca: Cornell University Press, 1988.

———. *Paratexts: Thresholds of Interpretation,* translated by Jane E. Lewin. Cambridge: Cambridge University Press, 1997.

Gerrig, Richard J. *Experiencing Narrative Worlds: On the Psychological Activities of Reading.* New Haven and London: Yale University Press, 1993.

Gibson, Andrew. *Towards a Postmodern Theory of Narrative.* Edinburgh: Edinburgh University Press, 1996.

Ginzburg, Carlo. *The Cheese and the Worms: The Cosmos of a Sixteenth-Century Miller.* Baltimore: Johns Hopkins University Press, 1980.

———. *Myths, Emblems, Clues,* translated by John and Anne C. Tedeschi. London: Hutchinson Radius, 1990.

Givón, Talmy. *Syntax,* vol. 1. Amsterdam and Philadelphia: John Benjamins, 1984.

Gledhill, Christine. "Image and Voice: Approaches to Marxist-Feminist Criticism." In

Multiple Voices in Feminist Film Criticism, edited by Diane Carson, Linda Dittmar, and Janice R. Welsch, 109–23. Minneapolis: University of Minnesota Press, 1994.

Gleick, James. *Genius: The Life and Science of Richard Feynman.* New York: Pantheon, 1992.

Goffman, Erving. *Forms of Talk.* Philadelphia: University of Pennsylvania Press, 1981.

———. *Frame Analysis: An Essay on the Organization of Experience.* New York: Harper and Row, 1974.

———. *The Presentation of Self in Everyday Life.* Garden City, NY: Anchor, 1959.

Goodman, Nelson. *Ways of Worldmaking.* Indianapolis: Hackett, 1978.

Goodwin, Charles. *Conversational Organization: Interaction between Speakers and Hearers.* New York: Academic Press, 1981.

Greimas, Algirdas-Julien. "Actants, Actors, and Figures." In *On Meaning: Selected Writings in Semiotic Theory,* translated by Paul J. Perron and Frank H. Collins, 106–20. Minneapolis: University of Minnesota Press, 1987.

———. "Narrative Grammar: Units and Levels," translated by Phillip Bodrock. *Modern Language Notes* 86 (1971): 793–806.

———. "Searching for Models of Transformation." In *Structural Semantics: An Attempt at a Method,* translated by Daniele McDowell, Ronald Schleifer, and Alan Velie, 222–56. Lincoln: University of Nebraska Press, 1983.

Grice, H. P. "Logic and Conversation." In *Syntax and Semantics, Vol. 3: Speech Acts,* edited by Peter Cole and Jerry Morgan, 41–58. New York: Academic Press, 1975.

Grisham, John. *The Rainmaker.* New York: Dell, 1995.

Grossberg, Lawrence, Cary Nelson, and Paula A. Treichler, editors. *Cultural Studies.* New York: Routledge, 1992.

Grosz, Barbara, and Candace Sidner. "Attention, Intentions, and the Structure of Discourse." *Computational Linguistics* 12 (1986): 175–204.

Gumperz, John J. *Discourse Strategies.* Cambridge: Cambridge University Press, 1982.

Halévy, Elie. *The Growth of Philosophic Radicalism,* translated by Mary Morris. Boston: Beacon Press, 1955.

Hancher, Michael. "How to Play Games with Words: Speech-Act Jokes." *Journal of Literary Semantics* 9 (1980): 20–29.

Haraway, Donna. *Simians, Cyborgs, and Women: The Reinvention of Nature.* New York: Routledge, 1991.

Harpham, Geoffrey. *Getting It Right: Language, Literature, and Ethics.* Chicago: University of Chicago Press, 1992.

Harris, Robert. *Fatherland.* New York: Random House, 1992.

Hasley, Louis. "James Thurber: Artist in Humor." *South Atlantic Quarterly* 73 (1974): 504–15.

Hawthorn, Geoffrey. *Plausible Worlds: Possibility and Understanding in History and the Social Sciences.* Cambridge: Cambridge University Press, 1991.

Hayles, N. Katherine. "The Materiality of Informatics." *Configurations* 1 (1993): 147–70.

Hayles, N. Katherine, editor. "Technocriticism and Hypernarrative." *Modern Fiction Studies* 43 (1997) [special issue].

Heintz, John. "Reference and Inference in Fiction." *Poetics* 8 (1979): 85–99.

Hendricks, William O. "On the Notion 'beyond the Sentence.' " *Linguistics* 37 (1967): 12–51.

Herman, David. "Existentialist Roots of Narrative Actants." *Studies in Twentieth-Century Literature* (forthcoming).

———. "Hypothetical Focalization." *Narrative* 2 (1994a): 230–53.

———. "Limits of Order: Toward a Theory of Polychronic Narration." *Narrative* 6.1 (1998): 72–95.

———. "Pragmatic Constraints on Narrative Processing: Characters, Actants, and Anaphora." Unpublished manuscript.

———. "Scripts, Sequences, and Stories: Elements of a Postclassical Narratology." *PMLA* 112 (1997a): 1046–59.

———. "Textual *You* and Double Deixis in Edna O'Brien's *A Pagan Place*." *Style* 28 (1994b): 378–410.

———. "Toward a Formal Description of Narrative Metalepsis." *Journal of Literary Semantics* 26 (1997b): 132–52.

———. *Universal Grammar and Narrative Form.* Durham: Duke University Press, 1995.

Hintikka, Jaakko. "Exploring Possible Worlds." In *Possible Worlds in Humanities, Arts and Sciences: Proceedings of Nobel Symposium 65,* edited by Sture Allén, 52–73. Berlin: de Gruyter, 1989.

———. *The Intentions of Intentionality and Other New Models for Modalities.* Dordrecht: Reidel, 1975.

Hockett, Charles F. "Jokes." In *The View from Language: Selected Essays,* 257–89. Athens: University of Georgia Press, 1977a.

———. "Where the Tongue Slips There Slip I." In *The View from Language: Selected Essays,* 226–56. Athens: University of Georgia Press, 1977b.

Hollowell, John. *Fact and Fiction: The New Journalism and the Nonfiction Novel.* Chapel Hill: University of North Carolina Press, 1977.

Holquist, Michael. *Dialogism: Bakhtin and His World.* London and New York: Routledge, 1990.

Hopper, Paul, editor. *Tense-Aspect.* Amsterdam and Philadelphia: John Benjamins, 1982.

Horwich, Paul. *Asymmetries in Time: Problems in the Philosophy of Science.* Cambridge: MIT Press, 1987.

Howe, Irving. *Leon Trotsky.* New York: Viking Press, 1978.

Hunter, I. Q., and Heidi Kaye. "Introduction—Trash Aesthetics: Popular Culture and Its Audience." In *Trash Aesthetics: Popular Culture and Its Audiences,* edited by Deborah Cartmell, I. Q. Hunter, Heidi Kay, and Imelda Whelehan, 1–13. London and Chicago: Pluto Press, 1997.

Hutcheon, Linda. *A Poetics of Postmodernism: History, Theory, Fiction.* London: Routledge, 1988.

Irele, Abiola. "Narrative, History, and the African Imagination." *Narrative* 1 (1993): 156–72.

Iser, Wolfgang. *The Fictive and the Imaginary: Charting Literary Anthropology.* Baltimore: Johns Hopkins University Press, 1993.

Ishiguro, Kazuo. *The Remains of the Day.* New York: Knopf, 1990.

Jackendoff, Ray. *The Architecture of the Human Language Faculty.* Cambridge: MIT Press, 1997.

———. *Consciousness and the Computational Mind.* Cambridge: MIT Press, 1987.

———. *Semantics and Cognition.* Cambridge: MIT Press, 1983.

———. "Semantics and Cognition." In *The Handbook of Contemporary Semantic Theory,* edited by Shalom Lappin, 539–59. Oxford: Blackwell Publishers, 1996.

Jacobs, Jane. *The Death and Life of Great American Cities.* New York: Random House, 1961; reprinted 1992.

Jahn, Manfred. "Frames, Preferences, and the Reading of Third-Person Narratives: Towards a Cognitive Narratology." *Poetics Today* 18 (1997): 441–68.

———. "The Mechanics of Focalization: Extending the Narratological Toolbox." Under review.

———. "Windows of Focalization: Deconstructing and Reconstructing a Narratological Concept." *Style* 30 (1996): 241–67.

Jahn, Manfred, and Ansgar Nünning. "A Survey of Narratological Models." *Literatur in Wissenschaft und Unterricht* 27 (1994): 283–303.

Jakobson, Roman. "Closing Statement: Linguistics and Poetics." In *Style in Language,* edited by Thomas A. Sebeok, 350–77. Cambridge: MIT Press, 1960.

———. "The Metaphoric and Metonymic Poles." In *Critical Theory since Plato,* edited by Hazard Adams, 1113–16. San Diego: Harcourt Brace Jovanovich, 1971.

James, Henry. *The Portrait of a Lady.* London: Penguin, 1970.

———. *The Turn of the Screw,* edited by Peter G. Beidler. Boston: St. Martin's Press, 1995.

Jameson, Fredric. *The Political Unconscious.* Ithaca: Cornell University Press, 1981.

Johnson, Richard. "What Is Cultural Studies Anyway?" *Social Text* 16 (1986–87): 36–80.

Johnson-Laird, Philip N. *Mental Models: Towards a Cognitive Science of Language, Inference, and Consciousness.* Cambridge: Cambridge University Press, 1983.

———. "Mental Models of Meaning." In *Elements of Discourse Understanding,* edited by Aravind K. Joshi, Bonnie L. Webber, and Ivan A. Sag, 106–26. Cambridge: Cambridge University Press, 1981.

Jolles, André. *Einfache Formen: Legende, Sage, Mythe, Rätsel, Spruch, Kasus, Memorabile, Märchen, Witz.* Tübingen: Niemeyer, 1965.

Joly, André. *Essais de systématique énonciative.* Lille: Lille University Press, 1987.

Jost, François. "L'oreille interne. Propositions pour une analyse du point de vue sonore." *Iris* 3 (1985): 8–15.

———. "Règles de je." *Iris* 8 (1988): 107–19.

———. "Le vu et le dit." *Fabula* 9 (1987): 31–43.

Joyce, James. "Eveline." In *Dubliners,* 36–41. London: Penguin, 1967.

Joyce, Michael. *Afternoon: A Story.* Cambridge, MA: Eastgate Press, 1987 [Hypertext Software].

Joyrich, Lynne. *Re-viewing Reception: Television, Gender, and Postmodern Culture.* Bloomington: Indiana University Press, 1996.

Kafalenos, Emma. "Functions after Propp: Words to Talk about How We Read Narrative." *Poetics Today* 18 (1997): 469–94.

———. "Implications of Narrative in Painting and Photography." *New Novel Review* 3 (1996): 53–64.

———. "Lingering along the Narrative Path: Extended Functions in Kafka and Henry James." *Narrative* 3 (1995): 117–38.

Kawin, Bruce. *Mindscreen: Bergman, Godard, and First-Person Film.* Princeton: Princeton University Press, 1978.

Kirkham, Richard L. *Theories of Truth: A Critical Introduction.* Cambridge: MIT Press, 1992.

Koch, Walter A., editor. *Simple Forms: An Encyclopedia of Simple Text Types in Lore and Literature.* Bochum, Germany: Brockmeyer, 1994.

Kozloff, Sarah. *Invisible Storytellers: Voice-Over Narration in American Fiction Film.* Berkeley: University of California, 1988.

Kripke, Saul A. *Naming and Necessity.* Cambridge: Harvard University Press, 1980.

———. "Semantic Considerations on Modal Logic." *Acta Philosophical Fennica* 16 (1963): 83–94.

Kristeva, Julia. "From One Identity to an Other." In *Desire in Language: A Semiotic Approach to Literature and Art,* edited by Leon S. Roudiez, 124–47. New York: Columbia University Press, 1980.

———. *Powers of Horror: An Essay on Abjection,* translated by Leon S. Roudiez. New York: Columbia University Press, 1982.

Labov, William. "The Transformation of Experience in Narrative Syntax." In *Language in the Inner City: Studies in Black English Vernacular,* 354–96. Philadelphia: University of Pennsylvania Press, 1972.

Labov, William, and Joshua Waletzky. "Narrative Analysis: Oral Versions of Personal Experience." In *Essays on the Verbal and Visual Arts,* edited by June Helm, 12–44. Seattle: University of Washington Press, 1967.

Lane, Michael, editor. *Structuralism: A Reader.* London: Cape, 1970.

Lang, Berel. *Act and Idea in the Nazi Genocide.* Chicago: University of Chicago Press, 1990.

Langacker, Ronald. *Foundations of Cognitive Grammar,* vols. 1 and 2. Stanford: Stanford University Press, 1987 and 1991.

Lanser, Susan S. *Fictions of Authority: Women Writers and Narrative Voice.* London: Cornell University Press, 1992.

———. *The Narrative Act: Point of View in Prose Fiction.* Princeton: Princeton University Press, 1981.

———. "Queering Narratology." In *Ambiguous Discourse: Feminist Narratology and British Women Writers,* edited by Kathy Mezei, 250–61. Chapel Hill: University of North Carolina Press, 1996.

———. "Sexing the Narrative: Propriety, Desire, and the Engendering of Narratology." *Narrative* 3 (1995): 85–94.

———. "Shifting the Paradigm: Feminism and Narratology." *Style* 22 (1988): 52–60.

———. "Toward a Feminist Narratology." In *Feminisms: An Anthology,* edited by Robyn R. Warhol and Diane Price Herndl, 610–629. New Brunswick: Rutgers University Press, 1991.

Larivaille, Paul. "L'analyse (morpho)logique du récit." *Poétique* 19 (1974): 368–88.

Le Corbusier, Eduard. *The City of To-morrow and Its Planning,* translated by Frederick Etchells. Cambridge: MIT Press, 1971.

Leder, Drew. *The Absent Body.* Chicago: University of Chicago Press, 1990.

Leech, Geoffrey N. *Meaning and the English Verb,* 2nd edition. London: Longman, 1987.

———. *Principles of Pragmatics.* London: Longman, 1983.

Legman, Gershon. *Rationale of the Dirty Joke: An Analysis of Sexual Humor.* Frogmore: Granada, 1973.

Le Guin, Ursula K. "Mazes." In *The Compass Rose,* 181–86. London: Grafton, 1986.

Lehnert, Wendy G. "The Role of Scripts in Understanding." In *Frame Conceptions and Text Understanding,* edited by Dieter Metzing, 79–95. Berlin: de Gruyter, 1979.

Lethcoe, Ronald James. "Narrated Speech and Consciousness." Ph.D. dissertation, University of Wisconsin, 1969.

Lévi-Strauss, Claude. *Anthropologie structurale.* Paris: Plon, 1958.

———. *Structural Anthropology,* translated by Claire Jacobson and Brooke Grundfest Schoepf. New York: Basic, 1963.

———. "The Structural Study of Myth." In *Critical Theory since 1965,* edited by Hazard Adams and Leroy Searle, 809–22. Tallahassee: University Presses of Florida, 1986.

Lewis, David. *Counterfactuals.* Cambridge: Harvard University Press, 1973.

———. *On the Plurality of Worlds.* Oxford: Basil Blackwell, 1986.

———. *Philosophical Papers,* vol. 1. New York: Oxford University Press, 1983.

———. "Truth in Fiction." *American Philosophical Quarterly* 15 (1978): 37–46.

Linde, Charlotte. *Life Stories: The Creation of Coherence.* Oxford: Oxford University Press, 1993.

Locke, John. *An Essay Concerning Human Understanding,* vol. 1, edited by Alexander Campbell Fraser. New York: Dover, 1959.

Lodge, David. "Analysis and Interpretation of the Realist Text." In *Modern Literary Theory: A Reader,* 3rd edition, edited by Philip Rice and Patricia Waugh, 24–41. London: Arnold, 1996.

Loux, Michael J., editor. *The Possible and the Actual: Readings in the Metaphysics of Modality.* Ithaca: Cornell University Press, 1979.

Lowes, John Livingston. *The Road to Xanadu: A Study in the Ways of the Imagination.* London: Pan, 1978.

Lubbock, Percy. *The Craft of Fiction.* London: Cape, 1963.

Lycan, William G. "The Trouble with Possible Worlds." In *The Possible and the Actual: Readings in the Metaphysics of Modality,* edited by Michael J. Loux, 274–316. Ithaca: Cornell University Press, 1979.

Lyons, John. *Linguistic Semantics.* Cambridge: Cambridge University Press, 1995.

Lyotard, Jean-François. *The Postmodern Condition: A Report on Knowledge,* translated by Geoff Bennington and Brian Massumi. Minneapolis: University of Minnesota Press, 1984.

Malinowski, Bronislaw. *A Scientific Theory of Culture and Other Essays.* Chapel Hill: University of North Carolina Press, 1944.

Marcus, Mitchell P. "Some Inadequate Theories of Human Language Processing." In *Talking Minds: The Study of Languages in Cognitive Sciences,* edited by Thomas G. Bever, John M. Carroll, and Lance A. Miller, 253–78. Cambridge: MIT Press, 1984.

———. *A Theory of Syntactic Recognition for Natural Language.* Cambridge: MIT Press, 1980.

Margolin, Uri. "Changing Individuals in Narrative: Science, Philosophy, Literature." *Semiotica* 107 (1995): 5–31.

———. "The Doer and the Deed: Action Basis for Characterization in Narrative." *Poetics Today* 7 (1986): 205–26.

———. "Narrative 'You' Revisited." *Language and Style* 23 (1993): 1–21.

Martens, Lorna. *The Diary Novel.* Cambridge: Cambridge University Press, 1985.

Martin, Wallace. *Recent Theories of Narrative.* Ithaca: Cornell University Press, 1986.

Martínez-Bonati, Félix. *Fictive Discourse and the Structures of Literature: A Phenomenological Approach.* Ithaca: Cornell University Press, 1981.

Mayr, Ernst. *The Growth of Biological Thought: Diversity, Evolution, and Inheritance.* Cambridge: Harvard University Press, 1982.

Mbalia, Dorothea Drummond. "Women Who Run with Wild: The Need for Sisterhoods in *Jazz.*" *Modern Fiction Studies* 39 (1993): 623–46.

McHale, Brian. *Postmodernist Fiction.* New York: Methuen, 1987.

McHale, Brian, and Ruth Ronen. *Narratology Revisited I and II. Poetics Today* 11.2 and 11.4 (1990) [special issues].

McKoon, Gail, Gregory Ward, Roger Ratcliff, and Richard Sproat. "Morphosyntactic and Pragmatic Factors Affecting the Accessibility of Discourse Entities." *Journal of Memory and Language* 32 (1993): 56–75.

Mey, Jacob L. "Pragmatic Gardens and Their Magic." *Poetics* 20 (1991): 233–45.

———. *Pragmatics: An Introduction.* Oxford: Blackwell, 1993.

Meyer, E. Y. *In Trubschachen.* Frankfurt: Suhrkamp Verlag, 1973.

Mezei, Kathy, editor. *Ambiguous Discourse: Feminist Narratology and British Women Writers.* Chapel Hill: University of North Carolina Press, 1996.

Miller, J. Hillis. *The Ethics of Reading: Kant, de Man, Trollope, Eliot, James, Benjamin.* New York: Columbia University Press, 1987.

Miller, Nancy K. *The Heroine's Text: Readings in the French and English Novel, 1722–1782.* New York: Columbia University Press, 1980.

Miller, Richard R. "There Is Nothing Magical about Possible Worlds." *Mind* 99 (1990): 453–57.

Miller, Robin Feuer. *Dostoevsky and "The Idiot": Author, Narrator, and Reader.* Cambridge: Harvard University Press, 1981.

Milroy, Leslie. *Observing and Analyzing Natural Language.* Oxford: Basil Blackwell, 1987.

Mink, Louis O. "History and Fiction as Modes of Comprehension." *New Literary History* 1 (1970): 541–58.

Minsky, Marvin. "A Framework for Representing Knowledge." In *Frame Conceptions and Text Understanding,* edited by Dieter Metzing, 1–25. Berlin: de Gruyter, 1979.

Mishler, Elliot. *The Discourse of Medicine: Dialectics of Medical Interviews.* Norwood, NJ: Ablex, 1984.

Monk, Leland. *Standard Deviations: Chance in the Modern British Novel.* Stanford: Stanford University Press, 1993.

Moore, Lorrie. *Self-Help.* New York: Alfred A. Knopf, 1985.

Morris, Pam. *Literature and Feminism.* Oxford: Blackwell, 1993.

Morrison, Toni. *Jazz.* New York: Plume, 1993.

Morson, Gary Saul. *The Boundaries of Genre: Dostoevsky's "Diary of a Writer" and the Traditions of Literary Utopia.* Austin: University of Texas Press, 1981.

———. *Hidden in Plain View: Narrative and Creative Potentials in "War and Peace."* Stanford: Stanford University Press, 1987.

———. *Narrative and Freedom: The Shadows of Time.* New Haven: Yale University Press, 1994.

———. "Tempics and *The Idiot.*" In *Celebrating Creativity: Essays in Honor of Jøstein Bortnes,* edited by Knut Andreas Grimstad and Ingunn Lunde, 108–34. Bergen: University of Bergen, 1997.

Morson, Gary Saul, and Caryl Emerson. *Mikhail Bakhtin: Creation of a Prosaics.* Stanford: Stanford University Press, 1990.

Mukherjee, Bharati. *The Holder of the World.* New York: Knopf, 1993.

Mumford, Laura Stempel. *Love and Ideology in the Afternoon: Soap Opera, Women, and Television Genre.* Bloomington: Indiana University Press, 1995.

Murray, Janet H. *Hamlet on the Holodeck: The Future of Narrative in Cyberspace.* New York: Free Press, 1997.

Natanson, Maurice. *Literature, Philosophy, and the Social Sciences: Essays in Existentialism and Phenomenology.* The Hague: Martinus Nijhoff, 1962.

Navon, David. "The Seemingly Appropriate but Virtually Inappropriate: Notes on Characteristics of Jokes." *Poetics* 17 (1988): 207–19.

Nell, Victor. *Lost in a Book: The Psychology of Reading for Pleasure.* New Haven: Yale University Press, 1988.

Newton, Adam Zachary. *Narrative Ethics.* Cambridge: Harvard University Press, 1995.

Nicolaisen, Wilhelm F. H. "The Past as Place: Names, Stories, and the Remembered Self." *Folklore* 102 (1991): 3–15.

Nolt, John Eric. *Informal Logic: Possible Worlds and Imagination.* New York: McGraw-Hill, 1984.

———. "What Are Possible Worlds?" *Mind* 95 (1986): 432–45.

Norton, Sandy Morey. "The Ex-Collector of Boggley-Wollah: Colonialism in the Empire of *Vanity Fair.*" *Narrative* 1 (1993): 124–37.

Nozick, Robert. *Philosophical Explanations.* Cambridge: Belknap Press, 1981.

Nünning, Ansgar. *Grundzüge eines kommunikationstheoretischen Modells der erzähler-ischen Vermittlung: Die Funktionen der Erzählinstanz in den Romanen George Eliots.* Trier: Wissenschaftlicher Verlag, 1989.

———. *Von historischer Fiktion zu historiographischer Metafiktion: Theorie, Typologie und Poetik des historischen Romans.* Trier: Wissenschaftlicher Verlag, 1995.

Nussbaum, Martha. *Love's Knowledge: Essays on Philosophy and Literature.* New York: Oxford University Press, 1990.

Nykrog, Per. "On Seeing and Nothingness: Balzac's *Sarrasine.*" *Romanic Review* 83 (1992): 437–44.

Odin, Roger. "A propos d'un couple de concepts: son in vs. son off." In *Sémiologiques: Linquistique et sémiologie,* edited by Michel Cusin, 93–125. Lyon: Presses Universi-taires de Lyon, 1978.

O'Neill, Patrick. *Fictions of Discourse: Reading Narrative Theory.* Toronto: University of Toronto Press, 1994.

Opie, Iona, and Peter Opie, editors. *The Oxford Dictionary of Nursery Rhymes.* Oxford: Oxford University Press, 1977.

Parker, William N., editor. *Economic History and the Modern Economist.* Oxford: Basil Blackwell, 1986.

Pavel, Thomas G. *The Feud of Language: A History of Structuralist Thought,* translated by Linda Jordan and Thomas G. Pavel. Cambridge: Basil Blackwell, 1989.

———. *Fictional Worlds.* Cambridge: Harvard University Press, 1986.

———. "Literary Narratives." In *Discourse and Literature,* edited by Teun A. van Dijk, 83–104. Amsterdam and Philadelphia: John Benjamins, 1985a.

———. *The Poetics of Plot: The Case of English Renaissance Drama.* Minneapolis: Uni-versity of Minnesota Press, 1985b.

———. "Possible Worlds in Literary Semantics." *Journal of Aesthetics and Art Criticism* 34 (1975–76): 165–76.

———. *La syntaxe narrative des tragédies des Corneilles.* Paris: Klinksieck, 1976.

Perry, Menakhem. "Literary Dynamics: How the Order of a Text Creates Its Meaning [With an Analysis of Faulkner's 'A Rose for Emily']." *Poetics Today* 1 (1979): 35–64, 311–61.

Peterson, Ivars. *Newton's Clock: Chaos in the Solar System.* New York: W. H. Free-man, 1993.

Petro, Patrice. "Feminism and Film History." In *Multiple Voices in Feminist Film Criti-cism,* edited by Diane Carson, Linda Dittmar, and Janice R. Welsch, 65–81. Minne-apolis: University of Minnesota Press, 1994.

Phelan, James. *Narrative as Rhetoric: Technique, Audiences, Ethics, Ideology.* Columbus: Ohio State University Press, 1996.

———. *Reading People, Reading Plots: Character, Progression, and the Interpretation of Narrative.* Chicago: University of Chicago Press, 1989.

Phelan, James, editor. *Reading Narrative: Form, Ethics, Ideology.* Columbus: Ohio State University Press, 1989.

Phelan, James, and Peter J. Rabinowitz, editors. *Understanding Narrative.* Columbus: Ohio State University Press, 1994.

Plantinga, Alvin. "Actualism and Possible Worlds." In *The Possible and the Actual: Readings in the Metaphysics of Modality,* edited by Michael J. Loux, 253–73. Ithaca: Cornell University Press, 1979.

———. *The Nature of Necessity.* Oxford: Clarendon, 1974.

Plotnitsky, Arkady. "Complementarity, Idealization, and the Limits of Classical Conceptions of Reality." *South Atlantic Quarterly* 94 (1995): 527–70.

Polanyi, Livia. *Telling the American Story: A Structural and Cultural Analysis of Conversational Storytelling.* Cambridge: MIT Press, 1989.

Powers, Richard. *Galatea 2.2.* New York: Farrar, Straus and Giroux, 1995.

Pratt, Mary Louise. *Towards a Speech Act Theory of Literary Discourse.* Bloomington: Indiana University Press, 1977.

Preston, Elizabeth. "Homodiegetic Narration: Reliability, Self-Consciousness, Ideology, and Ethics." Ph.D. dissertation, Ohio State University, 1997.

Price, Martin. *Forms of Life: Character and Imagination in the Novel.* New Haven: Yale University Press, 1983.

Prince, Ellen F. "Toward a Taxonomy of Given-New Information." In *Radical Pragmatics,* edited by Peter Cole, 223–56. New York: Academic, 1981.

———. "The ZPG Letter: Subjects, Definiteness, and Information-Status." In *Discourse Description: Diverse Linguistics Analyses of a Fund-Raising Text,* edited by William C. Mann and Sandra A. Thompson, 295–325. Amsterdam: John Benjamins, 1992.

Prince, Gerald. "Aspects of a Grammar of Narrative." *Poetics Today* 1 (1980a): 49–63.

———. "The Disnarrated." *Style* 22 (1988): 1–8.

———. *A Grammar of Stories.* The Hague: Mouton, 1973.

———. "Introduction to the Study of the Narratee," translated by Francis Mariner. In *Reader-Response Criticism,* edited by Jane P. Tompkins, 7–25. Baltimore: Johns Hopkins University Press, 1980b.

———. *Narrative as Theme: Studies in French Fiction.* Lincoln: University of Nebraska Press, 1992.

———. *Narratology: The Form and Functioning of Narrative.* Berlin: Mouton, 1982.

Pritchett, Bradley L. "Garden Path Phenomena and the Grammatical Basis of Language Processing." *Language* 64 (1988): 539–76.

Private Eye: Another Boob of Batches. ["Another selection of the misprints and absurdities culled from the press by *Private Eye.*"] London: André Deutsch, 1979.

Propp, Vladimir. *Morphology of the Folktale,* 2nd edition, translated by Laurence Scott, revised by Louis A. Wagner. Austin: University of Texas Press, 1968.

Rabinowitz, Peter. *Before Reading.* Ithaca: Cornell University Press, 1987.

———. "Canons and Close Reading." In *Falling into Theory: Conflicting Views on Reading Literature,* edited by David Richter, 218–21. Boston: St. Martin's Press, 1988.

———. "Truth in Fiction: A Reexamination of Audiences." *Critical Inquiry* 4 (1977): 121–41.

Radcliffe-Brown, A. R. "On the Concept of Function in Social Science." *American Anthropologist* 37 (1935): 394–402.

Rafferty, Terrence. "The Lesson of the Master." *The New Yorker,* 15 January 1990, 102–4.

Raskin, Victor. *Semantic Mechanisms of Humor.* Dordrecht: Reidel, 1985.

Raskin, Victor, and Salvatore Attardo. "Non-Literalness and Non-Bona-Fide in Language: An Approach to Formal and Computational Treatments of Humor." *Pragmatics and Cognition* 2 (1994): 31–69.

Raynaud, Jean-Michel. *Pour un Perec lettré, chiffré.* Lille: Lille University Press, 1987.

Rayner, Keith, and Sara C. Sereno. "Regressive Eye Movements and Sentence Parsing: On the Use of Regression-Contingent Analyses." *Memory and Cognition* 22 (1994): 281–92.

Rees, Martin J. "Our Universe and Others: The Limits of Space, Time and Physics." In *Possible Worlds in Humanities, Arts and Sciences: Proceedings of Nobel Symposium 65,* edited by Sture Allén, 396–416. Berlin: de Gruyter, 1989.

Reichman, Rachel. *Getting Computers to Talk Like You and Me: Discourse Context, Focus, and Semantics (an ATN Model).* Cambridge: MIT Press, 1985.

Rescher, Nicholas. *A Theory of Possibility: A Constructivist and Conceptualist Account of Possible Individuals and Possible Worlds.* Oxford: Basil Blackwell, 1975.

Rescher, Nicholas, and Robert Brandom. *The Logic of Inconsistency: A Study in Non-Standard Possible-World Semantics and Ontology.* Oxford: Basil Blackwell, 1980.

Richardson, Jane, and A. L. Kroeber. "Three Centuries of Women's Dress Fashions: A Quantitative Analysis." *Anthropological Records* 5 (1940); reprinted in *University of California Publications in Anthropological Records* 5 (1940–47): 111–53.

Ricoeur, Paul. "Narrative Time." *Critical Inquiry* 7 (1980): 169–90.

Riggan, William. *Picaros, Madmen, Naifs, and Clowns: The Unreliable First-Person Narrator.* Norman: University of Oklahoma Press, 1981.

Rimmon, Shlomith. "A Comprehensive Theory of Narrative: Genette's *Figures III* and the Structuralist Study of Fiction." *PTL: A Journal for Descriptive Poetics and Theory of Literature* 1 (1976): 33–62.

———. *The Concept of Ambiguity — The Example of James.* Chicago: University of Chicago Press, 1977.

Rimmon-Kenan, Shlomith. "How the Model Neglects the Medium: Linguistics, Language, and the Crisis of Narratology." *Journal of Narrative Technique* 19 (1989): 157–66.

———. *Narrative Fiction: Contemporary Poetics.* London and New York: Methuen, 1983.

Robinson, Sally. *Engendering the Subject: Gender and Self-Representation in Contemporary Women's Fiction.* New York: State University of New York, 1991.

Rodrigues, Eusebio L. "Experiencing *Jazz.*" *Modern Fiction Studies* 39 (1993): 733–54.

Roese, Neal J., and James M. Olson. "Counterfactual Thinking: A Critical Overview." In *What Might Have Been: The Social Psychology of Counterfactual Thinking,* edited by Neal J. Roese and James M. Olson, 1–55. Hillsdale, NJ: Lawrence Erlbaum, 1995.

Ronen, Ruth. "Completing the Incompleteness of Fictional Entities." *Poetics Today* 9 (1988): 497–514.

————. *Possible Worlds in Literary Theory*. Cambridge: Cambridge University Press, 1994.

Rorty, Richard. "The Contingency of Language." In *Contingency, Irony, and Solidarity,* 3–22. Cambridge: Cambridge University Press, 1989.

Ryan, Marie-Laure. "Allegories of Immersion: Virtual Narration in Postmodern Fiction." *Style* 29 (1995): 262–86.

————. "Embedded Narratives and Tellability." *Style* 20 (1986): 319–40.

————. "Fiction as Logical, Ontological and Illocutionary Issue." *Style* 18 (1984): 121–39.

————. "Narrative in Real Time." *Narrative* 1 (1993): 138–55.

————. *Possible Worlds, Artificial Intelligence, and Narrative Theory*. Bloomington: Indiana University Press, 1991.

————. "Postmodernism and the Doctrine of Panfictionality." *Narrative* 5 (1997): 165–87.

————. "A la recherche du thème narratif." *Communications* 47 (1988): 23–40.

————. "The Window Structure of Narrative Discourse." *Semiotica* 64 (1987): 59–81.

Sacks, Harvey. *Lectures on Conversation,* vols. 1 and 2, edited by Gail Jefferson. Oxford: Blackwell, 1992.

————. "Lectures on Storytelling." Paper presented at UC-Irvine, 1971.

Sacks, Harvey, Emanuel P. Schegloff, and Gail Jefferson. "A Simplest Systematics for the Organization of Turn-Taking in Conversation." *Language* 50 (1974): 696–735.

Sankoff, David. "Sociolinguistics and Syntactic Variation." In *Linguistics: The Cambridge Survey,* vol. 4, edited by Frederick J. Newmeyer, 140–61. Cambridge: Cambridge University Press, 1988.

Savan, David. "Toward a Refutation of Semiotic Idealism." *Recherches sémiotiques/ Semiotic Inquiry* 3 (1983): 1–8.

Scarry, Elaine. *The Body in Pain: The Making and Unmaking of the World*. New York and Oxford: Oxford University Press, 1987.

Schank, Roger C. *Tell Me a Story: Narrative and Intelligence*. Evanston: Northwestern University Press, 1995.

Schank, Roger C., and Robert P. Abelson. *Scripts, Plans, Goals and Understanding: An Inquiry into Human Knowledge*. Hillsdale, NJ: Lawrence Erlbaum, 1977.

Schank, Roger C., and Lawrence Birnbaum. "Memory, Meaning, and Syntax." In *Talking Minds: The Study of Language in Cognitive Sciences,* edited by Thomas G. Bever, John Carroll, and Lance A. Miller, 209–51. London: MIT Press, 1984.

Schenkein, James, editor. *Studies in the Organization of Conversational Interaction*. New York: Academic Press, 1978.

Schiffrin, Deborah. *Approaches to Discourse*. Cambridge: Basil Blackwell, 1994.

————. *Discourse Markers*. Cambridge: Cambridge University Press, 1987.

————. "Multiple Constraints on Discourse Options: A Quantitative Analysis of Causal Sequences." *Discourse Processes* 8 (1985): 281–305.

Schmidt, Arno. *Evening Edged in Gold: A Fairytale Arse. 55 Scenes from the C¦ou/u¦ntry-*

side for patrons of Er¦ra/o¦ta, translated by John E. Woods. New York: Harcourt Brace Jovanovich, 1980.

Schnitzler, Arthur. *Lieutenant Gustl.* 1900. Berlin: S. Fischer Verlag, 1965.

Schutz, Alfred. *On Phenomenology and Social Relations.* Edited by Helmut R. Wagner. Chicago: University of Chicago Press, 1973.

Schwarz, Daniel. "Performative Saying and the Ethics of Reading: Adam Zachary Newton's *Narrative Ethics.*" *Narrative* 5 (1997): 188–206.

Scollon, Ron, and Suzanne Wong Scollon. *Intercultural Communication: A Discourse Approach.* Oxford: Basil Blackwell, 1995.

Scott, James C. *Seeing like a State: How Certain Schemes to Improve the Human Condition Have Failed.* New Haven: Yale University Press, 1998.

Searle, John. *Speech Acts.* Cambridge: Cambridge University Press, 1969.

Segal, Erwin M. "Narrative Comprehension and the Role of Deictic Shift Theory." *Deixis in Narrative: A Cognitive Science Perspective,* edited by Judith F. Duchan, Gail A. Bruder, and Lynne E. Hewitt, 3–17. Hillsdale: Lawrence Erlbaum, 1995a.

———. "A Cognitive-Phenomenological Theory of Fictional Narrative." In *Deixis in Narrative: A Cognitive Science Perspective,* edited by Judith F. Duchan, Gail A. Bruder and Lynne E. Hewitt, 61–78. Hillsdale: Lawrence Erlbaum, 1995b.

Seiter, Ellen. "The Role of the Woman Reader: Eco's Narrative Theory and Soap Operas." *Tabloid* 6 (1981): 36–43.

Sennett, Richard. *The Conscience of the Eye: The Design and Social Life of Cities.* New York: W. W. Norton and Co., 1990.

Shaw, Harry E. "Loose Narrators." *Narrative* 3 (1995): 95–116.

Shklovsky, Victor. *Material I stil' v romane L'va Tolstogo "Vojna I mir"* [*Material and Style in Leo Tolstoy's Novel "War and Peace"*]. The Hague: Mouton, 1970.

———. *Theory of Prose,* translated by Benjamin Sher. Elmwood Park, IL: Dalkey Archive Press, 1990.

Shopen, Timothy, editor. *Language Typology and Syntactic Description, Vol. 2: Grammatical Categories and the Lexicon.* Cambridge: Cambridge University Press, 1985.

Shuman, Amy. *Storytelling Rights: The Uses of Oral and Written Texts by Adolescents.* Cambridge: Cambridge University Press, 1986.

Shuman, Amy, and Nan Johnson. "Rhetorical Indexes of the Natural." Paper presented at a conference on Inquiries in Social Construction, University of New Hampshire, 1993.

Simon, Herbert A. *Models of Thought.* New Haven: Yale University Press, 1979.

Slinin, J. S. "Teorija modal'nostej v sovremennoj logike" ["Theory of Modalities in Contemporary Logic"]. In *Logicheskaja semantika I modal'naja logika,* edited by Petr Vasil'evich Tavanec, 119–47. Moscow: Nauka, 1967.

Slobin, Dan, and Ayhan Aksu. "Tense, Aspect and Modality in the Use of the Turkish Evidentials." In *Tense-Aspect,* edited by Paul Hopper, 185–200. Amsterdam and Philadelphia: John Benjamins, 1982.

Smart, Robert Austin. *The Nonfiction Novel.* Lanham: University Press of America, 1985.

Smith, Barbara Herrnstein. "Narrative Versions, Narrative Theories." *Critical Inquiry* 7 (1980): 213–36.

———. *Poetic Closure: A Study of How Poems End.* Chicago: University of Chicago Press, 1968.

Smith, Barbara Herrnstein, and Arkady Plotnitsky. "Introduction: Networks and Symmetries, Decidable and Undecidable." *South Atlantic Quarterly* 94 (1995): 371–88.

Spanos, William V. "Breaking the Circle: Hermeneutics as Dis-Closure." *boundary 2* (1977): 421–57.

Squire, John Collings, editor. *If It Had Happened Otherwise: Lapses into Imaginary History,* 2nd edition. London: Sidgwick and Jackson, 1972.

Staiger, Janet. "The Politics of Film Canons." In *Multiple Voices in Feminist Film Criticism,* edited by Diane Carson, Linda Dittmar, and Janice R. Welsch, 191–212. Minneapolis: University of Minnesota Press, 1994.

Stalnaker, Robert C. *Inquiry.* Cambridge: MIT Press, 1984.

Stanzel, Franz K. *A Theory of Narrative,* translated by Charlotte Goedsche. Cambridge: Cambridge University Press, 1984.

Steiner, George. *Tolstoy or Dostoevsky: An Essay in the Old Criticism,* 2nd edition. New Haven: Yale University Press, 1996.

Stephenson, Neal. *The Diamond Age, or, A Young Lady's Illustrated Primer.* New York: Bantam Books, 1996.

Sternberg, Meir. *Expositional Modes and Temporal Ordering in Fiction.* Baltimore: The Johns Hopkins University Press, 1978.

———. "Temporal Ordering, Modes of Expositional Distribution, and Three Models of Rhetorical Control in the Narrative Text: Faulkner, Balzac, and Austen." *PTL: A Journal for Descriptive Poetics and Theory of Literature* 1 (1976): 295–316.

Stevenson, Randall. *Modernist Fiction: An Introduction.* Hemel Hempstead: Harvester Wheatsheaf, 1992.

Sukenick, Ronald. *98.6.* New York: Fiction Collective, 1975.

Suleiman, Susan Rubin. *Authoritarian Fictions: The Ideological Novel as a Literary Genre.* New York: Columbia University Press, 1983.

Tannen, Deborah. "What's in a Frame? Surface Evidence for Underlying Expectations." In *Framing in Discourse,* edited by Deborah Tannen, 14–56. Oxford: Oxford University Press, 1993.

Tedeschi, Philip, and Annie Zaenen, editors. *Syntax and Semantics, Vol. 14: Tense and Aspect.* New York: Academic Press, 1981.

Thomson, David. *A Biographical Dictionary of Film,* 3rd edition. New York: Knopf, 1994.

Thurber, James. "The Secret Life of Walter Mitty." In *The Thurber Carnival,* 69–74. Harmondsworth: Penguin, 1973.

Todorov, Tzvetan. *Grammaire du "Décaméron."* The Hague: Mouton, 1969.

———. "La Grammaire du récit." *Langages* 12 (1968): 94–102.

———. *Introduction à la littérature fantastique.* Paris: Editions du Seuil, 1970.

Toker, Leona. "Towards a Poetics of Documentary Poetics—from the Perspective of Gulag Testimonies." *Poetics Today* 18 (1997): 187–222.

Tolkien, J. R. R. *The Lord of the Rings.* London: Grafton, 1991.

Tolstoi, L. N. *Polnoe sobranie sochinenii [Complete Works],* edited by V. G. Chertkov. Moscow: Khudozhestvennaia literatura, 1929–58.

Tolstoy, Leo. *War and Peace,* translated by Alymer Maude, edited by George Gibian. New York: W. W. Norton and Co., 1966.

———. *War and Peace,* translated by Ann Dunnigan. New York: Signet, 1968.

Tompkins, Jane. *Sensational Designs: The Cultural Work of American Fiction, 1790–1860.* New York: Oxford University Press, 1985.

Torgovnick, Marianna. *Closure in the Novel.* Princeton: Princeton University Press, 1981.

Toulmin, Stephen. *Cosmopolis: The Hidden Agenda of Modernity.* New York: Free Press, 1990.

Traill, Nancy H. *Possible Worlds of the Fantastic: The Rise of the Paranormal in Literature.* Toronto: University of Toronto Press, 1996.

Trevor-Roper, Hugh Redwald. *A Hidden Life: The Enigma of Sir Edmund Backhouse.* London: Macmillan, 1976.

———. *History and Imagination.* Oxford: Clarendon, 1980.

———. *The Romantic Movement and the Study of History.* London: Athlone Press, 1969.

Turner, Mark. *The Literary Mind.* New York: Oxford University Press, 1996.

Turner, Scott. *The Creative Process: A Computer Model of Storytelling and Creativity.* Hillsdale, NJ: Lawrence Erlbaum, 1994.

Tynjanov, Jurij, and Roman Jakobson. "Problems in the Study of Literature and Language." In *Readings in Russian Poetics: Formalist and Structuralist Views,* edited by Ladislav Matejka and Krystyna Pomorska, 79–81. Cambridge: MIT Press, 1971.

Veyne, Paul. *Writing History: Essay on Epistemology,* translated by Mina Moore-Rinvolucri. Middletown, CT: Wesleyan University Press, 1984.

Virtanen, Tuija. "Issues of Text Typology: Narrative—a 'Basic' Type of Text?" *Text* 12 (1992): 293–310.

Volkogonov, Dmitri. *Stalin: Triumph and Tragedy,* translated by Harold Shukman. New York: Grove Weidenfeld, 1991.

Wall, Kathleen. "*The Remains of the Day* and Its Challenge to Theories of Unreliable Narration." *Journal of Narrative Technique* 24 (1994): 18–42.

Walton, Kendall. *Mimesis as Make-Believe: On the Foundations of the Representational Arts.* Cambridge: Harvard University Press, 1990.

———. "Spelunking, Simulation, and Slime: On Being Moved by Fiction." In *Emotion in the Arts,* edited by Mette Hjort and Sue Laver, 37–49. Oxford: Oxford University Press, 1997.

Warhol, Robyn R. "Feminine Intensities: Soap Opera Viewing as a Technology of Gender." *Genders* 28 (1998): http://www.genders.org.

———. *Gendered Interventions: Narrative Discourse in the Victorian Novel.* New Brunswick: Rutgers University Press, 1989.

———. "Toward a Theory of the Engaging Narrator: Earnest Interventions in Gaskell, Stowe, and Eliot." *PMLA* 101 (1986): 811–18.

Webber, Bonnie Lynn. *A Formal Approach to Discourse Anaphora.* New York: Garland, 1979.

Wenzel, Peter. "Joke." In *Simple Forms: An Encyclopedia of Simple Text Types in Lore and Literature,* edited by Walter A. Koch, 123–30. Bochum: Brockmeyer, 1994.

West, Candace. *Routine Complications.* Bloomington: Indiana University Press, 1984.

White, Hayden. *The Content of the Form: Narrative Discourse and Historical Representation.* Baltimore: Johns Hopkins University Press, 1987.

———. "Historical Emplotment and the Problem of Truth." In *Probing the Limits of Representation: Nazism and the Final Solution,* edited by Saul Friedlander, 37–53. Cambridge: Harvard University Press, 1992.

———. *Metahistory: The Historical Imagination in Nineteenth-Century Europe.* Baltimore: Johns Hopkins University Press, 1973.

———. *Tropics of Discourse: Essays in Cultural Criticism.* Baltimore: Johns Hopkins University Press, 1978.

———. "The Value of Narrativity in the Representation of Reality." *Critical Inquiry* 7 (1980): 5–27.

Willey, Basil. *The Seventeenth Century Background: Studies in the Thought of the Age in Relation to Poetry and Religion.* Garden City, NY: Doubleday, 1953.

Wilson, Edmund. "The Ambiguity of Henry James." In *The Triple Thinkers: Twelve Essays on Literary Subjects,* 2nd edition, 88–132. New York: Oxford University Press, 1948.

Winograd, Terry. *Language as Cognitive Process.* London: Addison-Wesley, 1983.

Wolf, Werner. "Intermedialität als neues Paradigma der Literaturwissenschaft?" *Arbeiten aus Anglistik und Amerikanistik* 21 (1996): 85–116.

Wolfe, Tom. *The New Journalism.* New York: Harper and Row, 1973.

Wolfram, Walt, and Natalie Schilling-Estes. *American English: Dialects and Variation.* Oxford: Basil Blackwell, 1998.

Wolfson, Nessa. *The Conversational Historical Present in American English Narrative.* Dordrecht: Foris, 1982.

Wolterstorff, Nicholas. *Works and Worlds of Art.* Oxford: Clarendon Press, 1980.

Woods, John. *The Logic of Fiction: A Philosophical Sounding of Deviant Logic.* The Hague: Mouton, 1974.

Woolf, Virginia. *A Room of One's Own.* New York: Harcourt Brace and Co., 1989.

Workman, Mark. "Paradigms of Indeterminacy." Paper presented at a conference on Inquiries in Social Construction, University of New Hampshire, 1993.

Wright, Georg Hendrik von. *An Essay in Deontic Logic and the General Theory of Action.* Amsterdam: North-Holland, 1968.

———. "The Logic of Actions: A Sketch." In *The Logic of Decision and Action,* edited by Nicholas Rescher, 121–36. Pittsburgh: University of Pittsburgh Press, 1967.

Yagisawa, Takashi. "Beyond Possible Worlds." *Philosophical Studies* 53 (1988): 175–204.

Yamaguchi, Haruhiko. "How to Pull Strings with Words: Deceptive Violations in the Garden-Path Joke." *Journal of Pragmatics* 12 (1988): 323–37.

Young, Katherine. *Presence in the Flesh: The Body in Medicine.* Cambridge: Harvard University Press, 1997.

———. *Taleworlds and Storyrealms: The Phenomenology of Narrative.* Dordrecht: Martinus Nijhoff, 1987.

Contributors

SEYMOUR CHATMAN is Professor Emeritus of Rhetoric and Film and Professor in the Graduate School at the University of California, Berkeley. He is the author of *A Theory of Meter* (1965), *The Later Style of Henry James* (1972), *Story and Discourse* (1978), *Antonioni, or the Surface of the World* (1985), and *Coming to Terms* (1990). He coedited, with Samuel R. Levin, *Essays on the Language of Literature* (1967), *Literary Style: A Symposium* (1971), *Approaches to Poetics: Selected English Institute Essays* (1973); with Umberto Eco, *Proceedings of the First International Congress on Semiotics* (1979); and, with Guido Fink, *Michelangelo Antonioni's l'Avventura: A Screenplay* (1989).

LUBOMÍR DOLEŽEL is Professor Emeritus of Slavic and Comparative Literature at the University of Toronto. He came to Canada in 1968, after receiving his Ph.D. from the Czechoslovak Academy of Sciences in Prague. He has published widely in stylistics, mathematical linguistics, poetics, semiotics, narratology, and fiction theory. His books include *O stylu moderní ceské prózy* (*On the Style of Modern Czech Narrative Prose,* 1960), *Narrative Modes in Czech Literature* (1973), *Occidental Poetics: Tradition and Progress* (1990); and *Heterocosmica: Fiction and Possible Worlds* (1998). He is interested in the possible-worlds semantics of literary fiction and is currently engaged in examining the relationship between fiction and history.

RUTH GINSBURG is Senior Lecturer of Comparative Literature at the Hebrew University of Jerusalem. She has written on narrative theory, Bakhtin, and psychoanalysis—all from a feminist perspective. Her current research concerns the fantasy of Mother and motherhood in the (Western, including Hebrew) novel. She is also currently working on a new Hebrew translation of Freud's *Interpretation of Dreams*.

DAVID HERMAN teaches critical theory, linguistics, and twentieth-century literature at North Carolina State University. The author of *Universal Grammar and Narrative Form* (1995) and of articles on topics in narrative and literary theory, the linguistics of literature, and modern and postmodern fiction, he is currently working on a book called "Story Logic: Problems and Possibilities of Narrative," as well as a study of North Carolina ghost stories.

MANFRED JAHN is a research assistant in the English Department of the University of Cologne, Germany. Current interests include natural language processing, cognitive, reception-theoretical and AI approaches to narratology, focalization theory, and techniques of consciousness representation. Recent publications include "Windows of Focalization: Deconstructing and Reconstructing a Narratological Concept" (1996), "Frames, Preferences, and the Reading of Third-Person Narratives: Towards a Cognitive Narratology" (1997).

EMMA KAFALENOS teaches comparative literature at Washington University in St. Louis. She has published articles on narrative and narrative theory in such journals as *Poetics Today, Narrative, New Novel Review, Nineteenth-Century Music,* and *Comparative Literature.* In her current work she is using function analysis to explore readers' satisfaction and ways that narratives bring comfort.

URI MARGOLIN is a professor of comparative literature at the University of Alberta, Edmonton, in Canada. His main areas of research include narratology, theory of character in narrative and drama, poetics, literature and philosophy, and methodology. His publications include over forty articles in international journals such as *Language and Literature, Language and Style, Poetics Today, PTL, Semiotica,* and *Style.*

GARY SAUL MORSON, Frances Hooper Professor of the Arts and Humanities at Northwestern University, is the author of *Narrative and Freedom: The Shadows of Time* (1994), *Hidden in Plain View: Narrative and Creative Potentials in "War and Peace"* (1986), *The Boundaries of Genre: Dostoevsky's "Diary of a Writer" and the Traditions of Literary Utopia* (1981, 1988), and, with Caryl Emerson, *Mikhail Bakhtin: Creation of a Prosaics* (1990). A member of the American Academy of Arts and Sciences, he is currently working on a study of contingency and process in Western thought.

MARY PATRICIA MARTIN is Assistant Professor of English at Ohio State University. Her area of research is the theory and history of the British novel in the eighteenth century, with a particular interest in women writers. She has published essays on Samuel Richardson's *Clarissa* and on the role of women writers in the controversy surrounding the novel in the mid-eighteenth century.

JAMES PHELAN is Professor and Chair of the Department of English at Ohio State University. He has written about style in the novel in *Worlds from Words* (1981); about character and narrative progression in *Reading People, Reading Plots* (1989); and about technique, audiences, ethics, and ideology in *Narrative as Rhetoric* (1996). He has also written a book of creative nonfiction, *Beyond the Tenure Track: Fifteen Months in the Life of an English Professor* (1991). Phelan has also edited *Reading Narrative* (1989), *Understanding Narrative* (with Peter J. Rabinowitz, 1994); and *Adventures of Huckleberry Finn: A Case Study in Critical Controversy* (with Gerald Graff, 1995), and is the editor of the journal *Narrative*. The essay in this volume is part of a larger project, a study of the ethics of homodiegetic narration.

SHLOMITH RIMMON-KENAN is Professor of English and Comparative Literature at the Hebrew University of Jerusalem. She chairs the Department of Comparative Literature and holds the Renee Lang Chair for Humanistic Studies. She is author of *The Concept of Ambiguity: The Example of James* (1977), *Narrative Fiction: Contemporary Poetics* (1983), *A Glance beyond Doubt: Narration, Representation, Subjectivity* (1996), and numerous articles on literary theory as well as on specific literary texts. She is editor of *Discourse in Psychoanalysis and Literature* (1987) and *Rereading Texts/Rethinking Critical Presuppositions* (with Leona Toker and Shuli Barzilai, 1997). Her current research concerns the concept of narrative in other disciplines (historiography, psychoanalysis, jurisprudence).

MARIE-LAURE RYAN is an independent scholar working in the areas of narrative theory and electronic textuality. A 1999 Fellow at the Society for the Humanities at Cornell University and the recipient of a postdoctoral fellowship from the National Endowment for the Humanities, she is the author of *Possible Worlds, Artificial Intelligence and Narrative Theory* (1991), and the editor of the forthcoming collection of essays *Cyberspace Textuality: Computer Technology and Literary Theory*. Her current project is a book-length study of immersion and interactivity in literature and electronic culture.

ROBYN R. WARHOL is Professor of English and Director of Women's Studies at the University of Vermont. She is author of *Gendered Interventions: Narrative Discourse in the Victorian Novel* (1989), and coeditor, with Diane Price Herndl, of *Feminisms: An Anthology of Literary Theory and Criticism* (1991, 1997). Her articles on feminist narratology have appeared in various journals, including *Style, Narrative, PMLA, Novel,* and *Studies in English Literature.* She is currently working on a book theorizing the relationship between "feelings," gender, and such popular cultural forms as soap opera and serial fiction.

KATHARINE YOUNG is a writer, scholar, and occasional lecturer at the University of California, Berkeley, and San Francisco State University. Her most recent book is *Presence in the Flesh: The Body in Medicine* (1997). She is currently investigating narrative and the body in somatic psychology. Her particular interest is gestures and their relationship to thought and emotion.

Index

Page numbers in italics mark key discussions of a particular topic. Literary narratives are indexed by title rather than author. Films are indexed by title rather than director.

Film: as exploiting information tracks of sight and sound, 315, *318–21*, 327–28; use of concurrent narration in, 334–35; use of unreliable narration in, 321, *338 n. 7. See also* Character-narrator; Modality; Narration, Narratology; Sound track; Voice-over narration

Firbas, Jan, 234

Fish, Stanley, 173, 191, 192, 281, 287, 311 n. 14

Fleischmann, Suzanne, 151, 155

Flesh-and-blood readers. *See* Authorial audience

Fludernik, Monika, 27 n. 2, 29 n. 7, 136–37, 150, 153, 162, 163, 166, 169, 191, 222, 234

Focalization: in Hemingway's "Cat in the Rain," 5–6; as vehicle for narrative anachrony, 54. *See also* Morphing; Story-line windows

Fodor, Janet Dean, and Atsu Inoue, 170–72, 193 nn. 1, 3, 8

Foerster, Heinz von, 193 n. 5

Forster, E. M., 280

Foucault, Michel, 66, 69–73, 86 n. 5, 168, 286, 302

Frames. *See* Garden paths; Recursivity

Frank, Joseph, 311 n. 18

Frawley, William, 145

Frazier, Lyn, 192 n. 1

Frege, Gottlob, 261, 263, 272 n. 20

French Lieutenant's Woman, The (Fowles), 134

Freudlieb, Dieter, 272 n. 23

Friedlander, Saul, 251, 253

Frye, Northrop, 311 n. 17

Füger, Wilhelm, 168

Functions: as defined by Propp, 33, *40;* as interdependent on configurations of events, 33, 38, *39–41,* 49–50, 55, 57; in *Sarrasine, 49–53,* 59; in *The Turn of the Screw, 42–48,* 58

Gaines, Jane, 345

Galatea 2.2 (Powers), 132–33

Galbraith, Mary, 140 n. 10, 185, 191

Gallie, W. B., 271 n. 10

Gaps: as forcibly imposed in totalitarian histories, 259–61; functioning of in history vs. fiction, 23, *257–61;* as result of deferred or suppressed information in narratives, *34–35,* 38, 45–46, 51, 53–57; as revealing the difference between fabula and sjuzhet, *36–*

38, 45–46, 48–49, 57–58. *See also* Fabula; Indeterminacy

Garden paths: as caused by ambiguous pronominal references, 179–80; cognitive approaches to, 172–78; and frame-based models of contextual knowledge, *173–75,* 176; and genre, 190; in jokes and riddles, 167, 169, *178–82;* in narratives, 19–20, 167, 169, *182–89;* and the need for processual vs. holistic (or final-state) models, *186–87,* 189, *190–91;* and preference-rule systems, *175–78,* 185, 189–90; and the question of individual readers' preferences, 191; and reading for maximum cognitive payoff, *177–78,* 189, 192; and script-based models of contextual knowledge, *173–75,* 176; in sentences (or sentoids), 19–20, 167, 169, *170–78;* and the shift from text-as-product to discourse-as-process, 169; structure and symptoms of, 171–72; vitality of across a history of rereadings, 190

Gardiner, Michael, 87 n. 12

Garfield, Jay L., 220

Gaudreault, André, 338 n. 3

Gearhardt, Suzanne, 263

Geertz, Clifford, 286

Gender: author- and narrator-oriented approaches to, 340–41, 343, *347–48;* reader- and audience-oriented approaches to, 341, 343, *348–49, 353–54. See also* Author; Narrative; Social constructionism

Genette, Gérard, 5, 61 nn. 3–4, 63 nn. 15, 20, 64 n. 24, 95, 108 n. 3, 109 n. 6, 140 n. 16, 165, 168, 169, 183, 184, 230, 247, 264, 317–18, 342, 355 n. 3

Gerrig, Richard J., 117

Ghost stories: as laboratory for studying reference in narrative, 225, *232–33;* as marked by a salient or stratified ontology, 237. *See also* Indeterminacy; Reference

Gibson, Andrew, 28 n. 2, 137

"Gift of the Magi, The" (O. Henry), 127

Ginsburg, Carlo, 264–65

Ginsburg, Ruth, and Shlomith Rimmon-Kenan, 14, 15–16, 29 n. 4

Givón, Talmy, 1984

Gledhill, Christine, 344

Gleick, James, 181–82

Goffman, Erving, 197, 199, 201–4, 224

Goodman, Nelson, 263

Goodwin, Charles, 206–7

The Theory and Interpretation of Narrative Series
James Phelan and Peter J. Rabinowitz, Editors

Because the series editors believe that the most significant work in narrative studies today contributes both to our knowledge of specific narratives and to our understanding of narrative in general, studies in the series typically offer interpretations of individual narratives and address significant theoretical issues underlying those interpretations. The series does not privilege any one critical perspective but is open to work from any strong theoretical position.

Misreading *Jane Eyre:* A Postformalist Paradigm
Jerome Beaty

Matters of Fact: Reading Nonfiction over the Edge
Daniel W. Lehman

Framing *Anna Karenina:* Tolstoy, the Woman Question, and the Victorian Novel
Amy Mandelker

Narrative as Rhetoric: Technique, Audiences, Ethics, Ideology
James Phelan

Understanding Narrative
Edited by James Phelan and Peter J. Rabinowitz

Before Reading: Narrative Conventions and the Politics of Interpretation
Peter J. Rabinowitz

The Progress of Romance: Literary Historiography and the Gothic Novel
David H. Richter

A Glance beyond Doubt: Narration, Representation, Subjectivity
Shlomith Rimmon-Kenan

Psychological Politics of the American Dream: The Commodification of Subjectivity in Twentieth-Century American Literature
Lois Tyson